Setting Up & Running

QuickBooks 2014

The Accountant's Guide for Business Owners

Philip B. Goodman CPA
Thomas E. Barich
Certified QuickBooks ProAdvsior

CPA911 Publishing, LLC
Jacksonville, FL

D1214536

Setting Up & Running QuickBooks 2014

ISBN-10: 1-932925-50-3

ISBN-13: 978-1932925500

Published by CPA911 Publishing, LLC October 2013

Copyright 2013 CPA911 Publishing, LLC

CPA911 is a Registered Trademark of CPA911 Publishing, LLC.

All rights reserved. No portion of the contents of this book may be reproduced in any form or by any means without the written permission of the publisher.

CPA911 Publishing LLC has used its best efforts to make sure the information in this book is reliable and complete. Because of the possibility of human or mechanical errors by our resources, we make no representations or warranties for the accuracy or completeness of the contents of this book, and specifically disclaim any implied warranties. The publisher disclaims any responsibility for errors or omissions or the results obtained from the use of the information in this book.

QuickBooks is a registered trademark of Intuit Inc., and is used with permission.

Windows, Microsoft Excel and Microsoft Word are registered trademarks of Microsoft Corporation, and are used with permission.

Acknowledgments

Cover Design: InfoDesign Services (www.infodesigning.com)

Production: InfoDesign Services (www.infodesigning.com)

Proofreading: Dancing Monkey Editorial Services (www.dancingmonkeyediting.com)

Indexing: Transcription Conniption (www.transcriptionconniption.com)

Introduction

QuickBooks is a feature-rich and user friendly program. Unfortunately, it's not enough to simply understand how the program functions. Maintaining accurate financial records requires a basic understanding of the underlying accounting principles as well. That's where this book comes in.

Setting Up & Running QuickBooks is the one book that combines the expertise of a Certified Public Accountant with the expertise of a Certified QuickBooks ProAdvisor®. It provides step-by-step QuickBooks instructions and basic accounting principles, side-by-side. As the ProAdvisor is walking you through the QuickBooks procedures, the CPA is explaining the accounting activities that are taking place. In addition, both provide expert advice, tips, and recommendations all the way through the book.

Being able to rely on accurate financial records is absolutely crucial to the success of any business. Accounting figures aren't just for preparing tax returns. All too many QuickBooks users think they can "fudge" the accounting stuff and have their accountants fix the books at tax time. In a way they're right. Their accountants can fix any problems, but at a price. Setting up and running QuickBooks the right way, from the start, will keep that price to a minimum.

While this book is not going to replace your accountant, it will significantly reduce those frantic phone calls for accounting help and, hopefully, keep your accounting fees at an affordable level.

Table of Contents

Acknowledgments iv

Introduction v

Chapter 1: Accounting Basics 1

The Ledger 2

Making Sense of the Debit and Credit Labels 3

Accounting Categories 4

Assets 4

Current Assets 4

Long-Term Assets 5

Liabilities 5

Current Liabilities 6

Long-Term Liabilities 6

Equity 6

Income 7

Expenses 7

Cost of Goods Sold 8

General and Administrative Expenses 8

Cash-Basis Vs. Accrual-Basis Accounting 9

Cash-Basis Accounting 10

Accrual-Basis Accounting 11

Selecting an Accounting Method 12

Fiscal Vs. Calendar Year 13

Chapter 2: QuickBooks Basics 15

What's Under the Hood? 16

QuickBooks Interface Components 17

Lists 17

Transaction Forms 17

Reports 17

Preferences 17

QuickBooks Centers 18

Account Registers 18

Utilities 18

Mastering the QuickBooks Interface 19

Home Page 20
Icon Bar... 20
   Customizing the Left Icon Bar 20
   Customizing the Top Icon Bar.. 21
   Adding the Active Window to the Icon Bar........................... 22
The Menu Bar 23
Using the Ribbon Bar in Transaction Forms 23
   Main Tab 24
   Formatting Tab... 24
   Send/Ship Tab 25
   Reports Tab 26
   Payments Tab.. 26

Getting Around in QuickBooks...27
  Mastering the Menu Bar... 27
  Client Collaborator 28
  Using the Icon Bar (Top or Left) 30
  Taking Advantage of Shortcut Keys 31

Understanding QuickBooks Centers.....................................33
  Customer, Vendor, and Employee Centers................................. 34
     Name List 34
     Transactions List... 36
  Payroll Center 36
  Lead Center 38
  Report Center... 39
  Bank Feeds Center 41
  Doc Center 42
  Collections Center.. 44

Setting QuickBooks Preferences 44
  Desktop View Preferences... 46
     My Preferences Tab... 46
     Company Preferences Tab 49
  General Preferences 50
     My Preferences Tab... 50
     Company Preferences Tab 53

Using QuickBooks Productivity Features...............................54
  Memorized Transactions 55
  Add/Edit Multiple List Entries 56

Create Batch Invoices 58

Create an Accountant's Copy 58

    Accountant's Copy Restrictions *59*

Create a Portable Company File 62

Prepare Letters with Envelopes 63

Customizing Transaction Forms 64

Making Minor Changes to an Existing Template 64

Advanced Customization 65

Using the Layout Designer 67

    Adding Elements *68*

    Modifying Elements *68*

    Moving Elements *69*

    Margins and Grids *70*

Chapter 3: Setting Up QuickBooks 71

Chart of Accounts 73

Naming Accounts 74

Using Account Numbers 75

    Account Numbering Options *76*

    Creating a Numbering Scheme *77*

Creating and Editing Accounts 78

    Creating New Accounts *78*

    Editing Existing Accounts *80*

Simulate a Divisionalized Chart of Accounts with Classes 80

    Creating the Class Divisions *80*

Setting Up Basic Lists 83

Terms List 83

    Creating Terms *84*

Customer Type List 85

Vendor Type List 87

Job Type List 87

Item List 89

Adding Custom Fields to Lists 89

    Item Custom Fields *89*

    Customer, Vendor, and Employee Custom Fields *90*

Sales Tax Setup 90

Enabling Sales Tax 91

Sales Tax Status 96

Sales Tax Code List 97

Sales Tax Items 98

Sales Tax Groups 99

Setting Up Customers 101

Preparing for Customer Setup 101

Naming Customers 102

Required Customer Data 103

Name and Address *103*

Terms *103*

Creating Customer Records 104

Adding Customer Jobs 106

Adding Vendor Records 108

Merging Records 111

Chapter 4: Tracking Income **113**

Creating Items Used on Sales Forms 114

Service Items 115

Inventory Part Items 116

Non-inventory Part 116

Other Charge Items 116

Subtotal Items 117

Group Items 117

Discount Items 117

Payment Items 118

Sales Tax Items & Groups 118

Creating Cash Sales 118

Daily Journals from Z-Tapes 120

Recording Sales in Batches *120*

Create Items to Match the Sales and Payments You Enter *120*

Create New "Register" Customers *122*

Creating A Daily Sales Summary Form *122*

Creating the Summary Sales Transaction *124*

Depositing the Day's Funds 125

Create Over and Short Accounts *127*

Create Over and Short Items *127*

Understanding Accounts Receivable 128

Invoicing Customers 129

Setting Sales-Form Related Preferences.. 130

Creating Invoices 131

Sending the Invoice... 133

Receiving Customer Payments...136

Setting Defaults for Receiving Payments...................................... 137

Automatically Apply Payments 138

Automatically Calculate Payments 138

Recording the Payment... 138

Applying the Payment 139

Applying a Credit.. 142

Customer Refunds 144

Creating Customer Credits & Refunds... 146

Applying Customer Discounts...148

Applying the Discount to the Sales Transaction 150

Applying the Discount to the Payment...................................... 151

Generating Customer Statements 153

Posting Miscellaneous Income 154

Tracking Interest Income.. 154

Tracking Refunds and Rebates Received................................... 155

Writing Off Receivables You'll Never Collect........................... 155

Bad Debt Expense.. 156

Running Income Tracking Reports 157

Income Tracker 158

Income Reports... 159

Chapter 5: Tracking Expenses in QuickBooks 161

Accrual Vs. Cash Expense Tracking...162

Entering Bills...164

Entering Header Data 165

Entering the Details.. 166

Using the Items Tab... 166

Using the Expenses Tab... 166

Accounts Payable Postings 167

Memorizing Bills..168

Creating a Memorized Bill... 168

Using the Memorized Transaction List.. 170

Modifying or Deleting Memorized Transactions....................... 170

Changing the Display of the Memorized Transaction List........................ 170

Marking a Memorized Bill for Payment.. 171

Creating Memorized Transaction Groups 171

Adding Transactions to a Group 172

Entering Vendor Credits...173

Managing Vendor Refunds 174

Paying Bills 175

Working in the Pay Bills Window.. 177

Paying Bills by Check.. 178

Paying Bills by Credit Card.. 179

Paying Bills by Online Payment.. 179

Selecting the Bills to Pay.. 179

Adjusting the Amounts to Pay 180

Applying Credits 180

Bill Payment Postings 180

Using Direct Disbursements 181

Using Manual Direct Disbursement Checks.................................... 182

Printing Direct Disbursement Checks 183

Printing a Single Check Quickly 183

Printing Checks in Batches... 184

Postings for Direct Disbursements 184

Petty Cash Expenses..184

Filling the Cash Box 185

Recording Petty Cash Disbursements 186

Tracking Petty Cash Disbursements for Expenses................................ 186

Tracking Petty Cash Advances.. 187

Refilling the Cash Box 190

Tracking Debit Cards 190

Running Vendor and Expenses Reports...193

Chapter 6: Managing Inventory.. **195**

Tracking Inventory Items..196

Setting Inventory Preferences.. 197

Naming Inventory Parts.. 198

Creating an Inventory Item Properly 198

Tracking Inventory Locations 202

Inventory Accounting Tasks 203

Creating Accounts for Inventory Accounting 203
Acquiring Inventory 205
   Using Purchase Orders *205*
Writing a Check.. 206
Receiving Items... 207
   Receiving Items without the Bill... *207*
   Receiving Items with the Bill... *208*
   Entering a Bill *209*
   Paying Bills *210*
Tracking the Quantity and Value of Inventory Items 212
Selling Inventory... 213
Valuation Methods for Inventory... 214
   Average Cost... *215*
   QuickBooks Average Costing.. *216*
   FIFO (First In, First Out) *218*
   LIFO (Last In, First Out).. *220*
   Specific Identification... *220*
Manufacturing Assembled Products 221
Creating Group Items.. 221
Adjusting Inventory 223
Counting Inventory 223
   Create an Inventory Count Worksheet *224*
   Freeze Inventory Activity During the Count *226*
Adjust Inventory Quantities after the Count 226
Managing Returned Damaged Inventory Items 227
Using an Item Designed for Damaged Inventory Returns........................... 228
Inventory Adjustments for Damaged Items 229
Adjusting Inventory for "Freebies" 229
Work In Process..230
The Theory of Work In Process 230
WIP Redefined for Small Businesses 231
   Tracking Production Costs in WIP.. *231*
   Moving WIP into Inventory.. *232*
Setting Up WIP in QuickBooks... 233
   Tracking WIP Transactions *234*
Running Inventory Reports 235
Inventory Report Tips 236

Tracking Inventory Reorder Points 236

Inventory Valuation Report Problem I 237

Inventory Valuation Report Problem II 238

Chapter 7: Managing Bank Accounts 241

Creating Bank Accounts 242

Entering Opening Bank Account Balances 243

Configuring Checking Preferences 244

My Preferences 244

Company Preferences 245

Transferring Funds between Accounts 247

Using the Transfer Funds Feature 247

Writing a Check to Transfer Funds.. 248

Handling Bounced Checks 250

Using the Record Bounced Check Feature.................................. 250

Adjusting Account Balances for Bounced Checks 252

Using the Bank Register 253

Using a Journal Entry 254

Recording Bank Charges for Bounced Checks............................ 255

Invoicing Customers for Bounced Checks 256

Creating an Item for a Bounced Check Replacement 256

Creating an Item for Service Charges.. 257

Creating the Invoice 258

Voiding Disbursements 258

Reconciling Bank Accounts 259

Examining the Bank Statement.. 260

Preparing to Reconcile.. 261

Adding Missing Disbursements to the Register........................ 261

Adding Missing Deposits to the Register................................. 262

Using the Begin Reconciliation Window....................................... 263

Entering Interest Income and Service Charges........................ 264

Reconciling Transactions 264

Eliminating Future Transactions 265

Clearing Transactions... 265

Viewing Transactions During Reconciliation............................ 266

Adding Transactions During Reconciliation 266

Deleting Transactions During Reconciliation 267

Editing Transactions During Reconciliation 267

Resolving Missing Check Numbers 268
Finishing the Reconciliation 268
Resolving Reconciliation Problems 269
Pausing the Reconciliation Process 270
Creating an Adjusting Entry 270
Resolving Differences in the Beginning Balance 271
Viewing the Previous Reconciliation Discrepancy Report 271
Imposing Bank Account Security Measures 273
Online Banking 275
Using the Bank Feed Setup Wizard 276
Using the Bank Feeds Center 278
Downloading Transactions 279
Using Renaming Rules 282
Setting Online Banking Preferences 284

Chapter 8: Tracking Assets **287**

Tracking Cash 288
Tracking Accounts Receivable 288
Tracking Loans Owed To You 289
Creating the Loan 289
Sending Loan Payment Invoices 290
Receiving Loan Payments 291
Vendor Deposits and Prepaid Expenses 292
Tracking Deposits Sent to Vendors 294
Returns of Vendor Deposits 295
Tracking Prepaid Expenses 296
Allocating Yearly Payments to Monthly Expenses 297

Inventory Asset 297
Fixed Assets 298
Creating Fixed Asset Accounts 298
Using the Fixed Asset Item List 300
When to Use the Fixed Asset Item List 300
What is Depreciation? 301
Purchasing a Fixed Asset 302
Cash Purchase of a Fixed Asset 303
Financed Purchase of a Fixed Asset 304
Intangible Assets 305

Intellectual Property 305

Organizational Costs 306

Goodwill 307

What is Amortization? 307

Chapter 9: Tracking Liabilities **309**

Accounts Payable 310

Customer Upfront Deposits.. 310

  Creating Accounts for Upfront Deposits 310

  Creating Items for Upfront Deposits... 311

  Recording an Upfront Deposit 312

  Applying a Customer Deposit to an Invoice 313

Client Retainers 314

  Receiving Retainers 315

  Applying Retainers to Invoices... 316

  Making Deposits into Subaccounts 318

Tracking Escrow 322

  Receiving Funds into an Escrow Bank Account.. 323

  Disbursing Escrow Funds 324

Sales Tax 325

  Remitting Sales Tax 326

    Adjusting Sales Tax Amounts 327

Loans to Your Company 328

  Current Liabilities Vs. Long-Term Liabilities 328

  Entering a Loan... 329

  Making Loan Payments... 332

Line of Credit... 335

  Entering a Draw on Your Line of Credit.. 336

  Using the Line of Credit to Pay Expenses.. 336

  Paying Interest on a Line of Credit.. 337

  Repaying Line of Credit Principal.. 338

Chapter 10: Managing Payroll **341**

Activating Payroll in QuickBooks 342

Setting Up Payroll in QuickBooks 344

  Preparing for Payroll Setup 345

Configuring QuickBooks Payroll 346

  Running the QuickBooks Payroll Setup Wizard.. 346

Configuring Payroll without the Wizard 348
  Using the Add New Payroll Items Wizard 349
  Adding Employees in the Employee Center 354
  Configuring Employee Defaults 356
Setting Payroll Preferences 358
Running QuickBooks Payroll 360
  Creating Payroll Schedules 360
  Running the Payroll 361
Understanding Payroll Accounting 364
  Gross and Net Pay 364
    Gross Pay 364
    Net Pay 365
  Payroll Liabilities 366
    Payroll Liabilities for Tax Withholding 366
    Payroll Liabilities for Employee Benefits 367
    Other Withholding Liabilities 367
  Payroll Expenses 368
    Payroll Expenses are Really Liabilities 369
    Posting Payroll Liabilities 369
    Paying Payroll Liabilities 370
    Posting Payroll Liability Payments 372
Working with Independent Contractors 373
  Reimbursing Independent Contractors for Expenses 374

**Chapter 11: Understanding & Customizing Important
          Reports 375**
Balance Sheet 376
  QuickBooks Balance Sheet Reports 377
    Balance Sheet Standard Report 378
    Balance Sheet Detail Report 378
    Balance Sheet Summary Report 379
    Balance Sheet Prev Year Comparison Report 380
  Balance Sheet Assets 380
    Balance Sheet Bank Accounts 380
    Balance Sheet Fixed Assets Accounts 381
    Balance Sheet Other Assets Accounts 382
  Balance Sheet Liabilities and Equity 382
    Balance Sheet Sales Tax Liability Account 383

Balance Sheet Loan Liability Accounts.. *384*

Profit & Loss Report..385

Net Profit or Loss 386

   Analyzing Your Business from the Profit & Loss Report 386

Accounts Receivable Report 388

   Proving the A/R Report Total against the Balance Sheet............................ 389

Accounts Payable Report 390

Inventory Reports...391

Setting Report Preferences 394

Customizing Reports..396

   Changing the Display Options... 397

     Detail Report Display Tab Options.. *397*

     Summary Report Display Tab Differences... *398*

   Creating Report Filters 400

     Using the Report Toolbar to Create Filters *400*

     Creating Custom Filters *401*

   Customizing Report Headers and Footers... 402

     Header Options *403*

     Show Footer Information *404*

     Page Layout *405*

   Modifying Fonts & Numbers Settings.. 406

Memorizing Reports...407

Importing a Report Template..408

Chapter 12: Year End Tasks **409**

Opening Balance Corrections..410

Opening Balance Equity Account 410

Basic Year-End Tasks 411

Depreciation and Amortization...413

   Creating a Depreciation/Amortization Transaction...................................... 414

   Fixed-Asset Dispositions... 417

     Sale of Fixed Assets *417*

     Retirement of Fixed Assets... *419*

Adjustments for Cash-Basis Tax Reports 419

Allocating Overhead Expenses to Divisions 421

Allocating Equity 421

Tax Forms and Tax Returns...422

Tax Forms 423
    Creating W-2s.. 423
    Generating 1099s 425
Business Tax Returns 429
    Proprietorship Tax Return.. 430
    Single Member LLC Tax Return 431
    Partnership Tax Return... 431
    LLP or Multimember LLC Tax Return 433
S Corporation Tax Return.. 434
C Corporation Tax Return 434
Closing the Books...435
Setting the Closing Date 435
Backing Up the Company File.. 437

Chapter 13: QuickBooks Maintenance 439
Backing Up with QuickBooks...440
Creating a Manual Backup... 440
    Configuring Manual Backup Options 440
Scheduled Backups 442
Offsite Storage of Backups 445
Restoring Backup Files 446
Cleaning Up Data File Corruption..448
Verify Data... 448
Rebuild Data 449
Managing Users and Passwords 450
Creating Users 451
Adding a User Name and Password 451
Setting User Permissions... 452
    Setting Permissions for Special Areas of QuickBooks 454
    Changing or Deleting Transactions Permissions.................... 456
    Closed Period Permissions 456
    Permissions Summary... 457
Changing User Settings 457
Updating QuickBooks 457
Configuring the Update Service 458
    Automatic Updates 459
    Shared Downloads 459
    Checking the Status of Updates 459

Updating QuickBooks Manually.. *460*

Importing and Exporting...460

    Import Utilities 460

    Export Utilities 461

    Third-Party Utilities... 463

Enabling Customer Credit Card Protection...464

Chapter 14: Managing Equity 467

Understanding Equity Accounts 469

Proprietorships..470

    Funding Proprietorships 470

    Withdrawing Money from a Proprietorship 471

    Personal Expenses Paid by a Proprietorship... 472

Partnerships..474

    Funding Partnerships 475

    Withdrawing Money from a Partnership 476

    Paying Personal Expenses for Partners 477

LLCs and LLPs 477

    Single-Member LLC 478

      Funding a Single-Member LLC.. *478*

      Withdrawing Funds from a Single-Member LLC...................................... *479*

Multi-member LLCs and LLPs 480

    Funding Multi-member LLCs and LLPs.. 480

    Withdrawing Funds in Multi-member LLCs and LLPs................................ 481

    Guaranteed Payments for Multi-member LLCs and LLPs 481

Corporations 483

    Funding Corporations... 483

    Loans from Stockholders 484

C Corporations..484

    C Corporation Stockholder Compensation.. 485

    C Corporation Profit Distributions... 485

    C Corporation Taxation 486

S Corporations..486

    S Corporation Stockholder Compensation.. 486

    Draws from S Corporations... 487

    S Corporation Taxation 488

CHAPTER 1:

Accounting Basics

- Understanding the Ledger

- Making Sense of Debits & Credits

- Accounting Categories

- Cash-Basis Vs. Accrual-Basis Accounting

- Fiscal Vs. Calendar Year

Business accounting is based on a double entry system of bookkeeping. This means that for every entry you make, there must be an equal and opposite entry. Opposite refers to the other side of the ledger.

The Ledger

The ledger sides are labeled DEBIT (always on the left) and CREDIT (always on the right), and you must make sure that every transaction has equal entries posted to both sides of the ledger.

Every transaction falls into a category that has a default, or "natural," side of the ledger, as seen in Table 1-1.

DEBIT	CREDIT
ASSETS	
	LIABILITIES
	EQUITY
	INCOME
EXPENSES	

Table 1-1: Each category has a "natural" side of the ledger.

QuickBooks understands this, so you only have to enter one side of the transaction. Your setup and configuration of the software pre-determines the postings. For most transactions, QuickBooks takes care of the "other side" of the entry for you automatically, without you having to think about it. (The exception is a journal entry, which is generally used to adjust existing figures in the ledger.) However, you do have to assign the appropriate account to a QuickBooks transaction, which means that you have to understand the way accounting transactions work in order to set up your software properly.

The information in Table 1-1 is the basis for all accounting, whether your business is a multinational corporation or an ice cream stand on the beach. All accounting processes follow the rules inherent in this chart, although large companies have many subcategories to refine and narrow the postings made in their accounting systems.

When a category *increases* as a result of a transaction, the amount is posted to its assigned (default) side of the ledger; when it *decreases* as a result of a transaction, the amount is posted to the opposite side of the ledger.

For example, when you enter a transaction that adds an amount to your bank account, the increase in your bank balance is posted to the Debit side of the ledger because your bank account is an asset and the Debit side is the default side for assets.

The offsetting entry is the "reason" for the transaction, which in this case is usually the receipt of business income (notice that income is on the Credit side of the ledger, and because income is increased, it is posted to its default side of the ledger).

On the other hand, when you remove money from your bank, that transaction decreases the value of that asset, so the amount is posted to the other (in this case, Credit) side of the ledger. The equal and opposite entry is the "reason" for the decrease, such as payment of an expense (notice that expenses are on the Debit side of the ledger, and since expenses have been increased by the transaction, you use the default side for that category).

Making Sense of the Debit and Credit Labels

The labels *Debit* and *Credit* can be confusing because they don't follow the logic of your generally accepted definitions for those words. How can an asset be a debit? Isn't *debit* a negative word?

These terms are used all over the world and date back to the 1400s, so it's too late to try to change them. Just live with them. The solution is to ignore your vocabulary skills and your logic and just memorize the rules and definitions. You'll be amazed at how fast you absorb the concepts once you've begun entering or examining business transactions. There are only two rules you have to memorize:

- Debits on the left, Credits on the right.
- Assets and expenses are debits by default; liabilities, equity, and income are credits by default.

ProAdvisor TIP: *If all else fails, here's a trick to remember the difference between debits and credits: Common sense tells you that a credit increases and a debit decreases. Well, that holds true for Liabilities, Equity, and Income, but it's just the opposite for Assets and Expenses. As long as you remember that Assets and Expenses are backward, you're OK.*

Accounting Categories

Every transaction posts to both sides of the ledger, using at least one category on each side. Some of the category labels are rather broad, so in this section we'll define them more specifically.

Assets

Assets are things that belong to (are owned by) your business. They are broken down into two main subcategories called Current Assets and Long-Term Assets. In turn, each of those subcategories has additional subcategories. Chapter 8 teaches you when and how to use asset accounts in transactions.

Current Assets

Current assets are best described as those things that you expect to be able to convert to cash or use as cash within one year. These are the assets that are commonly used when you're posting transactions. The following are examples of common current assets:

- **Cash**, which includes money in bank accounts, in the cash register, and in the petty cash box.
- **Accounts Receivable**, which is the money currently owed to you by customers.

- **Inventory**, which is the total value of the cost of products you purchased for resale or you purchased to create a product.
- **Loans** you make to others.
- **Prepaid expenses**, which are the monies you paid in advance of their actual use, such as prepayments on insurance premiums, payment of business tax estimates for the current year's taxes, deposits on utility accounts, etc.

Long-Term Assets

Long-term assets are those possessions that you expect to remain in use, without converting them to cash, for more than a year. The following are common examples of long-term assets:

- **Land**
- **Buildings** (and accumulated depreciation)
- **Leasehold Improvements** (and accumulated depreciation)
- **Equipment** (and accumulated depreciation)
- **Vehicles** (and accumulated depreciation)
- **Furniture and Fixtures** (and accumulated depreciation)
- **Start-Up Costs** (and accumulated amortization)
- **Goodwill** (and accumulated amortization)
- **Copyrights and Patents** (and accumulated amortization)

You will learn about tracking assets in Chapter 8, while Chapter 12 explains depreciation and amortization.

Liabilities

A liability is something that you may be holding or have the use of, but does not belong to you. It is something you owe to someone else. Like assets, liabilities are subcategorized into two groups: Current Liabilities and Long-Term Liabilities. Chapter 9 discusses the whens, hows, and whys of posting transactions to liability accounts.

Current Liabilities

Current liabilities are usually defined as debts that are due within a year. Following are the common current liabilities you track:

- **Accounts Payable**, which is money you owe vendors.
- **Payroll Liabilities**, which is money withheld from employees' pay, your business's share of taxes on that pay, and other payroll obligations due to government agencies, insurance companies, pension funds, etc.
- **Sales Tax** you have collected from customers and must turn over to the state tax authority.

Long-Term Liabilities

Long-term liabilities are debts that require more than a year to pay off. These are commonly loans, such as mortgages, business loans, equipment loans, vehicle loans, etc.

Equity

Equity tracks the value of business ownership and the value of the business. The way you track equity, including the types of categories and ledger accounts you create, depends on the way your business is organized. Following are some of the common equity categories:

- **Stock** in your company if you are a corporation.
- **Capital** invested by partners if you are a partnership.
- **Capital** invested by members if you are a limited liability partnership (LLP) or limited liability company (LLC).
- **Capital** invested by you if you are a proprietorship or single-member LLC.

- **Draws** (withdrawals of funds) if you are not incorporated.
- **Retained earnings**, which is the accumulated profit (or loss) since the business began. This is a calculated amount (income less expenses), not an account to which you normally post transactions.

Chapter 14 explains the various types of business organizations and explains when and how to post transactions to equity accounts.

Income

Income is the revenue your business receives. You can separate your income into various subcategories to analyze the source of funds. For example, if you sell both products and services, you may want to track those monies separately. If you sell services only, you may want to subcategorize your revenue by service type.

In addition to the subcategories you set up to track specific revenue sources, QuickBooks allows you to create an Other Income subcategory to cover receipts that aren't connected to your main source of revenue. For example, you may want to create accounts for Interest Income or Finance Charges Collected within QuickBooks in this category.

You may also want to track customer returns/refunds as a separate Income account instead of posting the amounts of those returns to the regular Income category in order to track gross sales. (QuickBooks will do the math for you in its report generator to calculate the net sales amount.) Chapter 4 discusses the ways to post income transactions.

Expenses

Expenses are the monies you spend to run your business. Expenses are subcategorized for the purposes of meeting the reporting requirements on tax returns and for your own analysis.

Generally we think of expenses in two main categories: Cost of Goods Sold and General and Administrative Expenses.

Cost of Goods Sold

Sometimes called Cost of Sales, this is an expense category that usually tracks what you spend to create a product that you sell from inventory. Commonly, the following expenses are tracked as Cost of Goods Sold:

- Cost of raw materials for manufacturing.
- Cost of goods you purchase for resale.
- Inbound shipping costs for raw materials or products for resale to your business.
- Cost of labor to manufacture and assemble materials into products by a manufacturing company or technician's compensation, included in billings to customers in a service industry.
- Other costs involved with creating an inventory item, such as packaging, crating, etc.

Sometimes businesses can track Cost of Goods even if they're not selling inventory items. Check with your accountant about the Cost of Goods subcategories that are appropriate for your business.

General and Administrative Expenses

The general expenses involved in running your business are tracked by category in order to calculate totals that are required for tax returns. You'll also want to track specific types of expenses so that you can analyze the way you're spending money to run your business. Some of the commonly used categories are the following:

- Advertising
- Bank service charges
- Business taxes and licenses
- Dues and subscriptions
- Employer payroll taxes
- Entertainment (of customers—not your own fun)
- Insurance

- Interest expense
- Legal and accounting services
- Office Supplies
- Payroll
- Postage and shipping
- Rent
- Subcontractors
- Telephone
- Travel
- Vehicle maintenance
- Web site expenses

You and your accountant can design the list of expenses you need to track your expenses intelligently and to prepare tax returns easily.

In addition, QuickBooks has an expense category called Other Expenses in which you can track accounts you would like to segregate when analyzing your reports. For example, you may want to segregate Income Taxes or expenses not deductible for tax purposes (e.g., Fines and Penalties).

For most businesses, the list of expense categories is quite long (the more detail-oriented you want to be as you track and analyze where you spend money, the longer it gets). Some individual transactions cover multiple expense categories (think about entering the transaction that occurs when you write a check to your credit card company). Chapter 5 covers the ways in which you use these expense categories when you're entering transactions.

Cash-Basis Vs. Accrual-Basis Accounting

An accounting method is a set of rules used to determine when income and expenses are reported to the IRS. You can use either cash basis or accrual basis as your accounting method.

There are limits to the choice on which accounting method you can use. You can't just flip a coin, nor can you decide based on what seems easier or more advantageous to your tax bill. There are rules about the accounting method you use, and those rules are created and enforced by the IRS. If you prepare your own tax returns, you should consult an accountant before determining which accounting method to use. See the section entitled "Selecting an Accounting Method," later in this chapter, for more information.

You declare your accounting method when you file your first tax return for your business. If you want to change your accounting method after that, you must apply to the IRS for permission to do so. The IRS provides forms for this purpose. (Sometimes, albeit rarely, the IRS will contact a business and order it to change its accounting method.)

You must use the same accounting method across the board, which means you can't opt to use the cash-basis method for income and the accrual method for expenses (or the other way around).

In this section, we'll explain the differences between these two accounting methods and then go over the guidelines for the types of businesses that must choose a specific accounting method.

ProAdvisor TIP: *One nice feature in QuickBooks is the ability to switch between cash– and accrual-basis reports. This means you can see the state of your business finances by creating accrual reports and then create cash-basis reports for filing your taxes. (Cash-basis is the prevalent tax accounting basis for a small business).*

Cash-Basis Accounting

The cash-basis accounting method is used by most small businesses. Cash-basis accounting means that you account for income when you receive it and account for expenses when you pay them.

In cash-basis accounting, your income for the tax year includes all revenue you receive during that year, regardless of when you sold services or products and sent an invoice to the customer. It's the date on which you receive the money that determines the year in which you report it. The date on which you deposit the money doesn't count, because you're not allowed to avoid increasing your revenue (and therefore not paying tax on it) by holding onto checks, cash, credit card sales slips, etc. and depositing them the next year. The operative word for declaring revenue is "received;" the customer's invoice date and the deposit date don't count.

For example, if you make a sale to a customer in November or December and create an invoice at that time, the amount of the invoice is not considered income if you use cash-basis accounting. Instead, you recognize the income when you receive your customer's payment, which may not be until sometime in the next year.

In most cases, states allow you to calculate and pay your sales taxes using the same method you use to report your income—cash-basis taxpayers when the customer payment is received, accrual-basis taxpayers when the customer invoice is processed. Sales tax laws are in constant flux, so you should check the current terms of your state sales tax license to learn how you should be tracking and remitting sales tax and read Chapter 4 to learn how to enter those transactions.

Your business expenses are deducted in the year you pay them. It doesn't matter when the vendor sent a bill, you deduct the expense in the year you write the check (the date on your check is what counts) or hand over cash (don't forget to get a dated receipt when you use cash).

Accrual-Basis Accounting

Accrual-basis accounting is a more precise way of keeping books than cash-basis accounting because it takes into consideration every transaction and event as it occurs. When you view your records or create reports, you see all the transactions you've created and posted, which makes it easier to analyze the health of your business.

In accrual-basis accounting, your income is recorded when you earn it, either by performing a service or selling a product. When you create an invoice for a customer, you've earned the income, and you report it in the year you earned it, even if the customer doesn't pay you until the next year.

Your expenses are recorded when you become liable for them, regardless of when you actually pay them. When you receive a bill from a vendor, you're liable for the expense, and you report the expense for the year in which you received the bill, based on the date of the bill, even if you don't pay the bill until the following year. The same is true for expenses for which you don't receive an invoice, but you know your date of liability, such as rent, interest payments on a loan, etc.

Selecting an Accounting Method

Determining your accounting method is a matter of matching your business operations with the IRS rules. Some of the rules are clear; others may seem a bit confusing and hard to interpret. Most small businesses use cash-basis accounting, but if you can't determine for sure which accounting method to use, consult an accountant.

Following is a very brief (and very oversimplified) summary of the scenarios in which the IRS insists on accrual-basis accounting for calculating your tax liability. In actuality, the rules are more complicated than set out here and include exceptions for certain business types. You must get professional advice for this decision. If your business clearly doesn't fit into one of these descriptions, you can almost certainly keep books and file taxes using the cash-basis accounting method.

- Any corporation (other than an S corporation) that has average annual gross receipts exceeding $5 million must use the accrual-basis accounting method.

- Any partnership that includes a corporation as a partner (other than an S corporation) and that has average annual gross receipts exceeding $5 million must use the accrual-basis accounting method.

- Most businesses that sell products tracked in inventory must use accrual-basis accounting for transactions that involve inventory. Some inventory-based businesses must use accrual-basis accounting entirely; other inventory-based businesses are permitted to use cash-basis accounting for non-inventory transactions. Check with an accountant to determine which of these scenarios applies to your inventory-based business. (Chapter 6 discusses the way you track inventory purchases, materials, and sales.)

CPA NOTE: *The IRS has a chart showing how to compute "average annual gross receipts."*

Fiscal Vs. Calendar Year

You don't have to use the calendar year as the basis of your bookkeeping reports and your tax filing. Instead, you may be able to use a fiscal year, determining the first month of the year for yourself. If you run your business on a fiscal year, you create year-end reports and file your taxes based on your fiscal calendar.

While it's not common for a small business to use a fiscal year instead of the calendar year (either because of habit or IRS rules), there may be circumstances in which this option is preferable.

CPA CAUTION: *If you opt to run your business on a fiscal year, you must still keep payroll records and file payroll forms on a calendar-year basis. The same rule applies to subcontractors you pay who receive Form 1099. Fortunately, QuickBooks is able to handle this scenario with ease.*

Most businesses that adopt a fiscal year do so because of their annual business cycle or in order to avoid facing year-end tasks and tax preparation chores during their busiest times of the year. This almost exclusively applies to retailers who have a surge of sales activity in November and December (and perhaps even part of January) and aren't prepared to devote the personnel and time needed to perform the intensive work involved in using a December 31 year-end date for closing the books and preparing reports for taxes.

Nonprofit organizations and government agencies almost always use a fiscal year that coincides with periods of activity and spending. School districts often adopt a fiscal year that begins July 1 and ends June 30. Governments use fiscal years, also; for example, the U.S. government's fiscal year begins October 1 and ends September 30.

CPA TIP: *If you use a fiscal year, you note that fact in reports by using the term FYxxxx, where xxxx is the year in which your fiscal year ends.*

CHAPTER 2:

QuickBooks Basics

- The QuickBooks Interface
- Getting around in QuickBooks
- Understanding QuickBooks Centers
- Setting Preferences
- Using QuickBooks Productivity Features
- Customizing Transaction Forms

QuickBooks is an extremely powerful, yet relatively easy to use piece of accounting software. You'll notice that we said "relatively." The reason for that is twofold. One, QuickBooks assumes that you have a basic understanding of accounting principles, and using it will be anything but easy unless you do. Two, QuickBooks is a feature-rich program that requires a certain amount of learning just to get the hang of all those features.

What's Under the Hood?

While we're not going to delve deep into technical details here, it's important that you understand the basic structure of QuickBooks. The first thing to understand is that QuickBooks is primarily a database that stores, manipulates, and regurgitates all your company and financial information. The database consists of three different types of tables.

- List. The list tables contain all the basic data used in transactions. For example, the Chart of Accounts table holds all the accounts to which different transactions are posted. The Item List table contains all of the inventory, services, discounts, and other line items of which transactions are composed. The Customer list table contains all the information about your customers. There are a great many lists in QuickBooks, each one containing important information about your finances.

- Transaction. The transaction tables hold the data from completed transactions. Here, you'll find the data from checks, bills, invoices, estimates, and so on.

- Information. The info tables contain your company information, your preference settings, and more.

The process is simple: you input the list information, use it in transaction forms, and retrieve the results via QuickBooks reports. QuickBooks uses the information tables to determine how QuickBooks performs certain tasks, a well as which information to use.

QuickBooks Interface Components

Between you (the user) and all those complex database tables and functions is the QuickBooks user interface. It provides comparatively uncomplicated ways to input, massage, and retrieve the information in the database.

Lists

To fill up all those list tables, you have to input the data used to create transactions. There are a lot of lists in QuickBooks, and most (not all) of them can be found on the Lists menu. There are basic lists that are found in every company file, such as the Chart of Accounts, the Item List, the Customer and Vendor lists (not on the Lists menu). What other lists you have available depends on which optional features you've enabled, such as sales tax or payroll. See Chapter 3 for details on configuring QuickBooks lists.

Transaction Forms

Whether you're writing a check, recording a cash sale, creating an invoice, or receiving inventory items, you're going to be using a QuickBooks transaction form. These forms offer fields for all the basic information you need to complete the transaction. This information—customers, products, services, taxes, prices, and so on—is pulled from the lists you've configured.

Reports

QuickBooks reports provide you with organized listings of details from lists and from transactions results. Happily, they are also quite customizable, which means you can produce reports to precisely meet your needs.

Preferences

Since not all users are alike, QuickBooks offers a number of options that allow you to control how certain actions are performed. The QuickBooks preferences are divided into 23 different categories, each one with various options related to those QuickBooks functions. Some preferences apply only to the user currently logged on, while others apply to the currently open company file (regardless of the logged-on user). Choose Edit | Preferences to open the Preferences dialog.

QuickBooks Centers

In an effort to boost productivity, QuickBooks offers a number of different centers, in which related activities are concentrated. For example, in the Customer Center, you'll find a listing of all customers and another listing of all customer-related transactions. In addition, you'll find links to related commands and reports. The centers can serve as central locations for reviewing related information and performing related tasks.

Account Registers

QuickBooks offers registers for all your bank accounts that perform very much the same function as the paper register found in your checkbook. You can view and edit information on all the transactions that have been posted to the associated bank account. Thankfully, account registers are not limited to your bank accounts. They are available for all asset (bank, A/R, inventory), liability (loans, A/P, sales taxes), and equity (owner's capital, owner's draws) accounts. To view a register, open the Chart of Accounts, highlight the account, and press Ctrl-R.

Utilities

QuickBooks offers a number of utilities that help you take care of maintenance and housekeeping chores. For example, there are utilities to check the QuickBooks database for corruption and repair it when necessary. There are utilities to assist you in importing and exporting information to and from QuickBooks. Backing up your company file on a regular basis is a very important task, and one for which QuickBooks provides another utility. Many (but not all) of the utilities are found on the Utilities menu (File | Utilities).

Mastering the QuickBooks Interface

In the 2013 version of QuickBooks, Intuit did all of its users a big favor by standardizing the user interface. In prior versions, there had been a lot of inconsistencies that were finally cleaned up in 2013. In the 2014 version, they've tweaked the interface, making it even cleaner and more efficient. The interface consists of some basic elements that we'll cover in this section:

- Home Page
- Top Icon Bar
- Left Icon Bar
- Menu Bar
- Transaction Form ribbon bar

Let's begin by taking a look at the QuickBooks interface as it first appears when you create a new company (see Figure 2-1).

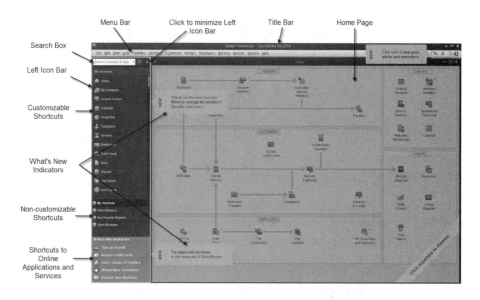

Figure 2-1: The QuickBooks interface is easy to use.

As soon as you click anywhere on the screen, the What's New boxes disappear and you're ready to get to work.

Home Page

The Home page provides a flowchart-type navigational tool. As you can see in Figure 2-1, it contains five different sections by default, each with its own tab and icons. Only three of the tabs are functional—Vendors, Customers, and Employees. Clicking those tabs opens the related centers. For example, if you click the Vendors tab, the Vendor Center opens. For more on using the QuickBooks centers, see the section later in this chapter entitled "Using QuickBooks Centers."

All of the icons on the Home Page are functional. Click any icon to open the related form or dialog box. The icons in each section provide quick access to features that are related to that section. Therefore, if you wanted to invoice an existing customer, you would click the Create Invoices icon in the Customers section to open the Create Invoices form.

Icon Bar

The Icon Bar, which used to be found only at the top of the QuickBooks window, now comes in two versions—top and left. Where you place it is entirely up to you. By default, it appears on the left, but you can easily move it to the top of the window. To do so, choose View | Top Icon Bar. While you're there, notice that there are two other Icon Bar commands— Left Icon Bar and Hide Icon Bar. That means that, in addition to putting it on the left side or the top of the window, you can hide it altogether. If you're comfortable using the menus and keyboard shortcuts, you can hide it and regain a little bit of screen real estate.

When you are using the Left Icon Bar, you can also regain a little real estate by minimizing it. Click the small, left pointing arrow next to the search box to minimize the Left Icon Bar. When you want to access it, click the top part of the bar, and it automatically expands.

Customizing the Left Icon Bar

If you decide that the default icons the Intuit programmers have added to it don't suit you, all you have to do is change them to meet your needs.

1. With the My Shortcuts displayed in the top of the bar, right-click anywhere in the My Shortcuts area and choose Customize Shortcuts. This opens the Customize Icon Bar dialog.

2. The first thing to do is get rid of shortcuts you don't use. In the Icon Bar Content list, select a shortcut to remove and click the Delete button. Don't worry, you're only hiding it. You can put it back anytime you want.

3. If you want to add a shortcut that's missing, click the Add button to display the Add Icon Bar Item dialog. Choose a command in the list to the left, select an icon to represent the command, and enter (or modify) the Label and Description fields. Click the OK button to add the icon to the Left Icon Bar.

4. To edit an existing icon (to change the icon graphic or text labels), choose the icon and click the Edit button. When the Edit Icon Bar Item dialog opens, make the necessary changes and click OK to save them.

5. To reposition icons on the icon bar, move them up or down in the Icon Bar Content list. Keep in mind that if you switch to the Top Icon Bar, the icons on the top of the list will appear to the left of the bar and those on the bottom will appear to the right.

ProAdvisor TIP: *While you can drag an icon up and down in the Icon Bar Content list to position it, there's an easy way to determine its placement before adding it: Select the icon below which you want the new icon to appear before clicking the Add button. When you add the icon, it automatically appears below the icon you selected in the Icon Bar Content list.*

Unfortunately, that's all the customizing you can do on the Left Icon Bar. To make any more changes, you'll have to switch to the Top Icon Bar.

Customizing the Top Icon Bar

When the Top Icon Bar is visible, you can make the same changes described in the previous section, as well as a few more. You'll notice that there are several options grayed out in the Customize Icon Bar dialog when accessed from the Left Icon Bar. However, if you access it from the Top Icon Bar (right-click and choose Customize Icon Bar), the same dialog appears with all the options available. The following three options can only be set from the Top Icon Bar:

- Add Separator. If you want to create groups of icons, you can place a separator bar between them. Select an icon in the Icon Bar Content list and click the Add Separator button. The separator bar is called "(space)" in the list and appears below the selected icon. On the Top Icon Bar, the separator appears as a dark, vertical line between icons. Separators do not appear in the Left Icon Bar.

- Icon Bar Display Options. You have two choices here— Show Icons And Text and Show Icons Only. The first displays both the icon and the Label text on the Top Icon Bar. The second displays the icon only. It lets you place more icons on the Top Icon bar. Enabling this option has no effect on the Left Icon Bar.

- Search Box Display Options. The Search Box appears on the right end of the Top Icon Bar as long as this option is checked. Uncheck it and the Search Box disappears from the Top Icon Bar. Disabling this option has no effect on the Search Box that appears at the top of the Left Icon Bar.

As you can see, the reason these options are grayed out on the Customize Icon Bar dialog box accessed from the Left Icon Bar is that they have no effect on the Left Icon Bar.

Adding the Active Window to the Icon Bar

If you scrutinize the Customize Icon Bar dialog box, you'll see that not all the QuickBooks commands are available in the Icon Bar Content list. Fortunately, that doesn't mean you can't add additional commands. For example, the Enter Sales Receipts command does not appear on the list, but it's a commonly used feature. To add it, follow these steps:

1. Select Customers | Enter Sales Receipts to open the Enter Sales Receipts transaction form.
2. With the form open and active (make sure it's in the forefront if you have multiple windows open), select View | Add <Enter Sales Receipts> to Icon Bar (see Figure 2-2). The Add Window To Icon Bar dialog appears.

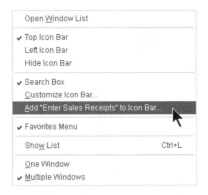

Figure 2-2: You can add most QuickBooks windows to the Icon Bar.

3. Accept or modify the Icon, Label, and Description fields.
4. Click OK to add the window to the Icon Bar.

The new icon appears on both the Top Icon Bar and the Left Icon Bar. While this works for most common windows, you may encounter some that refuse to cooperate.

The Menu Bar

The Menu bar is the one navigation tool that has been around since the early days of Windows programs. While it's being replaced in many applications with the ribbon bar, it is still a very useful means of getting around in QuickBooks. See the section later in this chapter entitled "Mastering the Menu Bar" for more information.

Using the Ribbon Bar in Transaction Forms

One of the "improvements" made in QuickBooks 2013 was the addition of ribbon bars to all the transaction windows (Create Invoices, Enter

Sales Receipts, and so on). While you may or may not like the concept of the ribbon bar, it was definitely an improvement in that it gave all the transaction forms a standard interface. In addition, it's fairly easy to use and includes all the necessary commands. To organize the different sets of commands, the ribbon bars have from two to five tabs, depending on the transaction form.

ProAdvisor TIP: *Transaction form ribbon bars have two handy icons tucked up in the top, right-hand corner. The first, the icon with four diagonal arrows, lets you view the transaction form full-screen. The second, a small up arrow, hides the ribbon bar, leaving only the tabs exposed.*

Main Tab

All ribbon bars have a Main tab with the basic commands used in conjunction with the form. As you can see in Figure 2-3, the Enter Sales Receipts ribbon bar contains buttons for saving, printing, e-mailing, and a variety of other actions.

Figure 2-3: Commonly used commands reside on the Main tab.

Most of the icons are self-explanatory. However, there a couple that warrant a little further discussion. For example, clicking the Save icon produces a menu with the options to simply save the sales receipt or to save it as a PDF file. The same is true with the Delete icon. Clicking it displays a menu with both Delete and Void commands.

Formatting Tab

The Formatting tab (see Figure 2-4) is found on forms that can be customized, such as Create Invoices, Create Estimates, Enter Sales Receipts, and others.

Figure 2-4: The Formatting tab lets you customize the form.

In addition to Preview, Spelling, and line command icons, the Formatting tab contains three buttons that provide quick access to the customization features. Click Manage Templates to open the Manage Templates window, where you can create a copy of the form template, change its name, or even download additional templates.

The Download Templates icon takes you to the Intuit Community Forms web page, where you can locate and download pre-designed form and report templates.

If you want to do some serious customizing of the current form template, click the Customize Data Layout icon to launch the Advanced Customization window. Here, you can make changes to the header, body, and footer of the form.

ProAdvisor NOTE: *If you attempt to customize a default form template such as the Intuit Product Invoice, you'll receive a message informing you that the template is locked and you must first make a copy. Most of the form templates with Intuit in the name are locked templates.*

Send/Ship Tab

You'll find the Send/Ship tab on invoice, sales receipt, and estimate forms, since they are the only ones used for recording transactions that might involve the shipping of products.

All three templates contain an Email icon that gives you the option to e-mail the current invoice or a batch of saved invoices. The shipper (FedEx, UPS, USPS) icons are found on the sales receipt and invoice templates, since items sold using either form might be shipped to the customer. The other icons found on the estimate and invoice templates are for creating and sending correspondence related to the templates. As you can see in Figure 2-5, the icons vary depending on the transaction form.

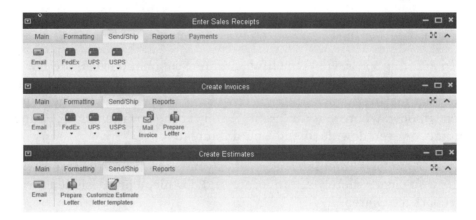

Figure 2-5: Tab icons may vary from template to template.

Reports Tab

As you'd imagine, the Reports tab contains icons for generating reports related to the transaction form. All templates with the ribbon bar contain a Reports tab; however, the available icons vary from form to form (see Figure 2-6). Only the Quick Report and Transaction History icons appear on all the templates.

Figure 2-6: Use the Reports tab to access common reports.

Payments Tab

The Payments tab is found on the Enter Sales Receipts form and the Receive Payments form, two forms used for recording customer payments. As you can see in Figure 2-7, the tab contains a single icon for adding credit card processing. This is an add-on service offered by Intuit for an additional fee. Click the icon to visit the corresponding web page to get information or to sign up.

Figure 2-7: Intuit offers fee based credit card processing.

Regardless of which form you're in, you don't have to rely entirely on the ribbon bar. You can still access some commands by right-clicking anywhere in the header area of the form and choosing a command from the context menu that appears.

Getting Around in QuickBooks

Navigating through the various QuickBooks lists, forms, and windows is done using one of four methods:

- Menu Bar
- Icon Bar (Top or Left)
- Shortcut Keys
- Home Page

If you're like most users, you'll probably end up using at least three of the four methods to some extent. It's almost impossible to fit all the commands you need on the Icon Bar. While keyboard shortcuts are very handy, not every command has one. Not only that, but most people would be hard-pressed to remember them all. QuickBooks beginners will probably use the Home Page for a while and then switch to some combination of the other methods.

Mastering the Menu Bar

To use the Menu bar, click the menu title to display a menu of related commands. An item on the menu with a small right arrow indicates that there's a submenu of additional commands related to that first item.

If you're a diehard keyboard fanatic (or your mouse battery happens to die), you can access the menu commands via the keyboard. Press the Alt key to activate the Menu bar. To display a menu, press the underlined letter on the keyboard. For example, to open the Vendors menu, you would press Alt-O. Once the menu opens, you can use a command by pressing its underlined letter on the keyboard. In other words, once you have the Vendors menu open, press the letter V to open the Vendor Center.

To make the most of the Menu bar, you should take advantage of the Favorites menu. It enables you to create a menu of all your most frequently used (favorite) commands. Click the Favorites menu title and select Customize Favorites to open the Customize Your Menus dialog box. Move any commands you want to appear on the Favorites menu from the Available Menu Items column to the Chosen Menu Items column. Click OK when you're done, and all the items appear on the Favorites menu. You can even include other menus on the Favorites menu.

New in QuickBooks 2014 are the three icons found on the right side of the Menu bar—Alerts, Reminders, and Client Collaborator. Clicking the Alerts icon (which is shaped like a bell) opens the QuickBooks Maintenance Alerts window, which displays alerts related to optimal running of QuickBooks. The Reminders icon displays the number of current reminders; when clicked, it opens the Reminders window.

Client Collaborator

The Client Collaborator is a handy feature that enables you and your accountant to correspond about specific QuickBooks transactions. It's free for you, but your accountant must be subscribed to the service for it to work. The two prerequisites are an e-mail invitation from your accountant, and a company file that is synced with Intuit's servers. When the e-mail arrives from your accountant, follow the instructions. In effect, you're both inviting the other to connect to your company file.

Once you and accountant are both connected to the service, open a transaction about which you want to ask your accountant, click the arrow next to the icon on the menu bar, and select a command (see Figure 2-8).

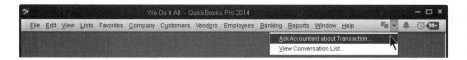

Figure 2-8: Ask your accountant a question.

Your choices are:

- Ask Accountant About Transaction. This command only appears if a transaction form is open and active. Selecting it opens the sign-in dialog (if you haven't already signed in), and then the Transaction Conversation dialog shown in Figure 2-9. Enter your question to the accountant, click the Add & Open Conversation List button, and then click the Notify Accountant button in the Transaction Conversations window. If you click the other button, the question is saved, but your accountant is not notified that you have left a question.

- View Conversation List. To review the ongoing thread(s) with your accountant, click the View Conversation List command to open the Transaction Conversations dialog. If you haven't received a timely response from your accountant, click the Notify Account button to send a reminder.

Figure 2-9: Use the Add & Open Conversation List button

Using the Icon Bar (Top or Left)

Basic navigation with the Icon Bar is the same whether you're using the Top or the Left Icon Bar. Click an icon to open the associated form or window. It doesn't get much simpler. As noted in the earlier section entitled "Icon Bar," you can minimize the Left Icon Bar so that it hugs the left side of the window and expands when you click it.

The advantage to using the Left Icon Bar over the Top Icon Bar is that it provides additional shortcuts not found on the Top Icon Bar. Clicking any of the following buttons displays the related content in the top half of the Left Icon Bar:

- My Shortcuts. Click this button to display the shortcut icons found on the Top Icon Bar.

- View Balances. Click this button to display the current balances for A/R, A/P, all your bank accounts, or any account in your Chart of Accounts. Click an account to display the account register. To add or remove accounts, click the Customize View Balances link to open the Customize Account Balances dialog box. Move an account from the Available Accounts pane to the Selected Accounts pane, and it will appear on the Left Icon Bar.

- Run Favorite Reports. This is a little like the Favorites menu on the Menu bar. However, it's only for reports. Click the button to display an icon for the Report Center and any reports you've previously selected. To add reports, click the Customize Reports link at the bottom or right-click and select Add Reports. This opens the Customize Favorite Reports dialog. Move the reports you want to appear in the Left Icon Bar from the Available Reports column to the Favorite Reports column and click OK.

- Open Windows. If you work with multiple windows open at the same time, you'll appreciate this button.

It lists all the currently open windows. Click a window name to bring it to the forefront.

ProAdvisor TIP: *You can reduce or expand the top section of the Left Icon Bar by dragging the bottom up or down. If you drag it as far down as it goes, the buttons turn into a row of small icons, giving you the maximum amount of space without losing access to those buttons.*

One last thing you'll find on the Left Icon Bar is the Do More With QuickBooks section. It's a marketing vehicle for Intuit's fee-based services. Unfortunately, you can't remove it, as it takes up valuable space that could be better used for shortcuts or other features.

Taking Advantage of Shortcut Keys

For those of us who prefer using the keyboard when possible, shortcut keys are a godsend. Rather than using multiple mouse clicks to accomplish a task, a quick combination of keystrokes does the same thing in a fraction of the time. For example, to open the Chart of Accounts window with the mouse, you have to click the Lists menu, locate, and then click the Chart Of Accounts menu item. Pressing Ctrl-A gets you to the same place with a minimum amount of work.

As you can see, there are a number of useful shortcut keys available in QuickBooks. Some of the shortcut keys work differently depending on which QuickBooks window you happen to be in. For example, if you are in an account window, Ctrl-R opens the related account register. Otherwise, it opens the Account Register dialog box, from which you select the account register you want to view.

You can also use standard Windows shortcuts like Ctrl-Z (undo), Ctrl-C (copy), Ctrl-V (paste) and so on. However, be careful as QuickBooks has co-opted a few Windows shortcuts for its own use. For example, Ctrl-A will surprise you if you expect it to "select all". Instead, it opens the Chart Of Accounts window.

There are quite a few handy shortcuts available for those features most frequently used. Table 2-1 provides a listing of them.

QuickBooks Feature	Shortcut Key
Chart of Accounts	Ctrl-A
Customer Center	Ctrl-J
Create Invoices	Ctrl-I
Write Checks	Ctrl-W
Memorized Transaction List	Ctrl-T
Find (opens the Find window)	Ctrl-F
Search (opens the Search box)	F3
Use Register	Ctrl-R
QuickReport	Ctrl-Q
Create New (item, account, customer, etc. in the related window)	Ctrl-N
Memorize current transaction	Ctrl-M
Insert Line (in transaction form)	Ctrl-Ins
Delete Line (in transaction form)	Ctrl-Del
Make General Journal Entries	Ctrl-U
Product Information	F2
Tech Help Window	F2, then F3
Get Payroll Updates	Ctrl-Shift-U
QuickBooks Help	F1

Table 2-1: Handy shortcut keys to know.

ProAdvisor TIP: *There's another shortcut that requires a little explanation, but can come in very handy. It only works when your cursor is in a drop-down list. Open a transaction form that contains a drop-down list of items from one of the many QuickBooks lists. For example, press Ctrl-W to open the Write Checks window. Move to the Expenses tab and click in the Account column. Now, press Ctrl-L, and the Chart of Accounts window opens. Select an account and press Ctrl-U to add the account to the Expenses tab of the Write Checks form.*

If you like a visual map of the principal QuickBooks features, you'll probably find the Home Page quite useful. It is basically a flowchart with links to the most commonly used features (see Figure 2-10). It clearly illustrates the normal workflow a business owner would follow in completing various accounting tasks.

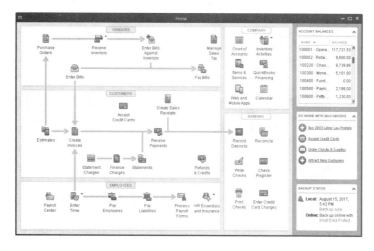

Figure 2-10: The Home Page offers quick access to basic features.

One thing to note is that the Home Page changes depending on the position of the Icon Bar. The Home Page seen in Figure 2-10 is from a company file with the Top Icon Bar displayed. When the Left Icon Bar is displayed, the right pane, with the Account Balances and Do More With QuickBooks sections, disappears, since they're on the Left Icon Bar itself.

Using the Home Page is a breeze. Click the tabs to open the related centers (Vendors, Customers, or Employees). Click an icon to open a form.

By default, the Home Page appears every time you open QuickBooks. To prevent it from appearing each time, disable the Show Home Page When Opening A Company File option. You'll find it on the My Preferences tab of the Desktop View preferences.

Understanding QuickBooks Centers

QuickBooks centers, of which there are as many as nine in QuickBooks Pro, provide central locations from which to manage related activities and data. For example, the Customer Center offers access to customer records, transactions, notes, to-dos, and more.

Customer, Vendor, and Employee Centers

These three centers are grouped together because they offer the same basic features, albeit for different groups. Take a look at the Customer Center, shown in Figure 2-11, to get an idea of the layout of all three centers.

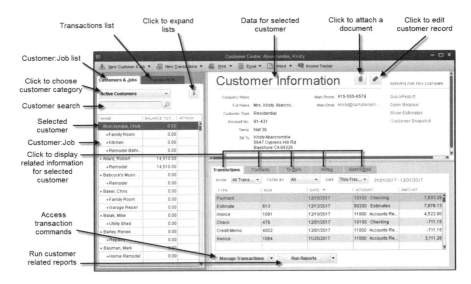

Figure 2-11: The Customer, Vendor, and Employee Centers contain most of the same features.

With some minor differences, the Customer Center and Vendor Center are practically identical. The Employee Center has one additional tab in the list pane on the left. That is the Payroll Center, which is covered in the next section. The Employee Center also is missing the Contacts tab in the bottom right pane, since the only legal contact for an employee is the employee.

Name List

Each of the three centers discussed here has a name list/tab in the left pane. When a name is selected from the name list, basic information for that name is displayed in the top right pane. The information is pulled directly from the record (for that name), which you can open and modify by clicking the Edit icon (pencil nub icon).

The bottom right pane displays additional information related to the selected name. The Customer and Vendor Centers display all five tabs discussed below, while the Employee Center is missing the Contacts tab.

- Transactions. By default, the Transactions tab displays all the selected customer's transactions for the current fiscal year. You can use the Show, Filter By, and Date drop-down lists to filter the list as needed. Double-click a line item to display the original transaction.

- Contacts. Click this tab to see a listing of all the contacts for the selected customer or vendor. (Remember, the Employee Center does not have a Contacts tab.) Double-click a contact name to open the Contacts dialog box, where you can view or modify the contact's data.

- To Do's. Click the To Do's tab to view or edit existing to-do items or to create new ones.

- Notes. Here's where you'll find existing notes attached to the selected record. The tab has three columns— Date, Notes, and a reading pane that displays the contents of the selected note. To add a new note, right-click in the Date or Notes column and select Add New to open the Notepad dialog box.

- Sent Email. This one's new in QuickBooks 2014 and is a welcome addition. If you're using Microsoft Outlook as your default e-mail client, QuickBooks now keeps track of all e-mails that you send to customers, vendors, and employees. Click this tab to see a listing of sent e-mails.

The two drop-down lists at the bottom of the pane contain commands that apply to the selected tab. For example, if the Transactions tab is activated, you have access to transaction-related commands and reports.

The drop-down lists and available commands vary depending on the tab selected.

Transactions List

To see the Transactions list, click the Transaction tab. As you can see in Figure 2-12, the Transactions list displays transaction categories in the left pane and individual transactions for the selected category in the right pane.

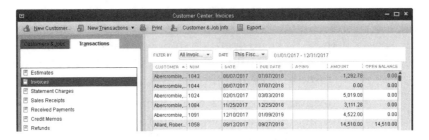

Figure 2-12: The Transactions tab in all three centers provides quick access to all related transactions.

Choose a category in the left pane, and all transactions of that type will appear in the right pane. By default, all transactions (for the selected category) for the current fiscal year are displayed. Use the Filter By and Date drop-down lists to filter the transactions as needed.

Double-click a line item to view the original transaction. To create new transactions, click the Manage Transactions button to display a list of transaction-related commands. Use the Run Reports button to create a report based on the list of displayed transactions.

Payroll Center

If you have a current payroll subscription from Intuit, you'll see that the Employee Center, unlike the Customer and Vendor Centers, has three tabs instead of two. The third tab, Payroll, opens the Payroll Center when clicked (see Figure 2-13). You can also access the Payroll Center by selecting Employees | Payroll Center from the Menu bar.

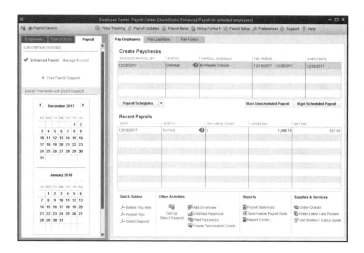

Figure 2-13: The Payroll Center is a center within a center (in the Employee Center).

As you can see if you refer back to Figure 2-13, the Payroll Center contains a left pane displaying the payroll subscription status and a calendar, while the right pane displays three payroll-related tabs:

- Pay Employees. The top section lists all payroll schedules you've created and a history of recent payrolls. In addition, it has buttons to work with schedules and to run both scheduled and unscheduled payrolls and a group of icons for payroll-related activities in the bottom section. See Chapter 10 for more on configuring payroll, including payroll schedules.

- Pay Liabilities. Here, you'll find a list of current payroll liabilities due, a history of past payments, and icons for liability payment activities.

- File Forms. With an Enhanced Payroll subscription, you can use this section to file your tax forms electronically with the appropriate tax agency. If you have a Full Service payroll subscription, the forms are filed for you, but you can view them here.

Lead Center

The Lead Center offers QuickBooks users an easy way to keep track of prospective customers. While it is by no means a full-fledged CRM (Customer Relationship Management) utility, it does provide some basics. Select Customers | Lead Center to open the Lead Center (see Figure 2-14).

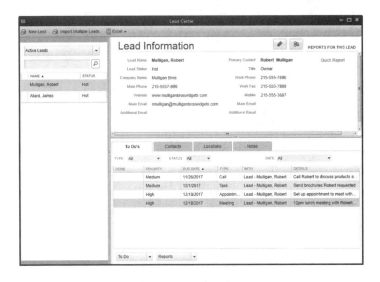

Figure 2-14: The Lead Center lets you track potential customers.

Here's what you *can* do within the Lead Center:

- Add new leads and edit existing leads.
- Copy and paste multiple leads from an Excel spreadsheet, Word document, or other source.
- Enter substantial contact information, including multiple contacts and locations.
- Add Notes and To Do items to each lead.
- Easily convert the lead into a QuickBooks customer.

Here's what you *cannot* do within the Lead Center:

- Create an estimate. A serious flaw, since an estimate is a useful tool in converting a lead to a customer.

- Use the Search Box to locate a lead. You can only search for leads from within the Lead Center.

- Use an advanced note feature like Date/Time Stamp, New To Do, or Print. The Lead Center notepad is a simple, no-frills notepad.

- Use Word to create correspondence with the lead or Outlook to e-mail the lead.

If prospecting and tracking potential customers is a significant part of your business, you'll want to look into a more robust Customer Relationship Manager (CRM). However, if you just need to retain a listing of leads with notes and to-do items, the Lead Center will do the job adequately.

Report Center

QuickBooks offers access to its large selection of pre-designed reports via the menu system and the Report Center. While the menu system is quick and easy, the Report Center is more visual and intuitive. To access the Report Center seen in Figure 2-15, Choose Reports | Report Center.

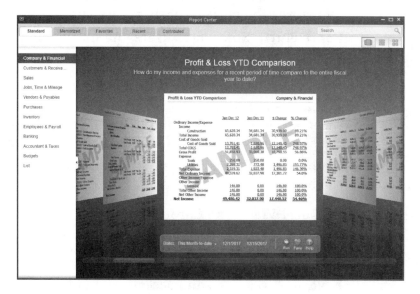

Figure 2-15: The Report Center offers easy access to QuickBooks reports.

Navigating the Report Center is easy. It contains two sets of navigational tools, which, when used together, provide quick access to all the reports available within QuickBooks and on the Internet.

First, there are the tabs:

- **Standard.** This is where you'll find the pre-designed QuickBooks reports. Select a category in the left pane to display the available reports in the right pane. What you see depends on the view you've selected.

- **Memorized.** When you memorize a report to preserve the customizations you've made, it gets parked on the Memorized tab.

- **Favorites.** Just like the Favorites on the Menu bar is used for quick access to frequently used commands, the Favorites tab in the Report Center is used for quick access to commonly used reports. Reports on this tab also appear in the Run Favorite Reports section of the Left Icon Bar.

- **Recent.** QuickBooks keeps track of the reports you run and stores the most recently run reports on this tab.

- **Contributed.** Since most users end up customizing reports at one time or another, Intuit decided to give them the opportunity to share those customized reports. If you access the Contributed tab while connected to the Internet, you'll see customized reports shared by users and by Intuit, separated into the same basic categories found on the Standard tab.

Next, there are the View buttons, located on the right side of the window, below the Search box:

- **Carousel View.** The Carousel View (refer back to Figure 2-15) displays a graphical sample of each report with buttons below the sample to change the date range, run the actual report, add it to your Favorites (reports), and access related help files. To navigate the Carousel View, you use the reports on either side of the central report as Next and Previous buttons. Click the report to the right to display the next available report. To return to a previous report, click the report to the left.

- List View. The graphical interface of the Carousel View is pretty, but it takes up a lot of real estate. If you can get by with descriptions of the reports, opt for the List View. It provides the report title, a brief description, and options for changing the date range, running the report, viewing a sample, adding it to the Favorites, and accessing help.

- Grid View. The Grid View is a cross between the other two. It offers small, sample report graphics, along with the same options found on the List View.

Bank Feeds Center

To access the Bank Feeds Center, you must have at least one bank account that is activated for online services. When you create a new bank account, QuickBooks asks if you want to set up online services and launches the Bank Feed Setup wizard that walks you through the process. As soon as you have at least one bank account configured for online access, you can use the Bank Feeds Center (see Figure 2-16).

Figure 2-16: Online banking was never this easy.

As you can see, the Bank Feeds Center has two panes. The left pane displays all the accounts that are configured for online access. The right pane displays the balances for those accounts, plus any new transactions that have been downloaded recently. Click the Transaction List button to open the Transactions List window (see Figure 2-17). If there are no transactions to add to the register, the Transaction List button changes to a Download Transactions button.

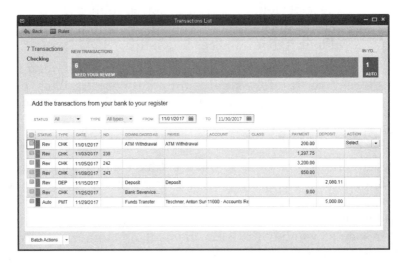

Figure 2-17: Select the transactions to match.

How you add transactions to your bank or credit card account register depends on whether the transactions already exist in QuickBooks. See Chapter 7 for more information about using the Bank Feeds Center.

Doc Center

The ability to attach documents and other files to QuickBooks records and transactions is very handy, indeed. The Doc Center is a central repository for attachments. You can either attach documents directly to individual records and transactions or store the documents in the Doc Center and make the links from there. To access the Doc Center, choose Company | Documents | Doc Center from the Menu bar.

Those documents attached to records or transactions appear with the record or transaction denoted in the Attached To column (see Figure 2-18).

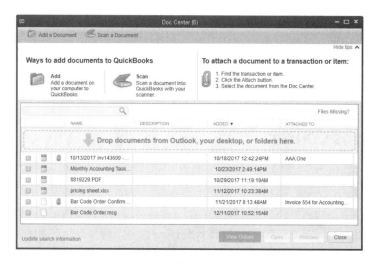

Figure 2-18: The Doc Center keeps track of all your attached
documents and files.

You can add documents/files to the Doc Center by clicking the Add button and searching your computer for files to add. You can also click the Scan button and use an attached scanner to scan a document into the Doc Center directly. If you have Windows Explorer or Outlook open, you can even drag items directly from either of those programs into the Doc Center.

From within a QuickBooks record or transaction, you can click the Attach icon (paperclip icon) and add the document/file from your computer, a scanner, or from the Doc Center itself.

ProAdvisor TIP: *A document that appears in the Doc Center can only be attached to one record or transaction at a time. Once it has been attached, it no longer appears when you click the Attach icon and then click the Doc Center icon. Fortunately, there's a way to link the same document to multiple records and/or transactions. Instead of using the Doc Center icon, simply drag the document/file into the Attachments window of the record or transaction. It will then appear twice when you open the Doc Center and denote the different records/ transactions to which it is attached.*

You can view the documents in the Doc Center by double-clicking each item to open it in the associated program. Of course, this will only work if you have the necessary program or viewer installed. If you try to open an Excel spreadsheet without having Excel or a viewer installed, you'll get an error message instead.

Collections Center

At first glance, experienced QuickBooks users will probably think the Collections Center has been eliminated. It used to automatically appear as an icon on the Customer Center menu bar. It's no longer there...by default, anyway. It's now an option that can be enabled in the Preferences dialog. To turn it on, click Edit | Preferences and choose Sales & Customers in the left pane and Company Preferences in the right. There, you'll see a new option called Enable Collections Center that, when checked, will put the icon back in the Customer Center.

To view the Collections Center (after the preference has been enabled), open the Customer Center (Ctrl-J) and click the Collections Icon that appears. You'll see that it provides a quick view of overdue and soon-to-be overdue invoices. Included are the customer, invoice number, amount, number of days overdue, and the customer's primary telephone. In addition, it has icons for sending overdue and near-overdue e-mail notices and for adding notes.

Setting QuickBooks Preferences

After its powerful accounting features, the QuickBooks Preferences are the next-most important features you'll want to take advantage of. These are the customization options for the program that allow you to dictate how QuickBooks responds in a multitude of ways. From using account numbers to pre-filling transaction forms to changing the display colors and a whole lot more, these options help you make QuickBooks work your way.

To access the QuickBooks Preferences, choose Edit | Preferences from the Menu bar. As you can see in Figure 2-19, the Preferences dialog consists of a left pane with an alphabetical listing of categories and a right pane with two tabs—My Preferences and Company Preferences.

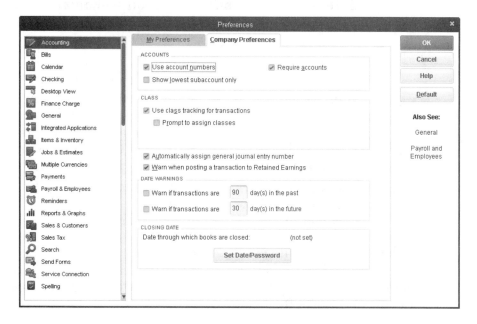

Figure 2-19: QuickBooks Preferences let you control the way many QuickBooks features work.

To access configuration options, click the appropriate category in the left pane and choose either the My Preferences or the Company Preferences tab. You'll find that not all categories have options on both tabs. For example, the Accounting category only has Company Preferences options, while the Calendar category only has options on the My Preferences tab.

The reason there are two tabs is because the effect of the options varies from tab to tab.

- • My Preferences. All options found on this tab are user-specific options. In other words, these options only apply when the user who sets them is logged into QuickBooks. Therefore, if you have multiple users on the same computer, one can set the Company File Color Scheme to Green-Forest, another to Orange, and a third to Pink. As one user logs off and another logs on, the color scheme changes to match the selection of the logged-on user.

- Company Preferences. The first thing to know about Company Preferences is that only the QuickBooks administrator can make changes to the options on this tab. The next thing to be aware of is that these options are applied company-wide. It doesn't matter which user is logged on, the settings on the Company Preferences tab will be in effect. So, if the QuickBooks administrator decrees that account numbers will be used in the Chart of Accounts, they'll appear regardless of which user is logged on.

Most of the preferences categories are self-explanatory and are covered in the chapters and sections in which they are most likely to be used. However, there are two categories that relate to basic QuickBooks operations. Those we will cover in the following two sections.

Desktop View Preferences

In QuickBooks, the main area of the window below the Menu bar and Top Icon bar (if selected) is considered the desktop. It's where the individual windows appear (transaction, record, list, and so on). The Desktop View category contains options on both the My Preferences and the Company Preferences tabs.

My Preferences Tab

Here, you'll find a number of very useful options that allow you to control how QuickBooks displays windows, colors, the state of the desktop, and more (see Figure 2-20).

Set the following options to your liking. Remember, these are My Preferences options, which means that every user can choose different settings that will take effect when he or she logs into QuickBooks.

Figure 2-20: Each user can decide how the QuickBooks desktop appears.

View Options

Here, you can decide whether you want your individual QuickBooks windows maximized or not.

- **One Window.** When this option is selected, each window you open expands to fill the desktop. It doesn't prevent you from opening multiple windows. However, if you have multiple windows open, you can only see the one in the foreground. To access other open windows, you have to use the Open Window List or the Window menu on the Menu bar.

- **Multiple Windows.** If you have a large monitor, you might want to choose this option, which allows you to arrange multiple QuickBooks windows on the desktop and access them individually. You can even use the commands on the Window menu to provide order to their arrangement (Tile Vertically, Tile Horizontally, or Cascade).

Desktop Options

You'll note that this section contains three different options that apply to what appears on the desktop when you open the current company file.

- Save Options. Initially, there are three choices here. Depending on the choice you make, a fourth may appear.
  - Save When Closing Company. Choose this option to save the desktop exactly as it appears at the time you close the company file.
  - Don't Save The Desktop. To open the current company with a clean desktop (no windows open), choose this option.
  - Save Current Desktop. If you work with the same windows open most of the time, choose this option. As soon as you have the desktop the way you want it, open the Preferences dialog, choose this option, and click OK. This sets the desktop to its present state, regardless of any changes you may make afterward. The next time you open the company file, the desktop returns to the state it was in when you set the option.
    - Keep Previously Saved Desktop. Once you've chosen the Save Current Desktop option, this option appears and stays selected until you reset the Save Current Desktop option.
- Show Home Page When Opening A Company File. If you like having the Home Page appear when you open the company file, check this option. Be advised, however, that this option takes precedence over all others. Therefore, regardless of which Save option you choose, the Home Page will always appear when the company file is opened.
- Switch To Colored Icons/Light Background On The Top Icon Bar. If you use the Top Icon bar and find the silver icons on the dark background difficult to see, check this option. The Top Icon bar background

becomes light, the icons colored, and the text black. This option has no effect on the Left Icon bar.

ProAdvisor TIP: *Although it may be handy to have the company file open with frequently used windows and reports displayed, it is also potentially dangerous. A corrupted report can prevent QuickBooks from opening. If it is part of a saved desktop, the problem will occur every time you try to open the company file. Therefore, it's generally best to choose the Don't Save The Desktop option. In the event that you ignore this advice and run into the problem, there is a way to bypass the saved desktop. When you log into the company file, hold the Alt key down when clicking OK.*

Windows Settings

Here, you'll find two buttons—Display and Sounds. They are not QuickBooks settings, but rather Windows settings. Therefore, use them judiciously. Most changes will apply to all programs, not just QuickBooks. The one set of options that will apply only to QuickBooks are the sounds associated with QuickBooks actions. Click the Sounds button and then choose the Sounds tab. Scroll down the list of Program Events until you find QuickBooks. There, you can choose which sound (or none) that you want to play when you perform an action (record a transaction, memorize a transaction, etc.) in QuickBooks.

Company File Color Scheme

If you have more than one company file, this is a very handy option to have. It changes the title bar and border color of all the windows in the company file. It makes distinguishing different company files very easy. Since it works instantaneously, you can preview the change before closing the Preferences dialog.

Company Preferences Tab

As noted earlier, the options on this tab can only be modified by the QuickBooks administrator and apply company-wide, regardless of the user logged on at the time. Unfortunately, the options found here are somewhat limited and not terribly useful. They all apply to which icons appear on the Home Page. The problem is that the icons are related to features which are either turned on or off. To remove most of the icons, you have to turn off the features. This is not a very practical solution if you actually need those features.

These options are primarily for those folks who have inadvertently turned on features they don't actually need.

General Preferences

There's lots of good stuff here on both tabs. These are options that cover a wide range of features and handle the small, but not unimportant details.

My Preferences Tab

Not all users are alike; they have different likes and dislikes. The options found here allow each user to fine-tune QuickBooks to his or her liking.

- Pressing Enter Moves Between Fields. By default, the Tab key is used to move between fields and the Enter key is used to record transactions and close windows. If you prefer to use the Enter key to move between fields, check this option. From then on, you must use Ctrl-Enter (or the mouse) to record transactions or close windows.

- Automatically Open Drop-down Lists When Typing. When checked, this option searches for matches as soon as you start typing in a drop-down list field.

- Beep When Recording A Transaction. If you want an audible confirmation that a transaction has been recorded, check this option.

- Automatically Place Decimal Point. This is one that people seem to love or hate. It assumes that when you enter numbers, you want QuickBooks to stick a decimal point in between the second and third digits from the right—in other words, entering 9995 results in the number 99.95. Without the option enabled, QuickBooks places the decimal point at the end— 9995.00.

- Warn When Editing A Transaction. When enabled, this option ensures that you don't edit a transaction and leave without saving your changes. It warns you and gives you the option to save the changes or discard them.

- Bring Back All One Time Messages. As you work in QuickBooks, you'll find there are a lot messages that pop up, either warning you about something or just providing information. Most of them have an option to stop displaying the message in the future. This option brings them all back.

- Turn Off Pop-up Messages For Products And Services. Unless you want to get bombarded with Intuit advertising for products and services, check this one.

- Show ToolTips For Clipped Text. Turning this option on enables you to view the entire text of a drop-down list item or a field's content when it is too wide to display within the list/box. A tooltip appears with the complete text when you hover your mouse over it.

- Warn When Deleting A Transaction Or Unused List Item. To keep from accidentally deleting transactions or unused list items (you can't delete list items that are in use), turn this option on. It warns you when you make such an attempt. Without it, QuickBooks lets you delete transactions or unused list items with no notice.

- Keep QuickBooks Running For Quick Startups. This is one of those options that sounds good in theory, but isn't all that great in practice. It keeps QuickBooks running in the background, even when you close the program. It makes for quick startups, but it also sucks up quite a bit of memory. Unless you have tons of memory and don't keep a lot of programs running all the time, you might want to leave this option unchecked.

Automatically Recall Information

This is a very useful option if your transactions for customers and/or vendors are consistently the same. It tells QuickBooks to bring forward information from the last transaction for the selected name. It has two suboptions, one of which must be selected.

- Automatically Recall Last Transaction For This Name. This option inserts the information from the last transaction form used for this name into the new transaction form of the same type.
- Pre-fill Accounts For Vendor Based On Past Entries. If you always (or almost always) post vendors' expenses to the same accounts, this will save you time by automatically inserting those accounts into Account fields of vendor transactions.

Default Date To Use For New Transactions

When creating new transactions (invoices, sales receipts, checks, and so on), you have two choices as to what date QuickBooks uses as the transaction date.

- Use Today's Date As Default. With this option enabled, QuickBooks always inserts today's date in the transaction, regardless of the date of the last transaction.
- Use The Last Entered Date As Default. This option is very handy if you frequently enter transactions with a date different from today's date. Suppose, for example, you're preparing to send monthly invoices that always display the last day of the month. You may be creating those invoices ahead of time to ensure they are sent out on time. With this option set, all invoices after the first will contain the date used

on the first invoice. Without this option enabled, each new invoice will contain today's date, which you'll have to change.

Keep Custom Item Information When Changing Item In Transactions

It is not uncommon to add items to the Item list without descriptions and prices. This enables you to enter a different description or price each time you use the item in a transaction. Occasionally, you may choose the wrong item, but enter the correct description and/or price. When you realize your mistake and choose a different item, QuickBooks can either retain the custom information entered or discard it, depending on the setting for this option.

- Ask. Select Ask to have QuickBooks query you each time this happens. You can decide at the time whether to retain or discard the custom data.

- Always. QuickBooks won't ask; it will just carry over the custom information for the new item.

- Never. If you want QuickBooks to always discard the custom information, choose Never.

Company Preferences Tab

The Company Preferences tab has a lot fewer, but still very important, options.

- Time Format. Decide how you want time displayed in QuickBooks. This is not how the clock displays time, but rather how time entries are displayed. For example, let's say you are tracking time and enter four and half hours into the time sheet. With the Decimal option selected, it will appear as 4.5 hours. If you choose Minutes instead, it will appear as 4:30.

- Always Show Years As 4 Digits (1999). The name says it all. Do you want the date to appear as 05/01/2018 (option enabled) or as 05/01/18 (option disabled)?

- Never Update Name Information When Saving Transactions. If you make changes to customer or vendor information in a transaction form, QuickBooks will ask if you want to modify the customer or vendor record to make the change(s) permanent. For example, if you change the Billing Address, Shipping Address, Terms, or other related data, QuickBooks will ask if you want to save this information for future use. When this option is enabled, QuickBooks no longer asks and uses the information for this transaction only.

- Save Transactions Before Printing. Don't think, don't hesitate, just make sure this option is enabled. It's an important safeguard against fraud. When this option is enabled, you cannot print a transaction form until it has first been saved. This means that an unscrupulous user/employee cannot create a transaction form, print it out, and then cancel the transaction. For example, a printed sales receipt and/or packing slip could be used to order and ship merchandise that has not been paid for. There is no practical reason for disabling this option.

Using QuickBooks Productivity Features

Of course, most of the QuickBooks features could be called productivity features, as they facilitate your bookkeeping and accounting tasks. However, there are certain features that go beyond that and help automate tasks which otherwise would be quite onerous. In this section, we're going to cover the major time-saving features QuickBooks has to offer:

- Memorized Transactions
- Add/Edit Multiple List Entries
- Create Batch Invoices
- Create an Accountant's Copy

- Create a Portable Company File
- Prepare Letters with Envelopes

Memorized Transactions

Computers have saved us a tremendous amount of time and ennui by simplifying the execution of repetitive tasks. Fortunately, smart computer programs like QuickBooks can automate such tasks even further. The Memorized Transactions feature in QuickBooks does that by allowing you to save a transaction template that you reuse without having to fill in the basic information each time.

Taking advantage of the feature is easy. For the following example, let's use a rent check sent to the landlord each month.

1. Press Ctrl-W to open the Write Checks window.
2. If you have multiple bank accounts, select the appropriate account from the Bank Account drop-down list.
3. Fill in all the pertinent information, including date, payee, amount, expense account(s), and so on.
4. Click the Memorize icon on the ribbon bar Main tab.
5. When the Memorize Transaction dialog opens, give the transaction a name (e.g., Monthly Rent Check).
6. Select one of the options to either remind you about the transaction (and how often) or to automatically enter the transaction. As you make your choices, other options appear. They are pretty self-explanatory.
7. Click OK to save the memorized transaction.

When it comes time to pay the rent again, all you have to do is recall the memorized transaction and modify any information that has changed (e.g., change the memo from "March 2018 rent" to "April 2018 rent"). To access a memorized transaction, press Ctrl-T to open the Memorized Transaction List. Either select the transaction and click the Enter Transaction button or just double-click the transaction to open it.

You can memorize all kinds of transactions, including invoices, bills, estimates, sales receipts, and more.

Add/Edit Multiple List Entries

The name of this feature, while not terribly creative, is perfectly apt. Entering data into individual records is fine when you only have a couple of records to add or edit. However, it is extremely tedious when you have a large number to do. The Add/Edit Multiple List Entries automates the process for the following QuickBooks Records:

- Customers
- Vendors
- Service Items
- Inventory Items
- Non-Inventory Items

Begin by selecting Lists | Add/Edit Multiple List Entries from the Menu bar to open the Add/Edit Multiple List Entries window shown in Figure 2-21.

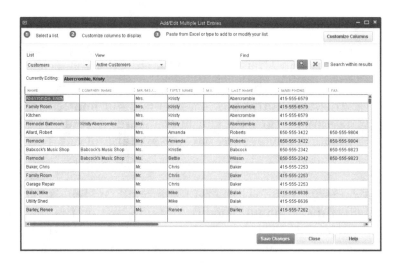

Figure 2-21: Speed up the data entry process with the Add/Edit Multiple List Entries feature.

The first thing to do is select the type of records you want to work on from the List drop-down list. Next, use the View drop-down list to filter the records. You can elect to view all records, active records, inactive records, unsaved records, records with errors, or records based on a custom filter that you create on the fly. To locate specific records, use the Find feature.

A nice feature that you'll find in many QuickBooks list windows is the Customize Columns feature, which is included here as well. Click the Customize Columns button in the top right corner of the window to display the Customize Columns dialog box. It offers two panes—Available Columns and Chosen Columns. Items listed in the Chosen Columns pane appear in the Add/Edit Multiple List Entries window. Therefore, all you have to do is move fields (columns) from one list to the other to make them appear in or disappear from the window. The higher the column appears in the Chosen Columns pane, the further to the left it will appear in the Add/Edit Multiple List Entries window.

You can enter data into any of the individual fields in the list, or you can copy (from any list document such as Excel or Word) and paste data into a column. There are also a couple of other handy features you'll find here, but which require a little understanding to be used effectively.

- Copy Down. This handy little time saver lets you copy the data from an existing field to the same field in all the rows (records) below it. For example, if you have a customer record with a Customer Type "Wholesale" and you add ten new customer records below it, you can right-click the field containing "Wholesale" and select Copy Down to fill in the Customer Type field for the rest of the records with "Wholesale." As great as it is, there's one caveat—you can't tell it when to stop, so you have to make sure that you want the value copied to every record that appears below the one with the data. The best way to do that is to apply a filter that leaves only the records you want affected.

- Duplicate Row. This command is also found on the right-click context menu. When selected, it does just what its name says—it duplicates the selected row.

- Clear Column. Use this one with caution, because it, too, does precisely what its name indicates. Regardless of where in the column you use it, the entire column, from top to bottom, is cleared of all data.

Create Batch Invoices

If you have to create multiple identical or similar invoices on a regular basis, you'll love this feature. It lets you select a template to use for as many of your customers as you need and create an identical invoice for each customer selected. It's great for invoicing rents, dues, membership fees, and more. For details on using the feature, see Chapter 4.

Create an Accountant's Copy

In the old days, before the Accountant's Copy, you had to send your accountant a copy of your company file and stop all data entry until she made her changes and returned the updated file to you. Now, it's so much simpler. You make an Accountant's Copy, send it to your accountant, and keep working while she makes her changes. When you get the file changes back, you incorporate them into your company file and just keep working.

To create an Accountant's Copy, follow these steps:

1. Choose File | Accountant's Copy | Save File to open the Save Accountant's Copy dialog.

2. With Accountant's Copy selected, click Next to proceed to the Set The Dividing Date screen (see Figure 2-22). Read about how the dividing date affects the work that can be done in the company file and enter a date. Keep in mind that you can view transactions created before the dividing date, but not modify them. You can, however, create and edit transactions dated after the dividing date.

3. Click Next and choose a location and file name for the Accountant's Copy.

4. Click Save to create the Accountant's Copy. QuickBooks saves the file with a .QBX extension and notifies you of the fact. Click OK to close the message.

5. Deliver the Accountant's Copy file to your accountant via e-mail, FTP, flash drive, or some other media.

Figure 2-22: Set a dividing date that works for you and your accountant.

You may have noticed another command called Send To Accountant on the Accountant's Copy menu. It will also create an Accountant's Copy file. The difference is that the Send To Accountant command creates the file and uploads it to an Intuit server, from which your accountant can then download it. Just make sure your accountant subscribes to the service. It's free for you but fee based for your accountant.

CPA NOTE: *The file sent to your accountant using this method needs a password for her to be able to open it. This is a password that should be separate from the password needed to open your file normally (if you have password-protected access to your data file). Talk to your accountant before assigning this unique password, as she may have a standard one for you to use.*

Accountant's Copy Restrictions

While an Accountant's Copy exists, you can work in the company file with certain restrictions. The restrictions cover three types of tasks:

- Working with transactions
- Working with lists
- Bank reconciliation

Transactions

You can create, edit, and delete transactions dated after the dividing date. You cannot work on transactions that are dated on or before the dividing date. This means that you cannot create transactions with a date on or before the dividing date and cannot edit or delete transactions that existed on or before the dividing date.

QuickBooks does not prevent you from opening a transaction that's dated on or before the dividing date, nor are you stopped if you make changes to any field in the transaction. When you close the transaction window, QuickBooks asks if you want to save the changes you made. If you select Yes, QuickBooks displays a warning message.

When you click OK, you're returned to the transaction window. Close the window and select No when you're asked if you want to save your changes.

This restriction applies to any changes, including those that may seem unimportant to the accounting processes involved in a transaction, such as changing the text in the Memo field.

Lists

The restrictions for working with list elements while an Accountant's Copy exists are not onerous. However, restrictions on the Chart of Accounts are a bit different from the restrictions on all other lists.

For the Chart of Accounts, the following rules apply (the term "existing" means that the account existed when the Accountant's Copy was created):

- You can create new accounts and perform any action (edit, merge, inactivate, or delete) on those new accounts except creating subaccounts.

- You cannot create new subaccounts for existing accounts.
- You cannot edit, merge, delete, or make inactive existing accounts or subaccounts.

For all other lists, the following rules apply:

- You can add new list elements to any list.
- You can edit any list element.
- You can merge, delete, and inactivate newly created items.
- You can edit and inactivate existing items. However, if the accountant modifies the same item, the accountant's changes will override the client's changes.
- You cannot delete a list element that existed at the time the Accountant's Copy was created.
- You cannot merge list elements that existed at the time the Accountant's Copy was created.

Bank Reconciliation

QuickBooks permits you to reconcile accounts (bank and credit card) while an Accountant's Copy exists, but when the reconciliation process starts, you see this message (Figure 2-23):

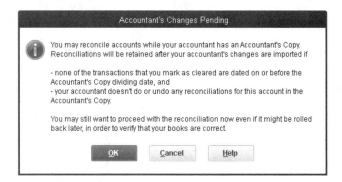

Figure 2-23: QuickBooks reminds you of the restrictions in force while an Accountant's Copy exists.

If your Accountant's Copy dividing date is only a few weeks before the current date, it's probable that some of the transactions in the bank statement are dated on or before the dividing date. In that case, wait until the Accountant's Copy has been returned and merged into your data file. The same is true if your accountant undoes a previous reconciliation. (You'll have to contact the accountant to ascertain whether this occurred.)

Create a Portable Company File

A Portable Company File is a compressed version of your company file. It is smaller in size and, therefore, easier to transport/send. The file size is reduced by excluding letters, logos, templates, graphics, and the .tlg (transaction log) file. To create a Portable Company File, follow these steps:

1. Choose File | Create Copy from the Menu bar to open the Save Copy of Backup dialog box.
2. Select Portable Company File and click Next. The Save Portable Company File dialog opens.
3. Choose a destination folder for the file, enter a new name (or accept the default name), and click Save.
4. QuickBooks displays a message that it must close and reopen your company file. Click OK.
5. QuickBooks creates the company file and displays a success dialog with the file location. Click OK to close it.

Be sure to make a note of the destination folder so that you can locate and utilize the folder. Remember, the file will have a .QBM extension. To restore a Portable Company File, choose File | Open Or Restore Company, select Restore A Portable File, and click Next. Then, follow the wizard steps.

ProAdvisor TIP: *Portable Company Files can also be used to rebuild a corrupt company file or to speed up file performance. The process re-indexes the file. Re-indexing can help resolve data problems, and it can make your company file run more efficiently. To use a company file for this purpose, you must first create a Portable Company File and then restore it. To be on the safe side, rename the file when restoring it. Once you're sure the restored file is okay, you can delete the original file.*

Prepare Letters with Envelopes

One of the great things about QuickBooks is the fact that it plays nicely with several Microsoft Office programs, including Outlook, Word, and Excel. The Prepare Letters With Envelopes feature works with Microsoft Word and allows you to create correspondence using your QuickBooks names lists (Customers, Vendors, Employees, and Other Names). It is basically a Word mail merge that is automated from within QuickBooks. Of course, this means that you can only use the feature if you have a compatible version (2003, 2007, 2010, or 2013) of Microsoft Word installed.

Select Company | Prepare Letters With Envelopes | <letter type> Letters to launch the Letters and Envelopes wizard. You can send collection letters, customer letters, vendor letters, employee letters, and letters to people on the Other Names List.

The first screen of the Letters And Envelopes wizard lets you set the criteria for choosing recipients. The choices are self-explanatory.

The next screen of the wizard displays the recipient(s) chosen based on the criteria selected in the opening screen. If everything looks okay, click Next to proceed or click Back to return to the previous screen and modify the selection criteria.

The third wizard screen lets you select an existing letter template or create your own. Make your selection and click Next to continue. If you choose an existing template, the Enter A Name And Title screen appears. In the Name field, enter the name you want to appear on the signature line of the letters. If the letter has a title, enter it in the Title field. If you elect to create your own, follow the wizard steps.

After you have selected or created a template, QuickBooks begins processing the data and creating the letter(s). If some of your QuickBooks records are missing information that is included in the letters, a QuickBooks Information Is Missing message appears, letting you know you'll have to correct that when the letters are created. Microsoft Word opens with all the letters ready to be printed and sent. Of course, if you received the missing information message, be sure to go through all the letters searching for **MISSING*INFORMATION** and replace it with the correct data.

Customizing Transaction Forms

It's easy to customize the transaction forms (called *templates* in QuickBooks) you use for invoices, sales receipts, and so on. You can use an existing template as the basis of a new template, copying what you like, changing what you don't like, and eliminating what you don't need.

Making Minor Changes to an Existing Template

You can make minor changes to a QuickBooks template by choosing the Edit Template function. Open the Templates list (Lists | Templates), right-click the transaction form you want to modify (for instance, the Intuit Product Invoice), and select Edit Template. This opens the Basic Customization dialog, which offers options that can be changed for any template.

You can modify the following elements:

- Logo. If you have a company logo in a .jpg, .gif, or .bmp file format, you can add it to the transaction form by clicking the Use Logo option, which opens the Select Image dialog.

- Color Scheme. QuickBooks offers several different color schemes that change the colors of the lines and the text on the transaction form. Choose a scheme from the drop-down list and click the Apply Color Scheme button.

- Fonts. You can change the font, font size, style, color, and effects by choosing a form element and clicking the Change Font button.

- Company Information. Check the pieces of company info you want to appear on the form and click the Update Information button to make the change(s). Click the Print Preview button to ensure that any new fields added are positioned properly on the form.

- Status Stamps. QuickBooks automatically applies the stamps (PAID, PENDING, and others), unless you deselect the Print Status Stamp option. They'll still appear onscreen, but not on the printed forms.

Advanced Customization

To perform anything beyond the basic customization, you must move to the Additional Customization window. You can access it from the Basic Customization window (click the Additional Customization button) or from the transaction window itself. To access it from the transaction window, click the Formatting tab and then click the Customize Data Layout icon.

ProAdvisor NOTE: *Some of the pre-designed templates are designed to work with preprinted forms from Intuit, and, therefore, cannot be modified beyond the basics found in the Basic Customization window. When you try to perform advanced customization using the Additional Customization window or the Layout Designer, QuickBooks notifies you that the template is locked and that you must make a copy to continue. Most of the templates with Intuit in the name fall into this category.*

When the Additional Customization window opens, you'll see that you have either four or five tabs on which you can set a variety of options.

- Header Tab. The Header tab lets you change the names of the various fields that appear in the header section of the form. For example, if you're a nonprofit organization, you'll probably want to change the Default Title from Invoice to Donation. You can also choose whether the fields appear in the onscreen or printed (or both) versions of the form.

- Columns Tab. This is where you decide what data appears in the body of the form (and what it's called). Here, again, you can choose whether it appears on the screen, print, or both versions of the form. You can also determine the order (from left to right) that the fields/columns appear by changing the Order number (see Figure 2-24). The lower the Order number, the further to the left the field appears.

- Prog Cols Tab. If you have enabled progress invoicing in the Jobs & Estimates preferences, you can set the options for those columns, as well. If the Progress Invoicing preference is disabled, this tab does not appear.

- Footer Tab. The Footer tab contains options for those elements that appear at the bottom of the form, such as the customer message, total, subtotal, tax fields, and more. The options here are basically the same as those found on the Header tab.

- Print Tab. Here, you can choose to use the default print settings for the form or create customized settings just for this one template. You can elect to change the orientation, number of copies, the paper size, and so on.

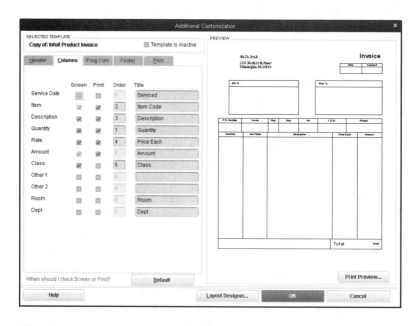

Figure 2-24: Customize the template to suit your needs.

As you make changes, keep an eye on the Preview window to the right. It will display changes that are made to the printed version of the form. If you make changes that affect the position of fields and labels on the form, QuickBooks will alert you that you may have overlapping elements. It will also show them in the Preview window. To correct them, you'll have to open the Layout Designer and reposition the elements.

Using the Layout Designer

The Layout Designer is a handy tool for adding new fields to a template and for repositioning elements on a template. We're not going to provide detailed instructions for the use of the tool, but rather give you a brief overview of its capabilities.

You can access the Layout Designer, shown in Figure 2-25, by clicking the Layout Designer button at the bottom of the Additional Customization window.

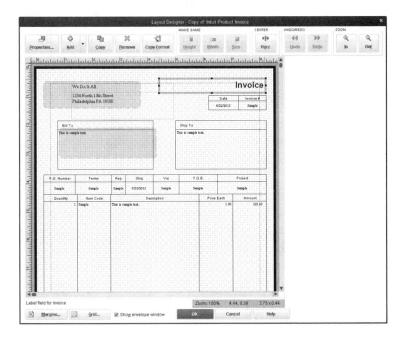

Figure 2-25: Use the Layout Designer to add, modify, and move template elements.

Adding Elements

You can add new elements to a QuickBooks template by clicking the Add button on the toolbar and selecting one of the following choices:

- Text Box. A text box contains no QuickBooks data. It is simply an input field into which a user can enter whatever text is desired.

- Data Field. A data field is a two-part element. It contains a label (text box) and the actual data field. The label contains the field name, which you can modify as you wish. The data field pulls information from the QuickBooks database.

- Image. You can add as many graphic images to the form as you wish. A company logo is the most common form of graphic used on templates.

New elements are automatically placed in the middle of the template and must be manually moved to their desired locations. See the section entitled "Moving Elements" later in this chapter for more information.

Modifying Elements

Once an element has been placed on the template, there are numerous ways to change the element. Some element types have more options for making changes than others.

- Resizing. All elements can be resized as needed. Begin by highlighting the element to show its outline and its resizing handles (small black squares). Grab one of the resizing handles and move it away from the center of the element to increase the dimension in that direction. You can also opt to make multiple elements the same size as another element. You use the Height, Width, and Size buttons to effect these changes.

- Arranging. Template elements can be placed on top of one another to create different design elements. For example, you could place a text box over a graphic element to add text to the image. To align an element, right-click the element, choose Order, and then select Bring Forward or Send Backward.

- Modifying Properties. To change an element's properties, right-click the element and select Properties. A Properties dialog box appears with options for changing the appearance of the element. For Text Box and Data Field elements, the properties you can change are text justification, fonts, borders, and background colors. The only thing that appears in an Image element Properties dialog is a Browse button so that you can select a different image file.

Moving Elements

You can move one or more template elements from one location to another by dragging with your mouse. Of course, you have to indicate which element(s) you want to move. If you're only moving a single object, you can grab it and drag it with no additional action. If you want to move multiple elements at the same time, you have to select them all first.

To select multiple form elements, highlight the first object, then hold down the Shift key and select the remaining objects. To move them, grab any one of the selected objects and drag. They all dutifully follow the object you're dragging. You can also draw a rectangle around the objects. However, you must enclose each entire object for it to be included in the group. You also have to be careful about accidentally dragging other objects around when attempting to make the enclosure.

Margins and Grids

Two last things to be aware of are the Margins button and the Grid button. Click the Margins button to open the Margins dialog, where you can set the top, left, right, and bottom margins of the template.

The Grid button opens the Grid And Snap Settings dialog. Here, you can choose to show or hide the grid, make objects snap to the grid, and set the size of the grid.

CHAPTER 3:

Setting Up QuickBooks

- Creating a New Company File

- Assembling the Chart of Accounts

- Using Account Numbers

- Configuring QuickBooks Lists

- Configuring Sales Tax

- Creating Bank Accounts

- Setting Up Customers in QuickBooks

- Setting Up Vendors in QuickBooks

Now that you've got the basics of accounting and QuickBooks under your belt, it's time to get to work. There are some simple setup tasks that will make working in QuickBooks much easier if you tackle them before jumping into the thick of it. For this chapter, we're going to assume that you're using QuickBooks for the first time and are creating your company file from scratch. If you have an existing company file, you can use the information in this chapter to update and modify your company file as needed.

When QuickBooks first opens, it displays the No Company Open dialog box, which gives you the option to create a new file, open an existing file, or open a sample company file. To get started, click the Create A New Company button, which opens the QuickBooks Setup window shown in Figure 3-1.

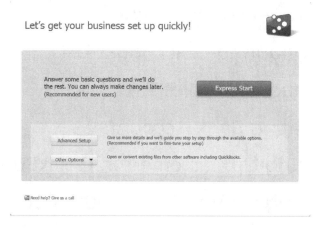

Let's get your business set up quickly!

Answer some basic questions and we'll do the rest. You can always make changes later. (Recommended for new users)   **Express Start**

Advanced Setup   Give us more details and we'll guide you step by step through the available options. (Recommended if you want to fine-tune your setup)

Other Options ▼   Open or convert existing files from other software including QuickBooks.

Need help? Give us a call

Figure 3-1: You can create your company file with a minimum of fuss.

As you can see, you have two choices for creating a new file:

- Express Start. Choose this option to fill out essential information only. You're only required to enter company name, industry type, business entity type, zip code, and phone number before creating your company file. It lets you get to work right away, but puts the burden of enabling the features you need on you.

- Advanced Setup. This wizard, called the EasyStep Interview, is great for beginners who may not be sure of exactly which features they need. It asks straightforward questions about your business and enables features based on your answers.

Whichever method you select, you're going to want to perform some essential setup tasks. While it's true that you can setup almost everything in QuickBooks "on the fly," you'll make your life a lot easier by getting organized right from the start. The basic areas that require at least some initial configuration are the following:

- Chart of Accounts
- Lists
- Customers
- Vendors

Chart of Accounts

The chart of accounts is the heart of your accounting system, and, as such, it needs to be created with careful consideration. It's the list of account names that you use to keep your accounting records. Each name in the list represents a category for the type of transactions that are collected for that name. For example, there are accounts for assets (bank account, equipment), liabilities (loans payable, sales tax payable), income (sales), and expenses (payroll, rent, etc.).

Although the chart of accounts is merely a list of names (and numbers, if you elect to use a numbered chart of accounts), it is the foundation of your ledger (usually called the General Ledger). All of your individual transaction postings make up the totals in your general ledger.

Linking a transaction to an account is called posting. For instance, when you deposit money from the sale of goods or services into your bank, you post the transaction amount to the bank that's in your chart of accounts (that's the debit side of the transaction), and the income category in your chart of accounts (that's the credit side). When you send a check to the landlord, you post the transaction to the expense named Rent (the debit side) in your chart of accounts, and remove the money from the bank (the credit side).

CPA TIP: *With the exception of General Journal Entries, QuickBooks knows whether to treat an amount you enter in a transaction as a debit or a credit, so it is not necessary for you to learn the posting conventions, but basically: Debits increase your assets and expenses or reduce your liabilities, equity, and income. Credits reduce your assets and expenses or increase your liabilities, equity, and income.*

When you create your company file using either method, QuickBooks installs a chart of accounts based on the type of business you selected. While the default chart of accounts may be a good starting point, it is rarely adequate to meet most users' needs without some tweaking.

Naming Accounts

When you name your accounts, create names that are descriptive and easy to recognize. This makes it easier to post transactions and to understand reports.

Use names that clearly describe the types of postings you'll make to the account. For example, an account named Telephone is a better choice than Communications Expenses. Computer Expenses is too generic as an account name if you want to analyze where your dollars are going; instead, create separate accounts for computer repairs & parts, computer support plans, computer software, and so on.

CPA TIP: *It's also very important to implement and enforce a strict naming convention for accounts, since the name you assign will be the way the account is presented in statements prepared by QuickBooks. For example, would you really want to see all capital letters in a report, or do you allow punctuation and spaces? Should it be Repairs & Maintenance, Repairs-Maintenance, or RepairsMaintenance? Set up clear rules and make sure everyone follows them.*

Be especially careful about clarity when you name your asset and liability accounts. For example, if you have a loan, name the account so that it's easy to determine which loan it represents. Some businesses name a liability account Bank Loan for a loan or line of credit, and then, when they have another type of loan from the same bank (perhaps for a vehicle), they call it Bank Loan 2. This makes it difficult for the person entering the transaction to know how to post it; unfortunately, rather than investigate, many users just guess.

CPA TIP: *You might want to include either the last four digits of the loan's account number (Loan Payable XYZ Bank-1234) or the monthly payment amount (Loan Payable XYZ Bank-123/ mo) in your account name. The same clarity should apply to naming assets. Don't name an asset Money Due to Company; instead, describe the purpose of the asset account, such as Deposits Held by Vendors or Loan to Employee.*

Using Account Numbers

QuickBooks does not require the use of account numbers, but it does make them available optionally. As a matter of fact, all the accounts generated automatically when you create a new company are numbered by default. The reason they don't show is that the account numbering option is turned off by default.

CPA TIP: *While account numbers are not required, they should be used. By default, QuickBooks lists accounts alphabetically within each of its major accounting categories (Bank, Accounts Receivable, Other Current Assets, Accounts Payable, Other Current Liabilities). Account numbers enable you or your accountant to design a well-organized and easily followed chart of accounts. They are especially helpful when it comes to generating effective financial reports.*

Using numbers means you can control the way the account names are sorted, because sorting alphabetically doesn't let you put related accounts together. For example, if accounts of the type Expense are arranged numerically instead of alphabetically, you can list related expense accounts contiguously. All of your insurance categories are together, as are your employer payroll expenses, your general office expenses, and so on.

When you use account numbers to make these related categories contiguous, you can generate subtotals that make it easier to analyze your cost of doing business by broad, general categories. If your related categories are numbered in a way that you can create subtotals that match the categories required on your company's tax return, this is also useful (especially to your accountant, who will spend less time on your tax return, which saves you money).

Account Numbering Options

If you want to use account numbers, you must enable the account numbering options in the Company Preferences tab of the Accounting preferences:

1. Select Edit | Preferences to display the Preferences dialog.
2. Click the Accounting category in the left pane and the Company Preferences tab in the right pane.
3. Place a check mark in the Use Account Numbers option to enable account numbering.
4. Check the Require Accounts option if you want to force users (including yourself) to always assign a number when creating an account. With this option enabled, you can't save a new account without an account number.
5. Do yourself a favor and check the Show Lowest Subaccount Only option. As you find more reasons to use subaccounts (and even sub-subaccounts), you'll find that the long account names become difficult to see and decipher in drop-down lists. With this option checked, only the last subaccount name appears. This means that if you have a sub-subaccount named Baseball Gloves: Right Handed: Catchers' Mitts, only Catchers' Mitts appears in related drop-down lists.

6. Click OK to save the new settings.

Creating a Numbering Scheme

The numbers you assign to accounts give you a quick clue about the type and category of the account you're working with. As you create accounts, you must use the numbers intelligently, assigning ranges of numbers to account types. The most common approach to account numbering uses the following pattern:

- 1xxxx Assets
- 2xxxx Liabilities
- 3xxxx Equity
- 4xxxx Income
- 5xxxx Expenses (can be of a specific type)
- 6xxxx Expenses (can be of a specific type)
- 7xxxx Expenses (can be of a specific type)
- 8xxxx Expenses (can be of a specific type)
- 9xxxx Other Income and Expenses (a way to track 'miscellaneous' income and expenses such as late fees, penalties, rebates, etc.)

You can, if you wish, have a variety of expense types and reserve the starting number for specific types. For example, some companies use 50000 for Cost of Goods Sold, especially if they track inventory, or Sales Expenses that are incurred in direct proportion to their income (they even separate the payroll postings between the salespeople and the rest of the employees), then use 60000 through 79999 for general operating expenses and 80000 for other specific expenses that are interrelated (such as business taxes).

You need to design an easy-to-understand format to break down assets. You might use 10000 through 10999 for cash accounts, 11000 through 16999 for receivables and other current assets, and 17000 through 17999 for tracking fixed assets such as equipment, furniture, and so on.

ɔllow the same pattern for liabilities, starting with current ɹabilities and moving to long-term. It's also a good idea to keep all the payroll-withholding liabilities together with a set of contiguous numbers.

CPA TIP: *As you create accounts, increase the previous account number by 100, so that if your first bank account is 10000, the next bank account is 10100, and so on. These intervals give you room to create additional accounts at a later date that belong in the same general area of your chart of accounts.*

Creating and Editing Accounts

Once you and your accountant have devised an appropriate chart of accounts for your business, you'll want to implement it in QuickBooks. Most likely, you'll have to create some new accounts that QuickBooks failed to include and modify some of the accounts that QuickBooks did include.

Creating New Accounts

Adding new accounts in QuickBooks is fairly easy. Just make sure that you have all the basic information handy for each account. You'll need to know the name, the account number, and whether it is a primary (parent) account or a subaccount of an existing account. Optional information includes a description and tax form information. Tax line mapping, as it's called, is a bit tricky, so be sure to check with your accountant before using it.

To create a new QuickBooks account, follow these steps:

1. Press Ctrl-A (or choose Lists | Chart Of Accounts from the menu bar) to open the Chart Of Accounts window.
2. Press Ctrl-N to open the Add New Account dialog box seen in Figure 3-2.

Figure 3-2: The first Add New Account dialog offers a choice of account types.

3. Select the Account type (use the Other Account Types option for account types not listed individually). For this exercise, we'll use an Expense account.

4. Click Continue to open a second Add New Account dialog with data fields for the new account.

5. Enter the necessary information. The fields are self-explanatory. Just keep in mind the CPA recommendations concerning account numbers and naming conventions.

6. To make this account a subaccount of another, check the Subaccount Of option and select the parent account from the drop-down list that appears to the right.

ProAdvisor TIP: *In the Add New Account dialog, for some account types you'll find a Select From Examples button next to the Account Name field. Click the button to display some common accounts of the type selected. When you choose one of these accounts, QuickBooks fills in the Number, Account Name, and Description fields automatically (all of which you can modify to fit your needs).*

7. Click Save & New to create another new account or Save & Close to return to your work in QuickBooks.

Editing Existing Accounts

When an existing account will suit your needs with a little modification, follow these steps to edit it:

1. Press Ctrl-A to open the Chart Of Accounts window.

2. Highlight the account you want to change and press Ctrl-E to open the Edit Account dialog box.

3. Make any necessary changes and click Save & Close.

Simulate a Divisionalized Chart of Accounts with Classes

Although QuickBooks does not officially support a divisionalized chart of accounts, you can do an adequate job of faking it by using the QuickBooks class feature.

CPA NOTE: *Using classes allows you to create divisions within your chart of accounts when generating financial statements. All account numbers are available within each class so that you have a single chart of accounts. Classes can be used to segregate information by location for a business with multiple stores; business segments, such as wholesale and retail, based on customer types; or construction and repairs for a contractor.*

Creating the Class Divisions

Unlike a true divisionalized chart of accounts, in which you assign additional numbers representing divisions to your accounts, QuickBooks utilizes classes to achieve a similar result. You need to create a QuickBooks class to represent each division. To do this, you must first enable the class feature, then create a list of classes, and finally assign one or more classes to every transaction you create.

Enabling the class feature is quite simple:

1. Select Edit | Preferences to open the Preferences dialog.
2. Click the Accounting icon in the left pane and the Company Preferences tab in the right.
3. Check the Use Class Tracking For Transactions option. This enables a sub-option called Prompt To Assign Classes (see Figure 3-3).
4. If you're serious about tracking your divisions, be sure to check the Prompt To Assign Classes option. It displays a reminder every time you try to close a transaction window without assigning a class.
5. Click OK to close the Preferences dialog box.

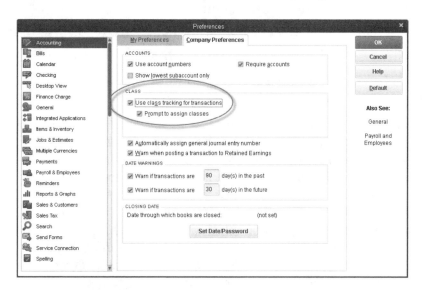

Figure 3-3: Begin creating your "divisionalized chart of accounts" by turning on class tracking.

Once class tracking is turned on, it's time to create the list of classes:

1. Choose Lists | Class List to open the Class List dialog box. If you don't see a Class List command on the Lists menu, it means you forgot to enable the Class Tracking feature. Do so now.

2. Press Ctrl-N to display the New Class dialog box.

3. Enter an appropriate name in the Class Name field.

ProAdvisor TIP: *If you have a large number of divisions, you might want to create classes and subclasses. For example, if you're located in Pennsylvania and have several stores throughout the state, you might add parent classes for each county first. You could then add a subclass for each individual store.*

---

4. To make the new class a subclass of an existing class, check the Subclass Of option and select the parent class from the drop-down menu that appears.

5. Click Next to create another class or OK to close the dialog box.

With the creation of classes, the prep work is done. Now, all that remains is to assign classes to all transactions.

ProAdvisor TIP: *One of the common complaints from accountants regarding the use of classes to mimic a divisionalized chart of accounts is the lack of a balance sheet by class report. While it's a valid concern for users of QuickBooks Pro (Premier and Enterprise have such a report), it's one that's easily remedied. If you're using QuickBooks Pro 2012 or later, you'll find the report you need on the Contributed tab of the Report Center. Simply do a search for "balance sheet by class" (be sure to include the quotation marks). When it appears, run it and save it as a memorized report (see Figure 3-4). If you're using an earlier version of QuickBooks, ask your accountant or another user of QuickBooks Premier to export the Balance Sheet By Class report template for you. You can then import it and save it as a memorized report.*

Figure 3-4: The Balance Sheet By Class report is available if you know where to look.

ProAdvisor CAUTION: *While it's true that you can create a "balance sheet by class" report by customizing a generic Summary report, the figures displayed will NOT be accurate. The true Balance Sheet By Class report available in the QuickBooks Premier Editions tracks all class assignments directly from the original transactions. The "custom" report does not.*

Setting Up Basic Lists

In this section, we're going to deal with those lists that should be created before adding customers or vendors. These lists contain information that you'll need in either the customer record, the vendor record, or, in some cases, both.

Terms List

We'll start with the terms list simply because it is used in both the customer record and the vendor record. You must specify the terms of payment as either the number of days available for payment from the date of the invoice or a specific date in the following month by which payment is due. If discounts are provided for early payment, note the amount of the discount and the time period for which the discount is valid. This is true for customers and vendors alike. You have to create the terms you offer your customers, as well as the terms your different vendors offer to you.

Creating Terms

Terms for your customers and from your vendors appear in the same list, called, appropriately enough, the Terms List. When you create a new company file in QuickBooks, the Terms List is automatically populated with some of the most common terms. If those terms work for you, you're all set. However, if those terms are not adequate, you can create your own by performing the following steps:

1. Choose Lists | Customer & Vendor Profile Lists | Terms List from the menu bar to display the Terms List dialog box seen in Figure 3-5.

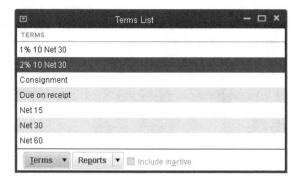

Figure 3-5: By default, QuickBooks creates a number of the most commonly used terms.

2. Press Ctrl-N to open the New Terms dialog.

3. Enter a descriptive name in the Terms field.

4. Select either Standard or Date Driven, depending on the type of terms you're adding.

   • Standard terms provide a certain number of days in which the payment is due. Net 30 is a common example. With Net 30 terms, payment is due within 30 days of the date of the invoice. Standard terms can also include discounts if payment is sent within a specified number of days from the invoice date. For example, with terms of 2% 10 Net 30, the payment is due within 30 days, but a discount of 2% is offered if payment is sent within 10 days.

- Date Driven terms require payment to be received by a specific day of the month. For example, if you send bills out by the last day of the month and want payment received by the 15th of the next month, you can create Net 15th terms. You can even specify that payment is postponed to the following month if the invoice is issued within a certain number of days prior to the due date. In other words, if you don't generate the invoices until the 10th of the month, it's hardly fair to expect the customer to pay by the 15th. As with Standard terms, you can include discount incentives for early payment.

5. Set the appropriate options (Due In, Due Before, Discount, etc) for the type of terms you're creating.

6. Click Next to create another set of terms or click OK to close the New Terms dialog box.

If you decide to modify terms already in the list, simply open the Terms List, highlight the terms you want to change, and press Ctrl-E to open the Edit Terms dialog. Make the necessary changes and click OK to save them.

Customer Type List

Like most accounting software, QuickBooks lets you specify a customer "type," which you can use any way you please. For example, you might use the customer types Wholesale and Retail, or separate customer types by the type of services you perform for them. You can produce reports by customer type and send correspondence about special sales or other information to specific customer types.

ProAdvisor TIP: *Customer types work best when you use similar categories. If you try to mix categories, you'll find that generating useful reports becomes difficult. For example, if you're going to use customer types to separate wholesale and retail customers, don't try to also separate walk-in customers, yellow-pages customers, and Internet customers. Since most customers will fall into both sets of categories, you'll end up with confusing reports. If you must, at least use subtypes to maintain order (e.g., Retail:Walk-in, Retail:Yellow Pages, Retail:Internet. Do the same for Wholesale.).*

Creating customer types is quite easy:

1. Select Lists | Customer & Vendor Profile Lists | Customer Type List from the menu bar to open the Customer Type List dialog box shown in Figure 3-6.
2. Press Ctrl-N to display the New Customer Type dialog.
3. Enter a name in the Customer Type field.
4. If you want to make the new type a subtype of an existing type, check the Subtype Of option and select the existing type from the drop-down list that appears.
5. Click Next to create another customer type or click OK to close the dialog box.

Figure 3-6: Create your customer types with some forethought.

When you create a new customer, you can assign a customer type by moving to the Additional Info tab of the New Customer form. As you can see in Figure 3-7, the Additional Info tab contains the Customer Type field with a drop-down list of choices.

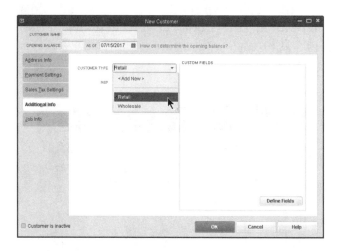

Figure 3-7: Be sure to assign a customer type to each new customer you create.

If you assign customer types consistently, you'll find that you can generate a number of helpful reports using the field.

Vendor Type List

The Vendor Type List is identical to the Customer Type List, except that it's used to categorize vendors from whom you purchase goods or services. Therefore, you can review the earlier section on the Customer Type List and substitute "Vendor" for "Customer" and follow the instructions you find there.

Job Type List

To properly use the Job Type List, you must first understand the concept of "jobs" in QuickBooks. Jobs are a subcategory of customers. They provide a simple way to track multiple projects for a single customer. For example, the Smith Brothers Electrical Contractors do a lot of work for the Carver Hills Construction Company, a general contractor. When setting up QuickBooks, Smith Brothers would add Carver Hills Construction as a customer. Then, each project they worked on for Carver Hills would be added as a job to the Carver Hills Construction customer. If they worked on the house on Elm Street, they would add an "Elm Street House" job to the Carver Hills Construction customer in the Customer Center (see Figure 3-8).

Figure 3-8: Use Customer:Jobs to track individual projects for each customer.

The Job Type List provides a way to further categorize the different jobs. In the example of the Smith Brothers, they might want to separate new construction jobs from renovation work, from historical restoration projects. Job types provide that opportunity.

Creating job types is similar to both customer and vendor types.

1. Choose Lists | Customer & Vendor Profile Lists | Job Type List to open the Job Type List dialog box.

2. Press Ctrl-N to open the New Job Type dialog.

3. Enter a name, and click OK to save it.

The Job Type List is used when creating a new job in the Customer Center. You'll find the Job Type drop-down list on the Job Info tab of the New Job record form. See the section entitled "Adding Customer Jobs" later in this chapter for more on creating jobs.

Item List

The Item List is one of the most important lists in QuickBooks. It enables you to create items for sale (both service and inventory), items to track supplies and other non-inventory goods, as well as a number of very handy, special items. However, with the exception of sales tax items, which are covered in the next section, there are no items that must be configured prior to setting up customers and vendors. See Chapter 4 for more information on working with the Item List.

Adding Custom Fields to Lists

As smart as the Intuit programmers are, they can't anticipate every user's need for different fields. That being the case, they've done the next best thing by providing users with the ability to create custom fields. Custom fields can be created in customer, vendor, employee, and item forms. Once you have data entered into those fields, you can add the fields to reports to display the data along with other QuickBooks information.

Item Custom Fields

You can add as many as five custom fields to items. The process is simple:

1. Choose Lists | Item List to open the Item List.

2. Right-click any service or inventory item and select Edit Item.

3. Click the Custom Fields button to display the Custom Fields For <item name> dialog. If no custom fields exist, QuickBooks alerts you and tells you to click the Define Fields button.

4. Click the Define Fields button to open the Set Up Custom Fields For Items dialog.

5. Enter a name in the Label column and place a check mark in the Use column if you want the field to appear in the Custom Fields For <item name> dialog.

6. Click OK three times to save the changes and close the item record.

Customer, Vendor, and Employee Custom Fields

Custom fields for customers, vendors, and employees are created in a similar fashion. In this case, you open any record of any type (customer, vendor, or employee), click the Additional Info tab, and then click the Define Fields button to display the Set Up Custom Fields For Names dialog. Enter a name in the Label column and decide which of the three record types (customer, vendor, and/or employee) you want to contain the custom field. Click OK to close the dialog and return to the record form.

Sales Tax Setup

If you're doing business in one of the 45 states (as of this writing) in the U.S. (or the District of Columbia) that has sales tax, it's almost guaranteed that you're dealing with the issue. Even if you're in one of the states that doesn't have a state sales tax, you may be faced with city or locality sales taxes. Therefore, configuring sales tax is an important issue for most businesses and should be dealt with before setting up customers and vendors.

Depending on how your company file was created, sales tax may or may not be turned on. If it's turned on already, that means either you or QuickBooks created at least one sales tax item. If QuickBooks created it, it's a generic item and should be modified to reflect your actual tax rate and tax agency. If you haven't yet enabled sales tax, now's the time to do it.

Enabling Sales Tax

If sales tax hasn't been turned on in your company file, you have two tasks to perform—enabling sales tax and creating/assigning your most common sales tax item:

1. Select Edit | Preferences to open the Preferences dialog.
2. Select Sales Tax in the left pane and the Company Preferences tab in the right.

ProAdvisor NOTE: *Only the Admin user can make changes to the Company tab, so be sure you're logged in as the Admin user. One other thing—changes made to the Company Preferences tab are applied to the company file and not the user profile. Unlike changes made to the My Preferences tab, changes made here apply to all users, not just the user logged on at the time the changes are made.*

---

3. Set the Do You Charge Sales Tax? option to Yes.

If you try to click OK and close the Preferences dialog box at this point, you'll get an error message informing you that you have to assign your most common sales tax item first. If this is the first time you're turning sales tax on, you won't have any sales tax items to choose. Therefore, you'll have to create a sales tax item to nominate:

1. Click the Add Sales Tax Item button to open the New Item dialog seen in Figure 3-9, in which the Sales Tax Item is automatically selected.
2. Click the Sales Tax Item listing to begin the process.
3. Enter a name for the tax item (e.g., PA State Sales Tax).
4. Enter a description if it will help differentiate this tax from others.

Figure 3-9: Sales tax items are required for each different tax
you're required to collect.

5. Enter the tax rate. QuickBooks knows you're entering a percentage, so you don't have to worry about the percent sign.

6. Enter the name of the agency to which you must remit the collected sales tax. If you are just now setting up sales tax, you probably don't have a tax vendor (agency) in your Vendors list yet. If that's the case, QuickBooks will offer to add the name you enter into the Vendors list for you (see Figure 3-10).

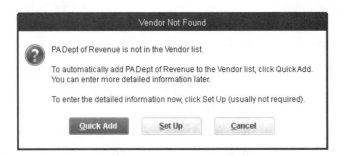

Figure 3-10: Click Quick Add and fill in the details later.

7. Click OK to save the sales tax item and return to the Preferences dialog.

QuickBooks assumes the new sales tax item is the most commonly used. If that's the case, click OK to save your changes and close the Preferences dialog box. If not, click Add Sales Tax Item again and create another sales tax item.

When you finally close the Preferences dialog by clicking OK, Quick-Books offers to make all your existing customers and/or your inventory and non-inventory items taxable (see Figure 3-11).

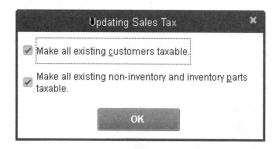

Figure 3-11: QuickBooks makes an offer that's hard to resist if most of your existing customers and items are taxable.

If you already have customers and items set up and most of them will be taxable, accept the offer. Otherwise, deselect the options and click OK.

CPA Sidebar
Understanding Sales-Tax Rates

You have to note the sales-tax rates for each customer. Depending on where you do business, the effort involved in determining a customer's sales-tax rate ranges from mildly confusing to totally baffling.

You need to make sure that you understand the sales tax rules in each locality you do business. Most states have adopted a series of confusing and convoluted rules defining "doing business." Consequently, you must also be aware of the rules in your customers' states and those states' definitions of whether you have a business presence in those states. Depending on the circumstances, you may be liable for charging, collecting, and remitting sales taxes to your customer's home state.

States have a base tax rate and then may impose an additional tax that you must assess for localities (county, city) within the state.

ProAdvisor TIP: *This is where QuickBooks Sales Tax Groups come in handy. See the section entitled "Sales Tax Groups" later in this chapter for more details.*

Sales tax will be due based on the state and locality "doing business" definitions. Consequently, a single transaction will only be assessed one set of taxes based on where the transaction is deemed to have been consummated (when goods sold are no longer yours, but are legally owned by your customer or where provided services are performed). As states and localities are in the constant search for additional revenue, you will need to be aware as they change the rules for taxable and nontaxable sales, as well as what action on your part may subject you to sales taxes in your customer's location instead of your own. You also need to be aware of changes in the assessed sales-tax rates.

ProAdvisor TIP: *Unfortunately, QuickBooks does not offer a simple solution for this problem. You can't create a different customer job for each location, since only the primary customer record contains the default sales tax item, which is inherited by all the associated jobs. That leaves you with two options. One, create a separate customer for each tax rate (Smith Brothers [8%], Smith Brothers [6.25%], etc.). Two, include the tax rate in the Note line of each different shipping address. The only drawback to this method is that the Note line appears on the printed invoice and shipping label.*

After you've determined the combination of state and local sales taxes for this customer, you can record the customer's tax rate in the customer's record. Then, things get muddy.

Remember that in order to add sales tax to a transaction, both the customer and the goods or services you're selling must be taxable. Even when you know the sale is taxable and you know the customer's tax rate, the confusion continues. Some states may have different tax rates for different types of goods or services; this means that each item on a sales transaction could have a unique tax rate.

ProAdvisor TIP: *If you run into this situation, you'll have to create a phony sales tax item with a tax rate of 0% to apply to the entire sale. Then you'll need separate sales tax items for each different rate applied to goods or services. These will be applied on a line-item basis (add the sales item to an invoice or sales receipt and on the next line, enter the sales tax item that applies). For multiple line items with the same sales-tax rate, enter a subtotal item first and then the sales tax item. Take a close look at Figure 3-12 to see how it works.*

When you change the tax rate for a transaction, QuickBooks displays a message asking whether you want to apply the tax rate to the customer. Click No unless this customer's purchases are always for specific items that have their own unique tax rates. If you're in a business in which specific tax rates are always applied in your state (such as a hotel or a bar), it's usually fine to assign a zero tax rate to all your customers, especially if you track your sales in a batch, using a generic customer name. Do not configure the customer as nontaxable, because the taxable items won't generate a sales tax. Instead, apply the zero percent tax to a taxable customer. (Remember, in order to apply sales tax, both the customer and the item must be taxable.)

Some states tax only the first XX dollars of a product, and then either reduce the tax or eliminate it. For example, only the first $5000.00 of the sale of tangible property may be taxable. However, if the state sales tax has a limit, the local surtax may not recognize that limit. Some local surtaxes may recognize the limit while others may not, and some may have a different limit.

Additional complications arise when you have to remit the sales tax to the state. Some states require you to send separate payments to each tax location. Most states want totals that show both the state's base tax rate and the location surtaxes, along with the total of nontaxable sales and taxable sales for each location.

Figure 3-12: QuickBooks can easily handle multiple tax rates.

Sales Tax Status

Some customers are taxable and other customers are not, and each customer's record must contain the tax status. The obvious "not taxable" list includes the following:

- Nonprofit organizations
- Government agencies

- Out-of-state customers whose addresses are not in a state that has a reciprocal agreement for sales tax with your state

- Customers who resell the products they buy from you and who have provided their sales tax license numbers to you (That sales tax license number must be part of the customer's record.)

Remember that a customer deemed "taxable" doesn't always owe tax on a sales transaction. The goods or services you're selling a taxable customer must also have a status of "taxable" for sales tax to be added to the sales transaction. Some states tax almost everything, including services. Some states eliminate some goods from taxation (usually necessities), and other states eliminate many services from taxation.

Sales Tax Code List

The Sales Tax Code List is extremely useful, especially if you're in one of those states that requires detailed reports on tax collections and exemptions. QuickBooks comes pre-configured with two sales tax codes—Tax for taxable and Non for non-taxable. The codes are applied both to customers and to sales items. For a sale to be taxable, both the customer and the item must be taxable. For many businesses, the default sales tax codes of Tax and Non are sufficient.

However, if your state requires you to separate the non-taxable sales by different categories, you'll need to create additional sales tax codes. For example, you might be required to break down your non-taxable sales by the categories provided in the previous section. In that case, you might have sales tax codes of Tax, Non, NPO (nonprofit organization), GOV (government agency), OOS (out of state), and WHL (wholesale).

Creating and modifying sales tax codes is pretty easy:

1. Choose Lists | Sales Tax Code List from the menu bar to open the Sales Tax Code List dialog box.
2. Press Ctrl-N to display the New Sales Tax Code dialog shown in Figure 3-13.

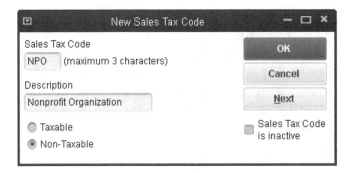

Figure 3-13: Name your tax codes so you can easily distinguish
between them.

3. Enter a three-character, recognizable code in the Sales Tax Code field.

4. With only three characters to use, it's a good idea to include a description that will help identify the code.

5. Select Taxable or Non-Taxable and click Next to create another tax code or OK to save this one and close the dialog box.

That's all there is to it. When you want to see a breakdown of your sales tax collections and exemptions, run the Sales Tax Revenue Summary report (Reports | Vendors & Payables | Sales Tax Revenue Summary). One thing to note about this report is that it uses the sales tax code Description field as the column header—another good reason to include a description when creating sales tax codes.

Sales Tax Items

If you collect sales tax, you must have at least one sales tax item. When you turn on sales tax in the Preferences dialog box, QuickBooks will not let you continue until you create at least one sales tax item to act as the default. If you do business in a state that has multiple tax rates (city, county, etc.), you'll have to create a sales tax item for each different rate.

As discussed in the earlier CPA Sidebar on Sales-Tax Rates, you could, conceivably, find yourself faced with a variety of different tax rates that you must charge, based not only on your business location, but also on the location of your customers.

Creating sales tax items is much like creating other list items. Open the Item List (Lists | Item List) and press Ctrl-N to display the New Item dialog box (see Figure 3-14). Select Sales Tax Item from the Type drop-down list and enter a name for the new item. A description can be helpful, especially if you have multiple sales tax items. Enter a tax rate in the Tax Rate (%) field. QuickBooks knows it's a percentage, so just enter the numbers (e.g., 8.25 for 8.25%) and QuickBooks will add the percent sign. Finally, select (or create) the agency to which this tax is remitted using the Tax Agency drop-down list. Click Next to save this item and create another item, or click OK to save the current item and close the New Item dialog.

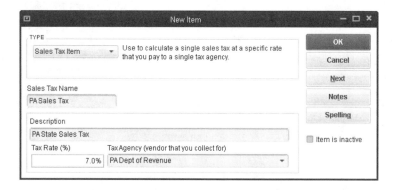

Figure 3-14: You must have at least one sales tax item if you collect sales tax.

Sales Tax Groups

Sales Tax Groups are very handy items to have if you have to collect multiple taxes on a single sale or single taxable item. For example, if you have to collect a state tax of 6%, a county tax of 1%, and city tax of 1.25%, you must create three separate tax items and use all of them on every sale. It works, but it's a pain.

Fortunately, QuickBooks Sales Tax Groups take the pain out of charging multiple sales taxes. A sales tax group is simply a collection of sales tax items to be applied simultaneously. Using the earlier example, you would create a sales tax group and include the state, county, and city sales tax items in the group, and then apply the group to each sale rather than the individual sales taxes.

Creating groups is similar to creating sales tax items:

1. Start by selecting Lists | Item list from the menu bar to display the Item List.

2. From the Type drop-down list, choose Sales Tax Group. The New Item dialog box appears with a field for the Sales Tax Group item (see Figure 3-15).

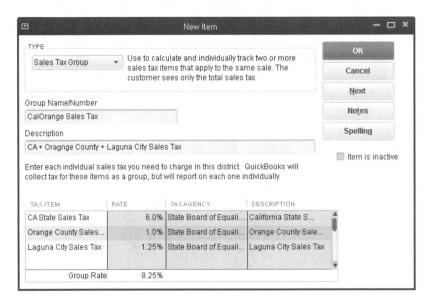

Figure 3-15: Collecting multiple sales taxes is easy when you use sales tax groups.

3. Enter a name and a description for the group.

4. Click the first row in the Tax Item column at the bottom of the dialog box to display the list of existing sales tax items.

5. From the drop-down list that appears, select the first item to include in the group. The rest of the fields (columns)

fill in automatically using data from the sales tax item record.

6. Repeat the process for each sales tax item you want to add to the group. If you need to create a new sales tax item, click the <Add New> item at the top of the drop-down list.

7. When you're done, click Next to create another group or OK to close the dialog box.

Setting Up Customers

Customers are the central focus of any business. Without them, you won't be in business for long. Whether you're running a retail business with hundreds or thousands of customers or a specialized service business with a limited number, customers are essential. Keeping track of them and configuring them properly is one of the most important setup jobs you have.

ProAdvisor TIP: *The first thing to decide is whether or not you need to keep track of every individual customer you do business with. If you have a customer base with whom you do a lot of repeat business or customers to whom you extend credit, you'll definitely want to keep track of each customer. However, if your customer base is made up of cash-sale (payment, regardless of type, at the time of the sale) customers, you might want to use a different method. If you only need to keep track of the sales and not the individual customers, you can simply create a customer called Cash and use it to record all your cash sales.*

Preparing for Customer Setup

Once you have your chart of accounts and basic list items squared away, it's time to think about adding customers to QuickBooks. Unless you're running a retail operation and never send invoices (instead, you collect all your money at the time of the sale), you have to keep track of customer activity. You need to know which customers are required to pay sales tax, the sales tax rate for each customer, and which customers have unpaid invoices.

In some businesses, customer prices differ (your retail customers might have a different price level than wholesale customers), so you should track the price level for each customer. You need to track the money you owe customers due to credits you issued for returned goods. Some customers have shipping addresses that differ from their billing addresses. All this information (and even more information, depending on your type of business) should be included in each customer's record.

Before you start adding customers to QuickBooks, it's worth spending a little time getting organized and collecting the customer data you'll need to create effective customer records.

Here's a brief list of some of the information you'll want to have handy when creating customers:

- Customer contact information (name, billing address, shipping address, phone number, etc.)
- Tax status & tax rate (if taxable)
- Customer account number and terms
- Customer shipping preferences

Naming Customers

Every customer in your system must have a unique name. QuickBooks does not allow duplicate customer names. Because each customer has to be unique, think of the customer name as the customer "code." The Company Name and Full Name fields in the customer record provide the company and contact names, address details, and so on.

Some businesses have a difficult time coming up with unique customer codes because so many of their customers have similar (or even identical) names. If you sell supplies to pizza stores, many of your customers might have company names that start with "Pizza."

> **CPA TIP**: *One way to ensure uniqueness is to use another reference that is unique; common solutions are to use the street name or the telephone number (including the area code) in the customer code/name.*

Required Customer Data

You must track all customer data that is related to customer transactions; in addition, you can maintain customer data that you can use for marketing and advertising.

Name and Address

If you send invoices, you must maintain information about the customer's company name (or full name if the customer is an individual), billing address, and shipping address. If you take credit cards on an Internet shopping cart or over the telephone, you will also need the name and billing address associated with your customer's credit card, which could be different from the business name and address (you don't need this information for over-the-counter credit card sales because you have the credit card).

> **ProAdvisor TIP**: *You should only retain credit card information for repeat customers who use the same card each time. If you are going to store credit card data in QuickBooks, you must enable Customer Credit Card Protection to ensure that you're in compliance with PCI DSS (Payment Card Industry Data Security Standards). Also, be sure only those users who need access to customer credit card information are provided with those permissions. See Chapter 13 for more on Customer Credit Card Protection and user permissions.*

Terms

See the section entitled "Creating Terms" earlier in this chapter for more information on using and creating terms.

Creating Customer Records

Once you've compiled the basic information needed for each customer, it's time to set up the customer records in QuickBooks. Begin by pressing Ctrl-J to open the Customer Center shown in Figure 3-16, which provides direct access to most customer-related information.

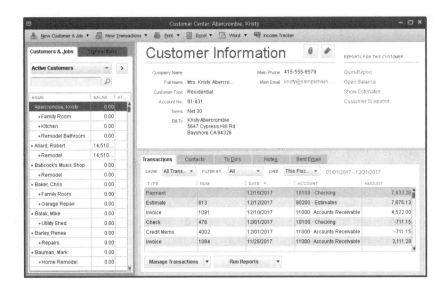

Figure 3-16: The Customer Center is your headquarters for customer-related activities.

Adding a new customer record is easy:

1. Press Ctrl-N to open the New Customer dialog box. As you can see in Figure 3-17, the New Customer dialog box contains a series of tabs offering access to a variety of input field types.

2. Enter basic contact information on the Address Info tab and move to the Payment Settings tab. Keep in mind that you can create multiple Ship To addresses for each customer. Click the Ship To drop-down list and choose <Add New> to open a new Add Shipping Address Information dialog.

Figure 3-17: Enter as much or as little customer information as you need.

ProAdvisor TIP: *Don't enter anything in the Opening Balance field. It is much better to create the opening balance by entering historical data for the customer.*

---

3. Use the Payment Settings tab to add an account number, terms, price levels, and more. You can also record customer credit card information here. However, if you are going to retain credit card data, be sure to enable Customer Credit Card Protection (see Chapter 13 for more on this feature).

ProAdvisor NOTE: *QuickBooks Pro users can only create Fixed Percentage price levels. You must be running QuickBooks Premier or Enterprise to employ Per Item price levels.*

---

4. Move to the Sales Tax Settings tab to include a sales tax code, a sales tax item, and a resale number if appropriate.

5. Click the Additional Info tab to enter a customer type and a customer rep. The Additional Info tab also allows you to create and use custom fields for important information for which QuickBooks does not provide fields.

6. If you are tracking only a single job for this customer, move to the Job Info tab and enter the details of the job. If you want to track multiple jobs, you can create separate job records and attach them to the customer. For more information, see the section entitled "Adding Customer Jobs" later in this chapter.

7. When you're done entering the customer information, click OK to save the new record.

If you have a computerized list of customers handy, you can speed up the input process by taking advantage of the Add/Edit Multiple List Entries feature. Select Lists | Add/Edit Multiple List Entries from the menu bar to open the Add/Edit Multiple List Entries window, into which you can paste columns of data from a Word or Excel document. See Chapter 2 for more on the Add/Edit Multiple List Entries feature.

Adding Customer Jobs

When you provide products or services for different projects for the same customer, you can use customer jobs to keep the projects organized and to print reports that separate the projects' costs, profits, losses, etc. Since jobs are really just sub-customers, the process is similar to creating customers:

1. Press Ctrl-J to open the Customer Center.

2. Right-click a customer in the Customers & Jobs list and select Add Job from the context menu that appears. The New Job dialog opens with the basic customer information already filled in (see Figure 3-18).

3. Enter a descriptive name for the job in the Job Name field.

4. Leave the Opening Balance field empty, even if you have a figure to input. As noted earlier, it's always preferable

to enter historical transactions to create opening balances. Your accountant will appreciate it.

Figure 3-18: You can enter a wealth of information about the new job.

5. Go through the first three tabs, all of which carry over some or all of the data from the customer record. Make changes as needed.

6. Open the Job Info tab and complete the fields with relevant information:

- Job Description. A good description here will enable anyone entering data to determine if this is the correct job.

- Job Type. If you work on different types of projects, use this field to organize them and create clear job reports.

- Job Status. To track the various phases of the job, select a status indicator from the drop-down list.

- Start Date. Enter the date on which the job is to start or has already started.

- Projected End Date. Enter the date you expect the job to be completed.

- End Date. Hopefully, this is the same or earlier than the Projected End Date. In any event, it's the date the job is actually completed.

7. Click OK to save the new job.

ProAdvisor TIP: *If you use specific jargon in your profession, you might want to customize the Job Status drop-down list to reflect the terminology you normally use. Select Edit | Preferences from the QuickBooks menu bar and click the Jobs & Estimates category in the left pane. Click the Company Preferences tab and make the necessary changes to the status descriptions you find there.*

If you need to make changes to an existing customer record, simply double-click the customer or job name in the Customers & Jobs list of the Customer Center to open the Edit Customer dialog. Make the necessary changes and click OK to save them.

Adding Vendor Records

Vendors are almost as important as customers when it comes to operating a successful business. Unless you are completely self-sufficient, you'll probably have to purchase products and/or services to maintain your business. As with customers, you need to gather the basic information for each vendor before creating vendor records. Once you have the information at your fingertips, the process of entering vendor information into QuickBooks is very similar to entering customer data.

1. Begin by selecting Vendors | Vendor Center from the menu bar. This opens the Vendor Center, which provides access to most vendor-related information and activities.

2. Press Ctrl-N to open a New Vendor Dialog box, which, as you can see in Figure 3-19, bears a strong resemblance to the New Customer dialog box.

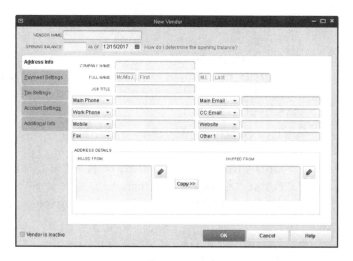

Figure 3-19: The New Vendor dialog looks a lot like the New
Customer dialog.

3. Select each tab and fill in the relevant data for the new
   vendor. While most of the fields are self-explanatory, a
   few could stand a little more explanation:

   - Address Info. All the fields on this tab are pretty
     straightforward. The only thing to note is that
     you can change the field names in the body by
     selecting different names from the various drop-
     down lists.

   - Payment Settings. The only field that bears
     closer scrutiny is the Print Name On Check As
     field. This is a great invention that enables you
     to create multiple vendors, all of whom are, in
     reality, the same vendor. For example, you may
     have to track and pay your state, county, and city
     sales taxes separately, but remit payment to the
     same tax agency. In that case, you'll be thankful
     this field exists. You can create three different
     vendors (e.g., PA State Sales Tax, PA Wage Tax,
     and Philly Sales Tax) for the different taxes

to maintain separate tracking and reporting. However, when it comes time to write the checks, they all go to the PA Dept of Revenue. You simply create three different vendors and enter the same payee name in the Print Name On Check As field.

- Tax Settings. Only two fields here—Vendor Tax ID and Vendor Eligible For 1099. You only need these fields if you employ 1099 vendors (e.g., consultants, subcontractors, etc.). See Chapter 10 for information on who qualifies and who doesn't.

- Account Settings. This tab provides three handy drop-down lists that let you assign default expense accounts to the vendor. For example, if you buy your house, car, and health insurance from the same agent, you could assign the three different insurance expense accounts to the agent's vendor record using this tab. The only problem with using all three default fields is that they all appear on the Expenses tab of the Enter Bills window when you select the vendor. It's perfect if your agent bills you for all three types of insurance on the same bill; otherwise, you'll have to delete one or two lines from the Expenses tab. In most cases, it is best to assign only the most commonly used account.

- Additional Info. This tab contains only a single default field—Vendor Type. However, the power in this tab resides in the ability to create custom fields. See Chapter 3 for details on creating and using custom fields.

4. Click OK to save the new vendor record.

Once you have your vendors set up, you may find that you need to make some changes. In that case, return to the Vendor Center, highlight the vendor name in the Vendors list, and click the Edit icon (it looks like a pencil nub) at the top of the Vendor Information pane on the right. The Edit Vendor dialog opens. Make your changes and click OK to save them.

Merging Records

As your lists of customers, jobs, and vendors grow, you'll probably find that you have duplicate records that need to be cleaned up. QuickBooks provides a simple solution for this problem—merging records. You can merge records of the same type as long as certain requirements are met. This means that you can merge two customer records, two job records, or two vendor records. You cannot merge among the different record types.

Vendor records have no restrictions, since they do not have subcategories. Therefore, you can merge any two existing vendors using the steps in this section.

Customer records and job records are the ones with the restrictions:

- Customer Records: Two customer records without jobs can be merged. A customer record without jobs can be merged with a customer record with jobs. Two customer records with jobs cannot be merged.

- Job Records: Two job records with estimates cannot be merged. If only one of the two has estimates, they can be merged.

Follow these steps to merge two records:

1. Open the record you want to eliminate.
2. Change the name to match (exactly) the name of the record you want to keep.
3. If there are no restricting conditions present, QuickBooks displays a message asking you if you want to merge the records (see Figure 3-20).
4. Click Yes to merge them or No to reconsider.

That's all it takes. All transactions of the eliminated record are transferred to the remaining record.

ProAdvisor NOTE: *You don't have to worry about losing attachments if either or both records have them. QuickBooks will ask to update the attachment link(s) during the merge.*

Figure 3-20: Eliminate duplicate records by merging them.

CHAPTER 4:

Tracking Income

- Creating Items Used in Sales

- Invoicing Customers

- Creating Cash Sales

- Receiving Customer Payments

- Managing Miscellaneous Income

- Writing Off Bad Debts

- Running Income Tracking Reports

With the basics out of the way, you're ready to start concentrating on the tasks of running and analyzing your business. Assuming you're in business to make money, which is the primary motivation for most business enterprises, you'll want to keep a close eye on the money coming in. In other words, you'll want to know how to track your income.

Creating Items Used on Sales Forms

In order to generate income, you have to make sales of some sort. Whether they are sales of services or goods, you will have to have "items" to sell. The QuickBooks Item List is the place to create those items. In addition to sales items, you may need other, nonsalable items such as discount items, subtotal items, other charge items, and so on, to complete the sale.

To create a new item, follow these steps:

1. Select Lists | Item List from the menu bar to open the Item List.

2. Press Ctrl-N to display the New Item dialog box shown in Figure 4-1.

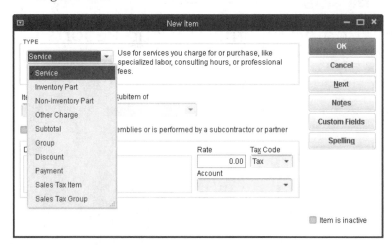

Figure 4-1: Create new items to start making sales.

3. From the Type drop-down list, choose the appropriate item type (see the sections later in this chapter for detailed explanations).

4. Fill in all the fields on the New Item dialog box as needed.

5. Click Next to save the new item and create another, or click OK to save the item and close the dialog box.

As you can see, the process is pretty simple. However, to help you use the different items properly, read the following sections that describe the different item types and their common uses.

ProAdvisor TIP: *You can use the Add/Edit Multiple List Entries feature to create multiple Service, Inventory Part, and Non-Inventory Part items in one fell swoop. Select Lists | Add/ Edit Multiple List Entries from the menu bar to access the feature.*

Service Items

The name pretty much says it all. If you provide services to your customers, you need service items to record and track them. For example, most lawyers, accountants, plumbers, electricians, and computer consultants are in the business of selling services. For each service they sell, they need to create a service item. The accountant might have Tax Prep, Bookkeeping, and Business Planning service items; the plumber, Heating, Plumbing, and Air Conditioning service items; and the computer consultant, Networking, Software Installation, and Computer Installation service items.

One thing to note about service items is that they have an option to make them two-sided, which allows you to include their costs and expense accounts as well as their prices and income accounts. The option is called This Service Is Used In Assemblies Or Is Performed By A Subcontractor Or Partner. For example, a general contractor who subcontracts the electrical work would want to track both the cost of the service (what the subcontractor charges her) and the income it generates (what she charges the customer).

Inventory Part Items

Inventory Part items are used for those tangible goods that you buy and keep in stock to resell. Unless you have inventory tracking turned on, you won't see Inventory Part in the Type drop-down list. Tracking inventory is a complex subject, and as such, it warrants a chapter of its own. See Chapter 6 for details on creating inventory items and tracking inventory.

Non-inventory Part

Use this type for supplies, special-order items, and materials used in the course of your work that do not fall into the category Inventory Part items. For example, a plumber might use fittings, lengths of pipe, and rolls of Teflon tape in the course of a job, but does not buy these things to resell. However, since they are an expense of the business, they need to be accounted for when purchased. For the most part, they will be used on purchase orders and/or bills. In that case, you only need enter an expense account in the Account field when creating the item.

If, on the other hand, you're using the item in an assembly or you've purchased a special-order item to resell, you'll want to track both sides of the transaction. To do so, enable the option called This Item Is Used In Assemblies Or Is Purchased For A Specific Customer:Job. Now you have the ability to enter the cost and expense account associated with the purchase of the item as well as the price and income account associated with the sale (or use in an assembly) of the item. Remember, only QuickBooks Premier and Enterprise users have the ability to create assemblies.

Other Charge Items

Use this item type for things like shipping charges or other line items that appear on your invoices. In fact, some people create a separate Other Charge item for each method of shipping. You can use the Other Charge item type for a variety of things, including over/short items, gift certificates, retainers, and more. If you use the item on a sales transaction, select an income account from the Account drop-down list. If you use the item on purchase transactions, choose an expense account from the Account drop-down list.

This is another item with an option to turn it into a two-sided item. If you're including the item in an assembly, or if it's an item for which you plan to get reimbursed by a customer, check the This Item Is Used In Assemblies Or Is A Reimbursable Charge option.

Subtotal Items

This is such a handy item when you need or want to see the total of two or more line items separate from the transaction total. This item type adds up everything that comes before it on a sales form. You can use it to calculate a subtotal before you subtract any discounts or prepayments, or apply a special tax.

This one is very easy to create. It only requires a name and description. QuickBooks takes care of the rest.

Group Items

You can use this item type to enter a group of items (all of which must already exist in your Item List) all at once. For example, you may sell something that is a package of separate items, and each of those items may be available for individual sale. Some service businesses, such as contractors, put individual services into a group in order to avoid lengthy invoices; for instance, you may want a group named Demolition that includes carpentry, hauling, cleaning, and other services that are individual items in your Item List. A retailer might create a Gift Basket group that includes several related items from different departments.

The individual items included in the group take care of the appropriate postings when the group item is sold. A group is merely a convenience that helps you avoid entering each item on its own line of the transaction form.

Discount Items

Use this item type to give a customer a discount as a line item. When you enter an item of the Discount type, you can indicate a percentage or a flat amount as the rate. Keep in mind that it only applies to the line (not lines) directly above it. If you need to discount multiple line items, use a subtotal item first and then discount the subtotal line item.

Payment Items

Use this item type to add a customer's prepayment to an invoice. QuickBooks automatically calculates the total appropriately, entering the amount as a negative number. As you'll see in the section on recording batch sales later in this chapter, payment items can also be used on cash sales.

Sales Tax Items & Groups

Use these item types to add sales tax to a sales transaction. Sales tax gets complicated in some states and localities, and you have to be extremely careful about the way you set up sales tax items. Chapter 3 explains how to set up Sales Tax Items and Sales Tax Groups.

Creating Cash Sales

A cash sale is a transaction in which the customer's money is received at the time the goods or services are received. Don't take the word "cash" literally; the payment may involve cash, a check, a credit card, a debit card, or a gift certificate.

Many companies that do most or all of their business as cash sales don't bother tracking customers for these sales. Some create a single customer, often named "Cash Customer," in QuickBooks. Some create customer records for repeat customers and a "Cash Customer" record to handle the rest.

To create a cash sale in QuickBooks, use the Enter Sales Receipts command found on the Customers menu. This opens the Enter Sales Receipts window seen in Figure 4-2.

1. From the Customer:Job drop-down list, choose the "cash" customer you've created.

2. Enter the Date, Payment Method, line items, Customer Message, and Memo as you would for any cash sale.

3. If you have a QuickBooks Merchant account and the customer is paying with a credit card, you can check the Process Payment option to automatically process the payment.

4. Click Save & New to save and process the sale and create another, or click Save & Close to save and process the sale and close the form.

The journal produced by this cash sale (the Cash Receipts Journal) looks similar to Table 4-1.

Account	Debit	Credit
10000—Bank Account	341.10	
40000—Income		322.50
22000—Sales Tax Payable		18.60

Table 4-1: A typical cash sale journal.

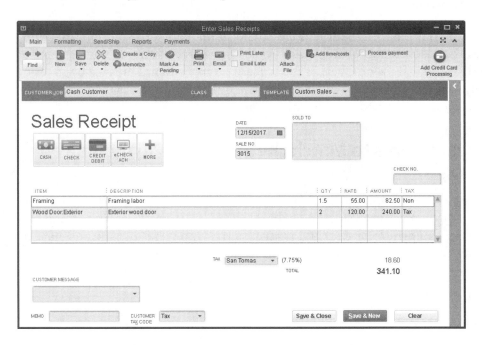

Figure 4-2: A cash sale is one that is paid for at the time of the sale, regardless of the payment method used.

Daily Journals from Z-Tapes

Businesses that use a cash register don't record each individual transaction in their books; instead, they enter all the daily sales as a batch.

Recording Sales in Batches

If your cash register gives you a breakdown of sales in terms of taxable and non-taxable and also provides payment information (cash, check, and each credit card you accept), you have everything you need to enter your totals in QuickBooks.

The best way to make use of a cash register report is to include sales and deposits information (bank deposit information) in one QuickBooks transaction form. The bottom line is zero (sales in, deposits out). To do this, you have to set up a couple of accounts and items so that everything posts properly.

If your cash register can track the items you sell, you don't need to track those items in your QuickBooks sales transaction. (You can periodically adjust item quantities separately, using journal entries or inventory adjustment transactions.) You use the daily summary transaction to get the numbers into your general ledger.

Create Items to Match the Sales and Payments You Enter

The first thing you need to do is create items to use on your batch sales receipt transaction. See the earlier section entitled "Creating Items Used On Sales Forms" for detailed instructions. Once you understand how it works, you can add any additional items you want to track.

Sales Items

For sales, you need the following:

- An item for taxable sales
- An item for non-taxable sales

Create them using a Non-Inventory Part Type. Just be sure to make the Taxable Sales item taxable and the Non-Taxable Sales item non-taxable.

Sales Tax Items

For sales taxes, you need the following:

- A sales tax item or group. You probably already have this item configured in your company file.
- If needed, a separate sales tax item to apply a line item for items subject to special taxes by your state or local tax authority, such as specific taxes for alcoholic beverages or other items your government agencies tax at a different rate).
- A "placeholder" sales tax item with a zero rate to apply to the batch transaction if tax items are applied as line items to specific types of items.

See Chapter 3 to learn how to set up sales tax items and groups, including special tax items for goods and services with separate tax rates.

Payment Items

Payment items track payments (money out of the till, including bank deposits). To do so, they deduct amounts from sales transactions. This means that you don't use a minus sign when you enter a Payment type item; QuickBooks automatically adds the minus sign. To track payments, you need the following Payment items:

- Cash
- Check
- Visa
- MasterCard
- Other credit cards you accept
- Debit cards

To set up Payment items, review the earlier section entitled "Creating Items Used on Sales Forms." Repeat this for every payment type you accept.

To set up these Payment items, you must have created the appropriate payment methods so that they appear in the drop-down list of the Payment Item dialog. To accomplish this, choose Lists | Customer & Vendor Profile Lists | Payment Method List. Press Ctrl-N to create a new payment method if the payment method you need isn't available.

Create New "Register" Customers

If you're using the register tape to record your daily sales summary, you might as well create a new customer for each register you have. That way, it will be easy to keep track of the origin of the sales data. Follow the instructions in Chapter 3 for creating new customers and name the new customers Register1, Register2, and so on. Make them taxable to ensure that tax is calculated on taxable sales.

Creating A Daily Sales Summary Form

Only QuickBooks Premier Retail Edition comes with a pre-designed Daily Sales Summary template, but creating your own is relatively simple. Here's how:

1. Choose Lists | Templates to open the Templates dialog box (see Figure 4-3).
2. Highlight the Custom Sales Receipt template and press Ctrl-E to open the Basic Customization window.
3. Click the Manage Templates button to open the Manage Templates window.
4. Click the Copy button at the bottom-left of the page.
5. Change the Template Name to Daily Sales (if you try to name it Daily Sales Summary, QuickBooks may balk), and click OK to return to the Basic Customization window.

6. Click the Additional Customization button to display the Additional Customization window.

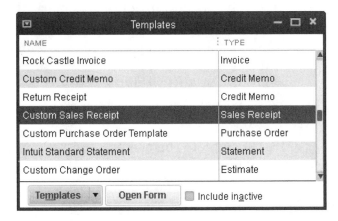

Figure 4-3: The Custom Sales Receipt template provides a good starting point for the Daily Sales Summary form.

7. Make the following changes to the Header tab:

  • Change the Default Title to Daily Sales Summary.

  • Deselect all the check marks in the Screen and Print columns except for Default Title and Date. There's no need to clutter the form header with unnecessary data.

8. Move to the Columns tab and make the following changes:

  • Check the Screen and Print columns for Item, Description, and Amount only. Deselect all the other items.

  • Change the Description Title to Sales, Sales Tax, and Payment Items.

9. Move to the Footer tab and make the following changes:

  • Check the Screen and Print column for Sales Tax and Total, and remove all other check marks.

- If the Overlapping Fields dialog appears after you check the Print column for Sales Tax, click the Default Layout button to automatically correct the overlap.
- QuickBooks warns you that you're about to lose all Layout Designer changes. Click Yes to agree and resolve the overlap issue.

10. Click OK to save the changes and return to the Basic Customization window.

11. Click OK to complete the process and return to the Templates dialog box.

Creating the Summary Sales Transaction

Armed with the report from the cash register, choose Customers | Enter Sales Receipts. From the Template drop-down list, select the Daily Sales template.

In the Daily Sales Summary template, select the generic "register" customer and fill out the form as follows:

1. Enter the total of nontaxable sales.

2. Enter the total of taxable sales (QuickBooks automatically calculates the tax and inserts the amount at the bottom of the transaction window).

3. Enter the total payments for each of the payment types. If QuickBooks displays a message informing you that you can use the Payment Method field to enter a single payment method, check Do Not Display This Message In The Future and click OK.

When you're finished entering sales and payments, the total for the transaction should be zero (see Figure 4-4). If the total isn't zero, use the Over or Short item discussed later in this chapter to balance the transaction, then save the transaction.

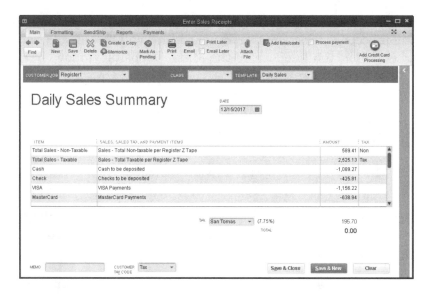

Figure 4-4: The Tax column appears the first time you use the form.

CPA TIP: To simplify the process of using QuickBooks to reconcile your bank account, it will be to your benefit to record the components as shown in Figure 4-4 (cash, checks, each type of credit card, debit card) individually. Below it will be explained how to move funds from Undeposited Funds to your bank account as a deposit so that you will be able to tie out your individual deposits to your bank statement.

Depositing the Day's Funds

When you choose Banking | Make Deposits, the Payments To Deposit window displays each payment method so that you can select each method separately, to match the way deposits are listed on your bank statement.

If you deposit cash and checks together, select Cash And Check and click OK to add them to the Make Deposits window, then click Save & New to return to the Payments To Deposit window.

If your credit card merchant accounts are fairly consistent about depositing proceeds, select each credit card that will be part of a single deposit and enter the total deposit in the Make Deposits window, but adjust the date to reflect the usual delay.

For a merchant card company that deducts the fee before depositing the proceeds, deduct the fee in the Make Deposits window before transferring the funds to the bank account:

1. In the line below the deposit, select your merchant card fee expense account in the Account column.

2. In the Amount column, enter the fee with a minus sign.

3. The deposit totals the net payments, which matches what will show up in your bank statement.

Since QuickBooks links the sales tax status to an item, and the item is linked to an income account, both taxable and non-taxable items may be linked to the same income account. The sales tax liability report is generated based on the item information in the sales transaction form, not the account to which the sale is posted.

Also enter the cash received that you're taking to the bank, which should result in a zero-based transaction. The resulting cash payments journal should look similar to Table 4-2.

Account	Debit	Credit
40000—Sales		3114.54
22000—Sales Tax Payable		195.70
10000—Operating Account	3310.24	

Table 4-2: In this case, both sales items (taxable and non-taxable) are linked to the same income account.

Of course, it rarely works this well because when you're ready to take the day's cash receipts to the bank, after you remove the money you want to remain in the till, the total in the cash bag doesn't always match the total sales, meaning your batch transaction doesn't zero out. The solution is to track overages or shortages so that the sales match the bank deposit.

CPA TIP: *To track over and short, it's best to create accounts named Over and Short of the type Other Income/Expense. Using income or cost of sales accounts distorts the gross profit and could affect commission calculations.*

Create Over and Short Accounts

To track Over/Short, you need to have some place to post the discrepancies, which means that you have to create some accounts in your chart of accounts, as follows:

- Create a parent account called Over/Short, using the account type Other Income.
- Create a subaccount named Over, using the account type Other Income.
- Create a subaccount named Short, using the account type Other Income.

If you use account numbers, make the three numbers sequential; for instance:

- 73000 Over/Short (parent account)
- 73010 Over (subaccount)
- 73020 Short (subaccount)

Create Over and Short Items

When you track cash sales in a Sales Receipt transaction, you need items for your overages and shortages. (In QuickBooks, you need items for everything that's connected with entering sales data in a transaction window.) Create items for overages and shortages using the following guidelines:

- Create two Other Charge items, one named Overage and the other named Shortage.
- Don't assign a price.

- Make the items non-taxable.
- Link each item to the appropriate subaccount that you just created for Over and Short. Don't link anything to the Over/Short parent account.

Now that you have the necessary accounts and items, use the Overage and Shortage items in the Sales Receipts window to adjust the difference between the amount of money you've accumulated in the cash-sale transactions and the amount of money you're actually depositing to the bank.

Remember to use a minus sign before the figure when you use the Short item. (In the transaction journal, an overage posts a credit and a shortage posts a debit.) The transaction journal posts the over/short amount properly, as seen in Table 4-3.

Account	Debit	Credit
40000—Sales		3114.54
22000—Sales Tax Payable		195.70
70320—Short	10.00	
10000—Operating Account	3300.24	

Table 4-3: The transaction total has to match the amount of the bank deposit.

Regardless of the total income, the amount posted to the bank has to match the amount you take to the bank. To make this happen, you have to track overages and shortages.

Over time, the over/short account usually balances; it's short one day and over another day. However, if you're short every day and the shortages are growing, you have an entirely different problem. You need to look at the person who stands in front of the cash register.

Understanding Accounts Receivable

Accounts receivable is the accounting terminology for money owed to you, and it's often abbreviated as A/R. (In the business community, the common jargon for A/R is money on the street).

A/R increases when you deliver a service or a product and send an invoice to the customer and the customer hasn't yet remitted payment. This is an asset because, as explained in Chapter 1, an asset is something that you own or something that belongs to you, even if you don't have it in your possession at the moment.

CPA NOTE: *Some companies (usually retail businesses) never have an A/R balance because the customer always pays for purchases at the time the sale takes place.*

A/R postings take place whenever the amount of money owed to you changes:

- A/R is debited (increased) when you create an invoice.
- A/R is credited (decreased) when you receive a payment on an invoice or issue a credit to a customer.

It's important to know that the entire amount of the invoice is posted to A/R, even if the amount includes items other than sales/income. For example, the sales tax you charge is not income, so while the A/R account posts the total amount of the transaction, the postings on the "other side" of A/R are made to multiple accounts. For details on invoice postings, see the section entitled "CPA Sidebar: Invoice Postings" later in this chapter.

Accounts Receivable is decreased whenever the amount of money owed to you is reduced by one of the following actions:

- The customer sends a payment for an invoice (covered in the next section).
- You issue a credit to a customer with an A/R balance (covered later in this chapter).

Invoicing Customers

An invoice is a document showing the details of goods and services purchased by the customer, and it includes a reference number (the invoice number), the goods and services sold, quantities, prices, taxes, total amount due, transaction date, and terms of sale.

In most cases, invoices are sent to the customer after the goods have been shipped to the customer or the services have been rendered. This differs from a cash sale, in which payment is handed over at the same time goods are sold.

Setting Sales-Form Related Preferences

Before jumping into the mechanics of creating invoices, it might be a good idea to set the QuickBooks preferences related to sales transactions.

Open the Preferences dialog (Edit | Preferences), and configure the following options found in the Sales & Customers category:

- Add Available Time/Costs To Invoices For The Selected Job. This option, found in the My Preferences tab, tells QuickBooks how to handle invoices and sales receipts for customers who have outstanding billable time, expenses, and so on. By default, it's set to ask you each time you create a sales transaction and select a customer with outstanding time/costs. However, if you always want to be informed, choose the first option, Prompt For Time/Costs To Add. If you don't ever want to be bothered with this information, , which is not a good idea, choose Don't Add Any.

- Sales Forms. This section of options, found in the Company Preferences tab, dictates how QuickBooks handles the default shipping method, the default FOB location, and whether to warn you when you try to use an invoice number already in use. The options are self-explanatory. If you have more than one packing slip template, you can also set the default template to use.

- Custom Pricing. Let QuickBooks know if you want to use price levels when creating sales transactions.

Creating Invoices

When you create an invoice, a journal of the transaction must be created (it's a Sales Journal) so that the postings can be transferred to the general ledger. The transaction is posted to all the affected accounts. Fortunately, QuickBooks takes care of this automatically.

Creating an invoice is easy:

1. Press Ctrl-I to open the Create Invoices window. For this example, we're going to use the Intuit Product Invoice. If you're using a different invoice template, there may be some differences in the form layout and fields present.

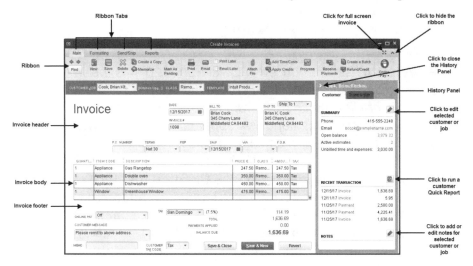

Figure 4-5: The Intuit Product Invoice template provides all the basics you need to create a good invoice.

2. Select the customer to invoice from the Customer:Job drop-down list.

3. If you're tracking classes, select a class from the Class drop-down list.

4. If you have multiple invoice templates, choose the appropriate template from the Template drop-down list.

5. Most of the invoice header fields are self-explanatory and filled in automatically if the information is in the customer record. Fill in missing information as needed.

6. Move to the body of the invoice and enter the sales as line items.

7. Enter a Customer Message that will appear on the printed invoice.

8. The Memo field is for entering additional information about the invoice. It will not appear on the printed invoice, but it WILL appear on statements you send to the customer, so be careful what you enter.

9. Click Save & New to create another invoice or Save & Close to close the Create Invoices window.

ProAdvisor TIP: *Introduced in QuickBooks 2014 is the ability to copy and paste line items in the body of the invoice form. Right-click the line you want to copy, and select Copy Line from the context menu that appears. Move to the next available line, right-click again, and select Paste Line.*

A very handy invoicing feature is the Create Batch Invoices feature. It enables you to create a single invoice that can be addressed and sent to multiple customers. It's great for businesses that do a similar billing on a regular basis—for example, professionals that bill for monthly retainers or landlords that bill for monthly rentals. To use the Create Batch Invoices feature, follow these steps:

1. Choose Customers | Create Batch Invoices to open the Batch Invoice wizard.

2. Select the customers for whom you want to create the invoices and click the Add button.

3. Click Next to move to step 2 of the wizard.

4. Enter the correct date for the invoice and select the invoice template to use.

5. Enter the line item(s) for the invoice.

ProAdvisor TIP: *Before adding customers, you can create a Billing Group by clicking the Billing Group drop-down list and selecting <Add New> to open the Group Name dialog. Give the group a name and click Save to create the group. After you add customers, you can save them as a group by selecting the group from the Billing Group drop-down list and clicking the Save Group button.*

6. Select a message from the Customer Message drop-down list and click Next to proceed to step 3.

7. Review all the invoices about to be created. If they're acceptable, click Create Invoices to build the invoices. If you want to make any changes, click the Back button to do so.

8. If the customers have a preferred send method in their records, the invoices are marked accordingly and a Batch Invoice Summary dialog appears with this information. Click the appropriate button(s) to send the invoices.

ProAdvisor TIP: *Since the current information in each customer record is used to create the invoices, you might want to double-check the records before using the batch invoicing feature to ensure that all information is up-to-date. One other thing to note is that batch invoicing is not available if you have Multiple Currencies turned on.*

Sending the Invoice

A QuickBooks invoice isn't going to do you much good unless you get it in the hands of the customer. Therefore, once you generate the invoice, you have a couple of options for sending it.

- Print and mail. When you're finished filling out the invoice, click the Print icon on the Main tab of the ribbon and select Invoice to generate a hard copy of the invoice. Notice while you're there, that you can also print an envelope, as well.

- E-mail. As long as your customer record contains a valid e-mail address, you can send a PDF copy of the invoice via e-mail. Complete the invoice form, click the Email icon, and select Invoice to automatically generate an e-mail message that includes the PDF copy of the invoice as an attachment.

ProAdvisor TIP: *If you use Outlook as your default e-mail client, you can automatically attach multiple files to the invoice e-mail. Before creating the invoice e-mail, make sure the additional documents/files are attached to the invoice (use the Attach File icon on the Main tab of the ribbon). Click the down arrow on the Email icon and choose Invoice And Files. All documents currently attached the invoice form are included in the e-mail as attachments.*

CPA Sidebar
Invoice Postings

As a business owner, you should understand how transactions are posted; otherwise, the data in reports can be confusing. The following examples are presented to clarify the way invoices are journalized as they feed the general ledger.

The journal for a simple sales transaction, involving no inventory or sales tax, is seen in Table 4-4. The posting to Accounts Receivable represents the total amount of the invoice.

Account	Debit	Credit
40000—Income		100.00
11000—Accounts Receivable	100.00	

Table 4-4: A journal for a simple sale of goods or services.

If you post certain types of sales to different income accounts as you create the individual items covered by the invoice, the journal for the invoice tracks those income accounts, as seen in Table 4-5.

Account	Debit	Credit
40100—Income for Services		60.00
40200—Income for Products		40.00
11000—Accounts Receivable	100.00	

Table 4-5: Journals reflect all the accounts used in the invoice.

When sales tax is involved, it doesn't affect income accounts in the journal because sales tax is neither income nor an expense to the seller; it is a liability, since you are merely acting as an agent/conduit for the tax authority. However, the tax affects the total amount due from the customer, which in turn affects the total of Accounts Receivable. The journal displayed in Table 4-6 is based on the fact that services are not taxable, and the products sold are taxable at the rate of 7%.

Account	Debit	Credit
40100—Income for Services		60.00
40200—Income for Products Sold		40.00
22000—Sales Tax Payable		2.80
11000—Accounts Receivable	102.80	

Table 4-6: The journal includes the sales tax liability.

Things get a bit more complicated when you're selling inventory, because the journal posts the cost of goods sold (usually abbreviated COGS), which is an expense and decreases the value of your inventory asset. As you can see in Table 4-7, those parts of the overall postings don't affect the amount of the invoice or the sales tax.

Account	Debit	Credit
40000—Income for Products Sold		40.00
22000—Sales Tax Payable		2.80
15000—Inventory Asset		18.00
50000—COGS	18.00	
11000—Accounts Receivable	42.80	

Table 4-7: Inventory postings are equal and opposite and don't affect the total amount of the invoice.

As you can see by the progression above, the A/R side of the entry is always the total amount of the sale that will be due to you from your customer. The rest of the entry provides as much detail as you desire to generate the reports to help you manage your business.

Receiving Customer Payments

When a customer sends a payment for an invoice that's in your accounting system, the payment reduces the A/R balance and increases the bank account into which you deposit the payment. For example, a payment of $100.00 is posted as seen in Table 4-8.

Account	Debit	Credit
10000— Bank Account	100.00	
11000—Accounts Receivable		100.00

Table 4-8: The journal for a customer payment is simple and straightforward.

The invoice for which the payment is received may be larger than the amount of the payment. If the original invoice was for $200.00 and the customer sends a partial payment of $100.00, the A/R balance is reduced by $100.00. The remaining balance of $100.00 remains in A/R.

In accounting, there are two ways to apply payments to invoices:

- Balance forward. This method considers the total of all the outstanding invoices as the amount due from the customer, and all payments are applied against that total. It doesn't matter which particular invoice is being paid, because it's a running total of payments against a running total of invoices.

- Open item. This method applies received payments to specific invoices. Usually, the customer either sends a copy of the invoice along with the check or notes on the check stub the invoice number that is being paid.

CPA NOTE: *It's important to understand that an invoice payment journal has no references to the accounts that are tracking income, inventory, or sales tax. Many accountants receive questions from clients who want to know why the payment doesn't show what products were sold or what general ledger income accounts were affected. All of that information was posted when the original invoice was created. The payment of the invoice is a second and separate transaction. The customer payment is trading one asset (A/R) for another (Cash); it is not a new sales transaction.*

Setting Defaults for Receiving Payments

QuickBooks offers some default settings for receiving payments from customers, and choosing the options that match your preferred methods can save you some keystrokes. The settings are available in the Company Preferences tab of the Payments category in the Preferences dialog (choose Edit| Preferences). The following options affect receipt of payments:

- Automatically apply payments
- Automatically calculate payments

ProAdvisor TIP: *The Preferences dialog also has an option labeled Use Undeposited Funds as a Default Deposit To Account. You should select that option, because it's difficult to track bank activity and reconcile your bank statement if you don't use the Undeposited Funds account. More information about this account appears later in this chapter.*

Automatically Apply Payments

This option, which is enabled by default, tells QuickBooks to apply payments to invoices automatically. If the payment matches the amount of an invoice, it is automatically applied to that invoice. If the payment doesn't match the amount of an invoice, the payment is automatically applied as a partial payment on the oldest invoice.

Automatically Calculate Payments

If you keep this option enabled (it's turned on by default), you can skip entering the amount of the payment in the Amount field at the top of the Receive Payments window and head directly for the list of invoices. As you select each invoice for payment, QuickBooks calculates the total and places it in the Amount field. If your customers' checks always match the amount of an open invoice, this saves you some data entry.

Recording the Payment

When a check arrives for which an invoice is in the system, you have to record that payment and apply it against the right invoice.

1. Choose Customers | Receive Payments from the menu bar to bring up the Receive Payments window (see Figure 4-6).

2. Click the arrow to the right of the Received From field to display a list of customers and select the customer or job who sent this payment. All the existing invoices for this customer or job appear in the body of the form.

3. If you have multiple A/R accounts, select the A/R account to which you posted the invoice(s) for this customer or job. If you don't have multiple A/R accounts, the A/R Account field doesn't appear in the Receive Payments window.

Pro Advisor TIP: *If you have multiple A/R accounts and you inadvertently posted an invoice to the wrong one, you can edit the original transaction to correct your error and change the A/R account.*

---

4. Enter the amount of the payment in the Amount field.

5. Select the appropriate payment method button and enter the details (e.g., credit card data) in the applicable field. To add a new payment method, click the More button, click Add New Type and fill in the information.

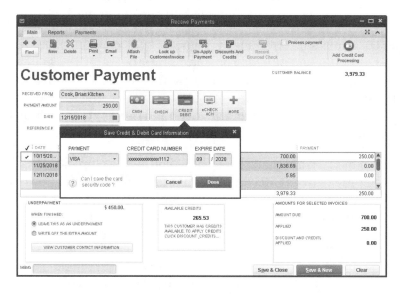

Figure 4-6: This customer has credits that can be applied to outstanding invoices.

Applying the Payment

Now you have to apply the payment against an invoice or multiple invoices for this customer. Numerous scenarios are possible when receiving customer payments:

- The customer has one unpaid invoice, and the payment is for the same amount as that invoice.

- The customer has several unpaid invoices, and the payment is for the amount of one of those invoices.

- The customer has one or more unpaid invoices, and the payment is for an amount lower than any single invoice.

- The customer has several unpaid invoices, and the payment is for an amount greater than any one invoice, but not large enough to cover two invoices.
- The customer has one or more unpaid invoices, and the payment is for a lesser amount than the current balance, but the customer has a credit equal to the difference between the payment and the customer balance.

If the customer's intention isn't clear, call the customer and ask how the payment should be applied. You can manually enter the amount you're applying against any invoice in the Payment column. You must apply the entire amount of the payment, no matter how many invoices you have to select, even if an applied payment is only a partial payment against an invoice amount.

If the payment exactly matches the amount of an invoice, or if only one invoice appears in the Receive Payments window, QuickBooks automatically applies it correctly. Otherwise, QuickBooks applies the payment to the oldest invoice. If you are using the balance forward system, just let QuickBooks apply payments against the oldest invoices.

If the payment is smaller than any single invoice amount, apply the payment to the oldest invoice unless the customer specified an invoice number for this payment.

If the payment is larger than any single invoice amount, but not large enough to cover two invoices, apply the payment amount to the oldest invoice and then select one or more additional invoices to apply the remaining amount toward.

After you finish applying the payment, if there are insufficient funds to pay off an existing invoice, the Underpayment section appears at the bottom of the Receive Payments window asking whether you want to leave the underpaid amount as an underpayment or write it off (see Figure 4-7).

Figure 4-7: QuickBooks lets you decide how to handle underpayments.

It's almost always best to retain the underpayment, which means that the invoice you selected for partial payment remains as a receivable with a new balance of the original balance less the payment you applied. When you save the payment, QuickBooks makes the appropriate postings. If you send statements to customers, the unpaid balance appears on the statement.

Occasionally, you may want to write off the unpaid balance. If the customer made a mistake in the check amount and it's off by pennies or nickels or dimes, you may decide it's not worth calling the customer to arrange for another payment. You may also have some reason to believe that an unpaid balance that is more substantial than small change will never be paid, and you might as well write it off.

When you select the option to write off the unpaid amount and save the transaction, QuickBooks opens the Write Off Amount dialog so that you can choose the posting account and, if applicable, apply a class to the transaction.

Discuss the account to use for a write-off with your accountant. You can create an Income or Expense account for this purpose, depending on the way your accountant wants to track receivables that you've decided to forgive. (Writing off a balance is not the same as managing bad debts, which are a whole other category of accounting).

Applying a Credit

If the customer has a credit, the Receive Payments window will contain an Available Credits section in the footer section with a number greater than zero (see Figure 4-8).

Figure 4-8: Don't forget to apply any available credits the customer may have.

To apply the credit and mark the invoice as paid, first enter the amount of the payment, then click the button labeled Discounts And Credits found on the Main tab of the ribbon bar. This opens the Discounts And Credits dialog for the customer.

If the invoices are for different jobs for the same customer, each job may have its own credits. You'll know this if you select all the credits for one job and click Done and the Available Credits section of the footer still contains a number greater than zero.

CPA Sidebar
Understanding Customer Credits

Let's look at what happens when you apply the credit or give your customer a discount after the original invoice was issued. Let's assume the customer has an outstanding invoice in the amount of $1000.00 and a credit/discount for $250.00. The customer sends a check for $750.00 and tells you to apply the $250.00 credit to make up the difference.

When you complete the task, the transaction journal shows the following postings:

- The bank account is debited for $750.00.
- Accounts Receivable is credited for $750.00

This is another occasion that often generates a telephone call from a business owner to an accountant. The question is, "I don't understand how a transaction that pays off an invoice for $1000.00 doesn't post the $1000.00-amount anywhere in my general ledger."

Let's look at what happens when you create an invoice, issue a credit, apply the credit to the invoice, and then apply the customer's payment. Follow the time line and transactions in Table 4-9 to understand how the accounting works.

Transaction	Account	Debit	Credit	Balance
Invoice created for $1000.00	Accounts Receivable	1000.00		
	Income		1000.00	1000.00
...time passes...				
Credit Created for $250.00	Accounts Receivable		250.00	
	Income	250.00		750.00
...time passes...				
Check for $750.00 is received	Bank	750.00		
	Accounts Receivable		750.00	00.00

Table 4-9: This invoice was paid by credit memo and check.

You can think of the credit that was applied as a payment made by the customer, but that payment wasn't in the form of a check or cash, so it couldn't be deposited in the bank. This means that on the "payment" side of this invoice, no single payment transaction in the amount of $1000.00 ever took place. However, following the time line, the credits to Accounts Receivable (the posting account for payments) add up to $1000.00, and that's the amount required to reduce the invoice balance to zero.

One additional note is that your accountant will probably suggest that you post a true credit (e.g., if there was an overcharge on the original sales posting) to one income account (Sales) and that you post a discount to a second income account for discretionary reductions in the original invoice provided to a good customer or on account of a promotion (Discounts and Allowances).

Customer Refunds

Refunds are easy to manage, because the refund process is usually a straightforward accounting transaction. Here's what happens:

- Cash is credited (reduced) and posted to the appropriate cash account.
- Sales are debited (reduced) and posted to the appropriate income account.

The appropriate cash account depends on the way you deliver the refund:

- If you write a check and post it to the appropriate income account, the transaction journal posts a debit to income and a credit to the bank account.
- If you take cash from the cash register, include the transaction (using the appropriate income account) in your daily Cash Receipts journal (covered earlier in this chapter). Don't forget to put a note in the cash register so the person creating the daily journal knows about it.
- A credit card refund could be considered a "negative" sale. Ideally, your cash register Z tape will allow you

to either record this as a credit, which will reduce your daily sales total (either as a single item or with details such as taxable sales, nontaxable sales, and sales tax), or will process the reduction in that day's credit card receipts in tandem with the increases that are part of your normal activities. If you maintain your daily Cash Receipts manually, again, treat the credit card refund above merely as a "negative" sale.

The appropriate income account depends on the method you want to use to track refunds:

- You can post the refund to the same income account you used for the original sale, which reduces total income for that account and displays the net income in reports.

- You can post the refund to another income account you set up specifically to track refunds.

CPA TIP: *It's best to track refunds via a specific account in the Income section of your chart of accounts. Name the account Refunds. Because the account is of the type Income, it's called a contra-sales account, which means it's an income account and appears in general ledger reports with a negative amount, which reduces total income, but lets you see (and analyze) the effect of refunds on your business.*

If sales tax was involved in the original transaction, you must also refund the amount of sales tax to the customer.

If the product the customer returns for the refund is an inventory item, you have to put the item back into inventory. This debits (increases) the inventory asset account and credits (decreases) the COGS expense that was posted when you sold the inventory.

As an example, Table 4-10 is a transaction journal for a refund by check for a returned inventory item that sold for $160.00. The refund amount is $171.20, including sales tax of $11.20. The COGS of the inventory item is $100.00. (If the refund had been a cash transaction, the credit to cash would have posted to the account linked to the cash register instead of to the bank account).

Account	Debit	Credit
41000—Refunds	160.00	
22000—Sales Tax Payable	11.20	
15000—Inventory Asset	100.00	
50000—COGS		100.00
10000—Operating Account		171.20

Table 4-10: Use a separate account to track refunds.

Notice that the inventory asset and COGS are equal and opposite, so they don't affect the amount of the refund. (You can think of it as a separate transaction within a transaction, used to manage inventory.) The sales tax debit reduces the sales tax payable amount that appears when you create the remittance to the state.

If the inventory was returned because it was damaged, you can't put the item back into inventory. Chapter 6 has information about handling damaged inventory.

Creating Customer Credits & Refunds

QuickBooks makes easy work of generating credits and refunds to customers. The same form is used for both—the Create Credit Memos/Refunds form.

1. Select Customers | Create Credit Memos/Refunds from the menu bar to open the Create Credit Memos/Refunds form.

2. Choose the appropriate customer or job from the Customer:Job drop-down list.

3. Enter or change the form header information as needed (Date, P.O. No., etc.).

4. Move to the body of the form and enter the line item(s) for which the credit is being given. Since it is a credit, you

don't have to add a minus sign; QuickBooks knows that the amount is a negative number.

5. Add any special line items, such as shipping and handling.

6. Enter the form footer elements (Customer Message, Memo, etc.) as needed.

7. Click Save & Close to save the credit memo. QuickBooks immediately displays the dialog box shown in Figure 4-9, asking how you would like to use the credit.

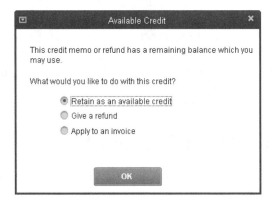

Figure 4-9: You have several ways to use the newly created credit.

8. Choose the manner in which you want to utilize the credit. Your choices include:

- Retain As An Available Credit. If the customer has no open invoices, you can choose this option to reserve the amount to apply to future invoices.

- Give A Refund. If the customer has no open invoices and has requested a refund, select this option to create a refund. QuickBooks displays the Issue A Refund dialog box, which offers you the opportunity to create the refund using any of your existing payment methods. If the refund is by cash or check, be sure to select the appropriate account from the Account field drop-down list.

- Apply To An Invoice. If the customer has any outstanding invoices, choosing this option displays the Apply Credit To Invoices dialog box. By default, the oldest invoice is automatically selected and the credit applied. However, if the credit is larger than the invoice total, the excess is applied to the next invoice. If no other invoices exist, the remainder is held as an available credit for the customer.

ProAdvisor TIP: *If you used the first option to retain the credit and later decide that you want to give the customer a refund, you can easily convert the credit into a refund. Simply open the credit and click the Use Credit To Give Refund button located on the Main tab of the form's ribbon bar. This opens the Issue A Refund dialog box.*

Applying Customer Discounts

Customer discounts are commonly applied for one of the following reasons:

- Either the customer earned a discount for volume purchases, or you're providing a discount for certain customers, such as wholesale customers.
- The customer earned a discount for timely payment of an invoice. The invoice total did not include the discount; instead, the discount is applied at the time of payment.

You can post discounts to the same income account you use to post sales, but it's better to create a discrete account for tracking customer discounts. You can then analyze the discounts as a percentage of total sales.

Name the account Discounts Given and put it in the Income section of your chart of accounts. (The reason you name the account Discounts Given instead of Discounts is that you also may need an account name Discounts Taken to track discounts you receive from vendors.)

To create a discount item:

1. Select Lists | Item List from the menu bar.
2. Press Ctrl-N to create a new item.
3. Choose Discount from the Type drop-down list that appears.
4. Enter a Name and Description for the new discount.
5. Enter the discount amount in the Amount Or % field using the following criteria:

   • If you are creating a specific percentage discount (e.g., 10% wholesale discount), enter 10%. You must enter the percent sign, or QuickBooks will assume it's a dollar amount.

   • If you are creating a specific dollar discount, enter the number of the discount. For example, if you want to create a $10.00 discount, enter the number 10 (without the dollar sign).

   • If you want to enter a discount (either percentage or dollar) at the time of the sale, leave the amount at zero. When you use the discount on a sales transaction, you only have to enter the percentage or dollar amount. Since it's a discount item, QuickBooks automatically makes it a negative number.

6. From the Account field drop-down list, choose (or create) the Discounts Given account. Remember, this should be an income account.

That's all there is to it. Click OK to save the discount item.

Applying the Discount to the Sales Transaction

If the discount is applied at the time you create the invoice or cash sale transaction, enter the discount as a line item on the transaction form (see Figure 4-10).

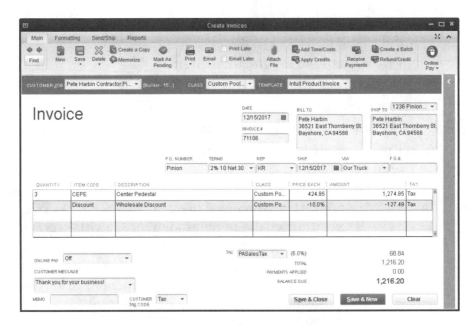

Figure 4-10: A discount item applies to the line item before it.

The transaction journal makes the postings seen in Table 4-11.

Account	Debit	Credit
40000—Income		1274.85
22000—Sales Tax Payable		68.84
41000—Discounts Given	127.49	
11000—Accounts Receivable	1216.20	

Table 4-11: Adjust the sales amount by applying a discount.

ProAdvisor TIP: *Remember, a QuickBooks discount item only discounts the single line item above it. If you want to discount multiple line items on a sales transaction, first use a subtotal item, and then discount the subtotal line item.*

Applying the Discount to the Payment

Some businesses, usually manufacturing and distribution companies, provide a discount for timely payment. The vendor (that's you) gives payment terms for the invoice (such as 30 days from the invoice date) and then offers a discount (commonly 2%) if the invoice is paid within a short time (such as within 10 days of the invoice date). The terms data in your invoice form for this type of discount should display as 2%10Net30; your customers know how to interpret that data.

You create the invoice for the full amount without any discount amount indicated. When the customer sends the payment, the discount has been taken, so the payment doesn't match the amount of the invoice or the amount for this customer in Accounts Receivable. When you process the payment, add the discount using the Discounts Given account. To process the payment, follow these steps:

1. Choose Customers | Receive Payments to open the Receive Payments form.
2. From the Received From drop-down list, select the customer.
3. Fill in the form header fields.
4. Place a check mark next to the invoice against which you want to apply the received payment. If the customer has earned a discount, you'll see a message in the footer of the form that says, "This Customer Has Discounts Available. To Apply Discounts Click Discount, Credits."

5. Click the Discounts And Credits button on the ribbon bar to open the Discount And Credits dialog (see Figure 4-11).

6. The discount information is pre-calculated, but you can change it if you wish. If you do so, make sure you communicate with the customer about the changes.

7. Select the Discounts Given account from the Discount Account drop-down list.

8. Click Done to apply the discount and return to the Receive Payments form.

9. Click Save & Close or Save & New to continue.

The invoice in Figure 4-11 was for $1216.20, and the customer took a discount of $24.32. You need to show the invoice as fully paid, but your bank deposit is only $1191.88. When you add the discount to the payment transaction, the postings make all of this work properly in the transaction journal, as seen in Table 4-12.

Account	Debit	Credit
10000—Bank Account	1191.88	
41000—Discounts Given	24.32	
11000—Accounts Receivable		1216.20

Table 4-12: Add the discount to the payment amount.

Figure 4-11: Payment discounts are also posted to the Discounts Given account.

Most of the time, probably always, customers send a check that takes the discount even if the payment arrives well after the discount date. You can apply the amount of the check to the invoice and leave a balance due, but most companies apply the discount even if the payment is late. This is what we call "goodwill."

Generating Customer Statements

One way to make sure that you and your customers are in agreement about the amounts they owe is to periodically create and send account statements to them.

Choose Customers | Create Statements to open the Create Statements window seen in Figure 4-12.

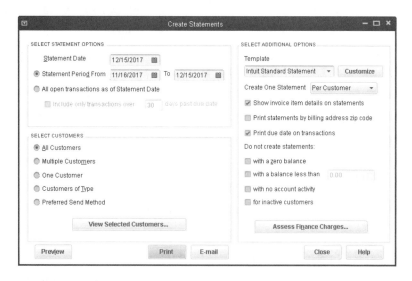

Figure 4-12: Regular customer statements minimize conflicts.

Most of the options in the Create Statements window are self-explanatory. However, a few options in the Template section on the right side of the window could use a little more explanation.

- Create One Statement. If you are tracking jobs as well as customers, you have the choice to create a single statement that includes all jobs for each customer or separate statements for each job.

- Show Invoice Item Details On Statements. When this option is deselected, the statement shows each invoice date, number, due date, and total amount. When you check this option, the specific line items for each invoice appear as well.

- Assess Finance Charges. Click this button to open the Assess Finance Charges window. Here, you'll see all customers with overdue balances based on their payment terms. Click the Settings button to open the Finance Charges section of the Preferences dialog. Select one or more customers from the list and click the Collection History button to view a report on the overdue balances. Finally, click Assess Charges to apply finance charges to the selected customers.

It's always best to preview the statements before either printing or e-mailing them. This is especially true if you are generating a large number of statements.

Posting Miscellaneous Income

Sometimes you receive income that is unconnected to sales of your services or products. Some examples of this are interest income, refunds for overpayments to vendors, and rebates from vendors.

Tracking Interest Income

Interest income is treated as part of your company's income for tax purposes, so you need to track it. Create an income account named Interest Income in your chart of accounts. When you create the transaction to put the interest into the bank account, the transaction journal looks like Table 4-13.

Account	Debit	Credit
10000—Bank Account	5.00	
42000—Interest Income		5.00

Table 4-13: The transaction increases the bank account and
increases interest income.

Tracking Refunds and Rebates Received

Judging by the queries many accountants receive, many business owners don't know how to post a rebate or a refund they receive for an overpayment. Following are some guidelines:

- If the money arrived in the same tax year as the payment was made, you can post the refund/rebate to the original expense you used when you created the payment or you can post the refund to your Other Income account. (Your accountant may have a preference, so be sure to ask.)

- If the money arrived after the end of your fiscal year, post the refund/rebate to an Other Income account. (You don't want to reduce this year's expenses.) The reason to use an Other Income account is that your Profit & Loss statement shows Other Income after a subtotal for the current year's ordinary income, and this makes it easier to analyze your "other income" activities.

Chapter 5 has more information on tracking refunds from vendors.

Writing Off Receivables You'll Never Collect

Sometimes, you have customers that aren't going to pay you. They may have gone out of business, they may have serious financial difficulties that seem to be permanent, or they may just be deadbeats.

At some point, you and your accountant will decide that you no longer want to show the uncollectible amount as an asset on your balance sheet. The way you perform this removal task depends on the way you file taxes.

If you file taxes on an accrual basis, you may be able to write off the amount as an expense to an account named Bad Debt Expense. This provides you with a tax deduction in the year you determine that there is no longer a possibility of collecting the customer account balance. You should note that the sale can take place in one tax year and the write-off in a subsequent year.

If you file taxes on a cash basis instead of accrual, there's no such thing as a bad debt. Many business owners assume that every uncollectible customer balance can be posted to the Profit & Loss statement as a bad debt expense, but that's an incorrect assumption. After all, in cash-basis reporting, you don't recognize the income from the unpaid invoice. If the income doesn't exist for tax purposes, how can you have a tax-deductible bad debt expense? Use a customer credit to reduce A/R and get rid of the uncollectible amount.

If you use accrual and cash-basis reports in QuickBooks (you always have the ability to look at both), using a customer credit to reduce A/R and get rid of the uncollectible amount will result in changes in your accrual-basis reports, but not in your cash-basis reports for the reason provided above.

Bad Debt Expense

If you file taxes on the accrual basis, the income was recognized and reported, so you may be able to use a bad debt expense to reverse the income that you recognized, but never received. To accomplish this, you need an expense account named Bad Debt Expense.

When you and your accountant agree that it's appropriate to post a bad debt expense, ask your accountant to give you the transactions needed to move the unpaid amount to your Bad Debt Expense account and clear the customer balance so that it no longer appears in A/R. Remember, it's not enough to post an amount to the Bad Debt Expense account; you must also clear the customer's A/R balance.

One method frequently used in QuickBooks is a four-step process:

1. Create the Bad Debt Expense account.
2. Create an item of the Other Charge type and call it BadDebt or WriteOff. Link it to the Bad Debt Expense account.
3. Create a credit memo for the customer using the BadDebt item. Enter the total amount due and deemed uncollectible. When QuickBooks asks, choose Retain As An Available Credit.
4. Open the Receive Payments window and apply the credit to the customer's unrecoverable amounts.

GAAP (Generally Accepted Accounting Principles) rules say that if you're on the accrual basis, you should create and maintain a reserve for uncollectible customer accounts. This reserve is held in an account named Allowance for Doubtful Accounts, which is an Accounts Receivable type of account. Many small businesses don't use an Allowance for Doubtful Accounts account. You should ask your accountant whether it's needed for your business and have him or her show you how to use it.

Don't let your accountant make journal entries against A/R to apply credits or write off open balances for specific customers. A/R changes should be made by creating transactions that are linked to the customer(s) in question. Have your accountant explain what has to be done and then create the appropriate transaction for the customer. The only acceptable journal entry against A/R is the year-end entry to provide a cash-basis report for tax preparation, and that journal entry must be reversed the next day, on the first day of the next fiscal year.

Running Income Tracking Reports

Many business owners fly by the seat of their pants and use their gut feelings to gauge how business is going. While that may be okay for some folks, it's not really the best way to get a handle on the status of your revenue stream. A much better way is to take advantage of the powerful QuickBooks reporting features.

Income Tracker

While not strictly a report, the new Income Tracker shown in Figure 4-13 deserves some mention here, because it provides a quick overview of some of the basic income tracking data you need to be on top of things. In reality, it eliminates the need to run some basic reports.

Figure 4-13: The new Income Tracker lets you quickly review the status of estimates, invoices, and payments.

The multicolor bar at the top of the window displays totals for four different categories—Estimates, Open Invoices, Overdue, and Paid Last 30 Days. To view the details for each category, click the colored bar corresponding to the category you want to view. The individual transactions for the category appear below the bar. Double-click a line item to open the original transaction.

By default, the window displays the totals for all customers. To show the totals for a single customer, choose the customer from the Customer:Job drop-down list and click the search button (the magnifying glass icon) next to the field. You can further customize the view by using the Type, Status, and Date drop-down lists. To return to displaying results for all data in the chosen category, click the Clear/Show All button that appears when you set any of the filters.

You can also print multiple transactions by selecting the transactions, which involves placing a check mark next to the transactions to include, and choosing the transaction type(s) from the Batch Actions drop-down list.

Income Reports

Tracking your income involves reporting on several different processes. You can track sales, accounts receivable, customers, and more. The income reports you generate depend on what you're looking for.

- Income by Customer (Summary and Detail). These reports are found in the Company & Financial section (Reports | Company & Financial). For a quick look at all income (which is the total sales minus credits and costs of goods) for a given period, use one of these reports. The summary report gives a breakdown of income by customer and job, with totals only. The details report includes every transaction generated within the selected time period.

- Customers & Receivables. This group of reports includes A/R aging reports, customer balance reports, open invoice reports, and more. They're great for seeing the true status of your income. Is it in the till, or are you still waiting for it?

- Sales. For a look at what you're selling, check out this group of reports. Here, you'll find reports that break down sales by customers, items, reps, and more.

CHAPTER 5:

Tracking Expenses in QuickBooks

- Accrual vs. Cash Expense Reporting
- Entering Bills
- Entering Vendor Credits
- Managing Vendor Refunds
- Paying Bills
- Using Direct Disbursements
- Petty Cash Expenses
- Tracking Debit Cards
- Running Vendor and Expenses Reports

Y ou have to track your business expenses carefully; otherwise, you'll have a difficult time preparing your tax returns and you won't be able to analyze the health of your business properly.

An important rule: Not every check you write is an expense. You have to understand when to post disbursements to expenses and when to post them to other types of accounts in your chart of accounts. This chapter explains the way expenses are posted to your general ledger.

Generally, you can define an expense as a product or service you buy from a vendor for the purpose of running your business. You have two ways to pay vendors:

- Enter the bill from the vendor into QuickBooks and then pay the bill (which is two steps).
- Don't enter the vendor bill; instead, just make the payment (write a check, wire funds, etc.).

CPA NOTE: *Your Accounts Payable (A/P) account represents the money you currently owe your vendors for goods and services you purchased to run your business. A/P accumulates when you enter vendor bills into QuickBooks. When you pay the bills (which are posted as bill payments), the A/P total decreases by the amount of the payments made.*

Accrual Vs. Cash Expense Tracking

In accounting, we say that books are maintained on either an accrual basis or a cash basis. The difference between the two is the way in which income and expenses are tracked. In this chapter, we're going to deal with the expense part of that equation.

Vendor bills get paid in one of two ways: you enter the bill in Quick-Books and then pay the bill later (hopefully before it's overdue), or you just write a check to pay the bill without first entering the bill (called a direct disbursement).

In accrual-based accounting, an expense is recognized as soon as it exists. When you get a vendor bill, that expense exists and must be entered into QuickBooks—you don't wait to pay the vendor bill to recognize the expense. The same is true of revenue because revenue is recognized when it exists, which means at the time you enter an invoice, not at the time the invoice is paid.

In cash-based accounting, an expense is recognized when it is paid. Often, the expense exists well before it's paid, but in a cash-based system, only the payment is tracked and reported on. For revenue, a cash-based system only recognizes revenue that is received—the point at which the customer's payment is recorded in QuickBooks.

One of the important distinctions between accrual and cash-based accounting is the way you file tax returns. Most businesses, especially small businesses, file cash-based tax returns. Businesses that have to manage inventory usually file accrual-based tax returns. Businesses that want to change the basis of their tax returns have to get permission from the Internal Revenue Service.

The truth is that cash-based accounting isn't a good system for evaluating your business because you never see an accurate state of your financial health. If you want to get a good picture of your financial position, it's useless to see reports on earnings without also seeing your upcoming expenses, as well as your future revenue. As a result, most businesses keep books on an accrual basis and then adjust the accrued amounts (e.g., Accounts Payable and Accounts Receivable) to create their tax returns on a cash basis.

QuickBooks users have an advantage in the fact that QuickBooks reports provide an option to perform calculations on either an accrual or cash basis. Business owners run accrual-based reports to keep an eye on the health of their businesses and run cash-based reports to prepare tax returns. (Not all accounting software applications have the ability to let users choose the basis of reports.)

Entering Bills

When the mail arrives, after you open all the envelopes that contain checks from customers, you need to enter the bills that arrived.

Before you do so, make sure the Bills preferences are set to your liking. Select Edit | Preferences to open the Preferences dialog. Click the Bills category in the left pane, the Company Preferences tab in the right, and set the options in the Entering Bills section.

- Bills Are Due. Choose the number days after the bill is entered that it becomes due. By default, QuickBooks sets this number to 10. This means that a bill entered on the 1st has a due date of the 11th. If you have payment terms configured for the vendor (e.g., Net 30), they will override this option.

- Warn About Duplicate Bill Numbers From Same Vendor. To ensure that you don't pay the same bill twice, you might want to enable this option. Then, if you enter a number in the Ref. No. field in the Enter Bills window that matches the Ref. No. for another bill from the same vendor, QuickBooks balks and asks if you really want to use that number.

Once your Bills options are set properly, it's time to enter the bills that arrived in the mail. To do so, choose Vendors | Enter Bills from the menu bar to open the Enter Bills window seen in Figure 5-1.

The Enter Bills window has two sections:

- The header section contains information about the vendor and the bill.

- The details section contains the data related to your general ledger accounts.

The details section has two tabs:

- Expenses, for ordinary expenses

- Items, for purchasing inventory items that you resell

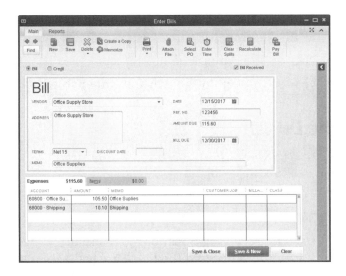

Figure 5-1: Use the Enter Bills transaction window to track details of each bill.

Entering Header Data

If you have multiple Accounts Payable accounts, an A/P Account field appears at the top of the transaction window. Use it to enter the A/P account to which you want to post this bill. If you don't have multiple A/P accounts, the field isn't displayed.

In the Vendor field, click the arrow to choose the vendor from the list that appears. If the vendor isn't on the list, choose <Add New> to add this vendor to your QuickBooks vendor list. Then, go through the fields as follows:

- Enter the [bill] Date, which is usually earlier than the current date by the number of days it took the bill to travel through the mail.

- The Due Date fills in automatically, depending on the terms you have with this vendor. If you have no terms entered for this vendor, the due date is automatically filled out using the default number of days for paying bills. QuickBooks sets this at 10 days, but you can change the default in the Preferences dialog in the Bills section.

- Enter the Amount Due.
- Enter the vendor's invoice number in the Ref. No. field.

Entering the Details

Depending on the type of bill you receive, you may use either the Items tab or the Expenses tab, or both.

Using the Items Tab

The Items tab is used for receiving inventory items that you need to track. The form is very straightforward and the fields are self-explanatory. Select an inventory item from the Item drop-down list and enter the quantity you've received in the Qty field. QuickBooks automatically fills in the Description, Cost, and Amount Fields if you entered them when you created the item. If they don't appear, or if you wish to change them, you can do so now.

Using the Expenses Tab

Click the small down arrow in the first row of the Account column to display a list of accounts in your chart of accounts. Select the account to which you're posting this bill. QuickBooks automatically enters the Amount Due you entered in the header into the Amount column.

If the entire amount of this bill is posted to the same account, the same job (if you're posting bills to jobs for job costing), and the same class, move through the rest of the columns and enter the data.

Depending on the bill, you may be able to assign the entire amount to one expense account or you may have to split the bill among multiple expense accounts. For example, your utility bills are usually posted to Utilities or to a specific utility account (electric, heat, and so on). Credit card bills are often split among numerous expense accounts.

Even if the entire amount of the bill is posted to one expense account, you may have to split the posting to accommodate multiple classes. In fact, you may have to split the bill across multiple accounts and multiple classes. We'll cover these scenarios in the following sections.

Posting to Multiple Expense Accounts

If the amount due has to be posted to multiple expense accounts, you need to enter the transaction over multiple line items. For example, you may have a vendor bill from your office supply company that includes supplies, printing expenses, and shipping expenses.

After you select the first expense account in the Account column, QuickBooks automatically enters the total amount due in the Amount column. Change the data in the Amount column to the amount you're posting to the selected account. Fill out the remaining columns in the row for Customer:Job if you're tracking that information for this bill and for Class.

Return to the Account column and enter the account to which the next amount you enter is posted. QuickBooks automatically changes the Amount column to reflect the remaining balance of the bill. If necessary, change the amount in the Amount column to the amount you're posting to the next account. Continue to add lines until you've split this bill among the appropriate accounts.

Accounts Payable Postings

When you enter a vendor bill into your books, the credit side of the transaction is posted to A/P. The debit side of the transaction is posted to the appropriate account(s) for the expense. The transaction is part of your purchases journal. Table 5-1 shows the purchases journal for a vendor bill that covers more than one expense. Many, if not most, bills cover a single expense, and you enter only that expense in the transaction.

Account	Debit	Credit
60600—Office Supplies	105.50	
68000—Shipping	10.10	
21000—Accounts Payable		115.60

Table 5-1: The total expenses equal the amount posted to A/P.

Although most vendor bills are posted to expense accounts, some transactions use an account type other than an expense account. For example, when you purchase equipment, you post the transaction to a fixed assets account. If you send a deposit against a purchase, you post the transaction to a current asset account that tracks advance deposits. When you make a loan payment, the part of the total that represents principal is posted to the loan's liability account and the interest is posted to the interest account, which is an expense account. In addition, QuickBooks posts the data to the appropriate Customer:Job record and Class record.

Periodically, you should run a report on A/P, which means you list all the vendors to whom you owe money. The total of the vendor A/P balances must match the total of the A/P account. To run the report in QuickBooks, select Reports | Vendors & Payables | A/P Aging Summary and choose All from the Dates drop-down list.

Memorizing Bills

Some vendors don't send bills. For example, your landlord, your mortgage company, and a bank that holds a loan may expect you to pay automatically, or they may provide a coupon book instead of sending bills.

Rather than rely on your memory to ensure these critical bills are paid each month, you can have QuickBooks perform this task for you with the memorized transaction feature.

Creating a Memorized Bill

Create the vendor bill in the Enter Bills transaction window, as described in the earlier sections. Split the bill among accounts, classes, and jobs if warranted. Use the upcoming due date for this vendor when you create the bill. Then, before you save the bill, press Ctrl-M to open the Memorize Transaction dialog (see Figure 5-2).

Use the Name field to enter a name for the transaction. QuickBooks automatically enters the vendor name, but you can change it. Choose a name that describes the transaction, so you don't have to rely on your memory to connect the vendor name to the transaction.

Figure 5-2: Memorize vendor bills to make sure the expense is counted when you report on future financials. Select the interval for this bill from the drop-down list in the How Often field, and then enter the next due date for this bill in the Next Date field.

Choose a reminder option from the following choices:

- Select Add To My Reminders List (the default) to tell QuickBooks to issue a reminder that this bill must be put into the system to be paid. Reminders only appear if you're using reminders in QuickBooks. Choose Edit | Preferences and click the Reminders category icon to view or change reminders options.

- Select Do Not Remind Me if you don't want a reminder and prefer to enter the bill in the Bills To Pay List yourself. (This requires an excellent memory or a note taped to your monitor.)

- Select Automate Transaction Entry to have QuickBooks enter this bill as a payable automatically, without reminders. (Most organizations find that this is the most efficient choice.)

If this bill is finite instead of perpetual, such as a loan that has a specific number of payments, choose Automate Transaction Entry and use the Number Remaining field to specify how many times this bill must be paid, after which, the memorized bill is no longer active.

Specify the number of Days In Advance To Enter this bill into the system. If you selected automatic entry instead of a reminder, at that time, the bill appears in the Select Bills To Pay list (see the section "Paying Bills," later in this chapter).

Don't select automatic payment for bills that don't have the same amount every month, such as utility bills. Use the Remind Me option so you can fill in the amount when the bill comes. On the other hand, you may not want to memorize the bill.

Click OK in the Memorize Transaction window to save it, and then save the bill. The memorized bill appears in the Memorized Transaction List on the Lists menu.

ProAdvisor TIP: *If you created the original bill only to create a memorized transaction and don't want to enter the bill into the system for payment now, save the memorized transaction, close the Enter Bills window, and choose No when QuickBooks asks if you want to save the transaction.*

Using the Memorized Transaction List

The Memorized Transaction List contains all the transactions you've memorized, which could include vendor bills, customer invoices, or other transactions. You can use this list to manipulate your memorized transactions. Press Ctrl-T to open the Memorized Transaction List.

Modifying or Deleting Memorized Transactions

Use the Memorized Transaction List to modify or delete a transaction. Select the transaction's listing and use one of the following actions:

- Press Ctrl-E to edit the memorized transaction. The original Memorize Transaction dialog opens so you can modify the data in any field or change any options.
- Press Ctrl-D to delete the memorized transaction.

Changing the Display of the Memorized Transaction List

By default, the Memorized Transaction List displays basic information about each transaction. You can add or remove columns as needed. To change the display, click the Memorized Transaction button at the bottom of the list window and choose Customize Columns. In the Customize Columns dialog (seen in Figure 5-3), remove, add, or change the order of any column.

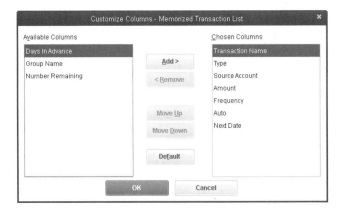

Figure 5-3: Change the data displayed in the Memorized Transactions List.

Marking a Memorized Bill for Payment

If you chose one of the "remind me" options when you created a memorized bill, you have to make the bill active. (If you told QuickBooks to enter the bill for payment automatically, you don't have to take this additional step.)

To include a memorized bill in the Pay Bills list, double-click the bill's listing in the Memorized Transaction List to open the bill in the usual Enter Bills window with the next due date showing. Fill in any missing data, and click Save & Close to save this bill so it becomes a current payable and is listed in the Pay Bills window you open when you write checks to pay bills.

Creating Memorized Transaction Groups

If you have many memorized transactions, you don't have to select them for payment one at a time. You can create a group and then invoke actions on the group (automatically invoking that action on every bill in the group). The steps to accomplish this are easy:

1. Press Ctrl-T to display the Memorized Transaction List.
2. Click the Memorized Transactions button at the bottom of the list window and choose New Group. In the New Memorized Transaction Group window, give this group a name (see Figure 5-4).
3. Fill out the fields to specify the way you want the bills in this group to be handled.
4. Click OK to save this group.

Figure 5-4: Create groups of memorized transactions to make it easier to manage them.

Adding Transactions to a Group

Now that you've created the group, you can add memorized transactions to it as follows:

1. In the Memorized Transaction List window, select the first memorized transaction you want to add to the group.
2. Press Ctrl-E to edit the memorized transaction.
3. When the Schedule Memorized Transaction window opens with this transaction displayed, select the option Add To Group, then select the group from the drop-down list that appears when you click the arrow next to the Group Name field.
4. Click OK and repeat this process for each bill in the list.

Once you've created a group, every time you create a memorized transaction in the future the Add To Group option is available in the dialog. That means you can add the transaction to a group when you create the memorized transaction instead of using the Edit function after you memorize the transaction.

If you have other recurring bills with different criteria (perhaps they're due on a different day of the month, or they're due quarterly or annually), create groups for them and add the individual transactions to the group.

Entering Vendor Credits

If you receive a credit from a vendor, you must record it in QuickBooks. Then you can apply the credit against an existing bill from that vendor, let it float until your next bill from the vendor, or ask for a refund.

QuickBooks doesn't have a vendor credit form; instead, you use the vendor bill transaction window by turning it into a vendor credit with a click of the mouse. Take the following steps to enter a vendor credit:

1. Choose Vendors | Enter Bills from the menu bar to open the Enter Bills window.

2. Select the Credit radio button at the top of the transaction window, which automatically deselects Bill and changes the fields in the form so they're appropriate for a credit (see Figure 5-5).

3. Choose the vendor from the drop-down list in the Vendor field.

4. Enter the date of the credit memo.

5. Enter the amount of the credit memo.

6. In the Ref. No. field, enter the vendor's credit memo number if one exists.

7. In the line item section, assign an account for this credit, which is usually the account you used when making the original purchase. QuickBooks automatically

fills in the amount to match the amount you entered in the top of the transaction window.

8. Click Save & Close to save the credit.

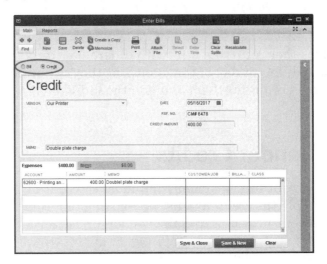

Figure 5-5: Select the Credit option to turn the Enter Bills transaction template into a Vendor Credit template.

ProAdvisor TIP: *If you're using classes, don't forget to assign the same class you assigned when you originally entered the bill.*

A credit from a vendor is a reverse purchase, and your transaction reflects that fact. The resulting transaction journal looks like Table 5-2.

Account	Debit	Credit
62600—Printing		400.00
21000—Accounts Payable	400.00	

Table 5-2: This credit removes the original expense and decreases A/P.

Managing Vendor Refunds

If a vendor elects to send a refund instead of a credit, entering the refund into QuickBooks is easier than tracking vendor credits. A refund doesn't affect the current balance due, doesn't affect your A/P balance, and isn't used in reducing the amount of future bills from the vendor.

A vendor refund is money that can be treated either as income or a reduction of an expense that you previously paid. You have two methods for posting this transaction:

- Post the money (a bank deposit) to an account named Other Income.
- Post the money (a bank deposit) to the original expense account you used when you paid the original bill.

Ask your accountant which method is preferred. If the refund arrived after the end of your fiscal year and the original payment was in the previous fiscal year, you might want to use the Other Income account so you don't skew the current-year expenses in your Profit & Loss statement.

Table 5-3 shows the transaction journal for a refund that is posted to the Other Income account.

Account	Debit	Credit
10000—Bank Account	100.00	
70000—Other Income		100.00

Table 5-3: This refund increased the amount in the bank account and the amount of other income received.

Paying Bills

At some point after you've entered the vendor bills into QuickBooks, you have to pay those bills. You don't have to pay every bill that's in the system, nor do you have to pay the entire amount due for each bill.

It's important to understand that there's a difference between making a bill payment and sending a payment to a vendor for whom no bill was entered in QuickBooks. These two methods for sending money to vendors are poles apart, because they post differently to the general ledger.

- A bill payment is a remittance that pays a bill that has already been entered into QuickBooks.

- A remittance to a vendor that is paying a bill that was not entered into QuickBooks is called a direct disbursement, and is discussed later in this chapter.

Before you start paying bills, you might want to check your Bills Preferences to make sure they are properly configured. Open the Preferences dialog (Edit | Preferences) and choose the Bills category in the left pane and the Company Preferences tab on the right. Change the options in the Paying Bills section to suit your needs.

- Automatically Use Credits. When this option is checked, QuickBooks applies any outstanding vendor credits without asking.

- Automatically Use Discounts. The same goes here. If you have any discounts available from the vendor, such as timely payment discounts, QuickBooks automatically applies them without asking.

- Default Discount Account. When you enable the Automatically Use Discounts option, this option becomes available. From the drop-down list, choose the account to which you want the vendor discounts posted.

CPA TIP: *Most discounts you will receive will probably come from vendors you purchase items from that you plan to resell. If this is the case, you will probably have a grouping of expenses called Cost of Goods Sold. It would be preferable to set up a "Purchase Discount" account as part of your Cost of Goods Sold and use it for these vendors' discounts. This will enable you to see the gross amount of your original purchases (to determine if you are due any volume-purchase discounts) more easily than if you post the discount in the same account as the original purchase. Discounts you receive for normal expenses (a rebate coupon you submit for a refund after a purchase, for example) are less frequent events, and posting those discounts directly to the original expense account is fine.*

When you're ready to pay bills, choose Vendors | Pay Bills. The Pay Bills window seen in Figure 5-6 appears, and each field in the window influences the bills that are displayed.

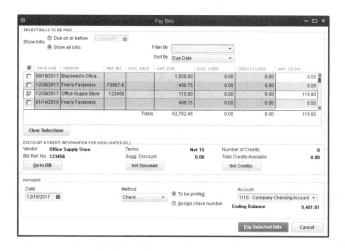

Figure 5-6: Set the options to match the bills you want to pay.

Working in the Pay Bills Window

The options in the Pay Bills window determine the list of bills you see. The Show Bills section of the window has two options: Due On Or Before and Show All Bills.

- Due On Or Before displays all the bills due within the next 10 days by default, but you can change the date specification to display more or fewer bills.

- Show All Bills displays all the bills in your system, regardless of when they're due.

The A/P Account field is where you select the accounts payable account to which the bills you want to pay were originally posted. If you don't have multiple A/P accounts, this field doesn't appear in the window.

The option labeled Filter By determines the vendors whose bills appear in the list. The choices are All Vendors or a specific vendor you choose from the drop-down list.

The option labeled Sort By determines the way your bills are displayed in QuickBooks. The choices are

- Due Date (the default)
- Discount Date (important if you receive a discount from the vendor for timely payment)
- Vendor
- Amount Due

At the bottom of the window, the Payment Account field is where you select the bank account you want to use for these payments.

In the Payment Date field, enter the date that you want to appear on your checks. By default, the current date appears in the field, but if you want to predate or postdate your checks, you can change that date.

ProAdvisor TIP: *If you select the bills today and wait until tomorrow (or later) to print the checks, the payment date set here appears on the checks. However, you can tell QuickBooks to automatically enter a check date that matches the day you print the checks by enabling the Change Check Date When Non-Cleared Check Is Printed option on the Company Preferences tab of the Checking preferences.*

In the Payment Method section, a drop-down list displays the available methods of payment. Choose one.

Paying Bills by Check

- If you print your checks, be sure the To Be Printed option is selected.
- If you're writing the checks manually, select Assign Check Number. When you finish configuring bill payments, QuickBooks opens the Assign Check Numbers dialog so you can specify the starting check number for this bill-paying session.

- If you use your bank's online ACH payment feature, select Assign Check Number and don't enter a check number in the Assign Check Number dialog, or enter ACH if you don't want to leave the check number field blank.

Paying Bills by Credit Card

- You can choose this option if you're tracking credit card transactions via a Credit Card account (a current liability account) in your chart of accounts.
- If you don't track each credit card transaction with this liability account, but enter the credit card bill when it arrives, you can't select Credit Card as a Payment Method.

CPA TIP: *It is preferable to set up credit card liability accounts as, for tax purposes, they act like a line of credit and allow the expenses to be deducted on the charge date.*

Paying Bills by Online Payment

This payment method is only available if you're signed up for QuickBooks's online payment services.

Selecting the Bills to Pay

If you made changes to the selection fields (perhaps you changed the due date filter), the list of bills to be paid may change. When all the bills displayed are to be paid either in full or in part, you're ready to move on.

Selecting a bill for payment is simple—just click the left-most column to insert a check mark. If there are bills on the list that you're not going to pay, don't select them. They'll return the next time you open the Pay Bills window.

If you want to pay all the listed bills in full, click the Select All Bills button. This selects all the bills for payment, and the Select All Bills button changes its name to Clear Selections in case you want to reverse your action.

Adjusting the Amounts to Pay

If you don't want to pay a bill in full, adjust the amount of the check by selecting the bill (click the left-most column to insert a check mark) and then changing the amount in the Amt. To Pay column.

The next time you pay bills or run an Accounts Payable report, the listing for this bill will display the balance due.

Applying Credits

If the list of bills includes vendors for whom you have credits, you can apply the credits to the bill. Select the bill, and if credits exist for the vendor, information about the credits appears in the Pay Bills window.

Click Set Credits to open the Discounts And Credits window. Select the credit and click Done to return to the Pay Bills window. QuickBooks automatically changes the Amt. To Pay column to reflect the credit.

When you've selected the bills to pay and perhaps adjusted the amounts, click Pay Selected Bills.

Bill Payment Postings

When you pay a vendor bill that you've entered into your books, the bill payment credits (reduces) the bank account and debits (reduces) the A/P account, as seen in Table 5-4.

Account	Debit	Credit
10000—Bank Account		115.60
21000—Accounts Payable	115.60	

Table 5-4: Paying an existing vendor bill reduces A/P.

Many business owners look at the posting for the check that paid a bill and wonder why they don't see the expense accounts covered by the transaction. When you use A/P to enter bills and pay them, the postings for the bill payment have nothing to do with the expenses incurred; those expenses were posted when you entered the bill.

You need to think of this process as two transactions that are both linked to A/P; the first transaction records the expense and increases A/P, and the second transaction reduces A/P and your bank account.

If you don't use A/P (you don't enter the vendor bills into Quick-Books), but instead just write checks, those checks are posted directly to the expense accounts.

ProAdvisor CAUTION: *All bills entered into QuickBooks must be paid using the Pay Bills feature. If you write a check (Ctrl-W) to pay a bill previously recorded in QuickBooks, you'll end up with incorrect postings and probably higher accountant fees for tracking down the problem.*

If you make a partial payment, the unpaid balance remains on the vendor's record and is included in the total of the A/P account in the general ledger. As additional bills arrive, the balance grows, and as you chip away at the balance with additional payments, the A/P reports track your progress.

You can, of course, make a vendor payment that covers multiple vendor bills; if so, QuickBooks keeps track of which bills are paid or partially paid. Tracking the vendor's bill number and date is important when you have to have a conversation with the vendor about your account.

Using Direct Disbursements

A direct disbursement is a disbursement of funds (usually by check) that is performed without matching the check to an existing bill.

If you pay a bill the same day it arrives, if you need to write a check to petty cash, or if you need to write a quick check when a delivery person is standing in front of you, it's silly and time-wasting to enter a bill and then pay it immediately.

CPA TIP: *Going the extra step and using the A/P system to enter this type of bill would not be silly if you might be due volume discounts for accumulated charges from a single vendor (one of the third-party delivery services, for example).*

Using Manual Direct Disbursement Checks

If you use manual checks, you can write your checks and enter the data in QuickBooks later, or you can bring your checkbook to your computer and enter the checks in QuickBooks as you write them.

To enter checks in QuickBooks, use the Write Checks window. While it's technically possible to work directly in the bank register, it requires more keystrokes because you have to click the Splits button to open line items, where you can enter the class. The line items are available in the Write Checks window.

ProAdvisor NOTE: *If you're paying for an item instead of posting the check to an expense account, you must use the Write Checks window. The register does not have an Items column.*

To use the Write Checks window (see Figure 5-7), press Ctrl-W or choose Banking | Write Checks.

In the Bank Account field at the top of the window, select the bank account you're using for this check. The next available check number is already filled in unless the Print Later option box is checked. If it is, click it to toggle the check mark off and enter the check number.

Fill out the check, posting amounts to the appropriate accounts, customers, jobs, and classes. If necessary, split the postings among multiple classes as described earlier for entering bills. Enter inventory items in the Items tab.

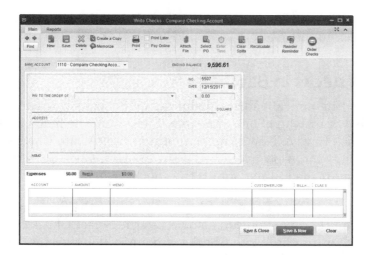

Figure 5-7: Fill out the fields to record the manual check you wrote. When you finish, click Save & New to open a new blank check. When you're through writing checks, click Save & Close to close the Write Checks window. All the checks you wrote are recorded in the bank account register.

Printing Direct Disbursement Checks

You can print direct disbursement checks quite easily, whether you need one quick check or you want to pay all your bills because you're not using the Pay Bills window to enter bills when they arrive.

Printing a Single Check Quickly

If you normally enter vendor bills and then print checks to pay those bills, you can print a check for a bill that isn't entered in your accounts payable system.

Open the Write Checks window and make sure the Print Later option is selected. Fill in the fields to create the check and then click the Print icon on the Main tab of the Ribbon bar.

A small window opens to display the next available check number. Make sure that number agrees with the next number of the check in the printer. If it doesn't, change it. Click OK to open the Print Checks dialog box. Set the printer and printing options and click the Print button to send the check to the printer.

Printing Checks in Batches

If you're creating multiple direct-disbursement checks, you can print them in a batch instead of one at a time. Fill out all the fields for the first check and click Save & New to open another blank Write Checks window. Repeat this step for every check you want to print. Click Save & Close when you are finished filling out all the checks.

Choose File | Print Forms | Checks and fill in the first check number to print all your checks. You can also access the Select Checks To Print window from within the Write Checks window. Click the small down arrow below the Print icon on the Main tab of the Ribbon bar and select Batch.

Postings for Direct Disbursements

The postings for direct disbursements are quite simple:

- The bank account is credited (reduced) for the total amount of checks written.
- Each posting account is debited (increased) for the amount posted to that account.

In addition, the data is recorded in the class record and in the record of any jobs involved in the transaction.

Petty Cash Expenses

Accountants frequently receive questions about how to handle cash layouts for business expenses. Usually, the questions involve one of the following scenarios:

- Someone used cash or a personal credit card to buy something for the company, and that person needs to be reimbursed.

- Someone used the debit card for the business account to withdraw cash and didn't use all of that cash for a business expense; the remaining cash needs to be tracked.

- Someone is going to be traveling for the company and needs cash in advance (and will need to return unspent cash).

There are other scenarios similar to these, but the ultimate question is, "How do I manage cash transactions that fall outside of the usual data entry for vendor bills and payments?"

The best solution is to have a cash box, which is a metal box that locks, in which you keep a certain amount of cash. Then, you track the cash that goes in and out of the box by creating a Petty Cash account in your chart of accounts. This account is treated like a bank account. As a matter of fact, if you haven't already done so, you should open the Quick-Books chart of accounts, create a new account of the type Bank, and call it Petty Cash. Here's how a petty cash box works:

1. You put money in it.
2. You account for the money that's disbursed.
3. When almost all the money is spent, you replenish the money in the box.

The Petty Cash account in QuickBooks doesn't represent a real bank account; it just represents the money that moved from the real bank account into the cash box.

Filling the Cash Box

You have to put money into the cash box, both literally (getting actual cash) and figuratively (record a withdrawal from your bank account to your petty cash account). Most of the time, the cash box is filled the first time by writing a check to Cash from your bank account, cashing the check at the bank, and bringing the cash back to the box. The check should be in the amount you want to use as the "base amount" for incidental cash expenses.

When you create the check in the bank account in QuickBooks, post the check to the Petty Cash account you created. You don't post a petty cash check to an expense; instead, the expense postings are recorded when you disburse cash from the box.

The transaction journal credits (reduces) the bank account and debits (increases) the petty cash account, as seen in Table 5-5.

Account	Debit	Credit
10000—Bank Account		100.00
10200—Petty Cash	100.00	

Table 5-5: Putting money into the petty cash box is like a transfer of funds between banks.

Recording Petty Cash Disbursements

As you take cash out of the petty cash box in the office, you must record those disbursements in the Petty Cash account in QuickBooks by writing checks on the Petty Cash account.

Make it a hard-and-fast rule that nobody receives cash for reimbursement without a receipt, and store the receipts in a large envelope marked with the current tax year (e.g., Cash Payments 2017). Store the envelope with your tax return, just in case you hear from an auditor.

ProAdvisor TIP: *If you're extremely meticulous in your record keeping, you can even scan each receipt and attach it to the corresponding check you write on the Petty Cash account. Just click the Attach File icon on the Main tab of the Ribbon bar in the Write Checks window.*

Tracking Petty Cash Disbursements for Expenses

When you create a check in your Petty Cash account (which is a fake check, of course), be sure to post it to the appropriate expense account. QuickBooks automatically inserts a check number, which you can delete, change to the word "cash," or accept. (Because you're never going to get a bank statement and have to reconcile this account, the check number reference doesn't matter.)

When you create a check for a petty cash disbursement, you usually don't need to enter a vendor name, because these expenses usually don't have to be tracked the way you track vendors that send bills and for whom you would need to keep a history. If you wish, you can create a single vendor named PettyCash for all petty cash disbursements.

You can keep the receipts in the cash box and create the fake check transaction weekly, or even monthly if you don't have a lot of cash disbursements. Just create a line item for each expense and post the total for that expense. Mark the receipt "ENTERED" and move it to your "cash payments."

Tracking Petty Cash Advances

You have to track advances you disburse from the cash box so that the Petty Cash account in QuickBooks always matches the amount of cash in the box. However, advances for future expenses aren't expenses yet, so they have to be posted differently.

Open the QuickBooks chart of accounts (Ctrl-A) and create an account of the type Other Current Asset and name it Petty Cash Advances. If you're using numbered accounts, select a number in the appropriate range for Other Current Asset.

When someone needs a cash advance, perform both of the following steps:

1. Have the person sign an IOU that says he or she took $XX.XX. Put the IOU in the cash box and disburse the money.

2. Enter the transaction in QuickBooks using a fake check from your petty cash fake bank account. Post the transaction to the account named Petty Cash Advances.

When the person who took the advance spends the money, one of the following scenarios occurs:

- More than the advance was spent, and the person has receipts for the entire amount spent, including the advance and the additional out-of-pocket expenses.

- Less than the advance was spent, and the person has receipts for the spent amount and has the leftover cash.

- The money spent is exactly equal to the amount of the advance, though it almost never works this way.

The best way to manage moving the advanced monies out of the Petty Cash Advances account and into the appropriate expense account(s) is to create a journal entry. You have a choice of two methods for doing this, and you should choose the one that's easiest and least confusing for you.

- You can move all the advanced funds back into the Petty Cash account, essentially voiding the IOU, and then create your disbursements from within the Petty Cash account as described earlier for tracking disbursements for expenses.

- You can include all the postings to expenses in addition to the return of any advanced funds in a single journal entry.

Note that no matter which way you enter the transaction, you are only tracking the money advanced to this person. There may be additional money in the Petty Cash Advances account representing other advances to other people. You are not emptying the Petty Cash Advances account; you are only moving the funds for this particular advance.

Let's say the advance was for $100.00. If you want to move the funds back into the Petty Cash account and create the transactions to cover the disbursements separately, create the journal entry seen in Table 5-6.

Account	Debit	Credit
10200—Petty Cash (ersatz bank account)	100.00	
13000—Petty Cash Advances		100.00

Table 5-6: Return the money to the Petty Cash account and post
the expenses in a separate journal entry.

If you want to perform both tasks (removing the advance and posting the disbursements) in one journal entry, Table 5-7 provides a sample transaction for the scenario in which the person spent $120.00 ($20.00 of her own money in addition to the $100.00 advanced) and has receipts. This transaction moves funds directly from the Petty Cash Advances account to the appropriate expense accounts and then takes the additional money spent from the Petty Cash account (because you have to give additional cash to the person from the cash box).

Account	Debit	Credit
13000—Petty Cash Advances		100.00
62000—Tolls & Parking	50.00	
61500—Office Supplies	40.00	
62200—Meals	30.00	
10200—Petty Cash		20.00

Table 5-7: This journal entry changes the money that was advanced into expenses.

If the person spent less than the advance and is returning money to the petty cash box, your journal entry must reflect that fact, as seen in Table 5-8. This transaction moves funds directly from the Petty Cash Advances account to the expenses and puts the leftover cash back into the Petty Cash account, reflecting the fact that you actually put money back into the cash box.

Account	Debit	Credit
13000—Petty Cash Advances		100.00
62000—Tolls & Parking	20.00	
61500—Office Supplies	20.00	
62200—Meals	30.00	
10200—Petty Cash	30.00	

Table 5-8: Remove the advance and dispense it to expenses, along with the cash returned to petty cash.

If the person spent exactly the amount advanced, then you remove the money from the Petty Cash Advances account and post the expenses (see Table 5-9). Since no money is returned to the cash box, nor is more money taken from the cash box, the Petty Cash account isn't included in the transaction.

Account	Debit	Credit
13000—Petty Cash Advances		100.00
62000—Tolls & Parking	30.00	
61500—Office Supplies	40.00	
62200—Meals	30.00	

Table 5-9: Move the money out of the Petty Cash Advances account and into expense accounts.

Refilling the Cash Box

As you dispense cash from the cash box, you need to replace it. The usual method is to bring the cash box back to its original balance (the amount of the first check you wrote to petty cash). Use the same steps you used to write the first check to petty cash, using the total amount of funds disbursed as the amount of the check. This brings the total available in the cash box back to the original amount.

You can write the check for less than the disbursed funds if you determine that you were putting too much money into the cash box, or you can write the check for more than the disbursed funds if you think you need to increase the amount of cash available in the cash box.

Tracking Debit Cards

Many accountants find that business owners who have a debit card attached to their business bank account are confused about the way to enter debit card transactions. There are two types of debit card transactions:

- The debit card is used at the cash register of a retail store to pay for a purchase.
- The debit card is used to withdraw cash from an ATM and the cash remains in the pocket of the person who withdrew it until it's spent for business expenses,

which can take days or weeks. Some business owners call this "walking around money."

A debit card withdrawal from your bank account is no different from a check you write or an automatic deduction by a vendor. A withdrawal is a withdrawal, no matter what form it takes. You have to enter every withdrawal from your bank account into QuickBooks, both so that you know your current bank balance and so that you can reconcile the bank account.

If the debit card is used at a retail location to pay for a purchase, entering the transaction is easy; essentially, it's a check with no number (because there's no physical check), and it's posted to the appropriate expense account. You may want to use DM (for debit memo), ATM, or another reference in place of the check number, depending on the way these transactions are noted on your bank statements. The resulting transaction journal resembles Table 5-10.

Account	Debit	Credit
10000—Bank Account		80.00
61500—Office Supplies	80.00	

Table 5-10: The transaction journal for a debit card withdrawal is the same as the transaction journal for a check.

If the debit card is used to withdraw cash that isn't spent immediately, it's more complicated. You must remove the money from the bank account, but there aren't any expenses to post. How do you accomplish this?

The process is similar to the process used for advances out of the petty cash box, as described in the previous section. This is money owed to the company, and it has to be tracked. (Money owed to the company is an asset.)

Some businesses tell people who withdraw money from the bank at an ATM that the cash has to be brought back to the office and put into the petty cash box. Then, it can be withdrawn from petty cash as needed and posted to the appropriate expenses.

If you adopt this policy, the transaction is easy to enter; just post the fake check to the petty cash bank account. In fact, this is a way to fill the petty cash box without writing a real check and sending someone to the bank to cash it. The transaction journal looks like Table 5-11.

Account	Debit	Credit
10000—Bank Account		80.00
10200—Petty Cash Account	80.00	

Table 5-11: You can use a debit card at an ATM to put cash into the petty cash box.

ProAdvisor TIP: *You can use the QuickBooks Transfer Funds Between Accounts feature to move the money. Choose Banking | Transfer Funds to open the Transfer Funds Between Accounts window. Because the Petty Cash account is set up as a bank, this works beautifully.*

Unfortunately, it's frequently the business owner who uses the debit card to get cash, and business owners frequently choose to ignore the rules. In that case, tracking the withdrawn cash is more complicated.

The only way to remove the cash from the bank and track its use is to follow the instructions in the previous section for tracking advances of petty cash. You need to post the transaction to an asset account and then use a journal entry to move it from the asset account to the appropriate expense(s) as the money is spent.

If you have a petty cash box and you also have people withdrawing money from the bank with a debit card, you should set up a separate Other Current Asset account for these ATM withdrawals. This is much less confusing than trying to track the petty cash box and the debit card withdrawal from one asset account. Name the account Bank Funds Held in Cash, Walking Around Money, or whatever seems logical. Then, as the money is spent, use a journal entry to move the expended funds into expense accounts, as seen in Table 5-12.

Account	Debit	Credit
13500—Bank Funds Held in Cash		80.00
62000—Tolls & Parking	25.00	
61500—Office Supplies	40.00	
62200—Meals	15.00	

Table 5-12: As the withdrawn money is spent, move the spent funds out of the asset account that's tracking the cash and into the appropriate expense accounts.

Running Vendor and Expenses Reports

Keeping your costs under control is just as important as maximizing your revenue. As a matter of fact, they go hand in hand. The truth is that you want to maximize your profit, which involves both.

QuickBooks offers a variety of reports that enable you to keep an eye on, and analyze, your expenses.

- Expenses by Vendor (Summary and Detail). For a look at total expenses (bills, payments, credits, and discounts) broken down by vendor, use these reports. The first gives totals for each vendor, while the second lists every transaction involved. You can access them by choosing Reports | Company & Financial from the menu bar.

- Vendors & Payables. The reports on this submenu include A/P aging reports, unpaid bills reports, vendor balance reports, and more.

- Purchases. Use this Reports submenu to access a variety of reports on purchases. Here, you'll find purchase reports broken down by vendor and by item. In addition, you'll also find purchase order reports.

- List. This submenu contains vendor contact and phone reports.

See Chapter 11 for details on running and customizing reports.

CHAPTER 6:

Managing Inventory

- Tracking Inventory
- Inventory Accounting Tasks
- Using Group Items
- Adjusting Inventory
- Understanding WIP
- Running Inventory Reports

Inventory is a complicated system. The financial processes involved in maintaining inventory include tracking inventory costs, additional costs added to inventory items, the total value of your inventory asset, and other financial processes. In addition, you have to understand how to keep track of the inventory items as they move into and out of your company.

QuickBooks provides a basic inventory feature, which is sufficient for many small to medium businesses. However, if you find that it just doesn't work for your business, you can purchase a QuickBooks add-on that's designed to provide more inventory functions. Check out the Intuit Marketplace for software that's been tested to make sure it works properly with QuickBooks (http://marketplace.intuit.com/).

Tracking Inventory Items

An inventory item is a physical product that you manufacture or purchase for the purpose of reselling to a customer. The main types of businesses that track inventory are manufacturers, wholesale distributors, and retailers. You only track the value of inventory that you own, so if you drop-ship to customers from a manufacturer or distributor without purchasing the goods from them (acting as their sales team), you don't track inventory, because it's not your asset.

Things you buy to immediately sell to customers in the normal course of business usually aren't tracked as inventory. This means that if you're an electrician and you buy wire, outlets, and various electrical parts that you sell to your customers as part of a job, you usually don't have to track those parts as inventory. On the other hand, a contractor with ten trucks, each carrying $10,000 in supplies/parts, might have to report inventory. If you fit that definition (or the amount of stock you have on trucks and/or in a warehouse comes close to that definition), ask your accountant if the amount still in stock at the end of the year is significant enough to add inventory to your tax return.

Every individual inventory item in your warehouse must be tracked carefully. That's the only way to make sure every customer gets exactly the inventory item ordered and that your supplier sends you exactly what you ordered. More importantly, it's the only way to make sure the financial data is accurate (the quantity and value of your inventory items).

CPA NOTE: *Many small businesses don't have real warehouses; instead, inventory is stored in a garage, a shed, a back room, the basement, or some combination of those places. When we use the word "warehouse," we mean any location in which you store your inventory. It would also include a fulfillment house that holds and moves inventory for you. The key to needing to track inventory is its ownership. If you own it, as opposed to merely serving as a sales agent for someone's products, you should track it on your books.*

Setting Inventory Preferences

Depending on how you create your new company file, inventory may or may not be turned on. If it's not, the first thing you have to do is turn it on. To do so, you have to access the inventory preferences.

1. Select Edit | Preferences from the menu bar to display the Preferences dialog.

2. Click the Items & Inventory category in the left pane and the Company Preferences tab in the right pane.

3. Set the Purchase Orders And Inventory options to suit your needs.

    • Inventory And Purchase Orders Are Active. This is the one that turns on inventory tracking. If you're going to track inventory, you have to enable purchase orders as well, even if you never use them.

    • Warn About Duplicate Purchase Order Numbers. If you use purchase orders, this is a good option to enable. Turn it on, and QuickBooks will warn you if you try to create a purchase order using a number that is already assigned to an existing purchase order.

- Warn If Not Enough Inventory Quantity On Hand (QOH) To Sell. This is a must for two reasons. One, you should always be aware of stock status when selling products so you don't disappoint your customers. Two, selling into negative quantity creates havoc with the calculations QuickBooks uses to determine the average cost of inventory items. See the section entitled "QuickBooks Average Costing," later in this chapter, for more information.

4. Click OK to save the changes and close the Preferences dialog box.

Naming Inventory Parts

Each inventory part you stock must have a unique code or name. Some businesses use "English" (such as Widget), and other businesses use numbers or a combination of letters or numbers (such as Wid97 or the sku number provided by its manufacturer).

In addition to the code/name, create a description of the item. For many inventory items, it's helpful to create a description for sales and a separate description for purchases, because the descriptions are often different. Sales descriptions tend to be plain English (e.g. Widget), while the purchase descriptions match the text your supplier uses (e.g. Widget88897).

CPA TIP: *If you create a catalog or printed price list for your customers, make sure that document uses the code/name you're using in your inventory tracking. That way, when customers want to place an order, you don't have to spend time translating the order into your official inventory codes, and you can be sure the customer receives the item that's expected.*

Creating an Inventory Item Properly

To create an inventory item, choose Lists | Item List from the menu bar to open the Item List. Press Ctrl-N to open the New Item dialog box, and select Inventory Part from the Type drop-down list. It's important to understand the fields in the inventory item record (see Figure 6-1).

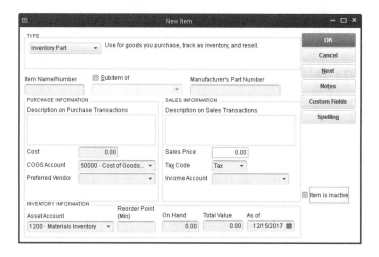

Figure 6-1: It's important to fill in data fields properly when you configure an inventory item.

Item Name/Number (required)

This is your name/code for the product. You can opt to create your own or use the manufacturer's. However, make sure the name is easily recognizable by everyone in your organization who uses QuickBooks.

Subitem Of (optional)

Creating parent items and subitems is a good way to keep groups of similar inventory items organized. It's also a good way to get reports that provide totals for the parent item and details for the subitems. For example, if you have a sporting goods store and sell baseball mitts, you might create a parent item called Baseball Mitts with subitems for Catchers' Mitts, First Base Mitts, Pitchers' Mitts, and so on. You could even have sub-subitems for Left-Handed and Right-Handed Mitts. This would enable you to generate reports that tell you how many baseball mitts you've sold, how many of each type, and how many left or right of each type.

Manufacturer's Part Number (optional)

Enter the number your vendor uses for this item. QuickBooks will automatically enter this data on purchase orders if you customize a PO template to display this field.

Description On Purchase Transactions (optional)

Enter the text that should appear in the Description field when you create a transaction for purchasing this item.

Description On Sales Transactions (optional)

Enter the text that should appear in the Description field when you create an invoice or a sales receipt. QuickBooks automatically copies the text in the Description On Purchase Transactions into this field, but you can edit the text if the description your customers see should differ.

Cost (optional)

The Cost field is not used for tracking financial data. QuickBooks does not use the data in this field to calculate the value of your inventory or the Cost of Goods Sold; it's irrelevant to the calculation of profit or loss. It's a "text" field that exists only to remind you of the cost of the item at the time you're creating a Purchase Order.

QuickBooks calculates the cost of inventory when you actually purchase an item, either by entering a vendor bill or a direct check to a vendor.

When you create a purchase transaction and enter a cost that's different from the text in the Cost field, QuickBooks asks if you want to update the Cost field. Your choice about updating the field has no effect on your financial records, because the data in this field isn't used in any calculations.

COGS Account (required)

Enter the COGS account that's used when you sell the item.

Preferred Vendor (optional)

This field is useful if you always buy this item from the same vendor. You can enter the item in the Item column in a purchase transaction (PO, direct check, or Vendor Bill) without filling out the top of the transaction window, and QuickBooks will automatically fill out the vendor information in the header section of the transaction window.

Sales Price (optional)

Use this field to enter the selling price of the item in a sales transaction window. You can change this amount while you're creating the transaction.

Tax Code (required if Sales Tax is enabled)

If you enabled Sales Tax, you must indicate whether the item is taxable or not. If you haven't enabled Sales Tax, the field doesn't appear.

Income Account (required)

Enter the Income account to which sales of the item are posted.

Asset Account (required)

Enter the inventory asset account to which purchases and sales are posted.

Reorder Point (optional)

Use this field to enter the minimum quantity you want to maintain for this item. When the QOH is down to this number, QuickBooks issues a reminder to order more. You must configure this reminder in the Reminders section of the Preferences dialog (Edit | Preferences | Reminders).

On Hand and Total Value (do not use)

These fields at the bottom of the window seem convenient, but filling them in can cause problems for your accountant. When you use these fields, QuickBooks posts the total value to your Inventory Asset account and posts the other side of the transaction to the Opening Balance Equity account.

A balance in the Opening Balance Equity account is a problem because it doesn't tell your accountant (or you) the source. Was it a purchase from your supplier? If so, when? This year? Last year? Is there an open A/P balance for that supplier? If so, is it connected to this amount in total or in part?

Skip these fields and enter transactions to bring in your inventory; if the transactions you enter are from a previous year, QuickBooks will use them in the calculation of your closing balances for the previous year. See Chapter 1 to learn about the effect of previous-year transactions on your opening trial balance in QuickBooks.

Tracking Inventory Locations

Sometimes, businesses with a great deal of inventory have to split the inventory into multiple locations. Some businesses use multiple locations to store some specific inventory items in one place and other specific inventory items in another place. Other businesses (those with multiple locations) store a full set of inventory items in each place.

CPA NOTE: *Businesses with a single location often track the location of each inventory item by shelf number or bin number.*

Tracking location makes it easier to find inventory when you're filling an order, as well as making it easier to count your inventory accurately.

Unfortunately, QuickBooks Pro and Premier cannot track multiple locations. You'll either have to purchase QuickBooks Enterprise or a third-party QuickBooks add-on or keep location information outside of your accounting software.

If you have only one location for inventory and you want to be able to track the shelf/bin number for each item, QuickBooks provides a feature called "Custom Fields," which you can use to create a custom field to track that information.

Inventory Accounting Tasks

The way you track financial data for buying and selling inventory items differs greatly from the way you track other purchases and sales.

When you purchase office supplies, you write a check and post the check to an expense named Office Supplies. Your Profit & Loss statement includes that expense, which reduces your taxable income. The same is true of rent, payroll, advertising, utilities, and most of your other purchases/expenses.

Inventory doesn't work the same way. Here are the guidelines for understanding accounting for inventory:

- Purchasing inventory (including inventory parts for manufacturing) is not an expense.
- Inventory is an asset.
- The value of your inventory asset is based on its cost, not its retail value.
- When an inventory product is sold, the expense (the cost of the inventory item) is posted to cost of goods sold and the value of the inventory asset is decreased by the same amount.

Creating Accounts for Inventory Accounting

In order to perform accounting tasks for inventory, you need several posting accounts devoted to inventory transactions:

- Inventory Asset, an asset of the type Current Asset
- Cost of Goods Sold (COGS), an expense account (a specific type of expense account; it appears before "regular" expenses in the Profit & Loss statement)

- Inventory Adjustments, which can either be an expense account or a COGS account (ask your accountant which type of account to use)

ProAdvisor TIP*: QuickBooks automatically creates an Expense account named Inventory Adjustments when you enable Inventory. When you select an account of the type Cost of Goods Sold as the adjusting account, QuickBooks displays a message telling you it expected an expense or income account. If your accountant wants you to use a COGS account, feel free to ignore the QuickBooks warning and continue. You also might want to check the Do Not Display This Message In The Future option so the message stops popping up.*

See Chapter 3 for details on creating accounts in QuickBooks.

CPA Sidebar
Inventory Adjustment Account

Some accountants use the expense account that QuickBooks creates, whether the adjustment is an increase or a decrease, and the account tracks the net changes. Other accountants prefer to create a COGS account named Inventory Adjustments and use that account for inventory adjustments whether the adjustment is an increase or a decrease. Very few, if any, accountants recommend using an income account as an inventory adjustment account. Most accountants agree that using an income account is wrong because increasing the quantity of inventory items does not increase your income; it reduces your expense.

There are circumstances under which accounts other than inventory adjustment accounts are appropriate when you adjust inventory quantities:

- If you send a sample to a potential customer, that's a marketing device; use the Marketing or Advertising expense account for the adjustment.
- If you send inventory to a charitable organization, use the Charitable Gifts expense account for the adjustment.

Be sure to check with your accountant regarding the inventory adjustment account to use.

In the following sections, we'll go over when and how each of the aforementioned accounts is involved in inventory transactions. Walking through the steps often makes it easier to understand the rather complicated accounting rules for inventory.

Acquiring Inventory

Bringing inventory into QuickBooks can be as simple as picking up or receiving the items and writing a check, or as complex as creating a purchase order, receiving the items, entering a bill, and paying the bill.

Using Purchase Orders

You can use a purchase order (PO) to order inventory items from your suppliers; in fact, many vendors require a PO. When you receive the bill, the PO number is on the bill.

A PO has no effect on your financial records. No amounts are posted to any account. Purchase orders are merely memo documents; they exist only to help you track what you've ordered so you can match your order against the items you receive and so you can tell whether more stock is due to arrive when the quantity of an item is low. You create the financial transaction when the vendor's bill arrives.

Purchase orders are a built-in feature of QuickBooks. When the inventory arrives, you can open the PO and create a vendor invoice automatically. If only part of your order arrives, the PO remains open and the number of items received is noted. When the rest of the order arrives, you finish receiving against the PO. If the missing items aren't going to be shipped to you, you can close the PO, and the outstanding quantity disappears.

To create a purchase order, follow these steps:

1. Choose Vendors | Create Purchase Orders from the menu bar to open the Create Purchase Orders window.
2. Select the vendor from the Vendor drop-down list.
3. Fill in the header fields.
4. Enter the inventory items you're ordering as line items.
5. Enter a Vendor Message if you wish.
6. Enter Memo text as needed. This is for your benefit, as it doesn't appear on the printed PO.
7. Click Save & Close or Save & New to continue.

Writing a Check

To pay for inventory purchases with a check, follow these steps:

1. Press Ctrl-W to open the Write Checks window.
2. Select the appropriate account from the Bank Account drop-down list (if you have more than one bank account).
3. Fill out the check with date, payee, amount, and so on. If the payee selected has any outstanding purchase orders, QuickBooks notifies you and asks if you want to receive items from the existing PO(s). If you say yes, the item information is automatically added to the Items tab at the bottom of the window.
4. Click the Items tab at the bottom of the window and enter the inventory items purchased. If QuickBooks filled in data from an existing PO, check to make sure the PO numbers match the quantity and cost of the items received.
5. Save the check and either print it or write a manual check.

When you buy inventory to resell or to create a manufactured product, the check you write is posted to the inventory asset account, as seen in Table 6-1.

Account	Debit	Credit
15000—Inventory Asset	300.00	
10000—Bank Account		300.00

Table 6-1: Purchasing inventory isn't an expense; instead, you're buying an asset.

The amount you enter is the total amount of the vendor's bill. This includes inbound shipping, sales tax, handling charges, and any other charges included in the bill. Do not separate the actual product cost from the other costs; post the total cost to the inventory asset account. The cost of your inventory includes everything you're charged to receive the inventory items.

CPA TIP: *If you have a sales tax license, be sure your suppliers have a copy of it so you aren't charged sales tax for any items you purchase for resale.*

Receiving Items

If purchases are shipped to you, chances are you won't be writing a check when they're delivered unless they arrive COD. In that case, you have two ways to enter the items into QuickBooks, depending on the status of the bill.

Receiving Items without the Bill

If the bill does not accompany the delivery, you still have to let QuickBooks know that you've received the items and add them to your inventory.

The process is relatively simple.

1. Choose Vendors | Receive Items to display the Create Item Receipts window.

2. If you have multiple A/P accounts, choose the appropriate one from the A/P Account drop-down list.

3. Fill out the Item Receipt information (vendor, date, etc.). If you select a vendor with outstanding purchase orders, QuickBooks informs you and gives you the option to receive against the PO. In that case, the data from the PO is automatically entered into the Items tab—check to make sure it's accurate.

4. Move to the Items tab, which is selected by default, and enter the inventory items delivered in this shipment.

5. Without the bill, there are probably no expenses (e.g., sales tax, shipping, handling) indicated. However, if they appear on the packing slip, enter them into the Expenses tab.

6. Click Save & Close or Save & New to save the data and continue working.

Receiving Items with the Bill

If the bill arrives with the shipment, the process is almost identical. Select Vendors | Receive Items And Enter Bill and follow Steps 2-5 in the previous section. As you can see in Figure 6-2, the Bill Received option has been checked automatically.

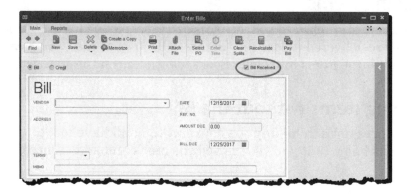

Figure 6-2: A single check mark converts the Item Receipt to a Bill.

This option turns an Item Receipt form into a Bill form. Try it yourself. As soon as you deselect the option, the Bill changes back to an Item Receipt. The form is basically the same, with the addition of Address, Terms, and Bill Due fields. The posting is also the same (see Table 6-2).

Account	Debit	Credit
15000—Inventory Asset	300.00	
21000—Accounts Payable		300.00

Table 6-2: If you enter the vendor's bill instead of writing a direct check, the amount is posted to A/P.

Entering a Bill

If you previously received items without a bill, you have to enter the bill into QuickBooks when it arrives. Choose Vendors | Enter Bill For Received Items from the menu bar to open the Select Item Receipt window. All item receipts you've created appear in the window. Choose the one for which you want to enter the bill. If you want the bill to have the same date as the item receipt, check the Use Item Receipt Date For The Bill Date option. Otherwise, the bill date will be either today's date or the last-used date, depending on the setting of the Default Date To Use For New Transactions option on the My Preferences tab of the General Preferences.

To enter a bill independently of items (e.g., for expenses), choose Vendors | Enter Bills to open the Enter Bills window. It is the same form seen in Figure 6-2. QuickBooks automatically checks the Bill Received option for you. Everything is the same as the previous section, entitled "Receiving Items With The Bill."

If you enter a vendor bill for later payment instead of writing a check, the posting is slightly different. As you can see in Table 6-2, the inventory asset is still increased (a debit), but the credit side is applied to Accounts Payable.

When you pay the bill, A/P is reduced (debited) and your bank account is reduced (credited) by the amount of the payment.

Paying Bills

Sooner or later, it comes time to pay those bills that have arrived. How you pay them depends on whether they've already been entered into QuickBooks.

Use the Write Checks Window

The only bills you should pay with the Write Checks window are those bills that have not been entered into QuickBooks. For example, items received COD, expenses that you pay without entering a bill, and so on. To pay those, you can simply write a check by pressing Ctrl-W and filling in the Write Checks form that opens. See the section entitled "Writing A Check," found earlier in this chapter, for more details.

Use the Pay Bills Window

Once bills have been entered into QuickBooks, you must use the Pay Bills window to pay them to ensure the postings are correct. If you try to write a check without using the Pay Bills feature, QuickBooks displays the Open Bills Exist dialog box, displaying all open bills for the selected customer (see Figure 6-3). If the check you're writing is for one of the open bills, select the open bill and click Go To Pay Bills. If it's not, click Continue Writing Check.

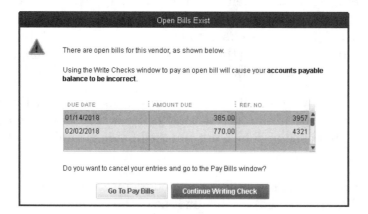

Figure 6-3: Never use the Write Checks window for an open bill.

ProAdvisor NOTE: *If you attempt to write a check to a vendor for whom open item receipts exist, QuickBooks displays a different warning, telling you to use the Enter Bills For Received Items window instead. If you don't, the item receipts will remain open until you void or delete them.*

1. To pay open bills, choose Vendors | Pay Bills to display the Pay Bills window shown in Figure 6-4.

Figure 6-4: Always use the Pay Bills window to pay open bills.

2. If you have a lot of open bills, you can make the list more manageable by using the Due On Or Before option, as well as the Filter By and Sort By options.

3. If you have multiple A/P accounts, choose the appropriate one from the A/P Account drop-down list.

4. Place a check mark next to the open bill(s) you want to pay now.

5. To view a particular bill, highlight it and click the Go To Bill button.

6. If you have any credits or discounts due to you (e.g., returns, early payments, etc.) click the appropriate button and apply them.

7. Set the date to appear on the payment, the payment method, and (if it's a check) whether the check is to be printed.

8. If you have multiple bank accounts, be sure to choose the appropriate account from the Account drop-down list.

9. Click Pay Selected Bills to complete the process.

The Payment Summary dialog box appears, offering the option to return to the Pay Bills window and pay more bills or to print the checks you just created.

When you pay the bill, A/P is reduced (debited) and your bank account is reduced (credited) by the amount of the payment (see Table 6-3).

Account	Debit	Credit
10000—Bank Account		300.00
21000—Accounts Payable	300.00	

Table 6-3: When you use the Pay Bills window, the amount is posted to A/P.

Tracking the Quantity and Value of Inventory Items

In addition to buying inventory and posting it to the inventory asset account, you must track the quantity and cost of your purchase.

It doesn't matter if the vendor's catalog says that each widget is $158.00. You determine the cost based on the vendor's charge to you, which may include sales tax, shipping, and other costs.

This means that when you receive items into QuickBooks or pay for a COD delivery with a check, you must enter both the items received and the expenses incurred. All the QuickBooks windows that deal with receiving inventory have two tabs—an Items tab and an Expenses tab. Therefore, if you buy 30 widgets that cost $158.00 each and the shipping charge is $60.00, you enter the widgets in the Items tab and shipping charge in the Expenses tab. The end result is that the cost of each widget is $158.00, plus $2.00 shipping ($60.00/30) for a total cost of $160.00.

Selling Inventory

An inventory item becomes an expense instead of an asset when you sell it. The expense is posted to an account named Cost of Goods Sold. (The name of that expense account is a reminder that you can't expense the cost of purchasing the inventory item until you sell it—the account isn't named Cost of Goods Purchased, it's Cost of Goods Sold.)

When you sell a customer an inventory item, you take the item out of inventory (reducing the value of your inventory asset account) and post the cost of the item to COGS (increasing your expenses). In addition, you post the income.

The total of the sale is not affected by the postings to the inventory asset and COGS accounts; these accounts wash (zero themselves out). The value of the inventory you sold is moved from the asset to the expense.

Let's say you sell a customer two of those widgets that cost you $160.00 each. You've priced the widgets at $190.00 each. Table 6-4 displays the postings for a simple cash sale of those widgets.

Account	Debit	Credit
40000—Product Sales		380.00
15000—Inventory Asset		320.00
49000—Cost of Goods Sold	320.00	
10000—Bank Account	380.00	

Table 6-4: Posting journal for a simple cash sale of inventory items.

The sale of inventory items can be more complex than this simple cash sale. You might create an invoice instead of receiving cash; you might charge the customer for shipping; the items and shipping might be taxable. Table 6-5 shows the posting journal for a more complex sale; notice that the Inventory Asset and COGS postings are the same as for the simple cash sale and don't affect the amount due from the customer.

Account	Debit	Credit
40000—Product Sales		380.00
22000—Sales Tax Payable		31.20
40900—Shipping Income		10.00
15000—Inventory Asset		320.00
49000—Cost of Goods Sold	320.00	
11000—Accounts Receivable	421.20	

Table 6-5: Posting journal for an invoiced sale of inventory items.

Valuation Methods for Inventory

There are several methods available for calculating the value of each inventory item. The common methods are

- Average Cost
- FIFO (First In, First Out)
- LIFO (Last In, First Out)
- Specific Identification

QuickBooks Pro and Premier only support a unique version of average cost. QuickBooks Enterprise (with Advanced Inventory) supports FIFO, as well. For any other method, you'll have to purchase a third-party QuickBooks add-on.

ProAdvisor TIP: *Beyond The Ledgers at www. beyondtheledgers.com offers an inexpensive FIFO Calculator program that integrates with QuickBooks and exports the results to an Excel workbook.*

The first time you buy any inventory item, it's easy to determine the cost: Divide the total cost by the total quantity to get the cost per item. In the widget purchase discussed in the previous section, it was easy to calculate the cost of each widget at $160.00; the vendor's charge for 30 widgets was $4800.00 (including all shipping, tax, handling charges, etc.).

After you sell 25 of the 30 widgets, you order 30 more, but the cost has changed and now the vendor's charge for 30 widgets is $5100.00. You have 35 widgets in stock; what's the cost per widget? Suppose the price changes quite a bit every time you purchase the item; sometimes it's lower than the last time, and sometimes it's higher than the last time.

What amount do you post to COGS if you sell a single widget? What amount do you post to COGS if you sell 30 widgets?

The answer is, "It depends on the method you're using for determining the value of inventory items." In the following sections, we'll give an overview of each of the four valuation methods listed at the beginning of this section.

CPA CAUTION: *Talk to your accountant before selecting a valuation method. The method you choose is global; it's part of the setup and configuration of QuickBooks, as well as your tax returns. You can't choose one method for some inventory items and a different method for other inventory items. Remember, if your accountant prefers a method other than average cost, you'll have to purchase a third-party add-on.*

Average Cost

The traditional average cost method takes the total amount spent on the inventory item and divides it by the total number of units purchased. If you were to track inventory manually, using an Excel spreadsheet, it would look something like Figure 6-5.

The formulas in the spreadsheet are quite simple:

- Column D is Column C divided by Column B (i.e., =C2/B2).

- The last row (the running calculation for the current average cost) SUMs Column B and Column C. The formula for Column D remains the same as the other rows (C/B).

▲	A	B	C	D
1	Date	Qty	Amount Spent	Avg Cost This Purchase
2	1/5/2017	30	$4,800.00	$160.00
3	2/10/2017	30	$5,100.00	$170.00
4	3/30/2017	20	$3,300.00	$165.00
5	5/25/2017	25	$4,000.00	$160.00
6				
7	Current Avg Cost	105.00	$17,200.00	$163.81
8				

Figure 6-5: You can compute the traditional average cost by entering the details of each purchase.

QuickBooks Average Costing

QuickBooks does not use the traditional average cost method. Instead, in QuickBooks, the average cost of an inventory item reflects the total history of that item since the last time that it had a quantity of zero. This is not necessarily the way you need (or want) to track average costing, so you must work with your accountant to come up with the correct figures for your tax return.

ProAdvisor TIP: *Beyond The Ledgers, at www. beyondtheledgers.com, has an excellent document explaining the way QuickBooks calculates the average cost. It also contains detailed explanations of the problems you may encounter when you sell inventory items to zero quantity and to a negative quantity. The document is located in the Papers section.*

The average cost that QuickBooks uses is calculated when you receive inventory, and that average cost is displayed at the bottom of the item record (you can't change it). The amount you enter in the Cost field is never used for calculating the cost/value of your inventory items.

You must be aware of the following QuickBooks "quirks" in computing average cost when you analyze your business financials and when you prepare tax returns. (The word "quirks" is our word, and it doesn't mean that there's anything illegal or unacceptable in the way QuickBooks manages average costing.)

Average Cost is not Calculated for a Fiscal Period

Calculations include the entire history of the item since the last time the quantity was at or below zero; there are no "period" (annual) calculations.

Selling All Items in Stock Erases Average Cost History

When you sell items to the point of having zero quantity, QuickBooks starts over. For example, if you've been buying a widget for years for $12.00, you've maintained an average cost of $12.00. If your quantity goes to zero and your supplier charges $14.00/widget for the next order, your average cost changes to $14.00, which is going to affect your P&L and Balance Sheet for the year. Unfortunately, this number is used to post COGS and inventory asset values (most 4th graders could understand the math needed to provide an accurate historical average cost).

Selling Stock That's not Available Creates Serious Problems

If you sell into negative quantity, QuickBooks gets confused. Later, if you receive more widgets, QuickBooks "catches up," but the numbers may not be acceptable to you or your accountant.

Unlike other accounting software, QuickBooks permits users to sell into negative quantity. The only way to avoid the mess this creates is to impose your own controls on user actions.

- Never sell into negative quantities.
- If you know that the QuickBooks quantity on hand is wrong (you've counted the stock and you know

you have enough to sell the quantity ordered by the customer), do an inventory adjustment before you create the sales transaction.

- If you know that new stock is arriving tomorrow, don't create the sales transaction until the receipt of the goods has been recorded in QuickBooks.

FIFO (First In, First Out)

Only QuickBooks Enterprise Solutions with Advanced Inventory supports FIFO, which tracks the quantity and amount of each purchase in chronological order. As you sell inventory, the cost of that inventory is posted against those "purchase lots." FIFO sells off inventory sequentially, starting with inventory from the oldest purchase and moving through the next purchase, the purchase after that, and so on. The cost of the item is taken from each set of purchases.

ProAdvisor NOTE: *As mentioned earlier, Beyond The Ledgers (www.beyondtheledgers.com) offers an inexpensive program called FIFO Calculator that integrates with QuickBooks Pro and Premier.*

For example, let's say you purchased 30 widgets at a cost of $160.00/widget in January. As you sell the widgets (at a price of $190.00 per widget), the COGS account is increased and the inventory asset account is decreased by the amount of the purchase cost. The income account is increased for the sales price of the widgets. The bank account or A/R (depending on whether it's a cash sale or an invoiced sale) is increased by the sales price of the widgets.

If you sell exactly 30 widgets before you purchase the next set of widgets at a cost of $170.00/widget, the next widget sale uses the new cost to post amounts to COGS and the inventory asset accounts.

Of course, it rarely works that neatly. The odds are that you'll have at least several of the January widgets left when you purchase more in February. Let's say you have 4 widgets from the January purchase in stock and 30 widgets from the February purchase in stock. Now a customer buys 6 widgets. When you create the sales transaction (charging the customer $190.00 per widget), the posting journal resembles Table 6-6.

Account	Debit	Credit
40000—Product Sales		1140.00
15000—Inventory Asset		970.00
49000—Cost of Goods Sold	970.00	
10000—Bank Account	1140.00	

Table 6-6: FIFO separates the cost per purchase to post amounts
to the COGS and inventory asset accounts.

The amount of $970.00 that is posted to the COGS and inventory asset accounts is a result of the following calculation:

- 4 widgets @ 160.00 = 640.00
- 2 widgets @ 170.00 = 340.00

As you continue to buy and sell widgets, the postings to the COGS and inventory asset accounts are calculated on a First In, First Out cost basis. This is a complicated procedure, difficult to do manually. Good software is the answer to maintaining FIFO.

You can change the price of the item (usually, you raise the price because your costs increased) without affecting the postings to the COGS and inventory asset accounts. If you raise the price before you sell off the oldest purchase lot, that just increases your profit for that lot.

You don't have to store the items by FIFO; it doesn't matter unless you're selling food or other date-sensitive products (in which case, you're also tracking lot numbers and dates). Store the items from all your purchases together and just pull the quantity needed for each sale from the group.

If you're using QuickBooks and your accountant feels that FIFO is better suited for your business, you can buy an inexpensive QuickBooks add-on named FIFO Calculator from www.beyondtheledgers.com. This add-on reads your transactions for inventory items and calculates inventory valuation as FIFO instead of average cost. The results are reported in Microsoft Excel. The program produces detailed reports for all inventory items, showing FIFO value calculation for each inventory transaction that affects valuation. Your accountant can use this data to adjust your general ledger and prepare your tax returns.

LIFO (Last In, First Out)

LIFO is appropriate if you sell the most recently purchased products first. The cost of the item is calculated in the opposite direction from FIFO. LIFO posts costs in reverse order of your purchase history because each sale is matched against the latest product purchase. Over time, if you haven't been purchasing new items regularly, COGS and the inventory asset postings could be calculated using the first purchase of the item (perhaps a long, long time ago).

The processes involved in calculating costs with LIFO are the same as those described in the previous section on FIFO, but in reverse chronological order. Like FIFO, this is a complicated mathematical process and works best with good software. None of the QuickBooks editions supports LIFO. Therefore, to use this method, you'll need a third-party add-on.

Specific Identification

Specific identification is a valuation method in which each physical inventory item has its own inventory name/code and has its own cost. When you sell the item, that cost is posted to the COGS and inventory asset accounts. (This means you have a profit/loss report for each individual sale.)

The specific identification valuation method is used for "made to order" products such as expensive hand-made jewelry or other unique products. Your inventory list contains every product, and each individual product has a quantity of one as well as a unique item name/code.

Each individual product is received into inventory with its specific cost, and when the product is sold, the quantity goes to zero and it cannot be sold again. (If another customer wants an identical product, you have to receive that new product into inventory with a different name/code.)

QuickBooks will support the Specific Identification method as long as you create a separate inventory item for each specific item you sell. Third-party add-ons can improve the process.

Manufacturing Assembled Products

Manufacturing businesses buy parts and then use those parts to create a new product; it's the new product that they sell to customers. When you buy parts to create a new product, the common term for the end product is an assembly.

ProAdvisor NOTE: *Only QuickBooks Premier and Enterprise editions offer assembly items. If you're using QuickBooks Pro, you're limited to using group items, which are similar, but definitely not the same. A group item is merely a collection of independent inventory items and not a discrete inventory item itself.*

The business process for manufacturers differs from wholesale and retail businesses that buy inventory items and resell them to customers. The process for manufacturers is "buy the parts, build the product." The process for wholesale and retail businesses is "buy it, mark it up, sell it."

When you manufacture an assembly from parts, both the parts and the finished product are tracked as inventory. In essence, you move all the items required for the product out of inventory as you build the assembly (often called Work in Process) and then bring the finished product into inventory. Usually, the value of your inventory asset doesn't change, because you've merely "swapped" the cost of the items from "individual inventory items" to "parts of an assembly inventory item." However, the quantities of the items change because the quantity on hand of the individual items is reduced and the quantity on hand of the assembly is increased.

Creating Group Items

Although group items are no substitute for assembly items, they do come in handy for retailers or wholesalers who want to create special packages of inventory items to sell. For example, a gift basket containing items from different departments (e.g., wine, jams, crackers, cheese, etc.), or several items that are frequently purchased together such as a baseball bat, glove, and ball.

To create a group item, follow these steps:

1. Choose Lists | Item List from the menu bar.
2. Press Ctrl-N to display the New Item form.
3. From the Type drop-down list, choose Group. As you can see in Figure 6-6, the New Item dialog for a group item is a little different from the other item dialogs.

Figure 6-6: Group Items are easy to create.

4. Enter a name for the group (e.g., Deluxe Gift Basket).
5. Enter a description for the group item. The description appears on sales transaction forms as long as you deselect the next option, Print Items In Group.
6. If you want the individual items in the group to appear on the sales transaction, check the Print Items In Group option. When this option is not checked, the group

description appears on the sales transaction form along with the total price of all the included items.

7. In the table at the bottom of the form, select the items to include in the group. Note that you can include multiples of any of the items.

8. Click OK to save the group item.

To use the group item in a sales transaction, select the group as you would any other item. The one thing to remember is that the group price is the sum of the individual item prices. You cannot assign a special price to a group item. Therefore, if you want to discount the group item (or perhaps increase the price), you'll have to adjust the individual prices on the sales transaction form.

ProAdvisor NOTE: *Regardless of the state of the Print Items In Group option (checked or unchecked), all the individual items appear on screen in the transaction form. The option only applies to the Printed (or Previewed) form.*

Adjusting Inventory

There are a variety of scenarios that require an adjustment to your inventory numbers. The most common is that the result of counting the inventory doesn't match the quantity on hand in your inventory records. When this occurs, you can use the Adjust Quantity/Value On Hand feature found in QuickBooks and discussed later in this chapter.

Counting Inventory

Counting inventory can be a complicated, time-consuming, boring process. However, it's imperative that you periodically perform a physical count of all your inventory items. At minimum, you must count inventory yearly, but many accountants suggest more frequent counts.

> **CPA TIP**: *If you have a large number of individual inventory items, periodically count groups of items instead of counting all of your inventory at a single time. You could also do this if you have separate inventory counts at multiple locations and do not want to close all of the locations down for an inventory count at the same time.*

Your inventory count and the quantity on hand reported by Quick-Books must match. Following are some guidelines to follow that will make this process easier and more efficient.

Create an Inventory Count Worksheet

Print a worksheet that lists every inventory item and has a space for entering the count. Fortunately, QuickBooks provides an excellent worksheet with which to take an inventory count.

Choose Reports | Inventory | Physical Inventory Worksheet to open the Physical Inventory Worksheet shown in Figure 6-7.

> **ProAdvisor TIP**: *Be sure to make all your items active before printing the worksheet. Items are often inactive because they're seasonal or because you've temporarily stopped selling them for some other reason, but inactive items may have quantities in stock, and they must be counted. Open the Item List, click the Include Inactive option, and then activate all inactive items.*

The nice thing about the Physical Inventory Worksheet is that it is a report that can be modified, like other QuickBooks reports. For example, you can change the position of the columns, add or remove columns, sort by different columns, and even include custom fields such as Bin or Dept. To make changes to the worksheet, click the Customize Report button and modify it as needed.

> **ProAdvisor TIP**: *Once you go through the trouble of customizing the worksheet, be sure to memorize it (click the Memorize button) so you don't have to do all that work again.*

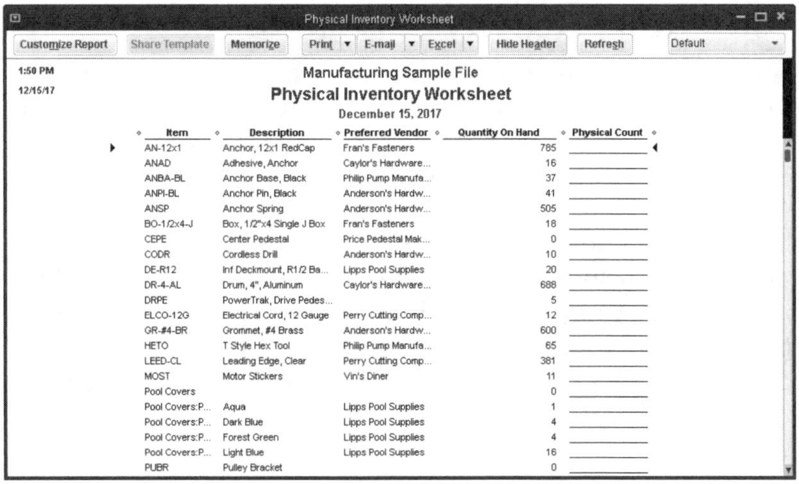

Item	Description	Preferred Vendor	Quantity On Hand	Physical Count
AN-12x1	Anchor, 12x1 RedCap	Fran's Fasteners	785	
ANAD	Adhesive, Anchor	Caylor's Hardware...	16	
ANBA-BL	Anchor Base, Black	Philip Pump Manufa...	37	
ANPI-BL	Anchor Pin, Black	Anderson's Hardw...	41	
ANSP	Anchor Spring	Anderson's Hardw...	505	
BO-1/2x4-J	Box, 1/2"x4 Single J Box	Fran's Fasteners	18	
CEPE	Center Pedestal	Price Pedestal Mak...	0	
CODR	Cordless Drill	Anderson's Hardw...	10	
DE-R12	Inf Deckmount, R1/2 Ba...	Lipps Pool Supplies	20	
DR-4-AL	Drum, 4", Aluminum	Caylor's Hardware...	688	
DRPE	PowerTrak, Drive Pedes...		5	
ELCO-12G	Electrical Cord, 12 Gauge	Perry Cutting Comp...	12	
GR-#4-BR	Grommet, #4 Brass	Anderson's Hardw...	600	
HETO	T Style Hex Tool	Philip Pump Manufa...	65	
LEED-CL	Leading Edge, Clear	Perry Cutting Comp...	381	
MOST	Motor Stickers	Vin's Diner	11	
Pool Covers			0	
Pool Covers:P...	Aqua	Lipps Pool Supplies	1	
Pool Covers:P...	Dark Blue	Lipps Pool Supplies	4	
Pool Covers:P...	Forest Green	Lipps Pool Supplies	4	
Pool Covers:P...	Light Blue	Lipps Pool Supplies	16	
PUBR	Pulley Bracket		0	

Figure 6-7: Customize the QuickBooks Physical Inventory Worksheet to facilitate the inventory count.

If you track bins, shelf numbers, or other location data, display that information on the worksheet. In fact, it's best to sort by location to make it easier for the people doing the counting to find the items.

If you have a lot of inventory and multiple counters, print a master sheet as a reference and then print the appropriate section for each person counting. As each person finishes counting and hands in the worksheet, copy those numbers to the master sheet so that all the numbers are in one place.

ProAdvisor TIP: *To print specific sections of the Physical Inventory Worksheet for each person counting, first apply the appropriate filter to the report. For example, if you use a custom field called Dept, you might want to print a separate set of pages for each department. In that case, click Customize Report and then click the Filters tab. Select the Dept field in the Filter list at the left. In the Dept text field that appears, type the first department name (e.g., Baseball, if you have a sporting goods store). Click OK, and the report/worksheet is filtered to display only those items for which the Dept field contains "Baseball." Print those pages and return to the Modify Report dialog and apply a different filter.*

Freeze Inventory Activity During the Count

While you're counting inventory, you can't remove items and you can't bring in items. That's true for your accounting records, and it's also true for your physical activities regarding inventory items. You have to freeze all sales and receipt of inventory transactions.

Unfortunately, QuickBooks does not have a "freeze" function, so you have to use a workaround. Create sales and inventory receipt transactions on paper. Don't unpack and shelve any inventory that's delivered during the count. When the count is finished and the inventory adjustment is entered, then enter the transactions in QuickBooks and stock your shelves.

Adjust Inventory Quantities after the Count

When the count is finished, use the numbers in the physical count column of the worksheet to create an inventory adjustment.

1. Choose Vendors | Inventory Activities | Adjust Quantity/ Value On Hand to display the Adjust Quantity/Value On Hand window (see Figure 6-8).
2. Select Quantity from the Adjustment Type drop-down list.
3. Select the adjustment account.

ProAdvisor TIP: *By default, QuickBooks creates an expense account named Inventory Adjustments. However, your accountant may prefer a COGS account. If you decide to use a COGS account, you have to force QuickBooks to accept it. It will warn you that it expects either an income or an expense account. If your accountant advises you to use a COGS account, ignore the warning and proceed.*

---

4. Fill in the remaining header fields, which are self-explanatory.
5. Move to the table in the middle of the window and start entering those items for which you need to change the on-hand quantities. Select the item and enter the revised

quantity from the inventory worksheet. QuickBooks calculates the new totals automatically.

6. Click Save & Close to save the changes.

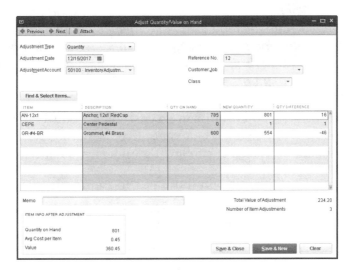

Figure 6-8: Making inventory adjustments is easy in QuickBooks.

If the physical count resulted in more inventory than the records in QuickBooks, the inventory adjustment increases (debits) the inventory asset account and decreases (credits) the inventory adjustment account.

If the physical count resulted in lower quantities than the records in QuickBooks, the inventory adjustment decreases (credits) the inventory asset account and increases (debits) the inventory adjustment account.

If the physical count matched the records in QuickBooks, you don't have to do anything (but that almost never happens).

Managing Returned Damaged Inventory Items

If a customer returns a damaged product, you can't put it back into inventory. However, when you issue a credit to a customer, that's just what happens. QuickBooks assumes that the inventory item is good and sticks it back into inventory. This increases the quantity on hand for the item, even though you're probably going to return it yourself, if possible, or destroy it if it's not returnable.

CPA TIP: *When the customer contacts you to report the damage, you can tell the customer to dispose of the item instead of returning it (assuming you cannot return it to your supplier for credit). This saves you the shipping costs for which you'd have to reimburse the customer.*

The standard method for entering a customer credit is to enter the inventory item being returned in the Create Credit Memos/Refunds transaction window, which produces the following undesirable postings:

- The quantity on hand of the item is increased.
- The inventory asset account is increased for the average cost of the item.
- The COGS account is decreased for the average cost of the item.

The credit also reduces accounts receivable, income, and sales tax liability if the customer and the item are taxable, which is appropriate.

There are two ways to make sure the damaged inventory isn't put back into inventory:

- Don't use the inventory item in the credit memo; instead, use an item designed for the return of damaged goods.
- Use the inventory item in the credit memo and then make an inventory adjustment to remove it from inventory.

Using an Item Designed for Damaged Inventory Returns

You can create an item for this purpose, but it cannot be an inventory part. Use an item of the type Non-Inventory Part or Service.

- Name this item "Credit for Damaged Goods," or something similar.
- Link the item to the income account you use when you sell inventory.
- Do not enter a price.
- Make the item taxable, so that if the customer is also taxable, the sales tax liability is automatically reduced.

Use this item in the Credit Memo. Enter an amount equal to the amount of the price you charged for the inventory item and the sales tax, if applicable, when you sold the item to the customer. In the Description field, enter the returned item name and description so that you and the customer know what the credit is for.

Inventory Adjustments for Damaged Items

You can use the inventory item when you create the credit memo, and then do an Inventory Adjustment to reduce the inventory.

Create an account named Damaged Inventory using either a COGS or Expense account, depending on your accountant's instructions. Having a discrete Damaged Inventory account provides a better audit trail for the transactions.

Use the Damaged Inventory account when you make the inventory adjustment after you receive the damaged inventory through a credit memo.

CPA TIP: *You can also use this account to adjust inventory if you find damaged items in your warehouse.*

Adjusting Inventory for "Freebies"

You must also adjust inventory when you remove inventory without selling it. Use the same inventory adjustment process described earlier for adjusting quantity after a physical count, but change the adjustment account as follows:

- If you send free products (samples) to customers, use your Advertising or Marketing expense account.
- If you provide an inventory product to a nonprofit organization, use your Charitable Contributions expense account.
- If you take inventory off the shelf in order to use it in your business, use the applicable expense account (Office Expense, Repairs and Maintenance, etc.).

Some or all of these "freebies" may require the payment of use tax, depending on your state's tax law.

Work In Process

Work in Process (commonly referred to as WIP) is an accounting concept that tracks resources that have been allocated to the process of building assembled products. The WIP account is a Current Asset account.

The Theory of Work In Process

The theory behind WIP is that when you know you're about to build new products, you should reserve the components needed in your WIP account. This means that inventory items are transferred from inventory to WIP. Sometimes other components, such as labor, non-inventory materials, and anything else that will be used to produce the finished product, are posted to the WIP account.

WIP is used in large manufacturing companies. Usually, the WIP account represents components that are waiting for everything to arrive in order to begin building the assembled products. Inherent in most WIP tracking is "delay;" one or more components are missing.

Frequently, the missing components are "pre-builds"—assembled products that aren't sold to customers; instead, they are used in the finished assembled product. In order to build the finished product, you have to build the pre-builds. In addition, some components may not be on hand; either they're en route or they haven't yet been ordered. WIP account balances are usually quite large because companies that use this account invest large amounts of money in components and manufacture large quantities of assembled products from these components.

WIP Redefined for Small Businesses

For small businesses, a WIP account is useful for tracking the costs of an inventory product that is created instead of purchased. The individual parts and services that are needed to create the product are purchased specifically to create the product. You don't need to track those parts as inventory because they're never going to be offered for sale; they exist only to produce another product.

For example, some businesses purchase individual items and improve or repair those items before offering them for sale. Antique dealers, furniture restorers, antique car dealers, and other similar businesses are a few examples.

Other businesses create an item by purchasing specialized services along with some parts. The services are specific to the creation of the inventory item, and the parts are never sold; they exist only to produce the finished product. For example, anyone who produces media such as books, CDs, videos, etc. purchases services and items over a period of time before merging everything into the finished product.

Tracking Production Costs in WIP

When you have components that are never sold to customers because they exist only to create a product, instead of creating an assembled product you can post the costs to a WIP account. When the product is ready to sell, receive the product into inventory using the total expenses as the cost of the inventory item.

You can use WIP for the same purpose even if you're not creating a single unique item. This works just as well for producing large quantities of an inventory item. As an example, Table 6-7 shows the postings for goods and services purchased to create thousands of copies of a book.

Date	Account	Debit	Credit	Memo
2/14/17	15500—WIP	1200.00		Editor
2/14/17	10000—Bank Account		1200.00	Editor
3/29/17	15500—WIP	1100.00		Artist—cover
3/29/17	10000—Bank Account		1100.00	Artist—cover
4/10/17	15500—WIP	1600.00		Printer—file production
4/10/17	10000—Bank Account		1600.00	Printer—file production
4/22/17	15500—WIP	1000.00		Color separations
4/22/17	10000—Bank Account		1000.00	Color separations
4/29/17	15500—WIP	6000.00		Paper
4/29/17	10000—Bank Account		6000.00	Paper
5/10/17	15500—WIP	2100.00		Plate & presswork
5/10/17	10000—Bank Account		2100.00	Plate & presswork
5/15/17	15500—WIP	8000.00		Printing & binding
5/15/17	10000—Bank Account		8000.00	Printing & binding
5/20/17	15500—WIP	700.00		Shipping to warehouse
5/20/17	10000—Bank Account		700.00	Shipping to warehouse

Table 6-7: You can track outsourced work and supplies in WIP
when you're creating inventory items.

Moving WIP into Inventory

When the product is ready to sell, you receive it into inventory using the total posted to WIP as the cost of the inventory. You also increase the quantity of the inventory item by the appropriate number.

This is really an inventory adjustment, similar to the inventory adjustments discussed earlier in this chapter. However, in this case, the offsetting account for the inventory asset is the WIP account instead of the inventory adjustment account. Table 6-8 represents the posting journal for bringing 4,000 books into inventory by moving the WIP cost total into the inventory asset account.

Account	Debit	Credit
15000—Inventory Asset	21700.00	
15500—WIP		21700.00

Table 6-8: WIP expenses become the cost of inventory received.

You must also track the quantity received of the new inventory item, using the total cost divided by the quantity of items to determine the cost of each item. Accounting software does this automatically in a single inventory adjustment transaction.

Setting Up WIP in QuickBooks

It's possible to set up a QuickBooks system to track Work in Process (WIP) and then transfer finished goods to inventory, but you have to do it manually because QuickBooks has no built in "WIP to Inventory" process. That's understandable, because QuickBooks is designed for use by businesses that have very simple inventory management needs.

WIP inventory is needed when a finished product is the result of multiple processes, such as subcontracted services and/or non-inventory products.

This book is an example of an inventory item that requires WIP tracking. It's created (manufactured) from a variety of services and products; it's not purchased or assembled from existing inventory items.

In the case of this book, the manuscript for each chapter is sent to editors; the edited manuscripts are sent to a production facility that transforms the documents into special files that the printer requires; an artist creates the cover; and the printer prints, collates, and binds the book and then ships cartons of books to our warehouse. Every company involved in these processes submits a bill for each task.

ProAdvisor CAUTION: *WIP processes are difficult in QuickBooks if your business has more than a few inventory products that are tracked this way. In that case, buy a separate software application to track these manufacturing steps. Check the QuickBooks Marketplace Solutions web pages to find a QuickBooks add-on that will work for you.*

Tracking WIP Transactions

To track WIP, create an account of the type Other Current Asset and name it Work in Process or WIP. Products or services purchased to create inventory items are posted to this WIP account.

Don't use POs for products and services for WIP to avoid having to create an item. (Items need expense and income accounts, which makes tracking WIP more complicated.) Use the Memo field on each transaction to note the product for which you're making the purchase.

ProAdvisor TIP: *If any of the companies involved in creating your product require a PO, you can generate a PO in your word processor or create the PO in QuickBooks, but don't receive items against it; in fact, you can void or delete it after you send it.*

Make sure you've created the inventory item for the finished product and the WIP account. When the finished products are ready, use an Adjust Quantity/Value on Hand transaction to bring them into inventory.

1. Select Vendors | Inventory Activities | Adjust Quantity/Value On Hand to open the adjustment window.

2. Choose Quantity And Total Value from the Adjustment Type drop-down list.

3. From the Adjustment Account drop-down list, select the WIP Inventory account.

4. Move to the table and choose the finished inventory item from the Item drop-down list.

5. Tab to the New Quantity field and enter the quantity of finished items. If you already have some finished items on hand, enter the new quantity in the Qty Difference field.

6. Move to the New Value field and enter the total of the bills for the original item plus improvements.

7. Click Save & Close to process the adjustment.

If you check the WIP Inventory account in the Chart of Accounts window, you'll see that the new inventory value has washed the amount of the original bills for the products and the improvements.

Running Inventory Reports

QuickBooks provides a number of inventory reports that enable you to keep a close eye on the status of your inventory.

- Inventory Valuation Summary. Run this report for a quick look at the value of your on-hand inventory. It tells you, at a glance, the total asset value (your cost) and the potential sales value (your sales price) of each of your inventory items.

- Inventory Valuation Detail. This report is for the terminally curious. It not only provides the total asset value of each inventory item, but also every individual item transaction recorded. You can see each transaction on which items were either received or sold.

- Inventory Stock Status by Item. When you want to see just how much inventory you have on hand, run this report. It provides a breakdown, by inventory item, of the on-hand quantity as well as the number of units currently on a purchase order. In other words, you can see what you have and what you have on order.

- Inventory Stock Status by Vendor. Here you'll find the same information, but broken down by vendor.

- Physical Inventory Worksheet. Print this report to use when taking a physical inventory. See the section entitled "Create an Inventory Count Worksheet" earlier in this chapter for more information.

- Pending Builds. While you can only create assemblies (or pending builds—assemblies missing a particular component or placed on hold for another reason) in QuickBooks Premier or Enterprise editions, you can

view, edit, sell, or report on them in QuickBooks
Pro. This means your company file would have to
have been opened in Premier or Enterprise and the
assemblies or pending builds created there first. In
that case, you can run the Pending Builds report to
see their statuses.

To run one of the inventory reports, select Reports | Inventory and
select a report from the submenu that appears.

Inventory Report Tips

Inventory reports are very important to the health of your business.
Therefore, we've included a few tips to help you better understand
QuickBooks inventory reports.

Tracking Inventory Reorder Points

If you only track reorder points for a limited number of your inventory items, you may want to create a customized report to eliminate the
need to scroll through entire Inventory Stock Status by Item or Item Listing reports. The easiest way is to start with an Item Listing report. You
have to use the Item Listing report because the Stock Status reports do
not allow you to filter by the Reorder Point field.

1. Choose Reports | List | Item Listing to open the report.
2. Click the Customize Report button (Modify Report in pre-
   2012 versions).
3. In the Display tab, deselect extraneous information in the
   Columns list. Usually, you only need the item, the reorder
   point, and the quantity on hand. You may also want to
   include the description, quantity on PO, and preferred
   vendor.
4. Move to the Filters tab and choose Item from the Filter list.
5. From the Item drop-down list, choose All Inventory Items.
6. Go back to the Filter list and select Reorder Point (Min).

7. Select the Greater Than option (>=) and enter .01 in the text box.

8. Click the Header/Footer tab to view the options for the report header and footer.

9. Change the Report Title to Reorder Point Report or something similar.

10. Click OK to save the changes and return to the report.

The report no longer displays items that don't have reorder points. Memorize the report (press Ctrl-M) so you don't have to go through the customization effort again.

Inventory Valuation Report Problem I

If your accountant tells you there's a problem with the inventory valuation because the numbers didn't make sense when compared to the sales reports, don't panic. More likely than not, the culprit is inactive items. By default, the inventory valuation report displays information for active items only. Therefore, you'll have to do the following to correct the problem:

1. Select Lists | Item List to open the Item List window.

2. Enable (check) the Include Inactive option at the bottom of the window.

3. Locate any inactive items that had a quantity greater than zero and make them active by removing the X to the left of the item name.

4. Rerun the inventory valuation report.

Sometimes users make items inactive even if there's stock left because they don't want to sell the item at the moment. Unfortunately, the QuickBooks inventory valuation report doesn't include inactive items, even if stock exists (nor does the report have an option to include inactive items with existing stock, which is a serious flaw). Because inventory that exists has value by the very fact of its existence, the QuickBooks inventory valuation report should be renamed Inventory Valuation of Active

Items, or the report should be fixed to match accounting rules and expectations.

Inventory Valuation Report Problem II

In theory, the total for Inventory Asset that appears on your Standard Balance Sheet report should exactly match the Total Asset Value that appears on your Inventory Valuation Summary reports. Sometimes it doesn't, which causes a lot of consternation for both users and their accountants.

Fortunately, it's usually an easy problem to both discover and to resolve. Here are the possible causes and solutions:

- Inactive items. As mentioned previously, the Inventory Valuation report does not include inactive items. Since the Standard Balance Sheet report does include them, the two will differ if you have any items marked "inactive." The solution is to return all inactive items to active status, at least for the running of the reports.

- Expenses assigned to the Inventory Asset account. For example, let's say you receive a shipment of inventory items, which you record on the Items Tab and correctly assign to the Inventory Asset account. On the bill accompanying the items, there's also a shipping charge. You naturally move to the Expenses tab and record the shipping charge. However, instead of assigning the charge to the Shipping & Handling expense account, you assign it to the Inventory Asset account, thinking that it's part of the cost of the inventory asset. You'll have a problem. It will appear on the Standard Balance Sheet report, but not in the Inventory Valuation report. To fix the problem, reopen the bill and assign the shipping charge to the Shipping & Handling expense account.

- Non-inventory items assigned to the Inventory Asset account. If you create non-inventory items and select the Inventory Asset account as the expense account, they will appear on the Standard Balance Sheet report but not on the Inventory Evaluation report.

The bottom line is that the Standard Balance Sheet report includes a wider range of items that are assigned to the Inventory Asset account.

CHAPTER 7:

Managing Bank Accounts

- Creating Bank Accounts
- Transferring Funds between Accounts
- Handling Bounced Checks
- Voiding Disbursement Checks
- Reconciling Bank Accounts
- Banking Online
- Using the Bank Feeds Center

Unless you're keeping all your money under the mattress, you're probably going to have at least one bank account. Clearly, you need a checking account to handle income and expenses. If you do payroll, you should have a separate payroll account. If you're raking in the dough, you'll want to have a money market or other interest-bearing account in which to stash the excess. Keeping track of all that money is essential to running a healthy and profitable business.

Creating Bank Accounts

All bank accounts you want to track in QuickBooks must first be created and configured in the Chart of Accounts:

1. Press Ctrl-A to open the Chart of Accounts window.
2. Press Ctrl-N to display the Add New Account dialog box.
3. Select Bank as the account type and click Continue to open another Add New Account dialog (see Figure 7-1).
4. Assign the account a number. If you have multiple bank accounts, using account numbers keeps them together in the Chart of Accounts. Otherwise, they'll be organized alphabetically.
5. Enter the name of the account. You can elect to enter a name such as Operating Account or Payroll Account and then provide the bank name in the Description field.
6. Enter the bank account number and routing number if you plan to use online banking. Both numbers are required.
7. If you use TurboTax to do your income tax, you might want to use the Tax-Line Mapping field. It's a good idea to check with your accountant before making the selection.
8. Do NOT enter an opening balance. Instead, read the section in this chapter entitled "Entering Opening Bank Account Balances."
9. Click Save & Close or Save & New if you want to create another bank account.

Figure 7-1: Name your bank accounts so all users can easily identify them.

Entering Opening Bank Account Balances

You should never use any of the Enter Opening Balance fields when creating accounts, including bank accounts. The problem is that QuickBooks automatically posts these amounts to the Opening Bal Equity account, which is a QuickBooks invention. Eventually, you or your accountant will have to go through that account and move everything to the correct accounts. Save yourself the time, aggravation, and accountant's fees by doing it right from the start.

Begin by getting the correct opening balance from your last reconciled bank statement. Now, create a journal entry using that amount:

1. Choose Company | Make General Journal Entries to open the Make General Journal Entries window.
2. Enter the date corresponding to the date of the last reconciled statement.
3. Select the bank account from the Account drop-down list on the first line of the table.
4. Enter the opening balance amount in the Debit column.
5. Enter "Opening Balance" in the Memo column.

6. Move to the next line and select an equity account such as Owner's Equity or Retained Earnings. You should check with your accountant to find out which equity account he prefers.

7. QuickBooks automatically enters the same amount in the Credit column, so all you have to do is click Save & Close.

After you finish and save the opening balances journal entry, use individual QuickBooks transactions such as Write Checks or Make Deposits to enter the previous, unreconciled transactions. You can also use the bank account register to add them. Then, when you reconcile the bank account in QuickBooks, you'll see the opening balance as well as the unreconciled transactions.

Configuring Checking Preferences

Whether you have one or multiple bank accounts, you can save yourself a little time and a lot of headache by setting the QuickBooks checking preferences. There are options on both the My Preferences tab, which apply only to the logged-on user, and the Company Preferences tab, which are applied company-wide. Select Edit | Preferences to open the Preferences dialog box. Then, click the Checking icon in the left pane.

My Preferences

The options here are great for companies with more than one bank account. The Select Default Accounts To Use section presents four different check-writing activities and lets you assign a default bank account to be used with each. Place a check mark to the left of the activity name and choose a bank account from the Account drop-down list on the right. After the default accounts are set, the activity window opens with the default account already selected.

If you're wondering why the payroll activity isn't listed, it's because it has been placed on the My Company tab for security purposes.

There is one final option that may or may not appear. It is an Online Banking option, but it only shows up if you have Classic Mode selected on the Company Preferences tab. For more information, see the section entitled "Setting Online Banking Preferences" later in this chapter.

Company Preferences

As you can see in Figure 7-2, there are a lot more checking preferences that apply to the company file, regardless of which user is logged on.

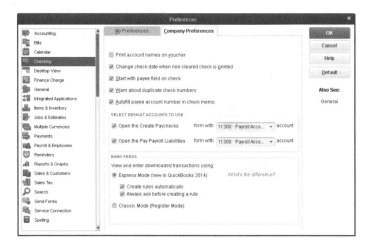

Figure 7-2: Use the Checking preferences to save time.

Here, your options include:

- **Print Account Names On Voucher.** When printing voucher checks, the account names do not automatically print unless this option is checked.

- **Change Check Date When Non-Cleared Check Is Printed.** If you create checks to be printed later and fail to print them until a later date, they will print with the original date unless this option is enabled. When checked, this option changes the check date to the date they are printed, not the date they were generated.

- **Start With Payee Field On Check.** By default, the cursor is placed in the Bank Account field when you open the Write Checks window. If you check this option, the cursor appears in the payee (Pay To The Order Of) field instead. If you only have one bank account, or if you've used the Checking preferences to configure default accounts, enabling this option will save a little time.

- **Warn About Duplicate Check Numbers.** Unless you want to use the same check number twice, you should probably check this option. It doesn't stop you from using a duplicate number; it just warns you when you're about to.

- **Autofill Payee Account Number In Check Memo.** If you utilize the Account No. field found in customer, vendor, and employee records, this is a good option to enable. It automatically prints the account number in the Memo field of the check. You'll find the Account No. field on the Payment Settings tab of the vendor and customer records and on the Additional Info tab of the employee record.

- **Select Default Accounts To Use.** There's nothing worse than printing an entire payroll run on the wrong bank account. If you have a separate bank account for payroll, these options are a must. Set the default account for the payroll checks themselves and for the payroll liabilities checks, as well.

- **Bank Feeds.** See the section entitled "Setting Online Banking Preferences" later in this chapter.

ProAdvisor TIP: *If you prefer not to set the default account options, or if you just like to have a visual clue as to which account you're using, you might want to assign a different color to each account. Press Ctrl-W to open the Write Checks window and then select the first account from the Bank Account drop-down list. Now, choose Edit | Change Account Color from the QuickBooks menu bar. Select a color for this account and click OK. The check image now has a border of the selected color. When you open the register for the account, you'll see that the color appears there as well. Repeat the process for all your bank accounts.*

Transferring Funds between Accounts

Moving money between bank accounts is a common procedure. Some organizations move funds from an operating account to a payroll account every payday. Some organizations have money market accounts and transfer the necessary funds to an operating account when it's time to pay bills. Others do it the other way around, moving money not immediately needed from the operating account to a money market account.

The difference between a regular transaction for income or disbursements and a transfer of funds between banks is that a transfer has no effect on your financial reports; it's neither a deposit nor a disbursement, and it has no effect on your Profit & Loss reports. Postings are made only to bank accounts, which are balance sheet accounts. However, if you don't handle a transfer properly in QuickBooks, you may inadvertently post amounts to income or expenses, which does affect your net assets.

There are three common ways to move funds between bank accounts.

- Using the telephone to notify a bank employee to transfer the funds or using the buttons on the telephone to effect the transfer via an automated transfer system.

- Going to your bank's web site and clicking the appropriate links to transfer funds between two accounts in that bank.

- Writing a check on the sending account and depositing the check to the receiving account when the accounts are in separate banks. (Checks are cheaper than an electronic transfer fee.)

Using the Transfer Funds Feature

If you use a form of automatic transfer, which means that no check is involved in moving money from one account to the other, use the QuickBooks Transfer Funds feature. Choose Banking | Transfer Funds to open the Transfer Funds Between Accounts dialog seen in Figure 7-3. Then, take the following steps:

1. In the Transfer Funds From field, select the bank account from which you're removing the money.

2. In the Transfer Funds To field, select the bank account into which you're depositing the money.

3. In the Transfer Amount field, enter the amount being transferred.

4. In the Memo field, enter an explanation for this transfer.

5. Click Save & New to enter another transfer; click Save & Close if you're finished.

Figure 7-3: The Transfer Funds dialog is essentially a journal entry between bank accounts.

QuickBooks posts the transaction to both banks, and if you open the bank registers, you see that the transactions are of the type TRANSFR. The sending bank is credited with the amount of the transfer (a credit removes funds), and the receiving bank is debited (a debit adds funds) with the amount of the transfer. This means the total for current assets on your balance sheet remains exactly the same.

Writing a Check to Transfer Funds

If you transfer funds by writing a check on one account and depositing the check into another account, you must be sure to post the transaction carefully. The safest way to do this is to pass the check through a transfer account in both directions. This means that you have to create an account for fund transfers with an account type of Bank. Use something like 10099 as the account number (the end of the numbers of your cash accounts, but before your next series of assets) and name the bank account BankTransfers.

To create a check for transferring funds, you need a payee. In most organizations, the payee for a transfer is the organization, the bank, or Cash. For fund transfers, it's best to create a payee as an Other Name, not a vendor.

If the payee name you want to use is already a vendor (common if you use the bank's name or Cash), don't use the existing vendor account because you don't want transfers showing up as part of the activity report for a vendor. Instead, create a new Other Name payee.

If you already have vendors named Cash and Bank (substitute your bank's name for Bank), use your organization's name as the payee (which is probably not a name in the vendor list).

If you write checks manually, you can create the check in either the Write Checks window or the bank register of the sending account (the latter is faster). If you print checks, use the Write Checks window (and be sure the To Be Printed option is selected). Post the transaction to the Transfers account you created.

After the deposit is made at the bank, enter the transaction in the receiving account using the following steps:

1. Open the account's register by double-clicking its listing in the Chart of Accounts window.
2. Enter the date.
3. Use the Tab key to move to the Deposit column and fill in the amount.
4. In the Account field, enter the BankTransfers account.

When you open the Chart of Accounts window, QuickBooks displays the current balances for balance sheet accounts. As a result, you know at a glance whether the deposit has been entered. If the deposit hasn't been entered, the Transfer account has a balance. When the deposit is entered, it washes the transaction (equal debits and credits) so that the Transfer account has a zero balance.

Handling Bounced Checks

Sometimes checks you receive bounce. When checks bounce, you have to perform the following tasks to adjust your QuickBooks records (all these tasks are covered in this section):

- Deduct the amount of the bounced check from your checking account.

- Record any bank charges you incurred as a result of the bounced check.

- Remove the payment applied to the invoice or pledge (if either existed) so the amount is once again due.

- Recover the money from the customer.

In addition, you should collect a service charge from the customer (at least for the amount of any charges your own bank assessed).

Using the Record Bounced Check Feature

New in QuickBooks 2014, the Record Bounced Check feature automates the process of recording a bounced check and issuing a replacement invoice. Unfortunately, at this time the feature is somewhat limited and lacks what we consider to be some necessary elements. Therefore, we're going to cover it here and include additional information for bypassing the feature and manually managing bounced checks in QuickBooks.

First, the limitations: To begin with, the feature only works with invoices. It will not work with Sales Receipts. The feature is only available from the Receive Payments window, and since a sales receipt payment is recorded with the Sales Receipt, there is no Receive Payments record available. The more serious limitation is that it simply recreates the original invoice (with original invoice number) and a new invoice for the bounced-check charge you levy against the customer.

The problem with this approach is that the customer already has this exact same invoice, and you are sending him a duplicate. This lays the groundwork for unnecessary confusion when trying to settle the issue. Instead, you should have an "Other Charge"-type item called Bounced Check, and the new invoice (with new invoice number) should be for two items only—the bounced check and the bounced-check charge. The original invoice is still valid.

The account postings made by the Bounced Check feature are correct, so you can use it as long as you're aware of its other limitations. Here's how:

1. Choose Customers | Receive Payments to open the Receive Payments window.
2. Locate the payment with the bounced check.
3. Click the Record Bounced Check icon on the Main tab of the ribbon bar to display the Manage Bounced Check dialog seen in Figure 7-4.

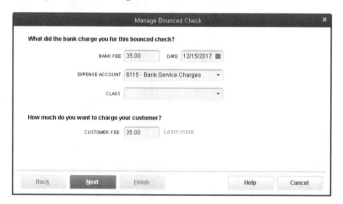

Figure 7-4: Be sure to include the fees your bank charges you.

4. Enter the fee your bank charges you in the Bank Fee field, and enter the date, expense account, and class as needed.

5. Enter the fee you charge the customer in the Customer Fee field.

6. Click Next to display the Bounced Check Summary dialog, displaying the changes that will be made in QuickBooks.

7. Click Finish to complete the process.

8. Resend the duplicate invoice and the new invoice for bank charges.

ProAdvisor NOTE: *There are two things that will cause the icon to either not function or not be enabled. If the payment has been placed in the Undeposited Funds account and not yet deposited (at least, not in QuickBooks), the feature will not work. QuickBooks lets you know about it. If you selected any payment type other than Check, the feature is grayed out. Obviously, it will only work if the invoice was paid by check.*

As we said at the beginning of this section, using the feature as outlined here (creating and sending duplicate invoices) may result in confusion when trying to resolve the issue with the customer. Therefore, it is suggested that you read the following sections and either use one of those methods or create a new invoice using a Bounced Check item (covered in the following sections).

Since the new feature does not address bounced checks from Sales Receipts, you'll still need to use one of the following methods when you encounter one.

Adjusting Account Balances for Bounced Checks

You must remove the amount of the check from your bank account and adjust the offset account that received the posting. Depending on the history of the bounced check, either you make the adjustment in the bank register or you create a journal entry.

For the following scenarios, use the bank register to make the adjustment:

- The bounced check was a payment against an invoice and you deposited the check directly into a bank account instead of using the Undeposited Funds account. The offset posting was to an Accounts Receivable account.
- The bounced check was a Sales Receipt (it didn't arrive as the result of an invoice) and you deposited the check directly into a bank account instead of using the Undeposited Funds account. The offset posting was to an Income account.

Use a journal entry to make the adjustment if the check's history matches these scenarios:

- The bounced check was a payment against an invoice and you deposited the check into the Undeposited Funds account and then used the Make Deposits window to deposit all the checks in that account. The offset posting was to an Accounts Receivable account.
- The bounced check was a Sales Receipt and you deposited the check into the Undeposited Funds account. The offset posting was to an Income account.

Using the Bank Register

If you deposited the check directly into the bank instead of using the Undeposited Funds account, you can adjust the bank account and the offset account from the bank register.

If the deposit was a payment for an invoice, its listing in the bank register has a type of PMT. You must delete the payment by pressing Ctrl-D or by choosing Edit | Delete Payment from the menu bar. (Unfortunately, there's no Void option for payments.)

QuickBooks displays a message warning you that the payment was used to pay an invoice and that deleting it will result in unpaid balances, which is exactly what you want to happen. Click OK, and the invoice that was paid returns to its balance due before the payment.

The Accounts Receivable account is also adjusted (the amount is added back). The invoice will show up as unpaid if you send a statement to the customer. You should also invoice the customer for any bounced-check charges you incurred (see "Invoicing Customers for Bounced Checks" later in this chapter.)

If the deposit was a sales receipt, its listing in the bank register has a type of RCPT. Right-click the listing and choose Void Sales Receipt. The amount of the transaction changes to 0.00, the bank balance is adjusted, the check is marked as cleared (so it won't show up in the next bank reconciliation as waiting to be cleared), and the Memo field displays VOID: in front of any text you entered in the field when you created the Sales Receipt. Click Record to save the changes.

Using a Journal Entry

If you used the Undeposited Funds account, create a journal entry to remove the amount of the bounced check from the bank. The alternative is to remove the original deposit from the Undeposited Funds account, which affects the Make Deposit transaction you created. If that deposit contained other payments, you have to recreate the entire deposit. Therefore, a journal entry is easier and less prone to mistakes.

To create a journal entry to adjust the amounts, choose Company | Make General Journal Entries, which opens the Make General Journal Entries window. Then, take the following steps:

1. Click in the Account column, then click the arrow and select the bank into which you deposited the payment.

2. Move to the Credit column and enter the amount of the bounced check.

3. Use the Memo column to write yourself a note (e.g., Jackson Ck #2345 bounced).

4. Click in the Name column and select the customer whose check bounced.

5. In the Class column, enter the class that was used in the original transaction.

6. On the next row, click in the Account column and choose one of the following accounts:

   - If the deposit was a payment of an invoice, select the Accounts Receivable account to which the invoice was posted.

   - If the deposit was a sales receipt, select the income account to which the sales receipt was posted.

7. QuickBooks automatically fills in the amount in the Debit column.

8. In the Class column, enter the class that was used in the original transaction.

9. Click Save & Close.

Don't forget to invoice the customer to collect the amount of the bounced check (see "Invoicing Customers for Bounced Checks" later in this section).

Recording Bank Charges for Bounced Checks

If your bank charged you for a returned check, you have to enter the bank charge. To do so, start by opening the register for your bank account. Then, fill out the fields as follows:

1. Click the Date field in the blank line at the bottom of the register and enter the date that the bank charge was assessed.

2. Delete the check number that's automatically entered.

3. Tab over to the Payment field and enter the amount of the service charge for the returned check.

4. In the Account field, assign this transaction to the expense account you use for bank charges.

5. Click the Record button in the register window to save the transaction.

Your bank account balance is reduced by the amount of the service charge. You should charge the customer for this, and in the following sections, we'll cover the steps needed to accomplish that.

Invoicing Customers for Bounced Checks

If you have to re-invoice your customer after a check bounces, you don't submit an invoice for the same item because you don't want to increase the activity for that item—this is a replacement for a previously entered transaction.

Instead, you have to create a specific item for bounced checks and another item for service charges. Then, use those items in the invoice. Those tasks are covered in the following sections.

Creating an Item for a Bounced Check Replacement

If you want to issue an invoice for the bounced check, you need an item for bounced checks. Open the Item List window and press Ctrl-N to open the New Item dialog. Then, fill out the fields using the following guidelines:

- The item Type is Other Charge.
- The item Name is Returned Check (or another phrase of your choice).
- The Description is optional.
- The Amount is blank (you fill in the amount when you create the invoice).
- The item is not taxable.
- Link the item to an income account.

The income account can present a problem. The bounced check was originally posted to an income account, and you may have multiple income accounts to track different types of revenue.

When you voided the check, you also removed the amount from the income account. When the customer pays the invoice for the bounced check, the same income account has to be credited.

If you have multiple income accounts, you have to create a bounced check item for each income account. That's because QuickBooks, unlike most accounting software applications, forces you to create a link between an item and an account.

Most software lets you specify the income account in the transaction window while you're creating the invoice. When you're creating an invoice for a bounced check, you merely select the income account that was used in the original transaction.

However, you're using QuickBooks, so you have to make a decision between the following choices:

- Create a subaccount named Returned Checks for each of the parent income accounts (Returned Checks-Products Income, Returned Checks-Services Income, and so on).
- Create a new parent account named Collections.

If you create a new parent account named Collections, when the customer sends the payment, deposit the money and then create a journal entry as follows:

1. On the first line, select the Collections income account.
2. In the Debit column, enter the amount of the payment for the bounced check.
3. In the Memo column, enter an optional description to remind yourself of this transaction's use.
4. In the Name column, enter the customer or job name.
5. On the second line, select the original income account you used for the transaction that resulted in the bounced check.
6. In the Credit column, QuickBooks has already entered the amount you entered in the Debit column of the previous line.

Before making a decision on subaccounts vs. parent accounts, check with your accountant.

Creating an Item for Service Charges

To create an item for invoicing customers for the bank service charges you incur when their checks bounce, use the following guidelines:

- The item Type is Other Charge.
- The item Name is RetChkChg (or something similar).
- The Description is optional.
- The Amount is blank (you fill it in when you create the invoice).
- The item is not taxable.
- The Account is an Income account you create for this purpose (or use the Collections account you created for the bounced checks item).

Creating the Invoice

Send an invoice to the customer for the bounced check. You can use the invoice template you normally use or create a new template for this type of invoice (see Chapter 2 to learn how to customize an invoice template). Then, take the following steps to complete the invoice:

1. Enter the name of the customer who gave you the bad check.
2. Enter the date on which the check bounced.
3. Click in the Item column and select the item you created for returned checks.
4. Enter the amount of the returned check.
5. If necessary, add another line item for the service charge you incurred for the bounced check, using the item you created for service charges.
6. Save the invoice.

Voiding Disbursements

Sometimes you have to void a check that you've written—you made a mistake in preparing the check, you decided not to send it for some reason, or you sent it, but it never arrived. Whatever the reason, if a check isn't going to clear the bank, you must void it.

To void a check, open the register of the bank account you used for the check and find the check's listing. If the check was written as payment for a vendor bill, its transaction type is BILLPMT. If the check was a direct disbursement, its transaction type is CHK.

Select the check's transaction line, right-click, and choose Void Bill Pmt-Check (for a bill payment) or Void Check (for a direct disbursement) from the shortcut menu, then click Record.

If the check you're voiding was a bill payment, QuickBooks displays a warning that your action will change previous transactions. This means the vendor bill, which had been paid, will be changed to unpaid and the Accounts Payable account will be incremented by the amount of this check. Since those are exactly the results you're looking for, click Yes to continue.

If the check you're voiding was a direct disbursement, QuickBooks merely voids the check. The expense account(s) to which you posted the check are credited with the appropriate amounts (the original posting was a debit).

The check amount is changed to 0.00, the check is marked as cleared so it doesn't show up as waiting to be cleared in your bank reconciliation, and the text VOID: appears in the Memo field in front of any existing text.

QuickBooks lets you delete a check instead of voiding it, which is a terrible idea. Deleting a check removes all history of the transaction, and the check number disappears into la-la land. This is not a good way to keep financial records. Voiding a check keeps the check number, but sets the amount to zero, which provides an audit trail of your checks.

(The ability to delete a check is a terrific feature for an embezzler who wants enough time to cash the check and run before you learn about the check in your next bank statement.)

Reconciling Bank Accounts

Reconciling bank accounts is bookkeeping jargon for "I have to balance my checkbook." In this section, we'll go over the steps required to reconcile your bank accounts in QuickBooks.

Business owners should always go over the bank statement and the bank register and compare them. Unlike the other reports discussed in this chapter, you don't view the bank statement to check figures and analyze them. Instead, this is a security check.

Unfortunately, statistics show that the rate of embezzlement in small businesses is much higher than you'd guess (and higher than embezzlement rates in large businesses). Even worse, a large percentage of embezzlers are family members who work in the family business.

According to a recent report from the Association of Certified Fraud Examiners, businesses lose 5% of their annual revenues to fraud, and small businesses are especially vulnerable. The median loss suffered by small businesses was estimated at $147,000.00 per business, which is higher, on average, than the amounts large companies lose.

According to the U.S. Chamber of Commerce, check tampering and fraudulent billing (the most common small-business fraud schemes) destroy many small businesses. The American Management Association estimates that one-third of small-business bankruptcies and at least twenty percent of business failures are due to employee theft.

Examining the Bank Statement

The bank statement contains check numbers (without names) for checks you sent to vendors and payee names for electronic transfers. Pictures of the checks (both front and back) are usually included in the statement or can be ordered from the bank.

Look for vendor names that appear frequently. Look for vendor names that only appear occasionally to which the amounts seem to be unusually large. Look for vendor names that aren't familiar to you. Check those vendor records in your accounting system. What's the address and telephone number, and what do you buy from them? Call the vendor if the name isn't familiar to you.

Look for bank transfers between bank accounts and make sure all the banks listed for these transfers are your own bank accounts.

Compare checks on the statement to the bank register and be suspicious of a check that was entered into the register months earlier than the check cleared; this indicates a back-dated check. A back-dated check is designed to be hard to spot, because the last time you checked the bank register, it didn't exist. This is especially suspicious if the check date in your system is for the previous year and the check was cashed this year (business owners hardly ever create reports for the previous year, so they don't see back-dated transactions).

Preparing to Reconcile

Open the register for the bank account you're about to reconcile by double-clicking the account's listing in the Chart Of Accounts window. If the bank statement shows deposits or checks (or both) that are absent from your bank register, add them to the register. If you miss any, don't worry. You can add transactions to the register while you're working in the Reconcile window, but it's usually quicker to get this task out of the way before you start the reconciliation process.

Interest payments and standard bank charges don't count as missing transactions, because the bank reconciliation process treats those transactions separately. You'll have a chance to enter those amounts during bank reconciliation.

Adding Missing Disbursements to the Register

The way you add missing disbursements to the register depends on whether the disbursements were checks or non-check withdrawals such as electronic payments or debit card withdrawals.

To enter a check, you can add the data directly to the register or use the Write Checks window (press Ctrl-W) and enter the check number, payee, and amount.

To enter a disbursement that isn't a check, add the data directly to the register. QuickBooks automatically enters the next check number, which you should delete and replace with an appropriate code (such as EFT for Electronic Funds Transfer, ATM for a debit card withdrawal, or

DM for a bank Debit Memo). You don't need to enter a payee for a debit card withdrawal, because usually, that's a cash purchase at a store that you're not tracking as a vendor, but entering the store's name will provide you a better audit trail. Enter the expense account (or petty cash account if you're refilling the petty cash box).

Adding Missing Deposits to the Register

You may see deposits on the bank statement that don't appear in your check register. This almost always means you forgot to make the deposit in QuickBooks. Check the Undeposited Funds account to see if you entered the deposits when they arrived but neglected to run the Make Deposits procedure.

Choose Banking | Make Deposits and see if the deposits are there (the odds are quite good that they are). Select the deposits that appear on your statement and deposit them into the appropriate bank account.

If you have multiple undeposited collections listed, deposit the funds in groups that match the deposited totals on the statement.

For example, your bank statement may show a deposit of $145.78 on one date and a deposit for $3,233.99 on another date. Both deposits still appear in the Make Deposits window. Select one of the deposits, process it, and then repeat the procedure for the other deposit. When you reconcile the account, your transactions reflect the transactions in your bank statement.

If a missing deposit isn't in the Undeposited Funds account, you have to create the deposit, which may have been a customer payment of an invoice, a cash sale, a transfer of funds between banks, a payment of a loan, or a deposit of capital.

For customer invoice payments or cash sales, fill out the appropriate transaction window.

- If you deposit the proceeds to the Undeposited Funds account, don't forget to take the additional step to deposit the funds in the bank so the transaction appears in the reconciliation window.

- If you deposit the proceeds directly to the bank, the transaction appears in the reconciliation window automatically.

If you made deposits unconnected to customers and earned income, such as a refund check or the proceeds of a loan, the fastest way to enter the transaction is to work directly in the bank account register.

Enter the deposit amount and post the transaction to the appropriate account (you can skip the payee, but, again, entering the payee will provide a better audit trail). If you're not sure which account to use for the offset posting, ask your accountant.

Using the Begin Reconciliation Window

Reconciling your bank account starts with the Begin Reconciliation window (see Figure 7-5), which you open by choosing Banking | Reconcile. If you have more than one bank account, select the bank account you want to reconcile from the drop-down list in the Account field.

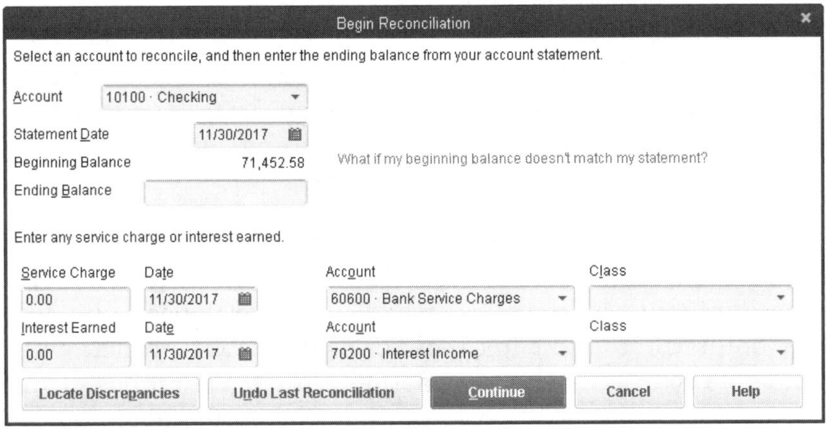

Figure 7-5: Bank Reconciliation starts in the Begin Reconciliation window.

Enter the statement ending date. Next, check the Beginning Balance field in the window against the beginning balance on the bank statement. (Your bank may call it the starting balance.) If the beginning balances don't match, see the section "Resolving Differences in the Beginning Balance."

If your beginning balances match, enter the ending balance from your statement in the Ending Balance field and enter the statement date.

Entering Interest Income and Service Charges

Your statement shows any interest and bank service charges if either or both are applied to your account. Enter those numbers in the Begin Reconciliation window and choose the appropriate account for posting (usually Interest Earned and Bank Charges).

ProAdvisor TIP: *If you have online banking and the interest payments and bank charges have already been entered into your register as a result of downloading transactions, don't enter them again in the Begin Reconciliation window. However, you may have to edit the original transaction(s) to allocate the proper amounts to the proper accounts.*

Bank charges refers to the standard charges that banks assess, such as monthly charges that may be assessed for failure to maintain a minimum balance, monthly charges for including checks in your statement, or any other regularly assessed charges.

Bank charges do not include special charges for bounced checks (yours or your customers') or any purchases you made that are charged to your account (such as the purchase of checks or deposit slips). Those should be entered into the bank register as discrete transactions, using the Memo field to explain the transaction. This makes it easier to find the transactions in case you have to talk to the bank about your account.

Reconciling Transactions

After you've filled out the information in the Begin Reconciliation dialog, click Continue to open the Reconcile window, shown in Figure 7-6.

Figure 7-6: The Reconcile window displays all the uncleared transactions for this bank account.

Eliminating Future Transactions

If the transaction list in the Reconcile window has a great many entries, select the option Hide Transactions After The Statement's End Date.

Theoretically, transactions that were created after the statement ending date couldn't have cleared the bank. Removing those listings from the window leaves only those transactions likely to have cleared.

If you select this option and your reconciliation doesn't balance, deselect the option so that you can clear the transactions, in case you made a mistake when you entered the date of a transaction. You may have entered a wrong month, or even a wrong year, which resulted in moving the transaction date into the future.

Clearing Transactions

All the transactions that are printed on your bank statement are cleared transactions. If the transactions are not listed on the statement, they have not cleared.

In the Reconcile window, click each transaction that cleared. A check mark appears in the left-most column to indicate that the transaction has cleared the bank. If you clear a transaction in error, click again to remove the check mark—it's a toggle. Use the following shortcuts to speed your work:

- If all, or almost all, of the transactions have cleared, click Mark All. Then, deselect the transactions that didn't clear.

- Mark multiple, contiguous transactions by dragging your cursor down the Cleared column.

- If the account you're reconciling is enabled for online access, click Matched to automatically mark all transactions that were matched when you downloaded data throughout the month. QuickBooks asks for the ending date on the statement and clears each matched transaction up to that date.

- To change the columns (fields) that appear in the tables, click the Columns To Display button and select or deselect columns to suit your needs.

- Clicking a column header in the reconciliation screen will sort by the items in that column. By default, the Checks And Payments side of the reconciliation screen sorts by date. You may find clearing items faster by sorting them by check number or amount.

As you check each cleared transaction, the Difference amount in the lower-right corner of the Reconcile window changes. Your goal is to get that figure to 0.00.

Viewing Transactions During Reconciliation

If you need to look at the original transaction window for any transaction in the reconcile window, double-click its listing (or select the listing and click the button labeled Go To).

Adding Transactions During Reconciliation

When you're working in the Reconcile window, if you find a transaction on the statement that you haven't entered into your QuickBooks software (probably one of those ATM transactions you forgot to enter), you don't have to shut down the reconciliation process to remedy the situation. You can just enter the transaction into your register.

Open the bank account register by right-clicking anywhere in the Reconcile window and choosing Use Register from the shortcut menu. When the bank register opens, record the transaction. Return to the Reconcile window, where that transaction is now listed (QuickBooks automatically updates the Reconcile window). Mark the transaction as cleared, because it was on the statement.

ProAdvisor TIP: *You can switch between the Reconcile window and the account register all through the reconciliation process. You might want to make it standard procedure to open the register of the account you're reconciling as soon as you start the reconciliation process, just in case.*

Deleting Transactions During Reconciliation

Sometimes you find that a transaction that was transferred from your account register to the Reconcile window shouldn't be there. This commonly occurs if you entered an ATM withdrawal twice. Perhaps you forgot that you'd entered a bank charge, or even a deposit, and entered it again.

To delete a transaction from the account register, select the transaction and press Ctrl-D. (QuickBooks asks you to confirm the deletion.) When you return to the Reconcile window, the transaction is gone.

Editing Transactions During Reconciliation

You may want to change some of the information in a transaction. For example, when you see the real check, you realize the amount you entered in QuickBooks is wrong. You might even have the wrong date on a check.

Whatever the problem, you can correct it by editing the transaction. Double-click the transaction listing in the Reconcile window to open the original transaction window. Enter the necessary changes and close the window. Answer Yes when QuickBooks asks if you want to record the changes, and you're returned to the Reconcile window, where the display has been updated to reflect the changes.

Resolving Missing Check Numbers

Most bank statements list your checks in order and indicate a missing number with an asterisk. For instance, you may see check number 1234, followed by check number *1236 or 1236*. When a check number is missing, it means one of three things:

- The check cleared in a previous reconciliation.
- The check is still outstanding.
- The check number is unused and may actually be missing.

If a missing check number on your bank statement is puzzling, you can check its status. To see if the check cleared previously, check the bank register, which shows a check mark in the Reconciled column if a check cleared.

To investigate further, right-click anywhere in the Reconcile window and choose Missing Checks Report from the shortcut menu to display the Missing Checks dialog. Select the appropriate account (by default, the first bank account in the Chart of Accounts appears, which may or may not be the account being reconciled) and click OK to run the report. You'll see asterisks indicating missing check numbers.

If the check number is listed in your Missing Checks Report, it's just uncleared and will show up in a future bank statement (unless someone is framing your checks instead of cashing them).

If the check never shows up in a future statement, you probably deleted the check instead of voiding it (don't do that anymore).

Finishing the Reconciliation

After all the transactions that cleared are marked in the Reconciliation window, the Difference figure at the bottom of the Reconcile window should display 0.00 (if it doesn't, read the following section). Click

Reconcile Now and select a report to print (Detail, Summary, or both) or click Close to skip a printed report.

Resolving Reconciliation Problems

If the Difference figure at the bottom of the Reconcile window isn't 0.00, try the following suggestions to locate the problem:

Count the number of transactions on the bank statement, then look in the lower-left corner of the Reconcile window, where the number of items you have marked cleared is displayed. Mentally add another item to that number for each of the following:

- A service charge you entered in the Begin Reconciliation box
- An interest amount you entered in the Begin Reconciliation box

If the number of transactions now differs, the problem is in your QuickBooks records; there's a transaction you should have cleared but didn't or a transaction you cleared that you shouldn't have. Find and correct the problem transaction.

Check the totals for deposits and withdrawals on the bank statement and make sure they match the deposit and withdrawal totals in the Reconcile window. If they don't match, do the following:

- Check the amount of each transaction against the amount in the bank statement.
- Check your transactions and make sure a deposit wasn't inadvertently entered as a payment (or vice versa). A clue for this is a transaction that's half the difference. If the difference is $220.00, find a transaction that has an amount of $110.00 and make sure it's a deduction if it's supposed to be a deduction (or the other way around).
- Check for transposed figures. Perhaps you entered a figure incorrectly in the register, such as $549.00

when the bank cleared the transaction as $594.00. A clue that a transposed number is the problem is that the reconciliation difference can be divided by nine.

When (or if) you find the problem, correct it. When the Difference figure is 0.00, click Reconcile Now.

CPA TIP: *If you can't immediately get the reconciliation difference to 0.00, go to another task and then come back to the reconciliation (you may be staring right through the error and not recognizing it) or let somebody else check over the statement and the register, because sometimes you can't see your own mistakes.*

Pausing the Reconciliation Process

If the account doesn't reconcile (the Difference figure isn't 0.00), and you don't have the time or the will to track down the problem at the moment, you can stop the reconciliation process without losing all the transactions you cleared.

Click the Leave button in the Reconcile window and go about your business. When you're ready to work on the reconciliation again, restart the process and everything will be exactly the way you left it.

Creating an Adjusting Entry

If you cannot find the problem, you can have QuickBooks make an adjusting entry to force the reconciliation to balance. The adjusting entry is placed in the bank account register and is offset in the Reconciliation Discrepancies expense account (which is created the first time you make an adjusting entry). If you ever figure out what the problem was, you can make the proper adjustment transaction and delete the adjusting entry.

To force a reconciliation, click Reconcile Now even though there's a difference. A message appears to offer the opportunity to make an adjusting entry. Click Enter Adjustment.

Resolving Differences in the Beginning Balance

The beginning balance that's displayed on the Begin Reconciliation window should match the beginning balance on the bank statement. That beginning balance is the ending balance from the last reconciliation, and nothing should ever change its amount.

If the beginning balance doesn't match the statement, you probably performed one of the following actions, all of which are major mistakes and should never happen:

- You changed the amount on a transaction that had previously cleared.
- You voided a transaction that had previously cleared.
- You deleted a transaction that had previously cleared.
- You removed the Cleared check mark from a transaction that had previously cleared.

These are all things you should never do, but if you did, you have to figure out which one of those actions you took after you last reconciled the account. QuickBooks has a tool to help you. Click the Locate Discrepancies button on the Begin Reconciliation window to open the Locate Discrepancies dialog. Select the bank account you want to check.

Viewing the Previous Reconciliation Discrepancy Report

Click Discrepancy Report to open the Previous Reconciliation Discrepancy Report. You can see any transactions that were cleared during a past reconciliation and then were changed or deleted. This report shows you the details of the transaction when it was cleared during a previous reconciliation and the change in the transaction since that reconciliation.

If the reconciled amount is a positive number, the transaction was a deposit; a negative number indicates a disbursement (usually a check).

The Type Of Change column provides a clue about the action you must take to correct the unmatched beginning balances.

- Uncleared means you removed the check mark in the Cleared column of the register (even though QuickBooks issues a warning when you do this).

- Deleted means you deleted the transaction.

- Amount is the original amount, which means you changed the amount of the transaction. Check the Reconciled amount and the amount in the Effect Of Change amount; the difference is the amount of the change.

Unfortunately, QuickBooks doesn't offer a Type Of Change named "Void," so a voided transaction is merely marked as changed. A transaction with a changed amount equal and opposite of the original amount was probably voided.

Open the register and restore the affected transactions to their original state. This is safe because you shouldn't have made the change in the first place. It's an absolute rule that a transaction that cleared should not be changed, voided, deleted, or uncleared.

ProAdvisor TIP: *You don't have to open the Begin Reconciliation window to see a Discrepancy Report. You can view the contents at any time by choosing Reports | Banking | Reconciliation Discrepancy.*

If you haven't found the problem that's causing the discrepancy in the beginning balances and want to search for it manually, you can compare the reconciliation report and the account register. Any transaction that is listed in the reconciliation report should also be in the register.

- If a transaction is there, but marked VOID, re-enter it using the data in the reconciliation report.

- If a transaction appears in the reconciliation report, but is not in the register, it was deleted. Re-enter it using the data in the reconciliation report.

Also, open the last reconciliation report and check the amounts against the data in the register. If any amount was changed after the account was reconciled, restore the original amount.

If you're not having any luck and you're determined to get to the bottom of the discrepancy problem, you can always cancel the previous reconciliation and start from there. First, make a backup of your company file, and then click the Undo Last Reconciliation button in the Locate Discrepancies dialog box. The Undo Previous Reconciliation dialog appears, suggesting that you make a backup and giving you the beginning and ending balances that will be restored. When you're ready, click Continue to complete the undo process.

Imposing Bank Account Security Measures

Large companies lose less to fraud than small companies because they have sufficient personnel to impose policies that make fraud more difficult. For example, the person with software permissions to add a new vendor to the accounting system does not have permission to write checks or approve vendor bills. The person with permission to approve vendor bills and enter them into the system does not have permission to write checks.

The budget and personnel constraints on a small business make security measures of this type difficult. There are, however, some security measures you can impose as the business owner.

Don't set up your bank accounts for electronic statements unless you can configure that feature for a different password than the password used for creating electronic transactions and viewing/downloading reports. Don't give anyone else the password. Unfortunately, most banks don't offer password security measures for different types of features, and if your bank doesn't offer this security measure, insist on paper statements.

If you receive paper statements, have the bank statement sent to your residence instead of the office. In fact, it's best if you reconcile the account every month yourself. If that's not possible, when you bring the statement to the person who reconciles the bank statements (probably the same person who writes the checks), stay in the room while the reconciliation proceeds. At a minimum, open the statement and take a general look at it. Ask questions about any transaction you're suspicious about. In fact, ask questions about most of the transactions, just to create the ambiance of "I'm watching carefully," because that reduces the level of temptation.

If your accountant is reconciling your bank accounts for you, the process is probably just a mathematical procedure to him or her. Accountants cross-reference the transactions on the bank statement to matching amounts in your ledgers. For the most part, they are only looking at the numbers presented, not the verbiage. Your own familiarity with vendors and customers makes it easier for you to spot potential security problems. Make sure you have looked at a copy of the statement before you give it to your accountant, scanning it for names or transactions you don't recognize or that seem out of the ordinary.

Look in the bank register for missing check numbers, then call the bank or check old statements to see if the check was presented. Look in the bank register for checks marked VOID and call the bank or check old statements to see if the check was presented. Keep a list of missing check numbers and voided checks and check future statements for these transactions.

Look at the checks you purchased and make sure the number of the last check matches the order you placed. It's not uncommon for people to help themselves to checks from the bottom of the pack for nefarious reasons.

You need to be especially vigilant since QuickBooks permits users to delete transactions (including checks). Most high-end accounting software permits users to void checks, but not to delete them (a check marked VOID, with a zero amount, is easy to spot when you look at the bank register, but a deleted check is just "not there").

However, QuickBooks does have a feature called "audit trail report" that produces a report for every transaction created, changed, voided, or deleted. Make it a habit to look at this report at least once a week. Choose Reports | Accountant & Taxes | Audit Trail to view the report.

Keep in mind that audit trails don't work unless users sign into the accounting software with unique names (the audit trail includes the name of the user who created each transaction). In addition to forcing the use of unique names, impose (and enforce) a rule that no user can leave his or her desk without closing the software. This prevents anyone else from accessing the software and creating transactions (or deleting transactions) under another user's name.

Not all "date lags" indicate a security issue. Sometimes there's a valid reason that a transaction is still uncleared after a long period of time. Are you storing a customer's check in your desk instead of depositing it (either inadvertently or for some reason) while QuickBooks shows that it was deposited more than a month ago? Is a vendor insisting the payment you sent months ago was not received, even though your books show that you paid the bill and don't have an outstanding balance? It's possible that the postal service failed (or maybe the check is stored in the vendor's desk).

Online Banking

Online banking is one of the true miracles of modern technology. From the comfort of your home or office, you can check balances, transfer money, pay bills, and do a lot more. Almost all banks today offer some form of online banking. In addition, most banks offer online banking features that include connectivity with QuickBooks. Those banks usually provide one or more of the following QuickBooks services:

- Web Connect. This is the basic service, which allows you to download transactions from the bank in a file that can then be imported into QuickBooks.

- Direct Connect. This is usually (but not always) a paid service to which you must subscribe. In addition to downloading transactions directly into QuickBooks, it offers additional features such as e-mail exchange with the bank, online money transfers, and online bill payment, all through QuickBooks. Not all banks offer all features, so be sure to check with your bank to see what features are available.

To determine the type of online banking service your bank offers, click Banking | Bank Feeds | Participating Financial Institutions. This launches the QuickBooks web browser and takes you to Intuit's Financial Institutions Directory web site. Scroll down the list on the left, locate your bank, and click the bank name to see what it offers.

ProAdvisor TIP: *If you want to allow users other than the QuickBooks administrator to access online banking, you must give them Sensitive Accounting Activities permissions. For more information on setting up users and user permissions, see Chapter 13.*

If the bank offers the Web Connect service, you'll have to access the bank's web site using a standard web browser and download a Web Connect file. If the Direct Connect service is offered, you can enable it using the Bank Feed Setup wizard, covered next.

Using the Bank Feed Setup Wizard

Using the Bank Feed Setup wizard is the way to configure your QuickBooks bank accounts for online access using the Direct Connect service.

1. Select Banking | Bank Feeds | Set Up Bank Feed For An Account to launch the Bank Feed Setup wizard.

2. Begin by entering your bank's name or selecting a bank from the "popular banks" list on the right. As soon as you click a bank name, the wizard moves to the next screen. What you see next depends on the service(s) offered by your bank.

   • Web Connect. An informational page with instructions appears. Close the window and access your account using a standard web browser.

   • Direct Connect. Some banks display an informational screen explaining how to enroll in the service. Others take you directly to the login screen.

3. Once you get to the login screen, enter your login information. It may be your User ID and password, or it may be your social security number and PIN. It varies depending on the bank.

4. Click Connect to open a list of your accounts (see Figure 7-7).

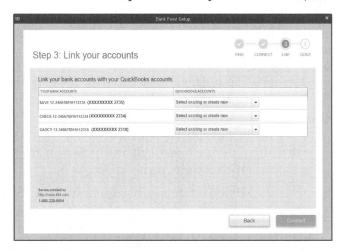

Figure 7-7: Link your online account(s) to the appropriate account(s) in QuickBooks.

5. From the QuickBooks Accounts drop-down list, choose either an existing account or <Create New Account>. If you opt to create a new account, the QuickBooks Add New Account dialog opens. Create the new bank account.

6. Click Connect to view the Success! screen, which displays the online accounts and the QuickBooks accounts to which they have been linked.

7. Click Close to shut down the wizard.

ProAdvisor NOTE*: While attempting to set up one account using the Bank Feed Setup wizard, we were told that the bank only offered Direct Connect. However, upon accessing the account through a standard web browser, we were able to download a Web Connect file. If the service you want doesn't appear in the wizard, double check with your bank online.*

Using the Bank Feeds Center

As soon as you configure at least one bank account for online banking, the Bank Feeds center (formerly the Online Banking Center) becomes available. Choose Banking | Bank Feeds Center to open it. What you see depends on the Bank Feeds (formerly Online Banking) preference setting. You'll find it on the Company Preferences tab of the Checking category in the Preferences dialog.

- Express Mode (formerly Side-by-Side Mode). This is the default mode selected when you create a new company. As you can see in Figure 7-8, it provides a list of bank accounts configured for online banking in the left pane and account information for the selected account in the right pane.

- Classic Mode (formerly Register Mode). Using this mode displays a split screen with the account register on top and the downloaded transaction on the bottom. The other difference is that it uses Aliases as opposed to Renaming Rules to automate the process of changing the payee names on incoming transactions.

Figure 7-8: Select an account on the left to view its details on the right.

Regardless of which type of online access your accounts have, they will appear in the Bank Feeds Center. However, Direct Connect accounts will display a Download Transactions button as well as a section containing options for sending and receiving messages from your bank. A Web Connect-configured account will only display the account totals. Both will display a Transaction List button if you have downloaded/imported transactions, but not yet processed them.

Downloading Transactions

For this section, we're assuming that you are using the Express Mode. How you download transactions depends on the type of online access your account has.

Downloading Direct Connect Transactions

If you've signed up for Direct Connect service from your bank, downloading transactions is done from within QuickBooks. Open the Bank Feeds Center, select the bank account in the left pane, and click the Download Transactions button in the right pane. If your bank requests a PIN number, enter it and click OK to begin the download.

Downloading Web Connect Transactions

The Web Connect method is a little more time consuming and is therefore usually without charge. It requires a couple of steps more than the Direct Connect method. Begin by accessing your bank's web site using your regular web browser and follow the bank's instructions for downloading transaction files.

1. Download the web connect file from your bank and save it to your hard disk.
2. In QuickBooks, select File | Utilities | Import | Web Connect Files to display the Open Online Data File dialog box.
3. Locate the Web Connect file (.qbo) and click Open to display the Select Bank Account dialog shown in Figure 7-9.

4. Choose an existing account or create a new one.

5. Click Continue to begin the import. When it's done, QuickBooks informs you that the transactions have been imported.

6. Click the account in the left pane and the Transaction List button in the right to display the list of imported transactions.

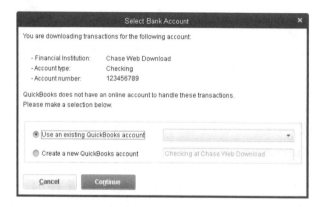

Figure 7-9: You can import transactions into an existing QuickBooks account or create a new one.

ProAdvisor NOTE: *When you download the Web Connect file, Windows first displays a dialog box asking if you want to open or save the file. The preceding steps assume that you elected to save the file. However, if you click Open, QuickBooks will automatically launch and offer you the opportunity to either import the transactions immediately or to save them to a file. If you have more than one company file, only choose the import option if the correct company file is open. The transactions are imported into the open company file and can only be removed manually.*

Adding Transactions

After you've either downloaded (Direct Connect) or imported (Web Connect) your transactions, a Transactions List button appears in the

Account Information section of the Bank Feeds Center. Click the button to display the Transactions List window shown in Figure 7-10.

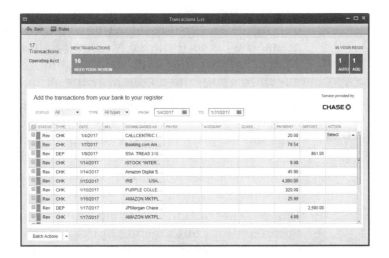

Figure 7-10: Use the Transactions List to process downloaded/ imported transactions.

As soon as you open the Transactions List, matched transactions are added to the bank register automatically. Matched transactions include those with the same check number, amount, date, or payee, or a combination of these criteria.

Transactions that remain in the list must be added manually:

1. Select an account from the Account drop-down list. QuickBooks will not enter transactions into the register without an account assigned.

2. Choose an action from the Action drop-down list. Your choices include:

   • Quick Add. Choose this option to add the transaction to the register without the payee name. You can return to the register later and enter the name.

   • Add More Details. Click this option to open the Add More Details dialog box, where you can enter/

change the transaction information to match that of an existing transaction.

- Select Bills To Mark As Paid. This option appears only if the selected transaction is a payment. It opens the Select Bills To Mark As Paid dialog, where you can choose an existing bill against which to apply the payment transaction.

- Match To Existing Transaction. To see (and match to) a transaction in the register, click this option. It displays the Match To Existing Transaction dialog, with all the currently unmatched (and uncleared) transactions from the account.

- Ignore. This option is misnamed. It is not an ignore option, but a delete option. If you use it, QuickBooks warns you that you are about to delete the transaction and will not be able to re-download it.

3. Follow the instructions in the window that opens.

4. Continue until all transactions have been matched or deleted.

ProAdvisor TIP: *You can add or delete multiple transactions by placing a check mark to the left of each transaction and choosing Add/Approve or Ignore (delete) from the Batch Actions drop-down menu.*

Using Renaming Rules

The Renaming Rules feature (formerly known as Aliases) is a handy tool for automating the matching process. Since the bank rarely gives the downloaded transaction the same description (Downloaded As) that appears on the transaction in your register, you can use renaming rules to link them. For example, if your vendor name is State of Florida Dept of Corps and the downloaded transaction is for Sunbiz.org, you can tell

QuickBooks that every downloaded transaction with Sunbiz.org in the name is really for the State of Florida Dept of Corps.

Here's what you do.

1. Choose Banking | Bank Feeds | Bank Feeds Center to open the Bank Feeds window.
2. Click the Rules icon on the top left of the window. This displays the Rules List window.
3. From the Manage Rules drop-down menu, click Add New to display the Add Rules Details dialog shown in Figure 7-11.

Figure 7-11: Use renaming rules to automate transaction matching.

4. Give the rule a unique and easily recognizable name.
5. Choose the matching criterion from the Description drop-down menu.
6. Enter the matching criterion in the text box to the right. To enter multiple matching criteria, click the plus sign to the right and enter another criterion.
7. Elect to rename or to assign an account to the transaction by making a choice from the Do This drop-down menu. Choose the existing vendor or account from the drop-down list to the right. To both rename and assign an account,

make one entry and then click the plus sign to the right to enter another.

8. Click Save to create the rule.

You can edit or delete existing rules by selecting the rule in the Rules List window and making the appropriate choice from the Select drop-down menu to the right of the rule.

Setting Online Banking Preferences

The online banking preferences provide a few options for customizing the Bank Feeds feature. You can choose between online banking interfaces, set options for how renaming rules are created, and opt to use the register when adding transactions. Select Edit | Preferences to open the Preferences dialog box and click the Checking icon in the left pane. There are online banking options on both tabs.

- **Bank Feeds.** Located on the Company Preferences tab, these options let you choose the interface used for downloading and processing transactions.
  - The Express Mode (refer back to Figure 7-8) lists accounts in the left pane and details in the right. You have to click the Transactions List button to view downloaded transactions.
  - The Classic Mode opens the Bank Feeds dialog box (see Figure 7-12), which lists the Items To Send and the Items Received From Financial Institution. When you view downloaded transactions, you can view a list of the transactions as well as the bank register for the account.

- **Always Use The Register When Adding Downloaded Transactions.** This option is found on the My Preferences tab only if you have selected Express Mode on the Company Preferences tab. When enabled, it bypasses the Add Unmatched Transaction window that normally appears when you select a downloaded transaction and click the Add One To Register button. Instead of giving you options, it heads right for the account register.

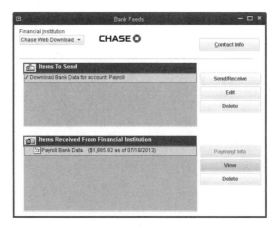

Figure 7-12: The Classic Mode offers a simple interface.

CHAPTER 8:

Tracking Assets

- Managing Loans Owed to You
- Tracking Vendor Deposits
- Tracking Prepaid Expenses
- Managing Fixed Assets
- Managing Intangible Assets

An asset is something your business owns that has value or usefulness. In accounting, assets are categorized and sub-categorized by various definitions.

Chapter 1 contains a complete list of all the asset categories; in this chapter, we'll discuss the asset categories you commonly encounter as you track business activities.

Tracking Cash

Don't take the word "cash" literally; in accounting, it means the money in your bank account(s) and cash that's in a cash register till or a petty cash box. Most of the transactions that take place as you run your business involve cash: You move money in and out of your cash accounts as you track sales and expenses.

Chapter 5 has detailed information on tracking petty cash. To learn more about tracking cash/bank accounts, see Chapter 7.

Tracking Accounts Receivable

Accounts receivable is the accounting terminology for money owed to you, and it's often abbreviated as A/R. (In the business community, the common jargon for A/R is "money on the street.")

A/R increases when you deliver a service or a product and send an invoice to the customer and the customer hasn't yet remitted payment. This is an asset because, as explained in Chapter 1, an asset is something that you own or something that belongs to you even if you don't have it in your possession at the moment.

A/R postings occur whenever the amount of money owed to you changes:

- A/R is debited (increased) when you create an invoice.
- A/R is credited (decreased) when you receive a payment on an invoice or issue a credit to a customer.

Accounts Receivable is covered in detail in Chapter 4.

Tracking Loans Owed To You

Your business may loan money to an individual (including you), another business, or an employee. You need to track the loan balance as well as the interest you're collecting on the loan.

When your business provides a loan to someone, it's an asset because the money belongs to your business. Your business is the creditor and the recipient of the loan is the debtor.

Creating the Loan

To track a loan you've made to someone, create an account of the type Current Asset for the loan.

1. Press Ctrl-A to open the Chart of Accounts window.
2. Press Ctrl-N to create a new account.
3. Choose Other Current Asset from the Other Account Types drop-down list and click Continue to enter the account details.
4. Enter the account number and name. Make the name easily recognizable (e.g., Loan to P.Goodman).
5. Enter a description that will help identify the loan.
6. Click Save & Close.

ProAdvisor TIP: *If you have multiple loans outstanding, you might want to create a parent account named Outstanding Loans and make each individual loan a subaccount of Outstanding Loans. It will be easier to track the total of all loans as well as each specific loan.*

If the loan is made to a customer, either create a new customer or use an existing customer. If the loan is for an employee, use the employee name. For someone who is neither a customer nor an employee, use the Other Names List.

When you give the loan (write the check) to the debtor, post the check to the loan asset account, as seen in Table 8-1.

Account	Debit	Credit
10000—Bank Account		3000.00
13010—Loan to P.Goodman	3000.00	

Table 8-1: A loan you make isn't an expense, it's an asset.

This means that when you write the check (Ctrl-W) in QuickBooks, you use the debtor's name as the payee and enter the loan amount in the Expenses tab. From the Account drop-down list, choose the current asset account you created to track the loan (13010—Loan to P.Goodman, in this case). If you extend the loan over multiple checks instead of writing one large check, each check is posted the same way. QuickBooks automatically makes the postings seen in Table 8-1.

Sending Loan Payment Invoices

You can, if you wish, send invoices to the debtor for each payment due. Note that since you can only send invoices to customers, the debtor will have to be set up in QuickBooks as a customer, even if he is not. In addition, you'll have to create a non-taxable Loan Payment item of the Other Charge type that is linked to the "Loan to P.Goodman" account.

Create the invoice (Ctrl-I) and select the debtor's name from the Customer:Job drop-down list. Select the Loan to P.Goodman item from the Item drop-down list, enter the amount, and click Save & Close. You can fill in additional fields (description, memo, etc.) as needed. Quick-Books posts the transaction to the loan asset account, as seen in Table 8-2.

Account	Debit	Credit
11000—Accounts Receivable	300.00	
13010—Loan to P.Goodman		300.00

Table 8-2: Sending an invoice reduces the amount owed on the loan and increases A/R.

If you're charging interest, the amount due for interest does not post to the loan asset (the principal); instead, it posts to an income account named Interest Income, as seen in Table 8-3.

Account	Debit	Credit
11000—Accounts Receivable	309.00	
49000—Interest Income		9.00
13010—Loan to P.Goodman		300.00

Table 8-3: Interest you charge on a loan is income.

Receiving Loan Payments

If the debtor is set up as a customer in QuickBooks and you have not sent an invoice, you can create a sales receipt transaction for the payment (Customers | Enter Sales Receipts). The postings are illustrated in Table 8-4. Note that this table includes posting for interest; if you're not charging interest, eliminate the interest amount.

Account	Debit	Credit
10000—Bank Account	309.00	
49000—Interest Income		9.00
13010—Loan to P.Goodman		300.00

Table 8-4: When a payment arrives that was not invoiced, it's posted to the loan asset to reduce the principal.

If the debtor is not set up as a QuickBooks customer, you'll have to create a journal entry to record the payment:

1. Select Company | Make General Journal Entries to open the Make General Journal Entries window (see Figure 8-1).

2. Enter the postings as shown in Table 8-4.

3. Include a memo and the customer name to help clarify the posting.

4. Click Save & Close to save the journal entry.

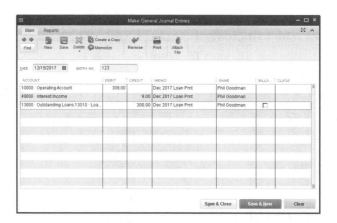

Figure 8-1: Use a journal entry to record a loan payment from someone on the Other Names List.

If you previously sent an invoice, use the Enter Sales Receipt window. The postings differ, as seen in Table 8-5. When you receive payment on an invoice, don't post amounts to the loan principal or the interest; that was accomplished when you created the invoice.

Account	Debit	Credit
10000—Bank Account	309.00	
11100—Accounts Receivable		309.00

Table 8-5: Invoice payments reduce A/R and increase the bank account.

CPA NOTE: *If the loan is to an employee and you want to deduct payments from the employee's paycheck, configure the payment as an after-tax payroll deduction that is posted to the loan's asset account.*

Vendor Deposits and Prepaid Expenses

It's not uncommon to face the requirement of an upfront deposit on some services such as rent or utilities. The deposits are usually held for a certain time, and then are either returned to you or applied as a credit to your balance by the vendor.

Sometimes, vendors want you to prepay all or part of an expense you're incurring. Prepaid expenses are usually tracked under the following circumstances:

- Some vendors may ask for a prepayment on a large order if you don't have a purchase history with the vendor.

- Some expenses (e.g., insurance) may require an annual or semi-annual payment that your accountant wants to expense one month at a time.

The funds you remit for any of these transactions fall into the definition of an asset; i.e., it's your money even though someone else is holding it. To track these remittances, you have to create an asset account for Deposits Held By Others and/or an asset account for Prepaid Expenses. Both of these are defined as Current Assets.

To create the account, press Ctrl-A to open the Chart of Accounts, then Press Ctrl-N to display the Add New Account dialog. Choose Other Current Asset from the Other Account Types drop-down list and enter the details for the new account.

The reason we suggest naming the asset account Deposits Held by Others is to make sure you don't confuse it with accounts that track deposits you're holding for customers, such as prepayments on orders, retainers, or other customer monies you're holding, all of which are liabilities. Naming an account Deposits or Deposits Held may be confusing—deposits to whom, from whom?

CPA NOTE: *It is very likely that you will have multiple prepayment or deposit accounts. It is preferable for you to have an account named "Prepaid Expenses," "Deposits," or "Deposits Held" and then create a subaccount for each individual prepayment or deposit.*

Tracking Deposits Sent to Vendors

Sending a deposit to a vendor is usually a straightforward transaction; you merely write a check. However, the check isn't an expense, it's an asset. Therefore, you post it to the Deposits Held by Others asset account to create the transaction journal seen in Table 8-6. The payee could be the landlord, a utility company, or any other vendor who requires a deposit.

1. Press Ctrl-W to open the Write Checks window.
2. Select the vendor from the Payee drop-down list.
3. Enter the amount of the deposit.
4. Move to the Expenses tab and select the Deposits Held by Others account from the Account drop-down list.
5. Enter data in the optional fields, such as memo, class, and so on (see Figure 8-2).
6. Click Save & Close to save the check.

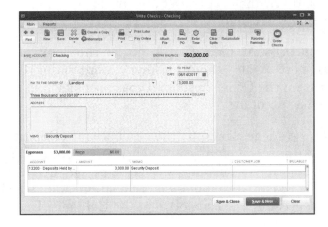

Figure 8-2: Assign vendor deposits to the correct asset account.

ProAdvisor TIP: *Watch out for vendors with default expense accounts assigned that automatically appear in the Account field of the Expenses tab when the vendor name is chosen. This check is not an expense, but rather an asset, and must be posted to the correct account.*

QuickBooks makes the following postings for you:

Account	Debit	Credit
10000—Bank Account		3000.00
13200—Deposits Held by Others	3000.00	

Table 8-6: This check isn't an expense, it's an asset.

Returns of Vendor Deposits

Usually, vendors return your deposit after a certain period of time. The common method for returning a deposit is to send you a check, but sometimes the vendor may apply the deposit against the next bill.

If you receive a check, all you have to do is deposit the check into your bank account and post the transaction to the Deposits Held by Others asset account. This creates a transaction journal that is the reverse of the journal that recorded the check you wrote for the deposit.

- Your bank account is debited (increased).
- The asset account is credited (decreased).

Follow these steps to enter the deposit:

1. Press Ctrl-R and select the appropriate bank account to open the associated account register.
2. Move to the first blank line in the register and fill in the date and the Payee (the vendor from whom you received the check) fields.
3. Move to the Deposit field and enter the amount of the check.
4. As soon as you do this, the Number field becomes blank and the Type field is changed to DEP.
5. Move to the Account field and select the Deposits Held by Others account.
6. Enter a memo if you wish and click the Record button.

You can also use the Make Deposits window (Banking | Make Deposits) to record the deposit.

If the vendor gives you a credit against the current expense (the amount due to the vendor) instead of sending you a check, you have to turn the asset into an expense. The method you use for this action is a journal entry. Open the Make General Journal Entries window and make the entries shown in Table 8-7. Be sure to select the vendor name from the Name field drop-down list.

Account	Debit	Credit
60000—Rent	800.00	
13200—Deposits Held by Others		800.00

Table 8-7: Change the asset to an expense with a journal entry.

If the amount of the deposit that's applied to the next bill is less than the amount of the bill, you have to write a check for the open balance. The check is posted to the appropriate expense, not to the Deposits Held by Others asset account. The total of the returned deposit and the check amount equals the expense that's posted for the month.

Tracking Prepaid Expenses

If you pay in advance when you purchase goods or services from a vendor, that payment is an asset. Create a Current Asset account named Prepaid Expenses to track these transactions.

When you create the check for the prepaid expense, post it to the Prepaid Expenses account. This credits (decreases) the amount in the bank account and debits (increases) the amount in the Prepaid Expenses account.

To turn the asset into an expense when the vendor's bill arrives (which may have a zero balance if your deposit was payment in full), create a journal entry that credits (decreases) the Prepaid Expenses account for the amount of your prepayment and debits (increases) the appropriate Expense account. Now, you have an expense on the books.

If there are additional charges on the vendor's bill such as shipping costs or the balance due if your advance payment was not for the entire amount, pay those charges the way you usually pay bills, posting the amount to the appropriate expense account.

Allocating Yearly Payments to Monthly Expenses

If you pay an annual fee for a service that's provided monthly, such as insurance, security services, technical support contracts, etc., your accountant may want you to track the expense on a monthly basis.

In this scenario, when you write the single check for the annual fee to the vendor, post it to the Prepaid Expenses asset account, not to an expense account. You then post the expense by creating a journal entry each month similar to the one seen in Table 8-8, which is the monthly expense for an annual premium of $1200.00. The journal entry reduces the Prepaid Expenses asset account and increases the expense account.

Date	Account	Debit	Credit
5/01/2010	85500—Insurance	100.00	
5/01/2010	13310—Prepaid Insurance		100.00

Table 8-8: This entry applies the current month's insurance cost to the Insurance expense.

Inventory Asset

The value of your inventory asset is the total costs expended for all inventory currently in stock (the current quantity on hand), including purchases from vendors, payments for freight delivery to your facility, labor paid on items you manufacture for sale, and other costs included in your manufacturing process. This means that the asset value changes often because you receive and ship inventory constantly. Inventory is a Current Asset.

The bookkeeping tasks involved in tracking inventory are not as straightforward as the tasks involved in creating sales or purchasing non-inventory goods and services. Therefore, we've devoted a separate chapter to the subject; read Chapter 6 to learn how to enter inventory-related transactions.

Fixed Assets

A fixed asset is something that a business owns and uses to run the business and produce income. Fixed assets are not expected to be consumed or sold in less than a year, and they are therefore categorized as Long Term Assets.

Fixed assets are tangible: you can see them, touch them, and point them out. The common categories of fixed assets are

- Equipment (office and plant equipment)
- Furniture & Fixtures
- Vehicles
- Buildings
- Leasehold Improvements (for improvements you make to real estate you're renting)

You should create Fixed Asset accounts for each category of fixed assets that are applicable to your business. (Almost all businesses track Equipment and Furniture & Fixtures; the other categories may not apply to your business.)

Creating Fixed Asset Accounts

Fixed Asset accounts are easy to create in QuickBooks. Open the Chart of Accounts window (press Ctrl-A), open the Add New Account dialog (press Ctrl-N), select Fixed Asset (Major Purchases), click Continue, and fill in the account number, name, and optional information.

What takes a little more thought is the opening balance for each Fixed Asset account. If you've been depreciating any of your fixed assets, the opening balance for the fixed asset is the current net value (the original cost, less the accumulated depreciation) as of the QuickBooks start date.

It's worth taking a bit of extra time to enter depreciation in a way that shows the history of the depreciation so that you can easily ascertain the original cost of the asset. To accomplish this, create accounts and subaccounts for each type of fixed asset you're tracking.

For example, if you're tracking vehicles, create a Fixed Asset parent account named Vehicle Assets. Then, create the following subaccounts:

- Vehicle (e.g., Van, if you want to track each vehicle individually) Cost, or Vehicles (if you want to track multiple vehicles in one account)
- Vehicle AccumDeprec

For the opening balance, enter the original cost of the vehicle in the Vehicle Cost subaccount and the current depreciation in the Vehicle AccumDeprec subaccount. Notice that you don't post any amounts to the parent account, but the parent account will show the net amount when you print balance sheet reports.

If you want to track individual vehicles, create a subaccount for each. If you wish, you can create a separate depreciation subaccount for each individual vehicle or post depreciation for all vehicles to the same subaccount. (Ask your accountant's advice.)

Take the same approach for other fixed asset accounts that require depreciation, such as equipment, buildings, leasehold improvements, and so on.

For information on entering depreciation in the future (now that the opening balances are recorded), see Chapter 12, which explains the tasks that have to be performed at the end of your fiscal year.

Using the Fixed Asset Item List

QuickBooks provides the Fixed Asset Item List to track information about the assets you depreciate. As you can see in Figure 8-3, the dialog for a fixed asset includes fields that allow you to keep rather detailed information.

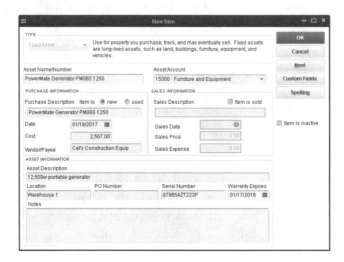

Figure 8-3: Track depreciable assets in the Fixed Asset Item List.

When to Use the Fixed Asset Item List

Unless you're using Premier Accountant Edition, the Fixed Asset Item List is inert. It doesn't do anything and isn't used for any type of transaction in QuickBooks.

When you enter a fixed asset in the Fixed Asset Item List, the financial information you enter isn't transferred to your Fixed Asset accounts, even though you must specify an account in the New Item dialog. You have to create separate transactions in your Chart of Accounts to enter that information into your fixed asset accounts. It doesn't work the other way around, either; the Fixed Asset Item List won't read the information from the fixed asset account you specify.

QuickBooks adds all the fixed assets you keep in this list to the Item drop-down list you see when you're creating a transaction. You have to scroll through all the fixed asset entries as well as your "regular" items to select an item for the transaction.

ProAdvisor TIP: *To keep the fixed asset items from cluttering your item drop-down lists, you'll have to mark all fixed asset items Inactive. Of course, when you want to use them, you'll have to reactivate them.*

On its own, the Fixed Asset Item List isn't terribly useful. However, it's very useful if you send your file to your accountant to depreciate your assets and your accountant is running the Premier Accountant Edition.

QuickBooks Premier Accountant Edition includes the Fixed Asset Manager, a tool that does use the information in the Fixed Asset Item List to generate depreciation.

Fixed Asset Manager automatically performs depreciation transactions, applying depreciation amounts to the appropriate fixed asset accounts. If your accountant uses the Fixed Asset Manager, you can send your company file or an Accountant's Copy file to automate the process of depreciating your assets. Since this may make your accountant's work easier and faster, it may reduce your bill for tax preparation. That trade-off may be worth the annoyances that come with the decision to use the Fixed Asset Item List.

What is Depreciation?

The Internal Revenue Service Publication 946 offers the following definition of depreciation: "An annual income tax deduction that allows you to recover the cost or other basis of certain property over the time you use the property. It is an allowance for the wear and tear, deterioration, or obsolescence of the property." The IRS doesn't let you post the cost of a fixed asset as an expense.

CPA NOTE: *One exception to this is Section 179 (the section of the IRS Code), which permits enhanced depreciation of your fixed assets, including the write off (expensing) of a fixed asset in the year that it is acquired. The rules change frequently enough that you should check with your accountant concerning whether or not this option is available to you.*

Most fixed assets are depreciated, which means that some or all of the cost of the fixed asset each year is transferred to an expense account, which reduces your taxable profit for that year. Technically, the idea of depreciation is to depreciate the fixed asset so that the expense is recorded for each year that the fixed asset is expected to be useful. How long will a fixed asset last before breaking or becoming obsolete? If the answer is five years, logic tells us that the cost is recovered at the rate of twenty percent of the original cost each year for five years.

Of course, it isn't that simple. Some fixed assets are hard to define in terms of deterioration or obsolescence. (We've never met anyone who could define, with absolute certainty, the useful life of a computer or the shelves in a warehouse.)

In addition, the Internal Revenue Service has devised a complicated set of rules and methods for taking depreciation for certain types of fixed assets.

Depreciation amounts should be computed by your accountant, who normally uses the IRS allowed amounts. When you have those numbers, you enter the depreciation expense and reduce the current value of the fixed asset in your books. This is usually done annually as part of tax preparation. The steps involved in this task are discussed in Chapter 10.

Purchasing a Fixed Asset

Depending on the type of asset, most businesses purchase a fixed asset in one of the following ways:

- Pay cash (write a check).
- Obtain a loan (or mortgage).

It's also common to combine these methods, using cash for a down payment and financing the rest.

CPA NOTE: *The cost of a fixed asset includes everything involved with buying it and putting it into service; this includes shipping, sales tax, and any other fees or costs (e.g., major electrical work to put a new machine into use).*

Because tracking fixed assets and their depreciation is a time-consuming task (and you're paying your accountant to perform the task), you and your accountant need to agree upon a minimum amount for posting equipment, fixtures, furniture, etc. as a fixed asset.

For example, if you buy a new computer monitor or a new router for your network, the cost is quite low compared to the cost of buying a major fixed asset. If you and your accountant have agreed on a $250.00 minimum threshold for treating a purchase as a fixed asset, purchases below $250.00 are posted to an expense account. You can create an expense account named Office Expenses, or Computer Expenses, or something similar and use that account to record the purchase as an expense.

Cash Purchase of a Fixed Asset

Most cash purchases of fixed assets are for the Equipment and Furniture & Fixtures categories, because the other fixed asset categories are usually for things too expensive to purchase without financing. When you write a check or post a credit card payment for something that qualifies as a fixed asset, post the payment to the appropriate fixed asset account.

If you're writing a check, be sure to use the Expenses tab and select the account for Equipment or Furniture & Fixtures. If you're using a credit card, the process is similar:

1. Select Banking | Enter Credit Card Charges to open the Enter Credit Card Charges window.
2. If you have more than one, select the appropriate credit card from the Credit Card drop-down list that appears.

3. Fill in the Date, Purchased From, Ref No., and Amount fields.

4. Finally, move to the Expenses tab and select the appropriate account from the Account drop-down list.

Either way, this creates a transaction journal that resembles Table 8-9.

Account	Debit	Credit
15010—Equipment	500.00	
10000—Bank Account		500.00

Table 8-9: If you use a credit card, the offsetting account is the Credit Card account rather than the Bank Account.

Financed Purchase of a Fixed Asset

If you're financing a fixed asset, you have to track both the value of the asset and the loan. For the portion of the cost that's financed, no bank account is involved because you didn't expend funds.

The loan is a liability to your business, and the easiest way to track both the asset and the loan is to create a journal entry that resembles the transaction seen in Table 8-10.

Account	Debit	Credit
15010—Equipment	5000.00	
23000—Bank Loan #1234		5000.00

Table 8-10: This asset comes with a bank loan; both the asset and the loan need to be entered in your books.

If you used a check or credit card for the down payment, the amount was posted to the fixed asset. When you create the journal entry for the loan, the amount of the loan is also posted to the fixed asset. Now, the total cost of the fixed asset appears in the fixed asset account. Tracking loan payments (including interest and principal) is covered later in this chapter.

Intangible Assets

Unlike a fixed asset, which is something you can see, an intangible asset is one that doesn't exist as a physical entity—it's not "fixed" the way furniture and equipment can be fixed in the workplace. An intangible asset has value because, like any asset, it is something that belongs to your company. Usually, an intangible asset is unique to your company.

Depending on the intangible asset and the manner in which it was acquired, you might be able to amortize the asset, which means you can create an expense that reduces your net profit (and therefore reduces your tax burden). A short explanation of amortization is included later in this chapter.

CPA NOTE: *Just as it was suggested to set up subaccounts for the cost of a fixed asset and its related accumulated depreciation, you should set up cost and accumulated amortization subaccounts for each of your intangible assets.*

Intellectual Property

For small businesses, the common intangible assets are patents, copyrights, and trademarks (called intellectual property).

Payments for intellectual property are normally paid by check against amounts invoiced by a vendor. In many cases, the total cost of the property is billed in sequential amounts over time. (For example, a deposit to an attorney to begin the process and then progress payments until the process is completed.) These partial payments are accumulated in a deposit account (a Current Asset) until the asset is fully acquired, as seen in Table 8-11.

Account	Debit	Credit
13020—Deposits on Patent	2000.00	
10000—Bank Account		2000.00

Table 8-11: Track payments made to acquire intellectual property in an Asset deposit account.

When the asset is fully acquired, create a new account for it. Press Ctrl-A to open the Chart of Accounts, and then press Ctrl-N to display the Add New Account dialog. Choose Other Asset from the Other Account Types drop-down list and click Continue. Fill in the details about the asset and click Save & Close.

Now, create a journal entry (Company | Make General Journal Entries) to reclassify the funds posted to the Deposit asset into an intangible asset, as seen in Table 8-12.

Account	Debit	Credit
18010—Patent	7000.00	
13020—Deposits on Patent		7000.00

Table 8-12: Reclassify the progress payments when the asset is fully acquired.

Organizational Costs

Organizational costs are the expenses you incurred to form and begin your business. This could include legal fees, incorporation charges, fictitious name registration charges, and other pre-operating costs.

Often, these costs are advanced by business owners before the business bank accounts are set up. In this case, create a journal entry to reflect money owed to the owner by the business for the payments (which is a liability to the business). Create the Organizational Costs as an Other Current Asset account type and the Advances Due To Owner account as an Other Current Liability account. Then, use the Make General Journal Entries window to create the postings seen in Table 8-13.

Account	Debit	Credit
19010—Organizational Costs	2500.00	
23010—Advances due to Owner		2500.00

Table 8-13: Record organizational costs that will be repaid to the owner as a liability.

If the advances are considered capital contributions from the owner, the credits are made to the applicable capital accounts (depending on the type of entity) instead of the advance account. Capital accounts are set up in QuickBooks using the Equity account type. Discuss this decision with your accountant. Chapter 14 covers owner contributions and capital accounts.

(If the payments for organizational costs are made directly from the business bank account, post the checks directly to the Organizational Costs asset account.)

Goodwill

Goodwill is the premium paid to acquire business assets in excess of their fair value. The Goodwill asset (of the Other Asset account type) is usually created when a new owner acquires an existing business. The amount is normally agreed upon between the buyer and seller, along with the value of the other assets being purchased. Table 8-14 shows how the acquisition of an existing business is usually recorded.

Account	Debit	Credit
12100—Inventory	2500.00	
15010—Equipment	5000.00	
19500—Goodwill	2500.00	
10000—Bank Account		10000.00

Table 8-14: Record the cost of purchasing a company by specifying each component of the purchase price.

What is Amortization?

Amortization for intangible assets is similar to depreciation for fixed assets. The rules concerning asset life spans and expensing rates are listed in Internal Revenue Service Publication 535.

Like depreciation of fixed assets, the entries required to record the annual amortization expenses that reduce the book value of your intangible assets should be provided by your accountant. Chapter 12 has additional information concerning amortization

CHAPTER 9:

Tracking Liabilities

- Customer Upfront Deposits
- Client Retainers
- Tracking Escrow
- Loans to Your Company
- Lines of Credit

A liability is something you owe to someone else. It is money or goods you may be holding, or have the use of, but that don't belong to you. For example, goods or services you've received but haven't yet paid for are recorded by matching liabilities (Accounts Payable). Also, money you are holding for someone else and will pass along to its rightful owner is a liability (payroll withholding or sales tax you've collected). In this chapter, we cover the common liabilities that small businesses encounter. (Payroll liabilities are covered in Chapter 10.)

Accounts Payable

Your Accounts Payable (A/P) account represents the money you currently owe vendors for goods and services you purchased to run your business. A/P accumulates when you enter vendor bills into QuickBooks. When you pay the bills (posted as bill payments), the A/P total decreases by the amount of the payments. Accounts Payable is covered in detail in Chapter 5.

Customer Upfront Deposits

If a customer gives you a deposit against a sale, the prepayment isn't income to you because you haven't earned it by delivering the goods or services. The money belongs to the customer until you earn it. Usually, customer deposits are requested for products that are custom made or for new customers who have ordered expensive goods or services. Because it's not your money (yet), a deposit is a liability. The liability is removed when you earn the money and present the customer with an invoice.

Creating Accounts for Upfront Deposits

To track customer deposits, you must create an Other Current Liability account named Customer Deposits. In addition, you must set up the customer record to track these deposits so that you know how much to deduct when you create the final invoice.

The amount of money posted to Customer Deposits represents the amount of your bank account balance you shouldn't spend. It's not your money yet. If you take many customer deposits, you should open a separate bank account to track and segregate these amounts. As you apply the prepayment to the customer's final invoice, the money becomes yours and you can transfer it to your regular bank account.

Creating Items for Upfront Deposits

Since you'll be recording upfront deposits on QuickBooks transaction forms, you'll need at least one Upfront Deposit item in the Item List.

1. Choose Lists | Item List to display the Item List.
2. Press Ctrl-N to open the New Item dialog box seen in Figure 9-1.
3. From the Type drop-down list, choose Service.
4. Name the item Upfront Deposits and enter a description if desired.
5. Leave the Rate at zero so you can enter it at the time you receive it.
6. Set the Tax Code to Non.
7. Select the Customer Deposits liability account from the Account drop-down list.
8. Click OK to save the new item.

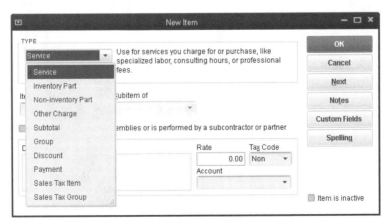

Figure 9-1: Use the Upfront Deposit item on QuickBooks transactions.

Recording an Upfront Deposit

Customer upfront deposits usually arrive in one of two ways: A conversation in which you ask the customer to send a deposit or an invoice you send to request the deposit.

If there is no invoice, you can use a sales receipt (Customers | Enter Sales Receipts) to record the deposit. Using the Upfront Deposit item ensures that the postings are correct. The income is posted to the Customer Deposits liability account and the Undeposited Funds account as seen in Table 9-1.

Account	Debit	Credit
12000—Undeposited Funds	200.00	
28000—Customer Deposits		200.00

Table 9-1: Deposit a customer's prepayment as a liability, not as income.

If you deposit funds directly into your bank account, bypassing the Undeposited Funds account, the debit in Table 9-1 will be to your bank account rather than the Undeposited Funds account.

If you create an invoice for the upfront deposit, post the invoice to the Customer Deposits liability account to create the posting journal seen in Table 9-2.

Account	Debit	Credit
11000—Accounts Receivable	200.00	
28000—Customer Deposits		200.00

Table 9-2: An invoice increases both A/R and the Customer Deposits totals.

CPA NOTE: *A customer deposit is not taxable; the taxes are charged when you send an invoice for the sale.*

When the customer pays the invoice, the posting for that transaction debits (increases) the bank account and credits (reduces) A/R.

Applying a Customer Deposit to an Invoice

When it's time to collect the money for the sale, you have to reduce the total amount of the invoice by the amount of the upfront deposit you received from the customer. However, you have to show the total amount of the sale, not the net amount collected, as income. Here's how to prepare the invoice:

1. Enter the item(s) of the sale, which are posted to Income.

2. On the last line of the invoice, enter the Upfront Deposit item and enter the amount of the original deposit with a minus sign to reduce the net amount of the invoice.

3. If the sale is taxable, the sales tax is applied to the total amount of sold goods (the amount posted to income). The customer deposit has no effect on the amount of sales tax; it only affects the amount due from the customer.

The resulting posting journal correctly reduces the Customer Deposits account and increases income and A/R. Table 9-3 displays the posting journal for a taxable (7%) sale of $1000.00, of which the customer prepaid $200.00. If you don't collect sales tax, the amount due is merely the total sale less the customer deposit.

Account	Debit	Credit
40000—Income		1000.00
28000—Customer Deposits	200.00	
21000—Sales Tax Payable		70.00
11000—Accounts Receivable	870.00	

Table 9-3: The invoice takes the upfront deposit into consideration.

> **ProAdvisor TIP**: *One thing that will make it a lot easier to apply upfront deposits (or retainers, for that matter) is a memorized report showing the available balance for each customer. Open the Customer Balance Report and click the Customize Report button. On the Display tab, deselect the Class and Balances columns (this makes the report easier to read). Move to the Filters tab and select Account from the Filter list. In the Account field, choose the Customer Deposits (and/or Retainers Held) liability account(s). Go to the Headers tab and change the name of the report to match its contents. Click OK to return to the report. Now, press Ctrl-M and memorize the report for future use.*

Client Retainers

Businesses that provide ongoing professional services (attorneys, accountants, financial advisors, technical support companies, and so on) frequently collect retainers against which they take their fees. The customer sends a certain amount of money that is held as a deposit against payment of future invoices. As you perform the work, your invoices "spend down" the retainer. When the retainer amount is too low to cover the next invoices, you collect another retainer from the customer.

If retainers are your normal method of doing business with clients, it's a good idea to open a separate bank account for them (a business savings account or money market that provides interest). If you deposit the money into your regular business account, you have to track the total amount of retainers (which matches the total in the Retainers liability account) to make sure that amount is always available in the bank account.

> **ProAdvisor TIP**: *If you accept both upfront deposits and retainers, you can simplify the process by creating a parent current liability account (Client Funds Held) and two subaccounts (Upfront Deposits and Retainers Held). Always use the appropriate subaccount and never the parent account.*

Receiving Retainers

To track retainers, you need an Other Current Liability account, named Retainers Held, and a nontaxable service item, called Client Retainers, which is linked to the Retainers Held liability account. When a client sends a retainer, you create a sales receipt to receive the retainer using the Client Retainers item. Depending on your default "deposit to" account (Undeposited Funds or your bank account), the posting appears as shown in Table 9-4.

Account	Debit	Credit
10000—Bank Account	2000.00	
29000—Retainers Held		2000.00

Table 9-4: If you use the Undeposited Funds account, the debit posting will be to it instead of the bank account.

Remember that the total of the funds in the Retainers Held liability account represents the amount of money in the bank account that isn't yours to spend. If you maintain a separate bank account for retainers, it's easy to make sure the amounts in the two accounts always match.

ProAdvisor Sidebar
Virtual Bank Accounts

If your retainer and regular funds are commingled in a single account, you should consider using virtual bank accounts to separate retainer funds from operating funds. That way, when you use the operating account to pay your business expenses, the balance won't include the retainer amounts you're holding. This makes it easier to avoid spending retainer money.

In addition, having a bank account (whether real or virtual) for retainer funds provides a quick way to check the status of retainer funds. The amount in the bank account should always equal the amount in the retainer liability account.

Virtual bank accounts are subaccounts of your business bank account. You must create two subaccounts under the parent account: an operating account and a retainer account. The operating account assumes the same role as a single bank account—it holds your operating funds. The retainer subaccount is where you deposit retainer fees. Move the appropriate amounts to the operating subaccount as the retainers are earned and turned into income. In the Chart of Accounts window, your subaccounts are listed (and indented) under your bank account.

After your bank subaccounts are created, you need to transfer the appropriate amounts from your original bank account into each subaccount. Create a journal entry to transfer the funds by choosing Company | Make General Journal Entries. In the Make General Journal Entries transaction window, credit (remove) the entire current balance of the parent bank account and debit (add) the appropriate amounts for each subaccount. Remember that this is a virtual exercise; the money is still in your real bank account.

Hereafter, when you open the Chart of Accounts window, the balance displayed for the main bank account is the total of the balances in the subaccounts. Balance sheet reports and trial balance reports display the balances of the subaccounts and the total for the parent account.

When you reconcile the bank account, use the parent account. Because your subaccounts are virtual bank accounts instead of real, separate bank accounts, the parent account actually maintains all the activity in the bank register.

Applying Retainers to Invoices

Money you received as a retainer becomes spendable when you earn it. At that point, the funds are changed from a liability to income. When you invoice your client for services performed, you transfer the retainer funds to income. Here's how to create an invoice for a client who has sent a retainer:

1. Press Ctrl-I to open the Create Invoices window.
2. Select the appropriate customer from the Customer:Job drop-down list.
3. Enter the item(s) for services rendered and the amount(s) due.
4. On the last item of the invoice, enter the Client Retainers item and make the amount applied a negative number.
5. Fill in the optional fields and click Save & Close.

If the retainer balance is larger than the invoice amount, only apply a retainer amount equal to the invoice amount. This creates a zero-amount invoice, but you've transferred these retainer funds into income and you can spend the money.

If the retainer balance is smaller than the invoice amount, apply the entire retainer balance to create an invoice for the net amount due from the client, and then issue a separate invoice for additional retainer funds.

The process of creating the invoice automatically turns the retainer funds into income by reducing the amount in the Retainers Held liability fund and increasing the amount posted to Income. Table 9-5 represents a posting journal for a client who sent a $2000.00 retainer that is being used to pay an invoice in the amount of $1400.00.

Account	Debit	Credit
40000—Income		1400.00
29000—Retainers Held	1400.00	

Table 9-5: The retainers account is decreased and the Income account is increased.

In this example, the client's bill is paid in full by retainer funds. Nothing posts to A/R because there's no balance due from the client. The Retainers Held account is decreased, and that amount is moved into Income, because now you've earned the money. (It's time to issue another invoice for retainer funds.)

Making Deposits into Subaccounts

Your QuickBooks company file configuration should specify the Undeposited Funds account as the default depository of monies. This means that when you create transactions for received funds (customer payments of invoices or cash receipts), the money is deposited into the Undeposited Funds account.

To deposit the funds in the bank, use the Make Deposits feature. This is the best way to manage bank deposits because it matches the way your bank statement reports deposits.

If you're using subaccounts, you have to separate regular income from retainer income so that the monies are deposited into the appropriate virtual account. First, select all the regular income and deposit that in the operating funds subaccount. Then, select all the retainer receipts and deposit them in the retainer funds subaccount.

Often, this isn't an easy task because you can't tell which receipt is for regular earned income and which is for retainer payments. The Payments To Deposit transaction window doesn't provide any clues about which receipts are for retainers and which are for regular income.

The way to resolve this dilemma is to come up with a solution that announces itself in the Payments To Deposit window. Using the Memo field in a customer payment transaction window doesn't work because memo text isn't displayed in this window.

Solve this problem with a new payment method (see Figure 9-2), named Retainer,which you create using the following steps:

1. Choose Lists | Customer & Vendor Profile Lists | Payment Method List
2. Press Ctrl-N to open the New Payment Method dialog.

3. Name the new payment method Retainer.

4. Select Other from the Payment Type drop-down list.

5. Click OK to save the new payment method.

Figure 9-2: Create a new payment method to handle retainer deposits.

When retainers arrive, either as a payment against an invoice you sent for retainer funds or as a sales receipt for retainer funds that arrived without an invoice, be sure the transaction window is marked with the Retainer payment type. The transaction window also has a field for entering the customer's check number (which is always important to record in case of any disputes with the customer).

- In the Receive Payment transaction window, when you select Retainer (or any other payment method classified as Other), the Check # field changes its name to Reference #.

- In the Enter Sales Receipts transaction window, when you select Retainer (or any other payment method classified as Other), the Check No. field doesn't change its label.

When you use the new Retainer payment method in transactions, the Payments To Deposit window is much easier to work with. As you can see in Figure 9-3, retainers are clearly discernible.

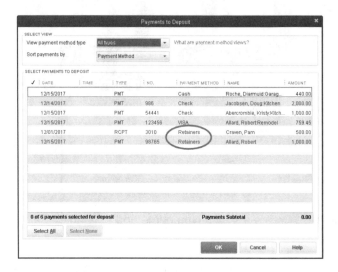

Figure 9-3: You can separate payments by type when depositing funds into a bank account.

Depositing the receipts in the proper accounts requires the following steps:

1. Select the Retainer payments and click OK.

2. In the Make Deposits window, select the Retainer Funds bank subaccount.

3. Select the date on which you took the receipts to the bank.

4. Click Save & New to return to the Payments To Deposit window.

5. Click Select All to select the remaining (non-retainer) receipts.

6. Click OK.

7. In the Make Deposits window, select the Operating Funds bank subaccount.

8. Click Save & Close.

You can automate the way you select payment types in the Payments To Deposit window, which is important in either of the following scenarios:

- You have a very large list of receipts in the window, and you don't want to click off the retainer methods one at a time.

- You have other types of payment methods that have to be deposited separately (such as credit card payments, which your bank handles separately on your statement).

To deposit different payment types in groups, use the following steps:

1. Click the arrow next to the View Payment Method Type field at the top of the Payments To Deposit window and choose Selected Types from the drop-down list.

2. In the Selected Types dialog, choose Other.

3. Click OK to return to the Payments To Deposit window, where only your retainer payments are displayed.

4. Click Select All to select all your retainer deposits, and then click OK to open the Make Deposits window.

5. Select the Retainer bank account and click Save & New to return to the Payments To Deposit window.

6. If you have credit card receipts to deposit, repeat Steps 1 and 2, selecting the appropriate credit card type in Step 2. Then, repeat Steps 3 through 5 (unless a credit card receipt was for a retainer, in which case it has to be handled separately and deposited in the Retainer Funds account).

7. Click OK to open the Make Deposits window and select the Operating bank account.

8. Click Save & New to return to the Payments To Deposit window.

9. In the Selected Types dialog, choose All Types, because all the remaining receipts should be standard income receipts.

10. Click Select All and click OK.

11. Choose the operating funds bank account.

12. Click Save & Close.

Tracking Escrow

Escrow funds (also called trust funds) are liabilities because they don't belong to you; they belong to your client. Managing escrow funds differs from managing retainers and customer deposits in two ways:

- The funds belong to your client, but are not collected from that client. Instead, they're collected from a third party on behalf of your client.

- The rules for managing escrow funds are mandated by state law and the rules of your professional association.

All states require attorneys to maintain a separate bank account for escrow funds and to impose strict bookkeeping procedures for tracking escrow funds as liabilities. Professional associations impose similar rules on other professions, such as realtors, agents, and others who collect funds from third parties on behalf of clients.

To manage escrow, you must open a separate bank account for escrow funds and add that bank account to your Chart of Accounts. Track each client's escrow carefully so that you always know the amount in the escrow fund for each client. (You can also open separate escrow bank accounts for each client).

You must also create a liability account for escrowed funds, usually named Funds Held In Trust. Because all transactions are linked to a client, your client records make it easy to track which funds in the liability account belong to which client. However, you may be more comfortable creating separate liability accounts for each client.

ProAdvisor TIP*: Opening a separate bank account can be rather cumbersome. It's a lot easier to either create sub-Escrow bank accounts (see the ProAdvisor Sidebar about virtual accounts earlier in this chapter) or one Escrow bank account and assign funds deposited and disbursed to each client. To do this, set up each client as a QuickBooks customer and always enter the Customer name in the Make Deposits window (Received From field) and on the disbursement check (Customer:Job field of the Expenses tab).*

Finally, you must create a nontaxable service item for escrow funds you receive. You can name it Proceeds Received or something similar. Link it to the Funds Held In Trust liability account.

The total of the funds in the liability account (or the combined totals of multiple liability accounts) must always equal the total of the funds in the escrow bank account (or the combined total of all the escrow bank accounts).

Every transaction that involves an escrow bank account, whether it's money coming in or money going out, must follow these rules, with absolutely no exceptions:

- The transaction must be posted to the Funds Held In Trust liability account.
- A client must be linked to the transaction.

Receiving Funds into an Escrow Bank Account

Money that is deposited into an escrow account comes from a third party for the benefit of a client. This is not income. Since escrow funds are not invoiced, they are usually recorded by using a Sales Receipt transaction similar to the one shown in Figure 9-4.

Figure 9-4: Record incoming escrow funds with a Sales Receipt.

The postings for this transaction depend on the "deposit to" account used in the Sales Receipt transaction. If you use the Undeposited Funds account as your default "deposit to" account, the postings will be as seen in Table 9-6.

Account	Debit	Credit
10500—Undeposited Funds	25000.00	
26000—Funds Held in Trust		25000.00

Table 9-6: Escrow funds are always posted to the liability account that tracks escrow.

You can then use the Make Deposits window to move the funds from the Undeposited Funds account into the Escrow Bank Account.

Disbursing Escrow Funds

Depending on your profession, a variety of payments may be due after funds have been deposited in an escrow account.

For example, real estate professionals track the buyer's down payment or "earnest money" (money accompanying the offer) as escrow when the buyer's offer is accepted. Usually, when the sale is complete (at settlement), the escrow funds are disbursed to the seller. If the sale falls through, the escrow money is disbursed in accordance with the terms of the contract that was signed by both the buyer and the seller (usually called the Agreement of Sale).

Attorneys usually have the most complicated set of disbursements from escrow, including repayments of costs paid in advance, internal costs incurred by the law firm, the legal fee due the law firm, and, of course, the client's proceeds.

Here are the guidelines for disbursing escrow funds:

- All checks are written from the escrow bank account.
- All checks are posted to the liability account for escrow.
- All checks are linked to and recorded in the client's record.

Most attorneys create separate checks for reimbursed expenses, internal expenses, and the firm's fee. The payee is the same. This is just a way to create an audit trail. The IRS advises that hard costs (real outlays for expenses) and soft costs (internal/overhead costs) should be tracked separately.

Sales Tax

If the goods or services you sell are taxable in your state (or in any state in which you are considered to have a presence), you must collect sales tax from your customers and remit the money to the state tax authorities.

Use tax applies when you buy something that is taxable in your state without paying sales tax upon purchase, usually because the vendor is in another state or because the item was used by you but originally purchased for resale. See Chapter 3 for detailed instructions on configuring and using sales taxes.

Remitting Sales Tax

Periodically (at the interval stated on your sales tax license), you have to remit the sales tax you've collected to the appropriate government agencies. This discussion assumes you've created the sales tax items you need and each item is linked to the right vendor (tax authority).

QuickBooks provides a feature called Manage Sales Tax (see Figure 9-5) that acts as a "home page" for information and help and contains links to the reports and payment forms covered in this section. You can open the Manage Sales Tax window by choosing Vendors | Sales Tax | Manage Sales Tax.

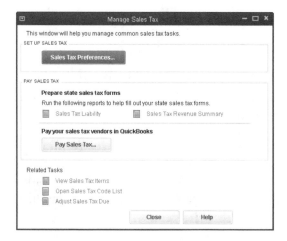

Figure 9-5: The Manage Sales Tax window has links to sales tax functions.

You can use the links in this dialog to display your sales tax reports and use the Pay Sales Tax function to remit sales tax to the appropriate tax authorities.

To make a sales tax payment, follow these steps:

1. Click the Pay Sales Tax button to display the Pay Sales Tax window shown in Figure 9-6.

2. From the Pay From Account drop-down list, select the checking account from which you want to write the check.

3. In the Show Sales Tax Due Through field, enter the end date for the tax period you want to pay.

4. The sales tax(es) due appear in the table below.

5. Select one or more taxes due to create the check(s).

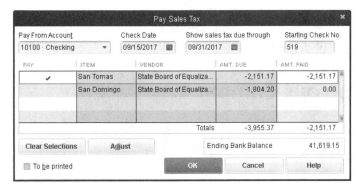

Figure 9-6: Select the sales tax(es) to remit.

Adjusting Sales Tax Amounts

If you need to adjust the amount of sales tax due (most states offer a discount for timely payment), select the appropriate sales tax item in the Pay Sales Tax window and click the Adjust button to open the Sales Tax Adjustment dialog seen in Figure 9-7.

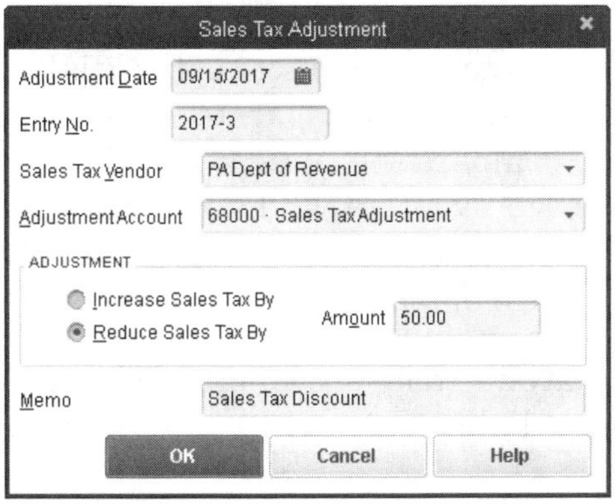

Figure 9-7: Adjust the sales tax amount before remitting the payment.

Specify the amount by which to reduce (or increase, if you're late and paying a penalty) the tax amount. Specify an adjustment account (you can create a specific account for this adjustment) and click OK to return to the Pay Sales Tax window, where the amount has been changed to reflect your adjustment.

If you remit sales tax to multiple tax agencies, create an adjustment for each tax vendor that requires an adjustment.

Loans to Your Company

Many businesses occasionally need loans to operate. Common reasons for loans include a vehicle purchase, a real estate purchase, expansion of inventory and/or staff, etc. You need to track the loan and your payments in QuickBooks.

Current Liabilities Vs. Long-Term Liabilities

The standard definition of a current liability is that the debt is expected to be paid within a year. Accounts Payable, payroll withholdings, sales tax payable, and other, similar debts are current liabilities.

Liabilities that are expected to be paid off over a period longer than a year are usually classified as long-term liabilities.

The reason to track current liabilities separately from long-term liabilities is that lenders, potential investors, financial analysts, and business owners frequently want to see separate totals for the two types of liabilities. They usually compare the current liabilities to the current assets (which include cash, A/R, Inventory, and any other asset that is expected to turn into cash within a year). These figures provide a quick way to determine the current health of a business.

These definitions aren't etched in stone, so check with your accountant to determine the type of liability account you should create for each loan.

Entering a Loan

Most loans are classified as long-term Liabilities, but your accountant may want to set up a short-term loan as a current liability, so check first. To track a loan, you'll have to set up a few new accounts. Press Ctrl-A to open the Chart of Accounts. Next, press Ctrl-N to display the Add New Account dialog. Create the following accounts:

- Long Term Liability. Use this account type for the loan itself. Name it so that you can easily identify the loan (e.g., Mortgage-Office Bldg or Vehicle Loan— Ford Van, etc.). The original loan amount, as well as payments on the principal, will be posted to this account.

- Expense. Create an expense account for interest. When you make a payment, the interest portion will be posted to this account.

- Other Current Asset. If your loan payment includes taxes and insurance, you'll need an escrow payment account of this type. When you make a loan payment, you'll post the tax/insurance portion to this account.

ProAdvisor TIP: *If you choose Loan as the account type when creating a new account, QuickBooks will create an account of the Other Current Liability type. Once the second Add New Account window opens, you can change the account type to Long Term Liability. As always, check with your accountant.*

CPA TIP: *When naming the account, you want to minimize errors in posting payments to the wrong account. You might want to include the monthly payment amount in the account name so that it will pop up in the drop-down menu when the account is selected while recording your payment (i.e. Vehicle Loan [$299.99]).*

You'll also need to set up the lending institution as a vendor in QuickBooks so that you can write checks to make payments. To create a new vendor, open the Vendor Center, click Ctrl-N, and fill in the relevant data.

If you received the proceeds of the loan in the form of a check or a direct deposit into your bank account, use the Make Deposits window to record the loan amount.

1. Choose Banking | Make Deposits to open the Make Deposits window. If the Undeposited Funds account is your default "deposit to" account and you have any undeposited payments, the Payments To Deposit window will appear first. Click Cancel to bypass it.

2. If you have multiple bank accounts, select the appropriate account from the Deposit To drop-down list.

3. In the From Account field, choose the long-term liability account you created to track this loan.

4. Enter the amount of the loan and fill in the other fields as needed.

5. Click Save & Close to record the deposit.

Table 9-7 represents the deposit of loan proceeds.

Account	Debit	Credit
10000—Bank Account	10000.00	
22200—Loan #887453		10000.00

Table 9-7: The money deposited into the bank is posted to the loan liability account.

Sometimes the loan doesn't result in a check; instead, the loan covers the purchase of an asset. In this case, create a journal entry to track both the asset and the loan.

1. Select Company | Make General Journal Entries from the menu bar to open the Make General Journal Entries window (see Figure 9-8).

2. Move to the first line of the table and select the asset account from the Account drop-down list.

3. Enter the amount of the loan in the Debit column.

4. Enter a brief description in the Memo field.

5. Move to the next line and enter the liability account you created for the loan. QuickBooks automatically inserts the amount in the Credit column.

6. Click Save & Close to record the journal entry.

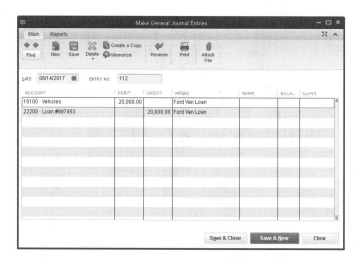

Figure 9-8: Use a journal entry to record a loan that you do not receive directly into your bank account.

The postings resulting from this journal entry are seen in Table 9-8.

Account	Debit	Credit
15100—Fixed Asset-Vehicle	20000.00	
22200—Loan #887453		20000.00

Table 9-8: This loan covers the purchase of an asset without the receipt of cash.

Often, a loan for a fixed asset or another large purchase is accompanied by a down payment. The down payment is also posted to the fixed asset to make sure the total cost of the asset is recorded. Check with your accountant to see how he or she wants you to create multiple transactions for the new asset.

Making Loan Payments

Loans are liabilities, but the interest you pay is a deductible business expense. As you make loan payments, you need to separate the amount applied to principal from the amount applied to interest.

Some loans have fixed amounts for principal and interest on the outstanding balance each month; other loans are set up to pay a constant amount that is less interest and more principal with each payment. For the latter, you need to get an amortization schedule from the lender so you know how to split each payment.

Whether you write a check or have your loan payment automatically deducted from your bank account, here are the guidelines for creating the payment:

- The amount of the payment is the total amount due to the lender (both principal and interest).
- The total amount of the payment is split between two posting accounts; post the principal to the loan's liability account and the interest to your interest expense account.

If you can't determine the amount of the principal and interest, post the entire payment to the loan's liability account. When the lender sends you a statement of interest, your accountant can instruct you on the steps to take to journalize the interest to an expense. Be sure the journal entry is dated in the appropriate year.

ProAdvisor Sidebar
Tracking Loans with the Loan Manager

QuickBooks provides a nifty tool for tracking loans called the Loan Manager. If you followed the instructions in the prior sections on entering loans, you have most of the prep work done for using the Loan Manager. Keep in mind that even though QuickBooks allows you to create accounts while the Loan Manager is open, they will not be available in the Loan Manager until you close and reopen it. Therefore, it's best to set everything up prior to opening the Loan Manager.

Use the following steps to set up your loan in the Loan Manager:

1. From the Banking menu, choose Loan Manager to open the Loan Manager utility.
2. Click the Add A Loan button to display the Enter Account Information For this Loan screen shown in Figure 9-9.

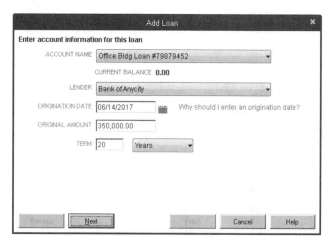

Figure 9-9: QuickBooks needs the basic loan information to start.

3. Select the liability account for the loan from the Account Name drop-down list.
4. From the Lender drop-down list, choose the lending institution vendor you created.
5. Enter the date you received the loan (Origination Date), the amount of the loan (Original Amount), and the length of the loan (Term) in weeks, months, or years.

6. Click Next to view the Enter Payment Information For This Loan screen (see Figure 9-10).

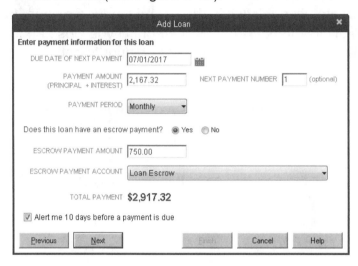

Figure 9-10: Enter all the data for your monthly payment.

7. The information here concerns the payment and should be supplied by the lending institution. Fill in all the fields from the data supplied by the lender.

8. Click Next to display the Enter Interest Information For This Loan screen.

9. Enter the interest rate of the loan and the compounding period. These should also be supplied by the lender.

10. From the Payment Account drop-down list, choose the bank account from which payments on the loan will be made.

11. Now, select the accounts to which interest expense and additional fees or charges will be posted.

12. Click Finish to complete the loan setup and return to the main window.

As you can see in Figure 9-11, the basic loan information is shown on the Summary tab. To see the amortization schedule for the loan, click the Payment Schedule tab. If you've entered contact information for the vendor, it will appear on the Contact Info tab.

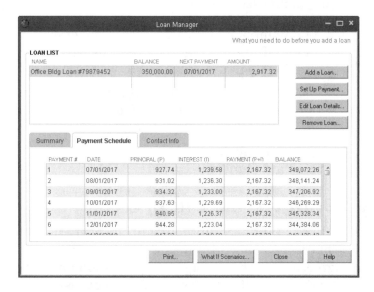

Figure 9-11: The Loan Manager creates an amortization schedule.

If you want to see what effect increasing your regular payment will have on your loan, click the What If Scenarios button at the bottom of the window. It opens the What If Scenarios window, where you can enter a new payment amount and recalculate the total payments and total interest you will have paid at the end of the loan.

Line of Credit

A line of credit is like a loan that you can use if and when the need arises. The advantage of a line of credit over a loan is that interest is charged only on the amount of the line of credit that you have drawn from the total amount available. A line of credit is issued with a maximum amount, but you only need to track the amount you've drawn and is, therefore, outstanding.

There are a variety of plans that financial institutions use to award and track a line of credit, but for this discussion we'll assume your line of credit follows the common scenario:

- When you need to draw on the line of credit, the financial institution transfers the amount you request into your bank account.

- The financial institution collects interest on the amount currently drawn. (Frequently, the interest is automatically deducted from your bank account.)

- There are no regularly scheduled payments for repaying principal.

Entering a Draw on Your Line of Credit

You need to create a liability account for your line of credit. Most of the time, a line of credit is categorized as a long-term liability, but the terms of your agreement with the financial institution and the maximum amount available may permit your accountant to suggest a current liability account (especially if it needs to be renewed on an annual basis).

Every time you draw on the line of credit, the transaction is a deposit to your bank account that is posted to the line of credit liability account. Either use the Make Deposits window (Banking | Make Deposits) or create a journal entry (Company | Make General Journal Entries). The posting will appear as shown in Table 9-9.

Account	Debit	Credit
10000—Bank Account	3000.00	
22300—Line of Credit #55567		3000.00

Table 9-9: When you draw on a line of credit, your bank account and your liability are increased.

Using the Line of Credit to Pay Expenses

As you write checks from your bank account to pay expenses, the payments have nothing to do with the line of credit. You post the transactions normally, ignoring the fact that the money came from a line of credit.

If your line of credit came with its own checkbook and you simply write checks to draw on the line of credit, you have to handle it a little differently. In that case, you have two choices as to how to enter the transaction.

The first is to use a journal entry to credit the liability account and debit the expense. Make sure to include the vendor name in the journal entry. For example, if you write a check from the line of credit to pay Contractor Joe for repainting the office, your journal entry will look like Figure 9-12.

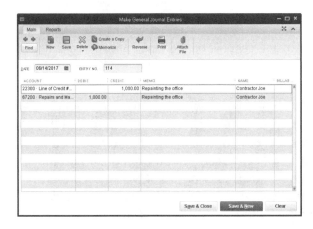

Figure 9-12: When you write a check directly from the line of credit, you use a journal entry to record the transaction.

The second, and the one preferred by most accountants since it will leave a more detailed trail, is to open up the liability account register to record the transaction. Press Ctrl-A to open the Chart of Accounts and double-click the liability account to display the register. Enter the vendor name as the Payee and select the expense account from the Account drop-down list. Since this is a credit to the liability account, enter the amount in the Increase column.

Paying Interest on a Line of Credit

The interest on your line of credit is based on the amount you've drawn. If you write a check for interest to the financial institution, post the check to your Interest expense account. If the money is automatically withdrawn from your bank account, create a "fake" check, which is a check with no number or with the text EFT (electronic funds transfer) used as the number.

Either way, the transaction journal shows the same posting. As you can see in Table 9-10, interest payments don't post to the liability account you created to track the line of credit.

Account	Debit	Credit
10000—Bank Account		110.00
62000—Interest Expense	110.00	

Table 9-10: Interest paid on the funds drawn from a line of credit is posted just like any other interest payment.

CPA TIP: *Since the IRS will allow you to deduct the interest charged on your Line of Credit on the date that it is charged (not necessarily the date it is paid), and because many Lines of Credit merely increase the amount drawn on the line on the date the interest is charged, it would be preferable to go through the following process to record the monthly interest: Open up the Line of Credit register and record the interest expense as an increase to the line on the date the interest is charged. When you make your payment from your checking account, record the payment against the Line of Credit instead of as an Interest Expense, since the expense will already be on your books.*

Repaying Line of Credit Principal

When you want to reduce your interest expense, you pay down your line of credit to reduce the outstanding line balance. Your payment is posted to the liability account, as seen in Table 9-11.

Account	Debit	Credit
10000—Bank Account		2800.00
22300—Line of Credit #55567	2800.00	

Table 9-11: Post principal payments to the liability account for the line of credit.

Of course, future interest payments are based on the remaining balance in the liability account.

ProAdvisor TIP: *You can also set the line of credit up in QuickBooks as a credit card account, which allows you to track the interest as the bank applies it.*

CHAPTER 10:

Managing Payroll

- Activating Payroll

- Configuring Payroll

- Setting Payroll Preferences

- Running QuickBooks Payroll

- Understanding Payroll Accounting

- Working with Independent Contractors

Some businesses with employees do the payroll themselves, which is called in-house payroll processing, while other businesses hire a payroll service company to take care of payroll, which is called outsourced payroll processing). Every employee receives a W-2 at the end of the year.

When business owners view the financial reports for payroll postings or view the government reports they have to sign, they frequently don't understand what they're looking at. Accountants receive a great many questions from business owners regarding the financial information for payroll, and in this chapter we'll explain the effects of payroll on your books.

Activating Payroll in QuickBooks

If you have employees, you have to create paychecks, track the liabilities and employer expenses related to those paychecks, and remit those liabilities and employer expenses. A great many postings to your general ledger take place as you perform these tasks. Even if you don't do your own payroll, you have to track those postings in your books (using the reports from your outside payroll company).

QuickBooks offers a variety of payroll solutions, one of which should fit your needs.

- Manual. If you only have a handful of employees and don't mind doing the tax calculations yourself, you can save the cost of a subscription and turn on manual payroll. No tax tables are available, which means you're responsible for any miscalculations.

- Basic. This is the bare-bones payroll service from Intuit that provides current tax tables so that you can create paychecks without having to do your own calculations. It creates paychecks, but does not fill out the payroll liability forms for you. You have to generate reports on the liabilities and then fill out and submit the forms yourself.

- Enhanced. To create paychecks, fill out the tax forms for payroll liabilities, and file those forms online, you'll have to sign up for the Enhanced Payroll subscription.

- Full Service. If you prefer to outsource your payroll, this is the plan for you. You keep track of your employees' hours and submit them to Intuit, and Intuit creates the paychecks and remits the payroll taxes for you.

To turn on manual payroll, see the sidebar entitled "Configuring Manual Payroll" later in this chapter.

To subscribe to one of the fee-based payroll services, choose Employees | Turn On Payroll In QuickBooks to be taken to the Intuit web site for payroll services. There, you can learn more about the different plans and sign up for one.

ProAdvisor Sidebar
Configuring Manual Payroll

Since no tax tables are available for manual payroll in QuickBooks, you must be sure you're up to the task of doing your own tax calculations. If you're confident and only have a few employees, manual payroll may work well for you. Due to the risks and the fact that Intuit would prefer you subscribe to one of its payroll services, manual payroll is a little tricky to enable.

1. Press F1 to open the help dialog called Have A Question?
2. Type "process payroll manually" into the text box and click the search button (magnifying glass).
3. Click the first help result that appears—Process Payroll Manually (Without A Subscription To QuickBooks Payroll).
4. Read the recommendation to ensure that you're ready to run manual payroll.

5. When you're ready, click the Manual Payroll Calculations link in the first step.

6. Move to the end of the dialog text and click the Set My Company File To Use Manual Calculations link.

7. QuickBooks informs you that you'll have to calculate your paycheck amounts manually. Click OK to proceed.

CPA CAUTION: *Tax tables, rates, and limits for your various payroll tax liabilities (federal withholding, social security, Medicare, state withholding, state unemployment, local, etc.) often change annually and can also change during the year without warning, so you run the risk of miscalculating your tax liabilities unless you stay on top of the changes. This, in turn, can expose you to penalty and interest charges from the taxing authorities. Be sure you're ready to assume the responsibility before you click that OK button.*

Setting Up Payroll in QuickBooks

Once you've subscribed to a payroll service (or turned on manual payroll), you're ready to begin the setup. You can do it a couple of different ways:

- QuickBooks Payroll Setup wizard. Payroll is a complex feature, and the wizard does a nice job of organizing the tasks and providing some handholding. That being said, you still must understand the basics of payroll setup, even with the wizard.

- Employee Center/Add New Payroll Item. You can ignore the payroll wizard and use two separate payroll related features:

  - Employee Center. Open the Employee Center, press Ctrl-N, and fill out a New Employee form for each employee.

- Add New Payroll Item wizard. If you know which payroll items you need, you can use this wizard to enter them individually. The only thing to be aware of is that this wizard does not offer the same level of handholding that the QuickBooks Payroll Setup wizard does. For example, the Payroll Setup wizard alerts you to the fact that you might need two deduction items for a benefit (e.g., health insurance) if both the employee and the company share the cost. The Add New Payroll Item wizard does not ask if you need both. It assumes that you know what you need.

Preparing for Payroll Setup

Before you jump in and start setting up payroll in QuickBooks, you should spend some time gathering the information you'll need to complete the setup. Whichever setup method you choose, you'll need the same information either way. Here's how the wizard is organized:

- Company Setup. This section covers both employee compensation and employee benefits. Are your employees paid an hourly rate, a salary, or both? What about bonuses, commissions, and tips—are they part of the compensation your employees receive? Do you offer health and retirement benefits? All of these things will have to be set up as payroll items independently or during the course of the wizard. If you have the information handy, the setup process will go a lot more smoothly.

- Employee Setup. Required information includes name, address, social security number, and hire date. Important information includes pay frequency and rate, vacation information, sick pay, overtime, deductions, and more.

- Taxes. QuickBooks needs to know which taxes (federal, state, local) apply, the agencies you file with, what the schedules are, and more.

- Year-To-Date Payrolls. Unless you're starting payroll on the first day of the year, you'll have to enter the historical payroll data into QuickBooks to ensure that your payroll information is accurate for the entire year.

Once you have this information pulled together, you're ready to start setting up payroll.

ProAdvisor TIP: *If you plan to use the QuickBooks Payroll Setup wizard or the EZ Setup method for adding payroll items, you might want to create vendors (tax agencies, benefit providers, etc.) before starting the wizard. The reason being that you cannot create them while the wizard is running. Unlike most other drop-down lists in QuickBooks, the vendor lists in the wizard do not provide an <Add New> command. That means you'll have to close the wizard, open the Vendor Center, create the new vendor(s), and return to the wizard. The Custom Setup method for adding payroll items does allow you to add new vendors on the fly.*

Configuring QuickBooks Payroll

As we mentioned earlier, you have two methods for setting up QuickBooks payroll—the QuickBooks Payroll Setup wizard or the manual method using the Employee Center and the Add New Payroll Item wizard. Whichever method you use, the end results are the same. Therefore, we're not going to go over each method in detail, but rather provide an overview of each method.

Running the QuickBooks Payroll Setup Wizard

The QuickBooks Payroll Setup method is the most comprehensive and user friendly of the two methods. It takes you through every possible scenario and holds your hand the entire way. The only drawback is that you have to slog through the entire wizard.

Starting the wizard is easy. Choose Employees | Payroll Setup to display the Introduction screen of the wizard (see Figure 10-1).

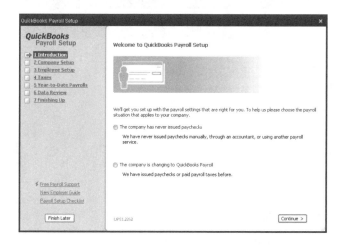

Figure 10-1: Take a look at the Payroll Setup Checklist (click the link) to make sure you have everything you need.

As you can see, the wizard first asks if you have previously run payroll. If you answer yes (The Company Is Changing To QuickBooks Payroll), the wizard includes a section in which you can enter historical payroll data. If you answer no (The Company Has Never Issued Paychecks), it ignores historical data.

ProAdvisor TIP: *If you prefer to enter summary information for the pre-QuickBooks payroll historical data, you can use the Set Up YTD Amounts wizard. To access the wizard, choose Help | About QuickBooks <version> to display the About QuickBooks screen. Press Alt-Ctrl-Y to launch the Set Up YTD Amounts wizard.*

The Payroll Setup wizard has a series of steps through which it walks you, giving guidance along the way. The first time you go through the wizard, it gives you a selection of choices for each category (see Figure 10-2). After you make your selection(s), the wizard walks you through the steps of configuring each one.

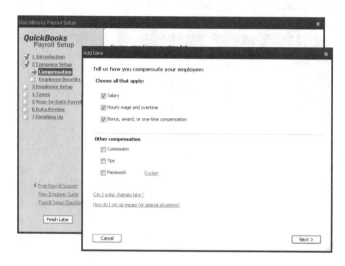

Figure 10-2: The wizard offers all the common choices for each different category.

Proceed through the wizard one step at a time until you've configured all the necessary items. You can close the wizard down anytime you want, saving the changes, by clicking the Finish Later button. The next time you choose Employees | Payroll Setup, the wizard picks up where you left off.

Configuring Payroll without the Wizard

The benefit to setting up payroll without using the wizard is that you can put it together in any order you wish. You can add employees one at time in the Employee Center or by importing them from an Excel spreadsheet. Wages, benefits, and other deductions can be entered individually using the Add New Payroll Item wizard. The downside is that you'll have less handholding than with the payroll wizard. If you go for the manual method, be sure you enter all the required data. As always, you should consult with your accountant.

Using the Add New Payroll Items Wizard

If you decide to bypass the Payroll Setup wizard, you'll have to use the Add New Payroll Item wizard (even if you try to create new items directly from the Payroll Item List). The wizard offers two different methods for creating new items—the EZ Setup method and the Custom Setup method (see Figure 10-3). To access the wizard, choose Employees | Manage Payroll Items | New Payroll Item.

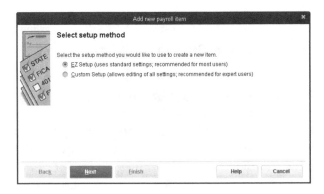

Figure 10-3: Use the Add New Payroll Item wizard to add payroll items manually.

EZ Setup Method

The EZ Setup method is a hybrid method that lets you pick the item type and then jumps to that spot in the QuickBooks Payroll Setup wizard to do the actual configuration. It eliminates the need to go through the entire wizard, but also cuts back on the amount of handholding offered.

Custom Setup Method

If you have a good grasp of payroll setup, you can save some time by employing the Custom Setup method. You choose the item type and then fill out the dialog boxes with all the information needed to create the item (see Figure 10-4).

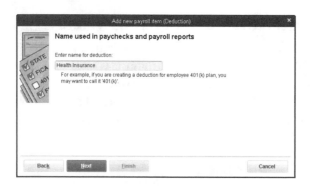

Figure 10-4: The Custom Setup method is the quickest.

CPA TIP: *By default, QuickBooks posts all of the standard tax withholding amounts to the Payroll Liabilities account. For better management of these amounts, it is preferable to set up subaccounts under Payroll Liabilities for the different groups of withholdings (e.g., Form 941, Form 940, State Withholding, State Unemployment, Local #1, Local #2, etc.) and an additional layer of subaccounts that reports each group's components. For example, Form 941 would have subaccounts for FWT, FICA ee, FICA er, Medicare ee, and Medicare er (in which "ee" is employee contribution and "er" is employer contribution). Your Balance Sheet report will then easily display the total amount due for each tax form for you. The Chart of Accounts is best set up before you add payroll items during the setup process, but can be added after the setup process. If they are added after the setup process, you will need to open up your list of payroll items and edit them so that their postings go to the new accounts that you have set up instead of to the generic Payroll Liabilities account.*

CPA Sidebar
Employee Vs. Independent Contractor

Most accountants will tell you that at some point, they've had a conversation with clients who want to hire independent contractors instead of employees. The clients point out that hiring workers as independent contractors is less expensive and less complicated than hiring employees. That's true.

Accountants have to explain that the description of an independent contractor is defined by the IRS, not by the employer. The definition is rather rigid and almost impossible to get around. If the IRS determines that the workers you've paid for years as independent contractors were really employees, the cost of catching up with unpaid liabilities and the attendant interest and penalties could be large enough to destroy your business.

We're not going to go over all the rules and the fine points that the IRS uses in making a determination about a worker's status; instead, we'll give you a brief overview. More information is available on the IRS website (http://www.irs.gov/). The following are some important questions to ask yourself:

Do you have the right to control what the worker does and how the worker does it?

Notice that we said "the right to control," which is not the same as asking, "Do you control?" or "Do you sometimes take the time to control?" Whether you exercise that right isn't the question; it's whether you and the worker both know that you have the right to control the work environment.

If you have the right to control what the worker does and direct how the worker does it, the worker is an employee.

If the worker is an independent contractor, the business has the right to control or direct only the result of the work and has no right to control the way the worker accomplishes the result. You don't set hours, you don't tell the worker where to work, and you don't have any control over the methods used by the worker.

Do you control the business and financial aspects of the worker's job?

The business and financial aspects of a worker's job include payment, providing tools and equipment, and other details (such as reimbursement of expenses).

If you decide the frequency of payment (e.g., you tell the worker, "We issue your check every Friday"), the IRS will probably determine that the worker is an employee. Most independent contractors present a payment schedule for the work they perform. Even if no formal payment schedule is presented, the frequency of payment for an independent contractor is determined by the agreement between you and the independent contractor (and if the payment schedule happens to be the same as your payroll schedule, that's a coincidence).

If you purchase and maintain the tools and equipment used by the worker, the IRS will almost certainly determine that the worker is an employee. Independent contractors usually have their own tools and equipment.

CPA NOTE: *A common "test" includes whether or not the worker can be doing similar work for others while doing work for you—having multiple customers for the same work is the mark of a true independent contractor.*

If you always reimburse the worker for money expended on behalf of the business, the IRS will probably determine the worker is an employee. Usually, independent contractors consider out-of-pocket expenses when they present their rate; they deduct the expenses on their own tax returns. If an independent contractor prefers to be reimbursed by the business, that fact is included in the agreement and the independent contractor usually submits an invoice for the out-of-pocket expenses.

Are your workers requesting independent contractor status?

It doesn't matter. The IRS doesn't care about personal preferences. Neither your workers nor you get to decide based on the perceived financial advantages. If workers want to be deemed independent contractors, they need to perform their work the way independent contractors do. They need to supply their own tools and equipment, maintain those tools and pieces of equipment (and, for some jobs, clothing or uniforms), and make a commitment to getting each job done within a time frame mandated by an agreement between you and them. No more nine-to-five days where the unfinished work can wait until tomorrow.

Many employees who make this request think they'll gain more net funds as independent contractors who operate as a business. They see their gross pay rate and think they'll get to bank and keep that amount. It doesn't work that way. In fact, they often end up with less money than the net pay they receive as employees.

- Federal taxes aren't withheld, but they have to be paid when the independent contractor files taxes. In fact, after the first year, they may have to send quarterly deposits against the federal income tax they'll owe.

- Medicare and social security aren't withheld, but they have to pay it; in fact, they have to pay double the amount of Medicare and social security that they're paying as employees (the employer matching amount is borne by the independent contractor).

- State income tax is due in the same amount it would be due as an employee.

- Local income taxes may be higher than the amount withheld for an employee. Many local taxing authorities levy taxes on business that aren't levied on employees. Usually, local tax authorities that impose wage taxes on employees impose a higher rate on businesses.

You are required to issue your subcontractors 1099s at the end of the year (the subcontractor's equivalent of an employee's W-2) reporting the gross amount paid to the subcontractor. Copies of these forms are submitted to the IRS and, frequently, to the state and local tax authorities, also. There are check-off boxes on your tax return asking whether you were required to issue 1099s and whether you did, in fact, issue them.

IRS publications on employee vs. independent contractor

You can learn more about the differences between employees and independent contractors by reading IRS Publication 1779, "Independent Contractor or Employee." To get this article, enter the following URL in the address bar of your browser: http://www.irs.gov/pub/irs-pdf/p1779.pdf

Both employers and workers can ask the IRS to determine whether a specific individual is an independent contractor or an employee by filing Form SS-8—Determination of Worker Status for Purposes of Federal Employment Taxes and Income Tax Withholding.

You can download Form SS-8 from the IRS web site and mail it after you fill it in or you can fill in the form online. The IRS uses the information in the form to work with you to determine the worker's status. Talk to your accountant before using the form.

Adding Employees in the Employee Center

Once you've determined that you have employees (see the sidebar entitled "Employee Vs. Independent Contractor" earlier in this chapter), you must let QuickBooks know about them. Begin by opening the employee center (Employees | Employee Center) and pressing Ctrl-N to open the New Employee dialog box shown in Figure 10-5.

> **ProAdvisor TIP**: Make sure your Employee Defaults are set up before you start adding new employees. See the section entitled "Configuring Employee Defaults" later in this chapter.

Figure 10-5: If you've enabled manual payroll (no subscription),
you'll see fewer fields than those shown here.

As you can see in Figure 10-5, the New Employee form contains six tabs, each of which holds a different type of information:

- Personal. This is where you record the employee name, social security number, and a bit more personal information. If you have an Enhanced Payroll subscription, you'll see additional fields for disability, work eligibility, and military service.

- Address & Contact. You'll need the employee address when it comes time to print and submit the W-2 forms at year-end. Enter it on this tab.

- Additional Info. There only two things on this tab. The first is the employee ID number (if you use one). The second is custom fields. If you previously created custom fields, they appear here. To create new custom fields, click the Define Fields button.

- Payroll Info. Be sure to fill this one out with accurate information, since QuickBooks pulls the data from here when creating paychecks. You can assign the employee to a payroll schedule, enter the hourly rate or salary, the tax and vacation data, and any deductions you may be withholding from the employee's pay.

- Employment Info. Keep track of when the employee was hired (and fired) and the type of employment assigned.

- Workers' Comp. If you subscribe to the Enhanced Payroll service, this tab appears automatically. However, you still have to activate the feature by enabling the Track Workers Comp option. To locate the option, choose Edit | Preferences | Payroll & Employees | Company Preferences. Now, click the Workers Compensation button to display the Workers Comp Preferences dialog. Finally, check the Track Workers Comp option.

Some businesses hire independent contractors instead of, or in addition to, employees. Independent contractors are paid an amount agreed upon in advance (and often there's a formal written agreement or contract). The independent contractor receives Form 1099 at the end of the year. In this chapter, we also discuss the accounting tasks involved in tracking independent contractors.

Configuring Employee Defaults

You can save yourself a lot of time when adding employees to QuickBooks if you setup the employee defaults ahead of time. Once the defaults are configured, they are automatically applied to each new employee you add. You can accept or change any of the information that QuickBooks adds automatically.

To set the employee defaults, follow these steps:

1. Select Employees | Employee Center to open the Employee Center.
2. Click the Manage Employee Information icon/button and choose Change New Employee Default Settings. This opens the Employee Defaults dialog shown in Figure 10-6.

3. In the Earnings section, choose the most common compensation item.

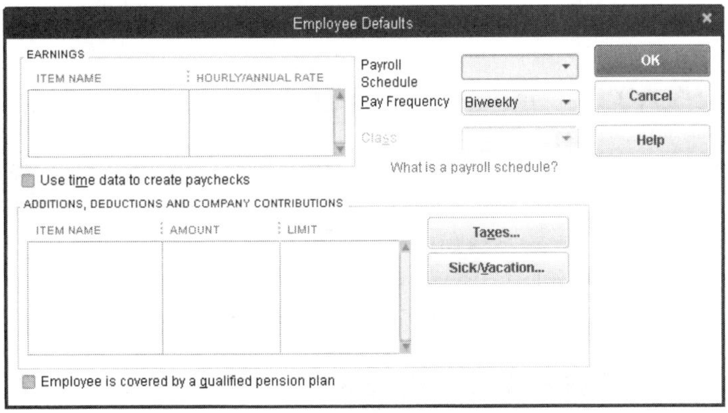

Figure 10-6: Setting up employee defaults can be a great time saver.

4. If you track time with QuickBooks timesheets and use it to create paychecks, check the Use Time Data To Create Paychecks option.

5. Enter the benefits, deductions, and miscellaneous items common to all or most employees in the Additions, Deductions, And Company Contributions section.

6. If you offer a pension plan to all your employees, check the Employee Is Covered By A Qualified Pension Plan option.

7. If you use payroll schedules, select the most common schedule from the Payroll Schedule drop-down list.

8. If you do not use schedules, select the most common pay frequency used from the Pay Frequency drop-down list.

9. Click the Taxes button to add common tax items.

10. Click the Sick/Vacation button to configure the most common accrual scenarios.

11. Click OK to save the defaults.

Although you can create payroll items on the fly while configuring the defaults, it will go a lot faster if you add the payroll items before setting the employee defaults.

Setting Payroll Preferences

Fine-tuning the payroll process is accomplished through the Payroll & Employees preferences. To access the preferences, choose Edit | Preferences to open the Preferences dialog box. Then, click the Payroll & Employees icon in the left pane. Next, click the Company Preferences tab to display the payroll options you can change (see Figure 10-7).

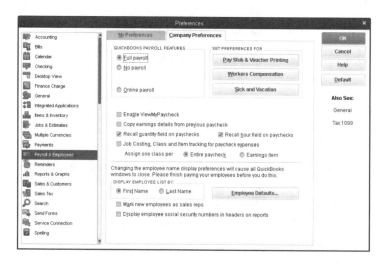

Figure 10-7: Configure the payroll preferences to enhance the payroll process.

The following preferences can be modified to suit your needs:

- **QuickBooks Payroll Features.** Let QuickBooks know that it is running payroll (or not). For manual, Basic, or Enhanced Payroll, choose Full Payroll. Select No Payroll if you're using an outside service or you don't have payroll. If you opted to subscribe to the online payroll service, choose the last option.

- Pay Stub & Voucher Printing. Let QuickBooks know exactly what information you want printed on pay stubs and vouchers.

- Workers Compensation. If you're using Enhanced Payroll and you're liable for Workers Comp, you can let QuickBooks track it for you.

- Sick And Vacation. This opens the Sick And Vacation Defaults dialog so that you can set the defaults for new employees.

- Enable ViewMyPaycheck. You'll only see this option if you subscribe to Enhanced Payroll. It gives employees online access to their current (and historical if you supply it) pay stub information. It's a free service for both you and your employees.

- Copy Earnings Details From Previous Paycheck. Do most of your employees' paychecks stay the same from paycheck to paycheck? If so, enable this option to fill current paychecks with the previous period's data.

- Recall Quantity Field On Paychecks. If you have an Other Payroll Item based on quantity, you can have QuickBooks automatically bring the previous quantity forward. This option works as long as the payroll item is part of the employee record (Payroll Info tab).

- Recall Hour Field On Paychecks. The same as the previous option for payroll items based on quantity.

- Job Costing, Class And Item Tracking For Paycheck Expenses. Use this option to track company-paid payroll expenses by job, class, or service item. The wording of this option changes depending on which other preferences you have enabled. With both time tracking and class tracking enabled, it appears as above. With only one enabled, the option name indicates which is enabled.

- Display Employee List By. How do you want the employee list in the Employee Center sorted?

- Employee Defaults. Click this button to open the Employee Defaults dialog. See the section entitled "Configuring Employee Defaults" earlier in this chapter for details.

- Mark New Employees As Sales Reps. Are most of your new employees sales reps? If so, check this option to have all new employees automatically added to the Sales Rep List (Lists | Customer & Vendor Profile Lists | Sales Rep List).

- Display Employee Social Security Numbers In Headers On Reports. When you generate payroll reports broken down by employee (Payroll Summary, Employee Earnings, etc.), you can elect to have the social security number displayed next to the employee name.

Running QuickBooks Payroll

After you have all your employees, payroll items, and preferences configured, you're ready to run payroll. Depending on the number of employees, the pay frequency, and how you pay them (check or direct deposit), you may opt to create payroll schedules or simply do an unscheduled pay run every pay day.

Creating Payroll Schedules

Payroll schedules let you group employees with the same pay frequency and other criteria into groups for which you can run payroll separately from other employees or groups. For example, if some of your employees are paid weekly and others are paid biweekly, you can create two payroll schedules and run each at the appropriate time. If all your employees are paid at the same frequency, but some receive a paycheck while others have their pay deposited into their bank accounts, you can create a schedule for each group and run one after the other on the day you generate payroll.

To set up a payroll schedule, follow these steps:

1. Choose Employees | Add Or Edit Payroll Schedules to open the Payroll Schedule List.

2. Press Ctrl-N to open the New Payroll Schedule dialog shown in Figure 10-8.

3. Give the schedule a name and select the pay frequency for employees on this schedule. The available options depend on the pay frequency selected.

4. Complete the remaining options, which are self-explanatory.

5. Click OK to save the schedule.

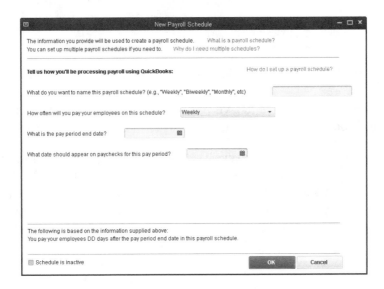

Figure 10-8: Payroll schedules can simplify the payroll process.

Running the Payroll

Once you have added employees and payroll items, you can process payroll in QuickBooks. How you process it depends on the payroll schedules you have set up and what type of payroll check you want to write. You begin by selecting Employees | Pay Employees from the menu bar. If you haven't yet created any payroll schedules, the command opens the Enter Payroll Information dialog seen in Figure 10-9.

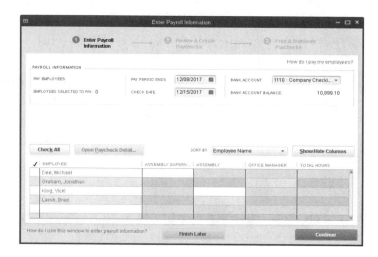

Figure 10-9: The first step in processing payroll is entering the info.

If you have at least one active payroll schedule configured, a submenu with three choices appears.

- **Scheduled Payroll.** Selecting this option opens the Payroll Center, which is the third tab on the Employee Center. It appears as soon as you activate an Intuit payroll subscription. (It does not appear if you use manual payroll without an Intuit subscription.) Once the Payroll Center opens, choose a payroll schedule and click the Start Scheduled Payroll button to open the Enter Payroll Information window.

- **Unscheduled Payroll.** If you have active payroll schedules but want to create a payroll run without using them, choose this option. It immediately opens the Enter Payroll Information window and displays all employees, regardless of their payroll schedule status.

- **Termination Check.** Use this option to create an immediate check when you terminate an employee. It brings up the Enter Payroll Information window with all employees. Choose the employee being terminated, enter the release date, and create the check.

Regardless of how you get there, running payroll (with or without schedules) is the same. When the Enter Payroll Information window appears, follow these steps:

1. Set the header fields for the payroll run:
   - Pay Period Ends. This is the last date included in the payroll run. If you pay your employees weekly and the week ends on Friday, use Friday's date.
   - Check Date. Enter the date that the payroll is actually being created. For example, if the payroll ends on Friday, but you don't print and hand out the checks until the following Wednesday, use Wednesday's date.
   - Bank Account. If you have more than one bank account (it's a good idea to have a separate payroll account), make sure you select the account you use for payroll.

2. Check the employee(s) that you want to include in this payroll run.

3. Enter the hours worked for hourly employees (and salaried employees, if you need to track their hours as well).

4. To preview a paycheck before moving on, click the employee name to display the Preview Paycheck window with details of all earnings, additions, and deductions.

5. Click Continue to assign check numbers and to review the paycheck information one last time.

6. Click Create Paychecks to generate the checks and open the Confirmation And Next Steps dialog.

7. For those employees who have their paychecks direct deposited, you can print pay stubs only. Click the Print Pay Stubs button, select the paychecks, and click Print (or Email). Click Close to return to the Confirmation And Next Steps dialog box.

8. Click the Print Paychecks button to send the checks to the printer.

9. Click Close to finish the run.

Understanding Payroll Accounting

The payroll process includes creating paychecks, tracking the liabilities and employer expenses related to those paychecks, and remitting those liabilities and employer expenses. A great many postings to your general ledger take place as you perform these tasks. Even if you don't do your own payroll, you have to track those postings in your books (using the reports from your outside payroll company).

In the following sections, we'll go over the accounting details that most business owners question their accountants about when they see Payroll reports, Profit & Loss reports, Balance Sheet reports, and tax returns.

Gross and Net Pay

Everyone knows the difference between gross pay and net pay: Gross pay is your pay rate, and net pay is the amount of your paycheck after all the deductions.

What's the difference in terms of your accounting books? Even if you outsource your payroll, you have to enter the financial data in your books. Where and how do all the amounts get recorded? What else gets recorded? What's deductible on your tax return?

Gross Pay

Gross pay is the total due to an employee based on his/her pay rate before any deductions. Gross pay is the amount you post to the expense account for salaries and wages. It doesn't matter how much money the employee actually receives, the gross pay is the tax-deductible expense and is usually posted to an expense account named Salaries & Wages.

If your business is a corporation, you must separate the gross-pay expense for officers from the gross-pay entry for all other employees. A corporation's Chart of Accounts needs two expense accounts to track gross pay:

- Salaries—Officers
- Salaries & Wages—Other

Net Pay

Net pay is the amount of the paycheck an employee receives, and it's the gross pay less the deductions. The amount of money deducted from employees' paychecks might stay in your bank account (albeit, not for long), but you can't spend it because it isn't your money. These are your payroll liabilities, and you have to remit the money to other entities.

CPA NOTE: *Net pay isn't posted to any payroll expense account; instead, it's posted to the bank account you use for payroll (as a check or as a direct deposit).*

In addition to the money withheld from employees' checks, there are payments related to payroll that you have to send to other entities (covered in the following sections of this chapter). These are your payroll expenses.

CPA NOTE: *The money you spend on an outside payroll company isn't a payroll expense; it's an operating expense.*

When you post your payroll, net pay is posted to the bank account. It's a credit to the bank account because it reduces the bank account balance. Table 10-1 is a simplified (actually, over-simplified) view of the way net pay is posted; the deductions and their postings are discussed in the following sections of this chapter.

Account	Debit	Credit
60000—Salaries & Wages	5000.00	
20100—Deductions from paychecks		2100.00
10500—Payroll bank account		2900.00

Table 10-1: The net pay is a credit to the bank account.

Payroll Liabilities

Payroll liabilities are defined the same way all liabilities are defined: A liability is something you have in your possession that doesn't belong to you; you're holding it for someone else. In this case, we refer to these liabilities as payroll liabilities.

All employers incur payroll liabilities for government agencies. Some employers also incur payroll liabilities for non-government entities such as insurance companies. The non-government liabilities depend on the benefits you provide for employees.

Payroll Liabilities for Tax Withholding

Government liabilities are those liabilities that are remitted to government agencies. The remittance always includes a form, even if the payment is remitted online. Your government payroll liabilities include the money withheld from employee paychecks as well as money due from you as the employer. The employer portion is turned into an expense and is covered in the section "Payroll Expenses." The liabilities for withholdings (called trust fund taxes) include some or all of the following:

- Federal income tax withheld from paychecks.
- Social security withheld from paychecks.
- Medicare withheld from paychecks.
- State income tax withheld from paychecks (if applicable).
- State unemployment tax withheld from paychecks (if applicable).
- State disability tax withheld from paychecks (if applicable).
- Local income tax withheld from paychecks (if applicable).

Social security withholdings have a limit; once the employee reaches a maximum gross pay for the year, social security is no longer withheld. (The maximum gross pay amount changes yearly.)

Some state taxes for unemployment and disability have a yearly maximum gross pay limit, after which tax is no longer due. Sometimes the limit is only applied to the employee, while other states apply a limit only to the employer (a payroll expense).

Payroll Liabilities for Employee Benefits

In addition to government liabilities, the benefits you provide employees may involve deductions from their paychecks. The withheld funds are sent to the applicable vendor, usually an insurance company and pension plan provider. The following are some of the common withholdings for benefits that small businesses offer:

- Contribution to medical benefits withheld.
- Contribution to retirement plan withheld.
- Contribution to health/legal savings plan withheld.

The company may also contribute to these benefits, and those contributions are posted as expenses (which is covered later in this chapter).

Other Withholding Liabilities

In addition to withholdings for taxes and benefits, your employees may have money withheld for other reasons. The two common withholding categories that are neither taxes nor benefits are

- Contributions to charitable organizations.
- Garnishments.

Withholding for Charitable Contributions

If your employees have contributions withheld for a charitable organization, you remit the donation periodically. Many businesses offer a matching amount (or a partial match) to these withheld funds, and those matching funds are an expense (posted to Charitable Contributions).

Withholding for Garnishments

A garnishment is a legal obligation owed by an employee that puts you in the middle of the employee's personal affairs. Garnishments are complicated and time consuming to administer, but they can't be avoided. If a garnishment order is delivered (paperwork is received from a federal, state, or local agency), employers are required to collect the garnished amount and remit it to the appropriate agency on behalf of the employee.

If you have a garnishment order for any employee and you post all your payroll liabilities to a single payroll liabilities account, don't include the garnishment in that posting; instead, create a specific payroll liability account for garnishments, or you'll drive yourself crazy tracking the remittances. If you use specific payroll liability accounts for each type of liability (which we suggest), add an account for garnishments.

Payroll Expenses

Payroll expenses are the payments due from the employer. Like liabilities connected to the withholding from paychecks, most of the expenses are sent to government agencies, and they vary depending on the state and local jurisdiction in which you do business. Employer expenses can also include non-government expenses, depending on the benefits you provide. Employer expenses commonly include the following:

- Matching payments for the social security withheld from paychecks
- Matching payments for the Medicare withheld from paychecks
- Federal unemployment tax (FUTA)
- State unemployment employer's tax (if applicable)
- State disability employer's tax (if applicable)
- Local employer tax (if applicable)
- Employer's contribution to benefits (if applicable)
- Workers' compensation insurance (if applicable)

CPA NOTE: *Employer payroll expenses are also called payroll burden.*

Payroll Expenses are Really Liabilities

Because payroll expenses are required expenses and are tied to the payroll, they're really payroll liabilities. You post these amounts as liabilities, but they end up as expenses, as you'll see in the following sections, in which we explain how your payroll is posted to the general ledger.

Posting Payroll Liabilities

Payroll liabilities are posted to payroll liability accounts, which are Other Current Liabilities. Some businesses post all liabilities to a single account named Payroll Liabilities. Other businesses post each liability to its own account (see Figure 10-10).

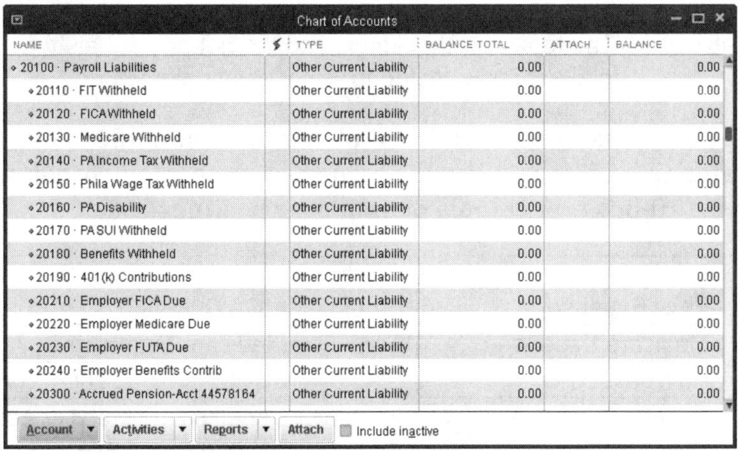

NAME		TYPE	BALANCE TOTAL	ATTACH	BALANCE
◆ 20100 · Payroll Liabilities		Other Current Liability	0.00		0.00
◆ 20110 · FIT Withheld		Other Current Liability	0.00		0.00
◆ 20120 · FICA Withheld		Other Current Liability	0.00		0.00
◆ 20130 · Medicare Withheld		Other Current Liability	0.00		0.00
◆ 20140 · PA Income Tax Withheld		Other Current Liability	0.00		0.00
◆ 20150 · Phila Wage Tax Withheld		Other Current Liability	0.00		0.00
◆ 20160 · PA Disability		Other Current Liability	0.00		0.00
◆ 20170 · PA SUI Withheld		Other Current Liability	0.00		0.00
◆ 20180 · Benefits Withheld		Other Current Liability	0.00		0.00
◆ 20190 · 401(k) Contributions		Other Current Liability	0.00		0.00
◆ 20210 · Employer FICA Due		Other Current Liability	0.00		0.00
◆ 20220 · Employer Medicare Due		Other Current Liability	0.00		0.00
◆ 20230 · Employer FUTA Due		Other Current Liability	0.00		0.00
◆ 20240 · Employer Benefits Contrib		Other Current Liability	0.00		0.00
◆ 20300 · Accrued Pension-Acct 44578164		Other Current Liability	0.00		0.00

Figure 10-10: This Chart of Accounts tracks specific payroll liabilities.

If you do your own payroll, the liabilities are posted by QuickBooks as you create the paychecks. If you have a payroll service, you use the report from the payroll service to post the liabilities by creating a journal entry. Table 10-2 represents the postings for the paychecks.

Account	Debit	Credit
60000—Salaries & Wages	Total Salaries and Wages	
20110—Fed Withholding Liability Account		Total Withheld
20120—Social Security (FICA) Liability Account		Total Withheld
20130—Medicare Liability Account		Total Withheld
20140—State Income Tax Liability Account		Total Withheld
20150—Local Income Tax Liability Account		Total Withheld
20160—State Disability Liability Account		Total Withheld
20170—State SUI Liability Account		Total Withheld
20180—Benefits Contrib Liability Account		Total Withheld
20190—401(k) Contrib Liability Account		Total Withheld
10500—Payroll Bank Account		Total Net Pay

Table 10-2: The total of withholdings and the net pay equals the total expense posted for salaries and wages.

In addition, QuickBooks and payroll service companies post the employer liabilities using the payroll expense account as the other side of the ledger. Table 10-3 is an example of employer postings.

Debit	Credit
20210—FICA Expense	Employer FICA Due Liability Account
20220—Medicare Expense	Employer Medicare Due Liability Account
20230—FUTA expense	Employer FUTA Due Liability Account
20240—Benefits Expense	Employer Benefits Due Liability Account
20300—Pension Expense	Employer 401(k) Due Liability Account

Table 10-3: Postings for employer payroll liabilities and expenses.

Paying Payroll Liabilities

If you are running manual or basic payroll, you'll have to run the payroll liability report (Reports | Employees & Payroll | Payroll Liability

Balances) to determine your liabilities, then fill out the appropriate forms
and submit them. If, on the other hand, you subscribe to the Enhanced
Payroll service, QuickBooks will track the liabilities and fill out the
forms for you. If you subscribe to the Full Service payroll, the forms
are automatically completed and submitted for you. For the rest of this
exercise, we are going to assume that you're subscribed to the Enhanced
Payroll service.

To pay your payroll liabilities:

1. Choose Employees | Payroll Taxes And Liabilities | Pay
   Scheduled Liabilities to open the Pay Liabilities tab of the
   Payroll Center (see Figure 10-11).

Figure 10-11: The Pay Liabilities tab lists all payroll liabilities
currently due.

2. In the Pay Taxes & Other Liabilities section, check the
   individual liabilities you want to pay and click the View/
   Pay button to create the check. A separate check is
   created for each liability selected.

3. Double-check the bank account, payee, and other
   important information.

ProAdvisor TIP: *If you have a separate bank account for payroll, be sure to set it as the default account for payroll liabilities. Open the Preferences dialog box and select the Checking category in the left pane and the Company Preferences tab in the right. Check the Open The Pay Payroll Liabilities Form With option and choose the payroll account from the drop-down list.*

4. Click Save & Close (Save & Next if you're paying more than one liability) to create the check(s) and open the Payment Summary window.

5. Click the Print Checks button to open the Select Checks to Print dialog.

6. Select the payroll account in the Bank Account drop-down list and enter the correct check number in the First Check Number field.

7. If other checks appear, only select the liability checks that get paid from the payroll account.

8. Click OK to open the Print Checks dialog.

9. Select the printer, printer settings, and check style.

10. Click Print to send the checks to the printer.

Posting Payroll Liability Payments

When you remit the payments to government agencies, insurance companies, pension plans, and so on, the postings "wash" (zero out) the amounts in the liability accounts. If you have a payroll service that remits your payments, you enter those transactions as a journal entry. Table 10-4 shows the postings for remitting a federal liability payment.

The same posting pattern occurs when you remit checks to other government agencies and to non-government vendors. You post to the liability accounts, and those postings remove ("wash") the liabilities.

Note that both the employee (withholding) and employer (expense) liabilities are "washed," but nothing touches the postings you made to the employer expenses. Those expenses remain and appear on your Profit & Loss report, and they are deductions on your tax return.

Account	Debit	Credit
10500—Payroll Bank Account		3824.00
20110—FIT Withheld	2600.00	
20210—Employer FICA Due	496.00	
20120—FICA Withheld	496.00	
20220—Employer Medicare Due	116.00	
20130—Medicare Withheld	116.00	

Table 10-4: Postings for remittance of federal payroll liabilities.

Working with Independent Contractors

All independent contractors, consultants, and other self-employed workers who perform work for you must fill out Form W-9–Request for Taxpayer Identification Number and Certification. This form provides you with the information you need to create Form 1099.

CPA TIP: *Make it company policy to not issue any payments to independent contractors until you have received their signed Form W-9s.*

You don't send Form W-9 to the IRS; you keep it in your files. You can get Form W-9 from the IRS by entering the following URL into your browser's address bar: http://www.irs.gov/pub/irs-pdf/fw9.pdf. When the file opens, save it to your hard drive or print it for distribution to independent contractors.

Posting payments to independent contractors isn't complicated; most of the time, you post the checks to an expense account named Subcontractors or Outside Services. However, for those independent contractors who receive Form 1099, you have to make sure you have the information you need to create and send the 1099s. This means that you have to set up your accounting components properly and post payments to match your 1099 setup. See Chapter 12 for more on generating and sending 1099s at year-end.

Reimbursing Independent Contractors for Expenses

If an independent contractor purchases something for your business as part of the job, it's normal to include reimbursable expenses in the check you send without separating out those expenses. You post the entire check to Outside Services (or whatever you've named the expense account for paying independent contractors). The independent contractor tracks the total amount of the check as income and indicates the expenses on his or her own tax return.

Some businesses and some independent contractors prefer to treat out-of-pocket outlays for the business as expenses to the business that should be reimbursed separately from payments for work.

If you adopt this approach for an independent contractor, posting the payment is slightly different, because the expense is your expense rather than the independent contractor's expense. When you pay the contractor, create a split transaction. As seen in Table 10-5, post the reimbursed expense to the applicable expense account in your Chart of Accounts and post the payment for work to the expense you use for outside services.

Account	Debit	Credit
64000—Outside Services	5000.00	
61500—Office Supplies	250.00	
10000—Bank account		5250.00

Table 10-5: You can split a payment to an independent contractor
to separate reimbursements from payments for work.

You have to be sure that the expense account you use in this situation is not linked to your 1099 configuration. That way, the amount posted for services is carried to the 1099, but the amount for reimbursement is not.

ProAdvisor TIP: *When entering a bill or writing a check that includes reimbursed expenses, you can use both the Expenses tab and the Items tab to record the 1099 expense and the reimbursed expense(s).*

CHAPTER 11:

Understanding & Customizing Important Reports

- Balance Sheet Reports
- Profit & Loss Reports
- Accounts Receivable Reports
- Accounts Payable Reports
- Inventory Reports
- Customizing Reports

Business owners should examine financial reports frequently, because reports are the key to gauging the financial health of a business. It's important to understand what data is in each type of report and what the data means. Accountants constantly receive questions from clients who don't understand why certain accounts aren't listed on certain reports or why accounts that appear on the reports have balances they don't understand. We've gathered a list of some of the most common questions of this type, and we'll include answers to those questions as we explain the important financial reports you should be keeping an eye on.

Balance Sheet

The balance sheet (see Figure 11-1) is a snapshot of your financial position at a particular moment in time. By "particular moment in time," we mean the date you choose when you create the report, which could be the current date or the last day of the previous year, quarter, or month.

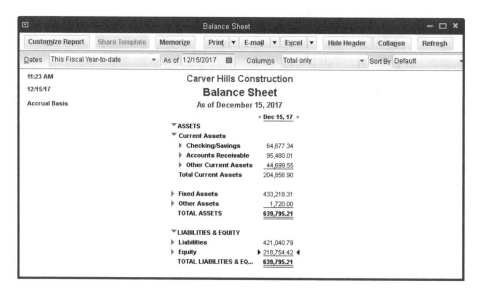

Figure 11-1: The Balance Sheet report at its most basic. Click a triangle to expand the category.

CPA NOTE: *Another term for balance sheet is statement of financial position.*

The balance sheet is the primary "health record" for your business. It shows what your business owns, what it owes to others, and its equity (a combination of owners/stockholders investments and the company's accumulated profit/loss). The balance sheet has two traits you have to be aware of:

- The word "balance" means that the numbers must balance using the formula **assets = liabilities + equity**.

- The totals in the balance sheet reflect the entire life of your business. The numbers roll on from year to year; they don't start fresh each year. Each account displays the "net balance" of all activity in that account since Day One.

Because the balance sheet has such important information about your company's financial health, it's usually the report that bankers want to see first when you apply for a loan. Investors (or potential investors) also typically start their investigations by looking at the balance sheet. For public corporations that have to make financial reports available to stockholders, the balance sheet is the first report investors want to see because the value of their ownership is reflected in the equity section of this report.

QuickBooks Balance Sheet Reports

Because the Balance Sheet report is so important, QuickBooks offers four different predefined versions.

- Balance Sheet Standard
- Balance Sheet Detail
- Balance Sheet Summary
- Balance Sheet Prev Year Comparison

Each report shows the same basic data, but in a different configuration.

Balance Sheet Standard Report

The Balance Sheet Standard report seen in Figure 11-2 is a cross between the Summary and Detail reports. It provides totals for all the individual accounts that are included in the report. Unlike the Balance Sheet Detail report, it does not display all the transactions for each account.

Figure 11-2: The standard report provides more detail than the summary report and less than the detail report.

Balance Sheet Detail Report

This one is for the terminally curious. As you can see in Figure 11-3, it lists every transaction generated for every account that appears on the report. It's not one you're going to run every day, but when you need to dig that deep, you'll be glad to have it.

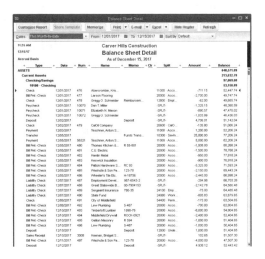

Figure 11-3: When you have to get down to the nitty-gritty, the
Balance Sheet Detail report does the job.

Balance Sheet Summary Report

When all you're looking for is a quick overview of your company's health,
run the Balance Sheet Summary report (see Figure 11-4). It provides
totals for each balance sheet category (Assets, Liabilities, and Equity), but
not for the individual accounts in the categories.

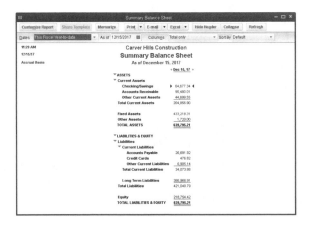

Figure 11-4: For the basic numbers, run the Balance Sheet
Summary report.

Balance Sheet Prev Year Comparison Report

After your first year in business, it's always helpful to see how you're doing compared to last year. That's where the Balance Sheet Prev Year Comparison report (see Figure 11-5) comes in. In addition to providing totals, it also displays both dollar and percentage change amounts.

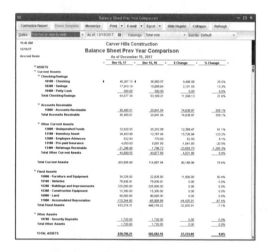

Figure 11-5: How does this year measure up to last year?

Balance Sheet Assets

What your business owns is displayed in the Assets section of your balance sheet (refer back to Figure 11-2).

Some of the accounts in the assets section of the balance sheet raise questions in the minds of business owners, and this is a good place to go over some of the most common questions that accountants receive.

Balance Sheet Bank Accounts

The balance sheet shows the bank balances in your bank registers as of the date of the balance sheet. Usually, the balance sheet is created for the last day of a year, quarter, or month.

If you have a copy of your bank statement for the same period, the bank's balance is almost certainly different from the balance on your Balance Sheet report. Many business owners call their accountants to get an explanation for the fact that their balance sheet amount and the closing amount on the bank's statement don't match.

Your bank register balance reflects all the activity in the bank account—every check you wrote and every deposit you entered. The bank statement reflects all the transactions you created that have cleared the bank. It does not include checks that haven't yet been deposited by the payees, and it does not reflect deposits you made that didn't clear the bank in time for the statement (usually, these are deposits made on the last or next-to-last day before the statement closing date or credit card payments that your merchant account doesn't deposit for a few days).

Eventually, those checks and deposits that weren't included in the bank's closing balance clear, but the bank's balance still won't "catch up" in the next statement because you'll have written more checks and made more deposits that didn't clear before you get the next statement.

Balance Sheet Fixed Assets Accounts

The purchase of fixed assets is posted to its own account (Fixed Asset-Purchases or Fixed Asset-Cost), and the depreciation is posted separately to its own contra-account (Accumulated Depreciation-Fixed Asset).

The balance sheet displays both posting totals and reports the current net value of the fixed assets. The history of the individual fixed assets within a category is usually kept in a separate schedule in order to keep the balance sheet presentation clean.

Some accountants and business owners prefer to consolidate the cost and accumulated depreciation into a single account for each type of fixed asset. In that case, the balance sheet displays the net value (cost less accumulated depreciation) in its fixed assets section.

If your fixed assets are posted to a single account for each category and the value of each category changes from year to year, it's because purchases, dispositions, and depreciation are posted to that single account and are included in the total you see. (Dispositions are assets that have either been sold or scrapped because they are no longer usable. Because the balance sheet assets include only things you own, ask your accountant how to remove these assets from your books.)

If you use a single account instead of separate accounts for purchases and depreciation, the displayed total is the current net value. The arithmetic is the same no matter how you set up your Chart of Accounts for fixed assets; the difference is only in the details that are displayed in the report.

Balance Sheet Other Assets Accounts

While fixed assets are tangible (you can touch them), you may have other assets that are intangible with a value that will last for more than one year.

Record these intangible assets similarly to the way you record fixed assets. It's best to have one account listing the original cost and a separate account (a contra-account) listing the accumulated amortization. Amortization is the term for the periodic writing down of intangible assets, and it's the same process as applying depreciation to fixed assets. (Amortization is covered in Chapter 12.)

These other assets are normally displayed below the fixed assets in the balance sheet, just before the total for all assets owned. Common other assets are

- Start Up Costs,
- Goodwill,
- Copyrights and Patents.

CPA NOTE: *The value of fixed assets and intangible assets on the balance sheet is the result of tracking your transactions, including the original cost and the accumulated depreciation/ amortization (figures are not related to current market value).*

Balance Sheet Liabilities and Equity

The section of the balance sheet that displays liabilities and equity looks similar to Figure 11-6. Notice that the total at the bottom matches the total for assets.

Figure 11-6: Liabilities plus equities must equal assets.

Some of the categories and accounts in this section of the balance sheet can also cause confusion, so in this section, we'll go over some of the most common questions accountants receive.

Balance Sheet Sales Tax Liability Account

Sales tax liabilities cause questions from business owners and also cause problems in accounting data files that accountants have to clean up (and sometimes, the cleanup isn't a cakewalk). In terms of the process, tracking sales tax is very logical.

- When you collect sales tax, you post the sales tax amount to a liability account (usually named Sales Tax Payable). Configuring sales tax is covered in Chapter 3.

- When you remit sales tax, you post the payment to the same liability account to reduce the balance. Remitting sales tax is covered in Chapter 9. If you remit sales tax monthly on the 10th day of the following month, the amount of sales tax displayed on your balance sheet on the 11th day of the month should be equal to the sales tax collected in the current month on days 1 through 11 (the balance left after you remit the previous month's tax).

However, many accountants find very large balances in the sales tax liability account (or business owners call to say the balance is way too large). How does this happen? The most common reason for this problem is that the client used the Write Checks window rather than the Pay Sales Tax feature in QuickBooks to create the payment, failing to "wash" the sales tax liability account.

Balance Sheet Loan Liability Accounts

A business sends a payment for a loan every month. Periodically, the bank sends a statement of the current loan balance. The bank's loan balance doesn't match the balance displayed on the balance sheet; the bank's loan balance is higher than the loan balance on your balance sheet. The business owner calls the accountant to get an explanation for the difference.

This happens when you post the entire loan payment to the loan liability account. Loans have interest, and the interest has to be posted separately from the payment to principal (interest is a deductible business expense and is posted to an expense account named Interest Expense). Instructions for creating transactions for loan payments are in Chapter 9.

Similar to the difference between the bank balance on the balance sheet and your bank statement, the difference between the loan balance on the balance sheet and the monthly statement may be a timing difference (a payment made late in the month is not reflected on the statement), or it may be that you failed to enter a monthly interest charge (so it is on the statement, but not reflected in your books, and needs to be recorded to correct your books).

Profit & Loss Report

The Profit & Loss report (nicknamed the P & L) shown in Figure 11-7 is the report that the majority of business owners rely on most (and look at most often). Choose Reports | Company & Financial | Profit & Loss Standard to run it. This report displays all your income accounts and their balances, all your expense accounts and their balances, and your net profit or loss. Like the balance sheet, the P & L has a formula: **Net Profit/Loss = Income – Expenses**.

CPA NOTE: *The Profit & Loss report is also called the Income Statement or the Statement of Operations.*

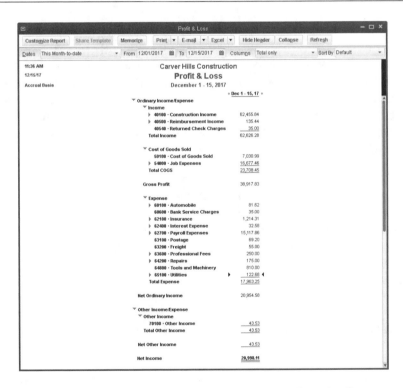

Figure 11-7: Your profit/loss is the last item in a P&L—the "bottom line."

Net Profit or Loss

Business owners and accountants usually move their eyes immediately to the bottom entry, Net Income, which is the net profit/loss. Note that this figure is the same as the Net Income figure in the Equity section of the balance sheet.

Your net profit on the P & L is part of your company's equity on the balance sheet when the two reports are created to show the entire year (which is really year-to-date when you create the report before the last day of the year). If you create a P & L report for a specific period (such as a month or a quarter), the P & L report profit/loss figure won't match the amount on the balance sheet report (which always displays year-to-date totals) unless you customize the report to show the same dates.

Unlike the balance sheet, which reflects the entire life of your business (the numbers roll over from year to year), the P & L report starts all over on the first day of your fiscal year. At the end of your fiscal year, the amount of the net profit/loss is transferred to the balance sheet and all the income and expense accounts are zeroed out. As you create transactions that post to income and expense accounts, the P & L rebuilds itself for the current year. QuickBooks takes care of this automatically when you run the year-end.

ProAdvisor NOTE: *Using the fiscal year entered in your Company Information window (Company | Company Information), QuickBooks automatically zeroes out your income and expense accounts at the end of the (fiscal) year. In addition, it automatically transfers your net income to retained earnings.*

Analyzing Your Business from the Profit & Loss Report

It's tempting to look at your P & L report and think, "I could increase my net profit if I increased my income and/or reduced my expenses." Unfortunately, it's not usually that simple.

You can increase your income by raising prices or by increasing the size of your customer base. Raising prices is a high-risk decision, because you could lose customers to your competition. If you lose enough customers, the higher prices result in less profit. The risk in increasing your customer base is that more customers and the higher volume of product sales also increase expenses, especially variable expenses.

There are different types of expenses, and you have to do your analysis with an understanding of their meanings. Basically, there are two types of expenses in your P & L report: *Variable expenses* and *fixed expenses.*

Variable expenses are those expenses that are directly affected by (and linked to) sales. Providing products requires raw materials, labor, space, shipping, commissions, and other expenses. (These are the expenses that are usually posted to Cost of Goods Sold.) Selling one more widget means paying for all of the costs to get one more widget on your shelf.

Fixed expenses are the expenses that are fairly consistent because they don't vary widely as a result of a change in sales figures. These are the fundamental overhead costs such as insurance, rent, and utilities. Fixed expenses are sometimes listed in the P & L report as General and Administrative Costs.

Some experts add a third category of expenses, called *discretionary expenses*, which includes wages, benefits, and other expenses that may be administrative, but can be changed to meet the needs of the company.

Many management consultants and small business experts warn that one of the largest causes of failure for a small business is the inability to manage growth. These businesses expand their customer base or product line (or both) and then don't have sufficient resources to handle the growth. Original customers don't get the attention they're used to and new customers don't get the attention they expect unless more employees are brought onboard. If there isn't sufficient capital to add employees, the customers start shopping elsewhere. The widgets you need to have on hand to sell to those new customers require capital, because usually you have to pay your vendor before your new customers pay you. Many businesses can't recover economically from the increased costs of producing more goods if the time period before those goods are sold is lengthy.

Accounts Receivable Report

The A/R reports show you how much money is owed by each customer and how long the unpaid invoices have been languishing. The length of time that money remains unpaid is called *aging*. Often referred to as "money on the street," a large balance in your A/R report can have a serious effect on your ability to continue operations. QuickBooks offers two A/R Aging Reports:

- A/R Aging Summary. This report (see Figure 11-8) displays each customer and job that has an A/R balance and shows both the current balances and the overdue balances. Overdue balances are sorted in columns by the amount of time the balance is overdue (1–30 days, 31–60 days, 61–90 days, and >90 days). This report is a good way to get a quick look at the amount of "money on the street."
- A/R Aging Detail. If you want to see all the transactions that make up your A/R balance, run this report. It breaks them down by aging category, starting with Current and working up to >90.

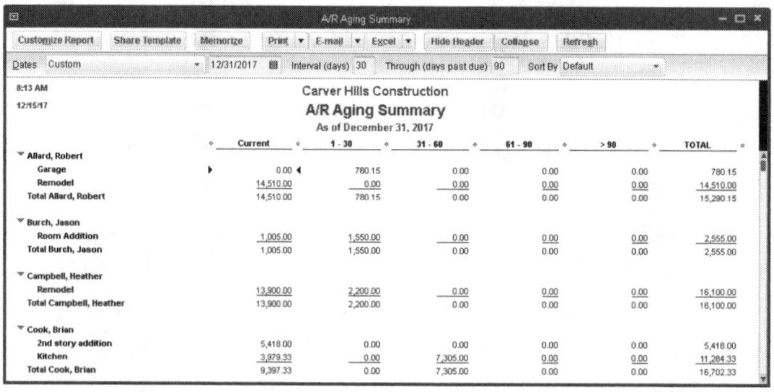

Carver Hills Construction
A/R Aging Summary
As of December 31, 2017

	Current	1 - 30	31 - 60	61 - 90	> 90	TOTAL
Allard, Robert						
Garage	0.00	780.15	0.00	0.00	0.00	780.15
Remodel	14,510.00	0.00	0.00	0.00	0.00	14,510.00
Total Allard, Robert	14,510.00	780.15	0.00	0.00	0.00	15,290.15
Burch, Jason						
Room Addition	1,005.00	1,550.00	0.00	0.00	0.00	2,555.00
Total Burch, Jason	1,005.00	1,550.00	0.00	0.00	0.00	2,555.00
Campbell, Heather						
Remodel	13,900.00	2,200.00	0.00	0.00	0.00	16,100.00
Total Campbell, Heather	13,900.00	2,200.00	0.00	0.00	0.00	16,100.00
Cook, Brian						
2nd story addition	5,418.00	0.00	0.00	0.00	0.00	5,418.00
Kitchen	3,979.33	0.00	7,305.00	0.00	0.00	11,284.33
Total Cook, Brian	9,397.33	0.00	7,305.00	0.00	0.00	16,702.33

Figure 11-8: Keep an eye on your receivables to ensure that you have a healthy cash position.

The best use of these reports is to develop a plan to contact the customers with the oldest and/or largest balances and make an effort to collect the money owed to you. You should also think about setting credit limits for customers who traditionally hold your money for a long time; once the credit limit is reached, orders must be paid for in advance or sent COD.

Too many business owners are reluctant to "cut off" customers who have owed a lot of money for a long time by insisting on advance payments or just refusing to continue to provide products or services until the customer has caught up. These owners are afraid that if they cut off a customer, they lose all chance of recovering the money currently owed. Many of these owners end up mired in customer debt, because these customers really aren't going to catch up, whether you continue to provide goods and services or not. Once it's obvious that a customer doesn't pay your invoices, stop selling to them (except for cash sales).

ProAdvisor TIP*: If you find that your A/R reports contain transaction listings for customers that have a zero balance, there's an easy solution. These customers have at least one credit transaction and one unpaid invoice transaction. Even though the balance is zero as a result of the arithmetic, when you add open balances and subtract credits, the transactions exist. You have to apply the credit to the invoice in the Receive Payments window, and then those individual transactions will no longer cause the customer to appear on QuickBooks A/R reports.*

Proving the A/R Report Total against the Balance Sheet

When you create an A/R report, make sure you also create a Balance Sheet report with the same date for both reports. The total aging in the A/R report must match the A/R amount on the balance sheet. If the amounts don't match, you must find out why. The following are some useful methods to track down the problem:

Change the date range of both reports, going back to the last day of the month prior to the date you originally selected for the reports.

- If the account totals match, you know that your problem is in the month ending on the original date for the reports.

- If the account totals don't match, go back another month (or several months) until you find a month-end date where the totals match. Your problem is in transactions later than that date.

- If you can't find any month in the recent past where the totals match, call your accountant for advice.

In the "problem month(s)," look for journal entries that contain a posting to the A/R account. Those amounts will be part of the A/R total on the balance sheet, but shouldn't show up in the A/R Aging report because the A/R Aging report is a report on transactions that went to sales journals and cash receipts journals. (The aging report is built up from transaction journals, not down from amounts in the general ledger.)

Make sure you haven't changed the report basis or set any customized settings for either the balance sheet or the A/R aging report to filter the report in any way.

Accounts Payable Report

The Accounts Payable (A/P) report displays all the vendor bills you've entered into your system that you haven't yet paid. The report also displays the length of time that each bill has remained unpaid.

QuickBooks provides plenty of A/P Reports that are useful for tracking the state of the money you owe. Select Reports | Vendors & Payables and choose the appropriate report from the submenu.

The commonly used A/P report is the Aging Summary Report shown in Figure 11-9, which provides a quick look at the state of your payables. The report lists each vendor for which unpaid bills exist and sorts the totals by 30-day intervals. You can double-click any total to drill down to see the original transactions.

Use this report to determine which bills should be paid if you don't have enough cash on hand to pay all your bills. The decision is based as much on your relationship with, or need for, vendors as on the amount of the balance due.

As with A/R, the total amount of A/P must equal the A/P amount displayed on the balance sheet for the same date. If the totals don't match, use the suggestions in the previous section on A/R to troubleshoot the problem.

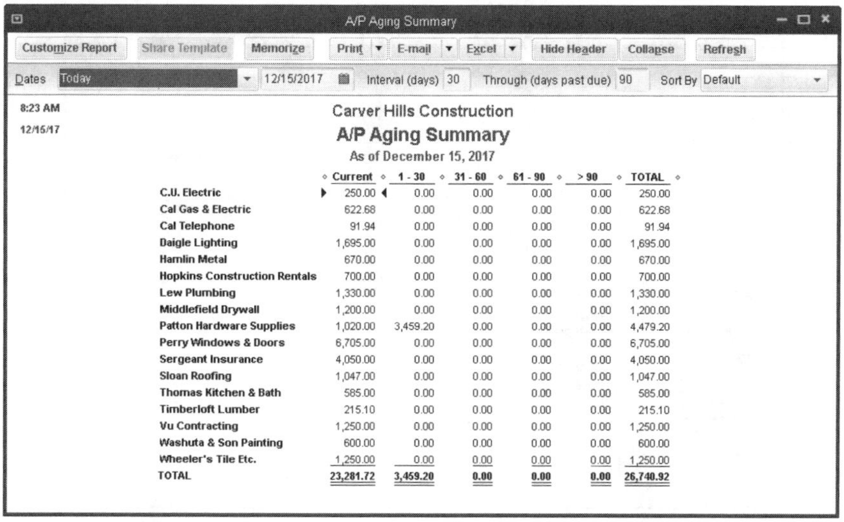

	Current	1 - 30	31 - 60	61 - 90	> 90	TOTAL
C.U. Electric	250.00	0.00	0.00	0.00	0.00	250.00
Cal Gas & Electric	622.68	0.00	0.00	0.00	0.00	622.68
Cal Telephone	91.94	0.00	0.00	0.00	0.00	91.94
Daigle Lighting	1,695.00	0.00	0.00	0.00	0.00	1,695.00
Hamlin Metal	670.00	0.00	0.00	0.00	0.00	670.00
Hopkins Construction Rentals	700.00	0.00	0.00	0.00	0.00	700.00
Lew Plumbing	1,330.00	0.00	0.00	0.00	0.00	1,330.00
Middlefield Drywall	1,200.00	0.00	0.00	0.00	0.00	1,200.00
Patton Hardware Supplies	1,020.00	3,459.20	0.00	0.00	0.00	4,479.20
Perry Windows & Doors	6,705.00	0.00	0.00	0.00	0.00	6,705.00
Sergeant Insurance	4,050.00	0.00	0.00	0.00	0.00	4,050.00
Sloan Roofing	1,047.00	0.00	0.00	0.00	0.00	1,047.00
Thomas Kitchen & Bath	585.00	0.00	0.00	0.00	0.00	585.00
Timberloft Lumber	215.10	0.00	0.00	0.00	0.00	215.10
Vu Contracting	1,250.00	0.00	0.00	0.00	0.00	1,250.00
Washuta & Son Painting	600.00	0.00	0.00	0.00	0.00	600.00
Wheeler's Tile Etc.	1,250.00	0.00	0.00	0.00	0.00	1,250.00
TOTAL	23,281.72	3,459.20	0.00	0.00	0.00	26,740.92

Figure 11-9: Run this report to stay on the right side of your vendors.

Inventory Reports

If you track inventory, you need to keep an eye on inventory data. The most important report is the Inventory Valuation report, which displays the asset value of the current quantity on hand for each item. The total asset value in this report must match the value of the Inventory Asset account on your balance sheet for the same date. QuickBooks offers two inventory valuation reports:

- Inventory Valuation Summary (see Figure 11-10). Here you'll find all inventory items with their On Hand numbers, average cost, and asset value. In addition, the report provides percentages of total assets and retail value information.

- Inventory Valuation Detail. To see the transactions (invoices, bills, etc.) that make up the summary report numbers, run this report. It provides all the individual transactions, as well as the totals.

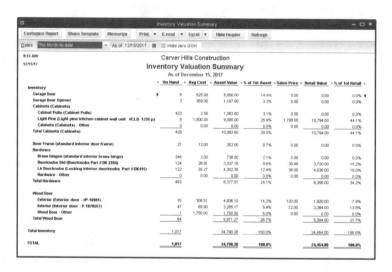

Figure 11-10: The inventory asset value must match the inventory asset amount on your balance sheet.

CPA TIP: *If the values don't match, you need to search transactions involving inventory to see where the problem occurred. Look for a journal entry with a posting entry to the Inventory Asset account (the most common cause of this problem).*

There is no situation in which the value of your inventory asset should be changed via a J/E (journal entry), because a J/E doesn't adjust quantity. If you find a J/E, ask the person who created it about the purpose of the adjustment. (Of course, that person may be you.) Void the J/E and enter a transaction that's appropriate to the purpose of the J/E to adjust the inventory. (Chapter 6 explains how to adjust inventory.)

An "appropriate" transaction is one in which both quantity and value are adjusted, and the most common adjustments are the following:

- An inventory adjustment transaction after a physical count.
- An inventory adjustment transaction when you remove inventory for your own use.
- A customer credit for the return of inventory.
- A customer credit for damaged inventory that isn't returned by the customer.

You should run other important inventory reports regularly. Here are some guidelines that most business owners find helpful:

- Periodically run reports that show the profit per item and adjust the pricing of items that are showing less profit because of rising costs. The Sales By Item Summary report (Reports | Sales | Sales By Item Summary) provides this information and more.
- If seasonal products lack enough quantity on hand to fill the rush of orders you expect, make sure you order more in a timely fashion. Your suppliers are probably facing large shipments of the same seasonal items to your competitors. The Inventory Stock Status reports (by Item and by Vendor) will give you the numbers you need. You'll find them on the Inventory submenu of the Reports menu.
- For non-seasonal products, make sure you've set realistic reorder points (the level of quantity on hand

at which you reorder) so that you don't ever lose a
sale because you're out of stock.

- Keep an eye on backorders to make sure enough
  product is due in to fill them and restock for future
  orders.

CPA TIP: *Make sure you track the backorders that are filled
to ensure that some customers aren't being neglected when
new products arrive in insufficient quantity to fill all backorders.
Some sales reps tend to manipulate the way backorders are
filled in favor of their own customers.*

Setting Report Preferences

To use report data effectively, it will help if you first set your report
preferences to suit your needs. You'll find them in the Reports & Graphs
section of the Preferences dialog box.

1. Select Edit | Preferences from the menu bar to display
   the Preferences dialog.
2. Click the Reports & Graphs icon in the left pane.
3. Click the My Preferences tab (remember, these options
   can be set by individual users and will be in effect every
   time those users log into QuickBooks).
4. Set the following options:
   - Prompt Me To Modify Report Options Before
     Opening A Report. If you find yourself
     customizing practically every report you run,
     you'll want to enable this option. When checked,
     each report you open appears with the Modify
     Report dialog box automatically displayed.
   - Reports And Graphs. This tells QuickBooks when
     and how to (or not to) refresh reports and graphs.
     If you always want to see current data in a
     report, choose Refresh Automatically. If you want

QuickBooks to alert you when data has changed, choose Prompt Me To Refresh. If you want to leave the report as is, even if the data changes, choose Don't Refresh.

- Graphs Only. If your graphs are based on a large quantity of data, or if your computer is slow, you might want to enable the Draw Graphs In 2D (Faster) option. The second option, Use Patterns, is very handy if you're printing a graph in black and white only. By default, QuickBooks displays and prints graphs using color. Of course, colors will not show on a black-and-white or gray print out. Patterns take the place of colors, allowing you to visually differentiate between the data.

5. Click the Company Preferences tab and set these options:

- Summary Report Basis. Do you want your summary reports to display income and expenses as of the dates they are recorded (Accrual) or as of the dates they are actually transacted (Cash)? In an Accrual Basis report, income and expenses will appear regardless of whether they have been received or paid. As long as an invoice or a bill is entered into QuickBooks, the data will appear on the report. Cash Basis reports only show income received and bills paid, ignoring outstanding invoices and bills.

- Aging Reports. Decide whether you want the aging to begin as of the date you create the transaction or as of the Due Date determined by the terms for the customer or vendor.

- Reports—Show Items By. When running reports that contain items, do you want to see the item name, its description, or both?

- Collapse Transactions. If you run a lot of really long reports with lots of details, you might want to select this option. It automatically collapses details. If you decide you need to see the details when running the report, you can display them by clicking the Expand button on the report itself.

- Reports—Show Accounts By. You can opt to display only the names of accounts or their descriptions, or both, when running reports.

- Statement Of Cash Flows. Click the Classify Cash button to display the Classify Cash window. The choices you make here determine the accounts that appear on the Statement Of Cash Flows report (Reports | Company & Financial | Statement Of Cash Flows). It is best to check with your accountant before making changes to this option.

- Default Formatting For Reports. If you like all or most of your reports formatted in the same manner, check the option and click the Format button. The Report Format Preferences dialog box appears with two tabs—Header/Footer and Fonts & Numbers. These tabs are covered later in this chapter.

6. Click OK to save your changes and close the Preferences dialog box.

Customizing Reports

One of the great things about QuickBooks reports is that you don't have to accept them as they are. You can make a variety of changes that enable you to view the data you need in the manner you want to see it. Depending on the whether the report is a summary report or a detail report, you will have different options. Where there are substantial differences, we'll cover them separately.

To customize an open report, click the Customize Report button, which immediately displays the Modify Report dialog. Depending on the type of report you're running, the Display tab will be different. The Display tab shown in Figure 11-11 is from a detail report (the Profit & Loss Detail report, to be exact).

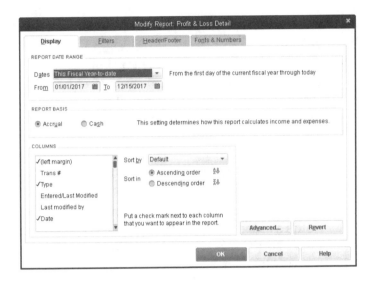

Figure 11-11: The Display tab options on a detail report allow you to add and remove columns.

Changing the Display Options

The Display tab options enable you to determine how the data in the report appears. It includes everything: which columns to display, the sort order, the report basis, and more. The Display tab found in detail reports differs significantly from the Display tab in the summary reports. Therefore, we'll go over them separately.

Detail Report Display Tab Options

As you can see in Figure 11-11, the Display tab options in a detail report include the following options:

- Report Date Range. You can choose a preset date range from the Dates drop-down list or enter your own custom date range using the From and To fields.

- Report Basis. Decide whether you want the report to display income and expenses when the invoices and bills are recorded (Accrual) or when the income is received and the bills paid (Cash). Only reports showing income and expense data will offer this option.

- Columns. Depending on the report you've chosen, there will be different columns (fields) for which you can show data in the report. The fields with check marks in the Columns pane appear on the report. Those fields without check marks do not appear. Go through the list and check the items you want to appear and uncheck those items you don't want to appear.

- Sort By. How do you want to sort the report? The fields you've selected (checked) in the Columns list appear in the Sort By drop-down list. Choose one to use as the sort basis.

- Sort In. Select Ascending Order to see the report data in an A-Z order or Descending Order to see the data in a Z-A order.

- Advanced. Click the Advanced button to display the Advanced Options dialog. It allows you to display either data for all accounts in your Chart of Accounts or only data for accounts that have activity for the date range of the report. To display open balances for customers as of today, choose the Current option. To display open customer balances as of the report date, choose Report Date.

When you've set the Display tab options to your satisfaction, move to another tab or click OK to save your changes and see the modified report.

Summary Report Display Tab Differences

Since summary reports provide totals without the accompanying detail, they require a few different options (see Figure 11-12).

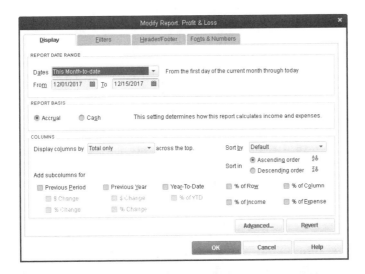

Figure 11-12: Summary report Display tab offers comparison
options.

Although you cannot choose the columns (fields) that appear in summary reports, you can elect to display data from previous periods and years. While some of the Display tab options are the same, others are different.

- Columns. The data in the summary report is predetermined by the report selected. However, you can use the Columns drop-down list to create columns that break the data down by criteria you choose. For example, you can create columns that break the totals down into date ranges (day, week, month, and so on). Depending on the report, you may have additional choices such as vendor, customer, item, and others.

- Add Subcolumns For. This option enables you to add data from previous periods to the report. It's great for making comparison reports such as current year totals to previous year totals. Some summary reports provide additional options for displaying percentages, as well.

- Advanced. The Advanced Options dialog box offers completely different options from the Advanced Options found on the detail report Display tab. Here, you'll be able choose the data that appears in rows and columns, as well as decide which reporting calendar to use for the report. The choices for rows and columns are Active (any fields with activity), All (all fields, regardless of activity), and Non-zero (all fields with totals that are either greater or less than zero). The Reporting Calendar options are Fiscal Year (the year selected as Fiscal Year in your Company Information dialog), Calendar Year (Jan–Dec), and Income Tax Year (year selected as Income Tax Year in your Company Information dialog).

Creating Report Filters

The ability to create filters enables you to set the parameters for what data is included in the report. While the Filters tab of the Modify Report dialog offers a wealth of filtering options, you can set basic filters using the options found right on the report window.

Using the Report Toolbar to Create Filters

The toolbar filter options are limited to a handful, but are probably the most frequently used. As you can see in Figure 11-13, they are either drop-down lists or calendars. Here's what you'll find:

- Dates. Choose the date range for the report. Your options include All, Today, This Month, Next Week, Next Fiscal Year, and a lot more.
- From/To. If the choices on the Dates drop-down list don't work for you, create your own date range. Just enter the beginning and ending dates in the From and To fields.

- Columns. This drop-down list appears on summary reports only. It provides a list of fields you can use to display data in columns on the report.

- Sort By. Your choice is limited in most summary reports to Totals. However, in detail reports, you can opt to sort the report by any of the visible columns.

Figure 11-13: The report toolbar provides basic filter options.

Creating Custom Filters

The toolbar filters are great for applying quick filters, but they don't offer a lot of options. When you need to create a detailed filter to display very precise data, you can use the sophisticated filtering options found on the Filters tab of the Modify Report dialog box. Begin by clicking the Customize Report button and then the Filters tab to display the Modify Report dialog seen in Figure 11-14.

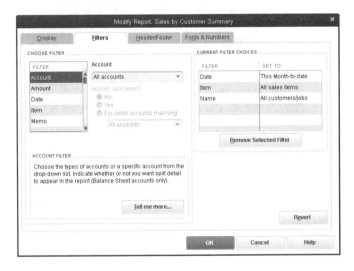

Figure 11-14: Set the advanced filtering options to display the report data you need.

Creating a new filter is a four-step process.

1. Review the preset filters in the Current Filter Choices and edit or remove those that are not suitable for your current needs. Highlight a filter and change the settings in the Choose Filter section or click the Remove Selected Filter button to delete it.

2. Create new filters by selecting the initial criterion to use from the Choose Filter list. Your choices vary depending on the report you're customizing.

3. Configure the additional options. Once you make your selection in the Filter list, additional options appear next to it. They may be in the form of a drop-down list with additional choices, text/number boxes into which you enter specific data (e.g., invoice number, memo text, etc.), date fields, or dollar amounts.

4. Click OK to save the filters and return to the report. Before you click OK, you can return the filters to their original state by clicking the Revert button.

If your default setting for refreshing reports (Edit | Preferences | Reports & Graphs | My Preferences) is to auto refresh, the report will automatically display the filtered data. If not, you may have to click the Refresh button to apply the new filter(s).

Customizing Report Headers and Footers

While the data presented in the report are the most important part of the report, they usually don't stand alone. To enable the recipient to quickly understand the purpose of the report, it needs a title and some additional information. This is where the Header/Footer options come into play. To view and modify these options, click the Customize Report button, then the Header/Footer tab (see Figure 11-15).

The options found on the Header/Footer tab are broken into three groups—header, footer, and page layout.

Figure 11-15: The Header/Footer options help make the report
more easily understood.

Header Options

The header options apply to the report information displayed above the
body of the report. Here's what you'll be able to configure:

- Company Name. QuickBooks grabs the company
  name you've entered into the Company Name field
  of the Company Information dialog (Company | My
  Company) and inserts it here. You can change it if you
  wish.

- Report Title. QuickBooks automatically enters the
  name of the report as the title. For example, when
  you open the Sales by Customer Summary report,
  QuickBooks names it Sales by Customer Summary.
  This is fine if you're just taking a quick look.
  However, if you do any customizing, you'll probably
  want to change the name (e.g., Sales by Customer
  Prev Year Comparison) and memorize the report for
  future use.

- Subtitle. This field is automatically populated with the date range chosen for the report. You can accept that or change it to something different (e.g., Philadelphia Customers Only).

- Date Prepared. Don't let this one throw you. It is merely an option for choosing the format of the date, not the date itself. From the drop-down list, choose from among five different date formats.

- Time Prepared. The name says it all. Check this option if you want the time prepared to show on the report.

- Report Basis. To show the report basis (cash or accrual) on the report, check this option.

- Print Header On Pages After First Page. If you deselect this, only the first page will display the title and other optional fields selected in this section. All subsequent pages will only display the body of the report and the footer information.

Show Footer Information

While the footer may not be as sexy as the header, it's important as well. Here, you'll find the following options:

- Page Number. This is another one of those fields for choosing the format of the field rather than the data itself. If you don't want to use page numbers, deselect the option. However, be advised that when you accidentally drop the report on the floor before stapling it, you'll wish you had checked it (especially if it's a really long report).

- Extra Footer Line. This is a great place to put the preparer's name or a disclaimer. ("If you don't like these numbers, contact Fred in accounting!")

- Print Footer On First Page. Unless you check this option, the first two options, page numbers and extra footer line, only appear on page two through the end of the report, but not on page one.

Page Layout

The only option available in this section is the Alignment option that allows you to change the position of the header and footer fields on the report. The Alignment drop-down list offers four choices (see Figure 11-16):

- Standard. The standard format is chosen by default and places the Time, Date, and Report Basis on the left side of the header, while the Company, Title, and Subtitle appear in the center of the header. The Extra Line appears on the left of the footer and the page number on the right.

- Left. The header fields switch sides with this choice, and the footer fields remain the same.

- Right. Both header and footer fields switch sides (from the Left alignment choice).

- Center. The header fields return to their original position (Standard) and the footer fields climb atop one another in the center of the footer.

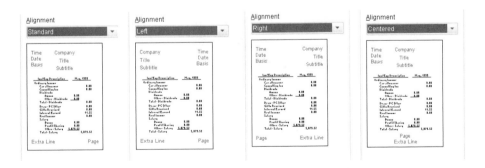

Figure 11-16: You get to choose how the header and footer fields are positioned on the report.

Modifying Fonts & Numbers Settings

The final tab in the Modify Report dialog, Fonts & Numbers, offers settings for dressing up the report (see Figure 11-17). Here, you change fonts, font sizes, and styles, as well as the way numbers are displayed.

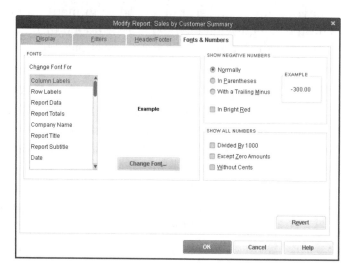

Figure 11-17: Use the Fonts & Numbers option to dress up your report.

The options on the Fonts & Numbers tab include

- **Fonts.** Select a report element from the Change Font For list and click the Change Font button to open the dialog box (named for the element selected) with font attribute options. Make the desired changes to font, style, size, color, and/or effects and click OK to save the changes.

- **Show Negative Numbers.** To ensure that negative numbers stand out on the report, set these options. When you choose an option, an example appears in the Example box. Regardless of which choice you make, you can elect to have all negative numbers appear in bright red. That will certainly make them stand out.

- Show All Numbers. If you're dealing with big numbers, you'll probably want to enable the first of these options—Divided By 1000. It makes those million-dollar numbers more manageable. The second option eliminates zero amounts. Finally, the third, Without Cents, removes all those annoying decimal points and trailing pennies. Use all three options to generate a nice, clean report that's easy to read.

Memorizing Reports

Once you've gone to the trouble of modifying a report, you should memorize it so that you don't have to start from scratch the next time you want to see the same report. It's a simple task. Make your changes to the report using either the toolbar filter options or the Modify Report dialog options and then click the Memorize button on the report. This opens the Memorize Report dialog seen in Figure 11-18.

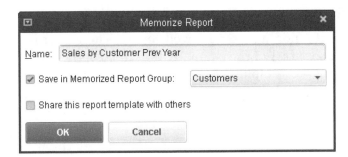

Figure 11-18: Save customized reports for future use.

Make sure you give the new report a name that will enable you to easily identify it the next time you want to use it. For example, Sales by Customer isn't going to tell you much. However, Sales by Philly Customers or Sales by VIP Customers will make it quite clear what data the report contains.

If you want to organize memorized reports, you can save them in special groups. Check the Save In Memorized Report Group option and select the group from the drop-down list. To create a new group, open the

Memorized Report List, click Memorized Report, and choose New Group from the drop-down list that appears.

If you think you've got a really hot report that other QuickBooks users might benefit from, check the Share This Report Template With Others to make it available online. When you click OK, the Share Template dialog box opens. Enter basic information about the report and click Share to upload it.

You can access memorized reports from the Reports | Memorized Reports menu or from the Memorized Report List (Reports | Memorized Reports | Memorized Report List).

Importing a Report Template

While QuickBooks Pro cannot export report templates, it can import them. QuickBooks Premier Editions can export customized report templates that can then be imported by all QuickBooks users.

Importing a report template actually does nothing more than convert the template file into a memorized report. The report is added to the Memorized Report List of the company file that's open during the import process. To import a template, use the following steps:

1. Choose Reports | Memorized Reports | Memorized Report List.
2. Click the Memorized Report button at the bottom of the window and select Import Template.
3. Navigate to the drive or folder that contains the template file (with a .qbr extension) and double-click its listing.
4. In the Memorize Report dialog, enter a name for the report or accept the displayed name (which is the name used by the person who exported the template).

The report is now available in the Memorized Report List.

CHAPTER 12:

Year End Tasks

- Cleaning Up the Opening Balance Equity Account

- Depreciation and Amortization

- Adjustments for Cash-Basis Tax Reports

- Allocating Overhead Expenses to Divisions

- Allocating Equity

- Tax Forms and Tax Returns

- Closing the Books

At the end of your fiscal year (which is usually the same as the calendar year for small businesses), you have to perform a number of tasks to make sure your financial information is ready for tax preparation and to get your books ready for your next fiscal year.

In this chapter, we'll discuss the common year-end tasks you face and also explain the various tax forms you have to think about as you prepare reports on your finances.

Opening Balance Corrections

Many accountants frequently have to change the opening balances for accounts because users have made changes to transactions that took place in the previous year. Accountants keep records of each year's closing balances so that they always know if you've changed the totals of the previous year by creating, deleting, or editing transactions. It is important for the prior year's closing balances to remain unchanged, because they agree with the amounts that are reported on your tax returns.

These accountants report that regardless of the controls built in to prevent working in previous years, users override the controls and change prior-year transactions. This is one of the things accountants have to accept, because QuickBooks, unlike almost all other accounting software, doesn't have a real "close" feature that absolutely seals the books. That deficiency is exacerbated by an apparently unstoppable urge of users to mess around with transactions that are dated in the previous year.

Opening Balance Equity Account

One correction you must make to your opening balances is the removal of any balance in the Opening Balance Equity account that QuickBooks automatically creates in the Chart of Accounts.

The Opening Balance Equity account you see in the Chart of Accounts is a QuickBooks invention. It should be named something like "garbage collection account invented by programmers who don't understand basic accounting principles." It doesn't have any connection to the phrase "opening balance" in the way that term is usually applied in accounting.

QuickBooks uses the Opening Balance Equity account as the offset account when you enter opening balances during setup. Those opening balances might have been entered during the company setup or when you manually created asset and liability accounts.

In this book, during the discussions of setting up your company file or creating accounts, customers, or vendors, we advised you to avoid filling in any opening balance data.

Instead, we suggested you create transactions that predate the Quick-Books start date to establish those balances (and post the amounts to the appropriate accounts). We advise accountants to take the same attitude when they work with QuickBooks users. If you followed our suggestion, your Opening Balance Equity account has a zero balance, which is the correct state of affairs.

If you opted to enter balances during setup, your Opening Balance Equity account has a balance, and your accountant will almost certainly create journal entries to reduce that balance to zero.

Even if the Opening Balance Equity account contains amounts that are linked to transactions dated before the QuickBooks start date, they may need to be journalized into the current year. Unless your Quick-Books start date was also the first day of your fiscal year, some or all of the balance in the Opening Balance Equity account may be current-year numbers. It takes a long time for your accountant to figure out which accounts should receive postings as the Opening Balance Equity account is emptied.

Basic Year-End Tasks

There are some QuickBooks tasks that you should be performing regularly during the course of the year, but which are a must at year-end.

- Reconcile Bank, Lines of Credit, and Credit Card Accounts. Keep an eye out for your December statements, which should arrive in January. Of course, if your fiscal year is not the same as the calendar year, the months will be different. When the statements arrive, reconcile all the accounts to ensure your year-end numbers are accurate. For statements that do not close on the last day of the month (many credit card statements do not), be sure to enter all transactions for the statement that includes your year-end closing date and reconcile that statement (since all activity on the statement is tax deductible based on the date of the charge, not the date of your payment). See Chapter 7 for details on reconciling accounts. By the way, don't forget to include petty cash accounts if you have any.

- Make Inventory Adjustments. If you track inventory, you'll want to make sure those numbers are accurate, as well. Take a physical inventory on the last day of the year or within a couple of days of the new year. Once you have the physical count, make the necessary adjustments using the last day of the fiscal year as the date. Chapter 6 provides instructions on inventory adjustments.

- Make Accounts Receivable Adjustments. If you use the accrual method of accounting, be sure that all of your customer invoices are entered. (You should do this every month.) Review your accounts receivable to see if you need to enter any balance adjustments for credits that may be due to your customers.

- Make Accounts Payable Adjustments. If you use the accrual method of accounting, be sure that all of your vendor invoices are entered. (You should do this every month.) Review your accounts payable to see if you need to enter any balance adjustments for credits that are due to you. Also, check to be sure that there are no errant balances (possibly an invoice was paid using the Direct Check method instead of through the Pay Open Invoices method).

- Generate Year-End Financial Reports. Your accountant is going to want to see your Profit & Loss and Balance Sheet reports for the fiscal year. They will be used not only for tax preparation, but for analysis and advice, as well. Make sure you run them after the last day of the fiscal year and select Last Fiscal Year as the date range. See Chapter 11 for more on running QuickBooks reports.

ProAdvisor TIP: *If you need more deductions, run the Vendor Balance Summary report before the year end to see if you have outstanding bills that can you can pay now (even if they're not due) and deduct for the current fiscal year. Of course, this only works if you're filing your taxes using the cash-basis accounting method.*

Depreciation and Amortization

Depreciation and amortization are expenses that you deduct against the costs of major purchases that have been recorded as assets. Depreciation is for tangible assets (things you can see and touch, such as equipment, furniture, etc.) and amortization is for intangible assets (such as patents, the organizational costs of starting a business, etc.).

Theoretically, you calculate the yearly expense/deduction by dividing the cost of the asset by the number of years the asset is expected to last or be useful. We use the word "theoretically" because it doesn't really work in a straightforward manner. First of all, some assets are hard to define in terms of useful life; you often can't predict with any confidence their rate of "wear and tear" or "obsolescence." Secondly, IRS rules, state laws, and court decisions have introduced many exceptions to the way depreciation and amortization amounts can be calculated for tax purposes.

The reason we have depreciation and amortization deductions is that when you spend money on a major purchase for something that will be used for a period of years, you're usually not allowed to deduct the total expense of the purchase the year you purchase it. If you'd declared the total cost as an expense, you'd have an understatement of your company's profit that year and an overstatement of profit in the following years. Since the asset is being used to operate the company for multiple years, that's not good accounting.

ProAdvisor TIP: *If your accountant is running QuickBooks Premier Accountant, s/he'll have access to the Fixed Asset Manager, which calculates depreciation. In that case, you'll probably want to use the Fixed Asset List in QuickBooks Pro to track your fixed assets. At the end of the year, your accountant can import the list and calculate your depreciation amounts for the year.*

Creating a Depreciation/Amortization Transaction

The transaction you create to record depreciation and/or amortization is different from most transactions in two ways:

- Unlike most transactions (such as selling a product or buying goods or services), no money is involved. You don't write a check and you don't deposit funds into the bank.

- Because of the complicated regulations for these deductions, the amount of the transaction is not easy to calculate; instead, you should ask your accountant for guidance.

Some businesses use one set of depreciation rules for keeping their books and another, more aggressive set of depreciation entries for reporting their taxes—this definitely requires input from your accountant.

The transaction for depreciation/amortization is a journal entry, reducing the value of the asset (a credit posted to the contra-asset account) and increasing expenses (a debit posted to the depreciation and/or amortization expense account). In effect, you're recognizing the wear and tear, obsolescence, or other decline in value of the asset by reducing its value and taking a tax deduction against that loss in value. Table 12-1 is a typical journal entry for depreciation; a journal entry for amortization takes the same form, using the appropriate accounts.

Account	Debit	Credit
17100—Accum Deprec-Furniture & Fixt		450.00
17200—Accum Deprec-Vehicles		600.00
17300—Accum Deprec-Equipment		550.00
66000—Depreciation Expense	1600.00	

Table 12-1: Depreciation and amortization are posted with a journal entry.

The journal entry displayed here uses asset accounts specifically created for the purpose of posting accumulated depreciation for each type of fixed asset. A separate asset account exists for posting the original purchases for each category (Furniture & Fixtures, Vehicles, Equipment, etc.).

To create the journal entry in Table 12-1, follow these steps:

1. Choose Company | Make General Journal Entries to display the Make General Journal Entries dialog box seen in Figure 12-1.

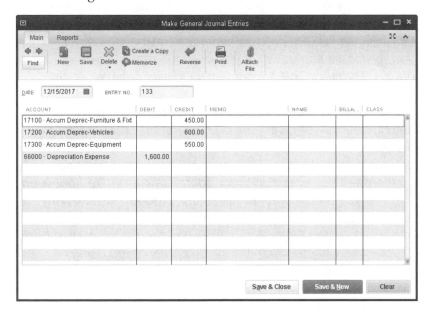

Figure 12-1: Use a journal entry to record fixed-asset depreciation.

2. Change the Date and Entry No. fields if necessary.

3. Select the Accum Deprec-Furniture & Fixt account from the Account drop-down list on the first line of the form.

4. Move to the Credit column and enter the appropriate amount.

5. Repeat for all depreciation accounts.

6. Select the Depreciation Expense account from the Account drop-down list.

7. Enter the appropriate amount in the Debit column.

8. Click Save & Close to record the journal entry.

ProAdvisor TIP: *If your accountant is using a current (2013 or 2014) version of QuickBooks Premier Accountant, s/he can create the journal entries for you and e-mail them to you. Then, you simply import them into QuickBooks, eliminating the need to create them yourself.*

CPA TIP: *To expand on the above ProAdvisor TIP, discuss with your accountant the use of an Accountant's Copy of your QuickBooks file. This allows him/her to review and adjust your historical entries while you continue making current entries. E-mailing the Accountant's Copy is seamless using QuickBooks servers and may save you time and money (your accountant doesn't need to travel to your office and might be able to have lower-level staff do some of the work at lower billing rates). The Accountant's Copy requires a password (separate from the data file's normal password if you use one), so there will be some additional coordination required between you and your accountant to utilize this program feature. Any adjustments made by your accountant are simply imported into your working QuickBooks file when they are e-mailed back to you. See Chapter 2 for details on creating and using an Accountant's Copy.*

Some businesses have only a single account for each asset category, instead of using separate accounts for cost and accumulated depreciation. When depreciation is posted, the single asset account balance is reduced.

A more detailed discussion of the choices for managing fixed-asset accounts and depreciation is in Chapter 8.

ProAdvisor TIP: *One way to provide a little more detail in your balance sheet is to create each fixed-asset account with two subaccounts—Cost and AccumDepr. When you purchase a fixed asset, post the amount to the Cost subaccount. When you depreciate the fixed asset at the end of the year, post it to the AccumDepr subaccount. Now, when you run your balance sheet reports, you'll have a history of each asset, including its cost, depreciation, and current value (the parent account).*

Fixed-Asset Dispositions

Fixed-asset dispositions occur when you sell a fixed asset or you stop using it because it's no longer useful (which is called retiring the asset). In either case, you need to remove the original cost and the accumulated depreciation associated with the asset from your books. To accomplish this, the amount of depreciation that was recorded against the fixed asset is added back and the original cost of the fixed asset is removed.

If you don't remove the fixed asset when you dispose of it, your Balance Sheet report shows the original costs and depreciation, inherently stating that the asset still exists. This can cause confusion when a lender, potential investor, or potential buyer relies on the assets included in your balance sheet. It can also cause a problem when an insurance agent tries to reconcile a listing of the assets included in your books with those included on your insurance policies.

Sale of Fixed Assets

When you sell a fixed asset, in addition to removing the original cost and the depreciation that was taken, you have to post the income you received from the buyer of the fixed asset. To remove the fixed asset and record the proceeds of the sale, your accountant makes the following journal entry:

1. Records any depreciation allowed for the final year of ownership.

2. Adds back all the depreciation taken over the years (including the final year, if any depreciation was recorded in Step 1).

3. Reverses the original cost of the fixed asset.

4. Records the bank deposit for the payment you received from the buyer.

At this point, the journal entry doesn't balance; the difference is the net gain or loss on the sale of the asset (which is not necessarily the amount you received from the buyer).

Let's use a real example so that you can follow the money.

- You purchased a fixed asset (a piece of equipment, a car, etc.) for $10,000.00. You recorded the purchase with a debit to the appropriate Fixed Assets account.

- Over the years, you took $7000.00 of depreciation. Each year, the depreciation was a credit to the asset account named Accumulated Depreciation and a debit to an expense account named Depreciation. (The expense reduced your taxable profit each year.)

- Now, you've sold the asset for $2400.00 and deposited the buyer's check into your bank account (a debit to the bank account).

Table 12-2 shows the postings for these amounts, but this is not yet a transaction because the debit and credit columns aren't equal. (Note that the postings for Accumulated Depreciation and Fixed Assets are the opposite of the original postings made when you purchased the asset and when depreciation was taken each year.)

Account	Debit	Credit
17300—Accum Deprec-Equipment	7000.00	
15300—Fixed Assets-Equipment		10000.00
10100—Bank Account	2400.00	
Totals	9400.00	10000.00

Table 12-2: This entry doesn't balance; the difference is the net gain or loss on the sale of the asset.

In this case, we need to add $600.00 to the Debit side of the entry to balance the transaction. The posting is usually to an Income account named Gain on Sale of Fixed Assets. Income is a credit, but in this case the posting is a debit. This means the amount is "contra-income," which is the same as an expense. You actually have a net loss of $600.00 for the fixed asset, which reduces your taxable income.

Of course, before your accountant creates this entry, you want to deposit the buyer's check in your bank account, and that means you have to post it in your accounting records. We suggest that you create an account specifically for the purpose of recording this sale. Add an Other Income account named Proceeds of Fixed Asset Sales to your Chart of Accounts and use it when you post the deposit. Isolating this transaction in this account highlights the sale so that your accountant can identify it. Your accountant creates the entries required to remove the asset from your books, record the profit or loss from the sale of the fixed asset, and adjust the entry you made to this "temporary" account.

Retirement of Fixed Assets

Fixed assets retirements occur when an asset is no longer in use. A common example is a computer that became obsolete and is sitting in a closet or has been thrown away.

Since a fixed asset that is being retired has already been completely depreciated, the cost of the fixed asset is the same as its accumulated depreciation. The combination of these amounts results in a zero balance carried on your books for the fixed asset; the individual account balances (the debit posting for the original cost and the credit postings for accumulated depreciation) are still appearing on your Balance Sheet report. Your accountant removes those individual balances from your books by posting a credit to the original purchase account and a debit to the accumulated depreciation account (the opposite of the original postings).

Adjustments for Cash-Basis Tax Reports

You'll find a complete discussion of the difference between accrual– and cash-based accounting in Chapter 1. For this discussion on year-end tasks, we'll assume that you keep your books on an accrual basis (a better way to get a handle on the financial health of your business), but you file your taxes on a cash basis.

In the old days, you'd have to create a couple of reversing journal entries to get the figures you need for your cash-based tax return. However, with QuickBooks, all you have to do is change the basis of your reports.

1. From the Company & Financial submenu (Reports | Company & Financial), choose the financial report to run (P&L, Balance Sheet, etc.).

2. Assuming that you're running the report at the beginning of the new year, select Last Fiscal Year from the Dates drop-down list.

3. Click the Customize Report button to open the Modify Report dialog box (see Figure 12-2).

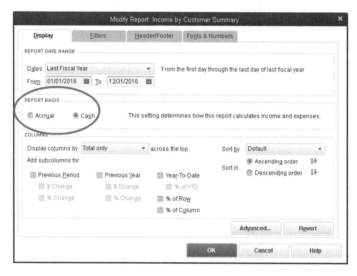

Figure 12-2: Set the basis for financial reports to match the way you file your taxes.

4. On the Display tab, locate the Report Basis options.

5. Select Cash.

6. Click OK to return to the report.

7. If the report does not update, click the Refresh button.

Allocating Overhead Expenses to Divisions

If you're tracking divisions by using QuickBooks classes, you can allocate overhead expenses to those divisions at year-end. This gives you a more precise Profit & Loss report for each division. (Chapter 3 has information about simulating a divisionalized Chart of Accounts with QuickBooks classes.) To see these figures, run the Profit & Loss By Class report found on the Company & Financial submenu (Reports | Company & Financial).

The specific expenses incurred by each division (class) were posted to that division's expenses as you paid them, but there are always some overhead expenses that are company-wide and can be allocated across the divisions. Usually, allocation is either calculated to each division evenly or you allocate a percentage of the expense to each division. If you allocate by percentage, you need a formula, which can be based on the size of the division (such as number of employees, the total of specific expenses, or the total of income). Some expenses are easier to calculate, such as automobile insurance, which is allocated depending on the number of vehicles used by each division.

Allocation is effected by a journal entry that removes an amount from the top-level (company-wide) expense account and posts it to the same expense account for the division, as seen in Table 12-5.

Account	Debit	Credit	Class
64500—Insurance-Vehicles		4200.00	
64500—Insurance-Vehicles	1800.00		East Philly
64500—Insurance-Vehicles	2400.00		West Philly

Table 12-5: Allocate expenses to divisions (classes) to get a more realistic Profit & Loss report for each division.

Allocating Equity

Companies that have multiple owners need to allocate the company's profit or loss among the owners at the end of the year. (A proprietorship, a single member LLC, or an S Corporation with only one stockholder obviously doesn't have to worry about this.) The allocated amount appears on the tax form provided to each owner/partner.

CPA NOTE: *Regardless of the number of stockholders, C corporations don't allocate equity because the profits aren't passed to the stockholders' tax returns. A C corporation files a tax return for the business and pays its own taxes.*

For an S Corporation with more than one owner, the distribution must be made in the same percentage as the stock ownership of each stockholder. An owner of 50% of the stock is allocated 50% of the profits; a 10% stockholder gets 10% of the profits; and so on.

For a partnership, an LLP, or a multimember LLC, the operating agreement created by the owners sets the allocation percentage. (These agreements don't always use the amount of capital contributed as the allocation basis.)

In addition to allocating the profit/loss to multiple owners, your accountant may choose to consolidate each owner's financial data into a single account. The total in that account becomes the opening balance for each owner/partner in the new year. This task is only performed if you maintain separate accounts for capital contributions and draw for each owner/partner. To accomplish this, your accountant takes the totals of each individual account and merges them so that the new single account holds the net amount (capital less draw).

For all types of businesses (single owner or multiple owners), Quick-Books rolls the current year's profit/loss into an historical retained earnings account and starts the new year with a zero balance in the profit/loss account.

Tax Forms and Tax Returns

Your business may have to produce tax forms and/or tax returns. Tax forms are those forms you provide to employees and independent contractors. A tax return is the method by which you report your business earnings and pay taxes on the profits. Some businesses file tax returns that stand on their own. Others file forms reporting the business activities as part of the owners' personal tax returns.

Tax Forms

At the end of the year, your company may have to produce some tax forms, specifically Form W-2 if you have employees and Form 1099 if you pay independent contractors, attorneys, and unincorporated vendors. (Information about tracking payroll and independent contractors is in Chapter 10.)

You can file these forms on paper or electronically. If you have 250 or more forms to file, you must file electronically. In this section, we'll go over these tax forms; in the sections following, we'll discuss business tax returns.

Creating W-2s

Every employee must receive Form W-2. Employees attach the W-2 to their personal tax returns, and you file copies with the Social Security Administration, your state revenue department, and any other tax entity that requires a copy (e.g., a local tax authority). You also keep a copy for your files.

When you send the forms to the Social Security Administration, you must include Form W-3—Transmittal of Wage and Tax Statements. This is a summary form that indicates the number of W-2s you are filing and the totals for each box on the W-2s you issued.

If you have an outside payroll service, the service produces the W-2s and sends them to the appropriate recipients. If you do payroll in-house and have a QuickBooks payroll subscription, you can prepare your own. You buy the forms (online or at an office supply store), and QuickBooks prints the forms and produces the reports.

1. Select Employees | Payroll Tax Forms & W-2s | Process Payroll Forms to display the File Forms tab of the Payroll Center.

2. Select Annual Form W-2/W-3-Wage And Tax Statement/ Transmittal in the File Forms list.

3. Click the File Form button to display the Select Payroll Form dialog shown in Figure 12-3.

4. Choose the employee(s) to include in the printing using the Process W-2s For options.

5. Enter the ending fiscal year in the Select Filing Period option.

6. Click OK to generate the forms and the report.

Before printing the forms and reports, you're given the opportunity to review the employees and the data and to make any needed changes.

Figure 12-3: Creating W-2 forms and reports is easy if you have a payroll subscription.

CPA NOTE: *It is extremely important that the employees' names match their social security records. Nicknames are not acceptable and will result in correspondence from the IRS. If, in the review process, you see an error with an employee's name, you'll need to go back to the employee's QuickBooks record, correct the name there, and then rerun the review file prior to printing the W-2s.*

If you do in-house payroll manually, you can buy the forms with software that sends the forms to a printer. You can also file W-2s and W-3s electronically. Learn more about this service by visiting the SSA website at http://www.socialsecurity.gov/employer/.

Generating 1099s

You must issue Form 1099 to every independent contractor who qualifies for the form (see Chapter 10 for more information on tracking payments to independent contractors). QuickBooks makes the process of filing 1099 forms and reports at the end of the year *almost* painless. You'll notice that we said "almost." That's because you still have to do the quality assurance to ensure that the recipients and the numbers are accurate.

ProAdvisor TIP: *QuickBooks offers a few reports that will help you verify the 1099 vendor information: the Vendor 1099 Review, the 1099 Summary report, and the 1099 detail report. They can all be accessed from the Vendors | Print/E-file 1099s submenu.*

The first thing to do is check the vendor records for all 1099 contractors and be sure that you have their current addresses and that they have two things on the Tax Settings tab of the Edit Vendor record:

- Vendor Tax ID. All independent contractors must supply you with their vendor tax IDs, whether they are EIN numbers or social security numbers. You cannot file 1099s unless these numbers appear in the vendor records.

- Vendor Eligible For 1099. Make sure this option is checked. If not, the vendor will not appear on the list of 1099 vendors.

ProAdvisor NOTE: *If you don't see these options in the vendor record, it means you haven't turned on the 1099 feature in QuickBooks. Choose Edit | Preferences, scroll down the left pane, and click the Tax: 1099 icon. Next, click the Company Preferences tab and set the Do You File 1099-MISC Forms option to Yes.*

CPA NOTE: *As with W2s, it is extremely important that 1099 recipients' names match their legal names on file with the IRS. Frequently, a business will operate using a street name ("doing business as") that is not its legal name. The W-9s you receive from them should provide you with their legal names. If, in the review process, you see an error with a contractor's name, you'll need to go back to the QuickBooks vendor record and correct the name there and then rerun the review file prior to printing the 1099s.*

Who Gets Form 1099?

Most independent contractors and unincorporated vendors that earn money from your business need to receive a 1099. The IRS also requires that all payments to attorneys, regardless of the amount, need to receive a 1099. The IRS has a very long list of Yes and No categories for the types of businesses that receive 1099s. In addition, there are multiple 1099 Forms for a variety of types of income.

Rather than fill a lot of space in this book listing all the 1099 forms, we'll deal with the most common form that businesses send to independent contractors: Form 1099-MISC. In fact, most businesses (large, small, and in-between) will only need to prepare Form 1099-MISC.

Form 1099-MISC has multiple uses; there are boxes on the form for rents, royalties, and other income sources. For reporting payments to independent contractors, the applicable box is Box 7—Nonemployee Compensation. A 1099 is required for Box 7 when the minimum amount earned is $600.00 (the minimum amount is called the threshold).

Following is a brief overview of the guidelines for Form 1099-MISC Box 7, although there are some exceptions to the broad statements made here and you must check with your accountant when you're ready to create the 1099.

You must send a 1099-MISC to any individual or business that is not a corporation that you paid during the calendar year. Among the common types of transactions requiring you to send a 1099-MISC for Box 7 are

- Payment for services, including payment for parts or materials used to perform the services if supplying the parts or materials was incidental to providing the service.

- Professional fees, such as fees to attorneys, accountants, architects, contractors, engineers, etc.

- Fees paid by one professional to another, such as fee-splitting or referral fees.

Running the QuickBooks 1099 Wizard

When it's time to generate and file 1099s, you can use the QuickBooks 1099 wizard to automate the process. After you create the forms, you can either print and mail them or you can file them online (for a fee). To run the wizard, follow these steps:

1. Choose Vendors | Print/E-File 1099s | 1099 Wizard to display the opening screen of the wizard. It briefly describes the wizard steps.

2. Click Get Started to move to the Select Your 1099 Vendors screen. All your vendors are displayed, but the only ones selected are those that have the Vendor Eligible For 1099 option checked in their vendor records (on the Tax Settings tab).

3. Select (or deselect) all the vendors who are to receive 1099s and click Continue to view the Verify Your 1099 Vendors' Information screen.

4. Review and, if necessary, edit the vendor information on this screen. As you can see in Figure 12-4, any required information that is missing is outlined in red.

5. Click Continue to open the Map Vendor Payment Accounts screen. Choose the 1099 form boxes in which the totals from accounts used for 1099 should appear. Review the section entitled "Who Gets 1099s?" earlier in this chapter for more information on assigning 1099 boxes.

ProAdvisor TIP: *Box 7 is the most commonly used box on the 1099 form. If, as is often the case, all the earnings are to be reported in Box 7, you can check the Report All Payments In Box 7 option to speed things up.*

6. Click Continue to display the Review Payments For Exclusions screen. If you paid any 1099 vendors using a credit card, debit card, gift card, or PayPal, you cannot include them on the 1099. The vendor will receive a 1099 from the credit card, debit card, or other provider for payments made to them by these third-party services.

7. Verify that any such payments have been excluded and click Continue to view a summary of the 1099s about to be created. Double-click an entry in the summary table to view a report of the details.

8. If you encounter any errors or problems, click Back to review and change those entries.

9. If everything is accurate, click the Continue button to select a filing method. Your choices include

   • Print 1099s. If you plan to print the forms and mail them, click this button. It opens a date range selection dialog first and then a Select 1099s To Print dialog. After you've selected both, click the Print 1099 button to print the forms and then the Print 1096 to print the report.

   • Go To Intuit 1099 E-File Service. If you'd rather not print the forms yourself (or if you have more than 250 forms to submit—an IRS regulation), choose this option to submit the forms electronically. QuickBooks connects you to the Intuit 1099 E-File Service web site, where, for a fee, you can file the forms electronically. Also note that the 1096 form is not needed if you e-file.

10. Click Save & Close to exit the wizard.

Figure 12-4: One vendor is missing the Tax ID.

If you printed the forms, send them to the IRS along with Form 1096—Annual Summary and Transmittal of U.S. Information Returns. (Form 1096 contains the total amount reported from all forms being submitted.)

CPA NOTE: *Some states and localities require that you file copies of 1099s that you prepare.*

Business Tax Returns

Business owners have to file tax returns that include the profit/loss of their businesses. However, not all businesses file tax returns in the business name; some forms of businesses report taxable income on the personal tax returns of the owners or members.

QuickBooks has a few features that will facilitate filing your taxes:

- Tax Line Mapping. When you create your Chart of Accounts, QuickBooks automatically assigns some tax lines based on the tax form selected from the Income Tax Form Used field in the Company Information dialog (Company | My Company). You can manually assign the rest. Check with your accountant to ensure that both the automatic and manual tax line mappings are accurate.

- **Income Tax Reports.** If you've assigned tax lines to your accounts, you can run several different income tax reports. Under the Accountant & Taxes submenu, you'll find an Income Tax Preparation report that lists all your accounts with their tax line assignments. In addition, you'll find two income tax reports (summary and detail). The summary report provides totals for each account broken down by tax line assignment. The detail report lists every transaction for each income and expense account, broken down by tax line assignment.

- **Import QuickBooks Data Into Tax Software.** If your accounts have tax assignments, you can import the data into TurboTax or ProSeries Tax. Follow the instructions in those tax preparation programs.

In the following section, we'll provide a brief overview of the tax return methods used by each type of business entity.

Proprietorship Tax Return

Proprietorships don't file a federal or state income tax return. Instead, the profit of the business is reported, and the tax paid, on the owner's personal tax returns.

For federal tax returns, the profit is normally reported on Schedule C and the net profit/loss amount on Schedule C is included on Form 1040. One major exception would be real estate rental operations, which would be reported on Schedule E. The owner pays the income taxes personally (along with self-employment taxes, if applicable, as a way of being included in the social security system).

Any state and local tax returns are handled in the same fashion, with the owner remitting taxes based on the profit of the business as reported on his/her applicable federal schedule.

It's important to note that the amount included for income tax reporting purposes is the calculated profit of the business, not the draw taken by the owner during the year.

Single Member LLC Tax Return

A single member LLC isn't recognized as an independent entity by the IRS, and federal tax returns are prepared and filed as if the business were a proprietorship. This means that just like a proprietorship, the single member files Schedule C and reports the profit on Form 1040. State and local tax returns are also based on the profit of the business, not the amount the owner withdrew.

CPA NOTE*: There is no limitation to the number of proprietorships or single member LLCs that can be included on an individual federal tax return. Each business requires its own Schedule C. The amount reported on page 1 of Form 1040 is the sum of all Schedule Cs included with the tax return.*

Also, some states and localities may have an additional business tax return filing that is not based on the income of the business.

A single member LLC can elect to be treated as a corporation, although this is not very common, and can file corporate tax returns. You should note that the "C" in LLC stands for "company," not "corporation."

Partnership Tax Return

At the end of the year, a partnership prepares and files its own federal tax return (Form 1065) but pays no income taxes on its own behalf. The partners are responsible for paying the taxes due on their shares of the business's income on their personal tax returns. The information recorded in Form 1065 comes from the partnership's Profit & Loss statement as well as its balance sheet (both of which are discussed in Chapter 11).

Each partner receives Schedule K-1, which reports his or her share of the profits. (You can think of this as similar to a W-2.) Each partner's share of the profits is based on the Profit & Loss report and not the amount of the partner's draw. If the profit is larger than the draw, the amount of the profit is treated as if the partner had drawn all profits and then contributed the amount not drawn back to the partnership to fund its continuing operations. These funds are available for withdrawal by the partner at a later time with no additional income tax consequences.

If applicable, Schedule K-1 also reports other transactions specific to that partner:

- Interest and dividend income
- Health insurance premiums
- Retirement plan contributions
- State income tax payments for partners who are not residents of the state in which the partnership does business (and the partner can take credit for those payments on his or her personal return)

Each partner reports the net profit reported on the Schedule K-1 on his or her personal tax return using Schedule E. The other income and payments from the partnership that appear on Schedule K-1 are also reported on Form 1040, but not normally on Schedule E.

Your state may require partnerships to file a tax return; some states collect income taxes from the partners as well as business taxes and/or fees imposed on the partnership. These funds are remitted with the partnership return that you file with the state.

State business fees are deductible as a business expense by the partnership. Income taxes that are paid by the partnership for the benefit of the partners are not deductible expenses for the partnership; instead, they are treated as a draw. Some states only require estimated income tax payments for nonresident partners. Nonresident partners file income tax returns in any nonresident states in which they have reportable income (receiving credit for the estimated nonresident state taxes paid on their behalf). When these partners file state income tax returns in their home state, they receive credit for taxes paid to any other state.

When you remit business tax returns and payments to the state, you post the partners' tax payments to each partner's draw account. Regular business fees owed to the state by the partnership are business expenses. Table 12-6 represents the postings for state business taxes, as well as nonresident state income tax payments made for the benefit of nonresident partners B and C (partner A is a resident of the state).

Account	Debit	Credit
36020—Draw-Partner B-State Tax	300.00	
36030—Draw-Partner C-State Tax	200.00	
85000—Business Taxes and Licenses	100.00	
10000—Bank Account		600.00

Table 12-6: Only state taxes imposed on the partnership are business expenses.

LLP or Multimember LLC Tax Return

The returns and procedures for LLPs and Multimember LLCs are the same as for partnerships for both federal and state taxes. The business files Form 1065, but pays no federal business taxes. Any taxes paid are personal taxes for the partners/members and are based on the information on Form K-1 (see the discussion on partnership returns earlier in this section).

The IRS treats a multimember LLC as a partnership by default. However, a multimember LLC can elect to be treated as a corporation, including an S corporation, by filing Form 8832—Entity Classification Election. This isn't a common action, but if your company has elected to be treated as a corporation, the information in the following sections for corporate tax returns applies.

S Corporation Tax Return

An S Corporation tax return is similar to that of a partnership (S corps are hybrid organizations, mixing some corporate conventions with partnership conventions). The corporation files a tax return (Form 1120S), but usually pays no income taxes on its own behalf. Included with the return is Schedule K-1, which reports the profit for each stockholder and a summary of any other transactions specific to that stockholder. (Many S corporations have a single stockholder.)

As with partnerships, LLPs, and multimember LLCs, a stockholder's share of the profits is based on the Profit & Loss report and not the amount of the stockholder's draw. To the extent that the profit is larger than the draw, you can look at it as if the stockholder had drawn all of his/her profit share out and then contributed the amount not drawn out back to the business to fund its continuing operations; the funds should be available for withdrawal at a later time with no income tax consequence.

The stockholder reports the net profit on page 2 of Schedule E of his or her personal tax return. Other financial transactions reported on Schedule K-1 are reported on the stockholder's tax forms, the same as if they had been received from or paid by a sole proprietor.

The S Corporation also files state income tax returns for every state in which it conducts business. As with partnerships, LLPs, and multi-member LLCs, most states impose state income tax for each stockholder who is not a resident of that state. The amount of the tax is based on the stockholder's share of the business profit. These payments to the state are often made by the S Corporation, but are not a business expense; instead, they are posted as a draw for those stockholders. Nonresident stockholders can take credit for these payments on their personal tax returns.

C Corporation Tax Return

A C Corporation files federal Form 1120 and applicable state corporate tax returns. The corporation pays taxes on the corporation's profits.

Stockholders may receive other tax forms, depending on the situation: W-2 for wages, 1099-MISC for directors' fees, 1099-INT for interest, and

1099-DIV for dividends. The amounts on these forms are reported on the stockholders' personal tax returns, the same as they would be if they were received from any other entity.

Closing the Books

Closing the books is something you should do at the end of the fiscal year. However, QuickBooks does not force you to do so. You can keep running for years without ever closing the books. The main reason to close the books in QuickBooks is to prevent users from making changes to transactions from the prior year.

ProAdvisor NOTE: *Even if you don't close the books, QuickBooks still automatically transfers your profit/loss to retained earnings and resets income and expense accounts to zero.*

Setting the Closing Date

Once the fiscal year is over, all transactions for the period should be left untouched. Unfortunately, users have a tendency to forget this rule and return to those earlier numbers to tidy up. The one way to make sure they don't give in to this temptation is to set the closing date in QuickBooks. Here's how:

1. Choose Company | Set Closing Date to open the Company Preferences tab of the Accounting preferences.

2. Move to the Closing Date section at the bottom of the tab and click the Set Date/Password button to open the Set Closing Date And Password dialog box (see Figure 12-5).

3. Since estimates, purchase orders, and sales orders may carry over into the next year, you may choose to allow changes to them by checking the Exclude Estimates, Sales Orders And Purchase Orders From Closing Date Restrictions option.

4. Enter the cutoff date for changes in the Closing Date field. This is usually the last day of the period you're closing.

5. Enter a password to keep other users from making changes to transactions from the closed period.

6. Click OK to save the new closing date and password.

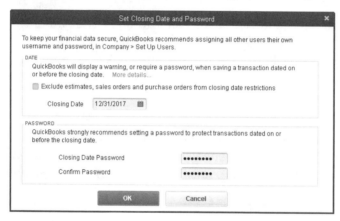

Figure 12-5: Set a closing date and password to prevent unauthorized changes to transactions.

If users attempt to make changes to transactions from a closed period, they are allowed to make the changes. However, when they try to save the changes, they are presented with the dialog box shown in Figure 12-6.

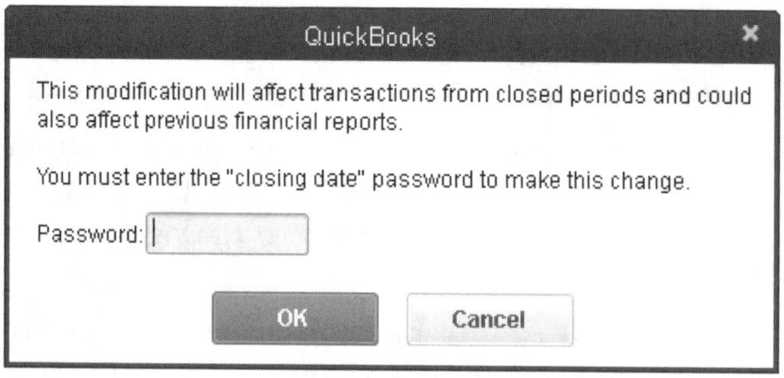

Figure 12-6: Changing a closed period transaction requires the password.

CPA NOTE: *While entering the password above will allow the change to the closed period, your balances will not agree to the ones used by your CPA when your tax return was prepared. This will require additional work and explanation when the CPA works on your next tax year's returns.*

Backing Up the Company File

As you know, backing up your data on a regular basis is extremely important. Making a year-end backup and storing it offsite is critical. In the event that disaster hits (robbery, fire, etc.), you'll want to be able to restore the data for previous years.

Follow the standard backup procedures using a CD or DVD to ensure that the data is secure. You can also make an online backup if you subscribe to the service.

CPA NOTE: *It is also a good idea to make a backup (call it "20xx Archive") that can be used in case of an audit. The IRS has begun requesting copies of QuickBooks files during the audit process (as it does with the major accounting software programs), and it would be preferable to provide the IRS with a data file that does not include more information than requested (e.g., subsequent year activity).*

CHAPTER 13:

QuickBooks Maintenance

- Backing Up and Restoring

- Verifying and Rebuilding Data

- Managing Users and Passwords

- Updating QuickBooks

- Importing and Exporting

- Enabling Customer Credit Card Protection

In addition to bookkeeping chores in QuickBooks, you have some computer housekeeping chores. It's important to keep your data safe, your company file clean, your software up-to-date, and more. QuickBooks provides tools to help you with these tasks.

Backing Up with QuickBooks

QuickBooks offers three types of backups:

- Manual
- Automatic
- Scheduled

We'll cover all three in the following sections.

Creating a Manual Backup

Begin by choosing File | Back Up Company | Create Local Backup to open the QuickBooks Create Backup wizard.

By default, the Create Backup wizard selects Local Backup. However, you can also use Intuit's fee-based service to backup online by choosing the Online Backup option. You can learn more about it (and sign up) by clicking the link labeled Try Now Or Learn More. For this discussion, we're assuming that you selected the option labeled Local Backup.

Configuring Manual Backup Options

Click the Options button to display the Backup Options window seen in Figure 13-1. If you click Next and haven't yet configured the options, the backup wizard opens the Options window for you.

Choose a Location for Manual Backups

Select a default location, which should be an external drive, a removable drive, or a shared folder on another computer on your network. The location in Figure 13-1 is an external hard drive.

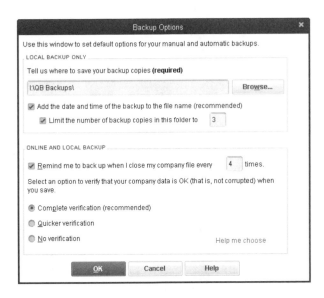

Figure 13-1: Let QuickBooks know where and how to save the
backup file.

You can choose a folder on the same hard drive on which QuickBooks is installed, but you'll get a warning message about the lack of safety and will be asked to confirm your choice. To ensure that the misfortune that befalls your original file doesn't affect your backup, store the backup on a separate device.

Add a Timestamp to a Manual Backup Filename

Select the option to add a timestamp to the backup filename to ensure you don't overwrite the last good backup every time you save a backup.

Use the option labeled Limit The Number Of Backup Copies In This Folder to set a limit on the number of backups saved to the target location. When the limit is reached, the new file replaces the oldest file.

If you don't set a limit, QuickBooks saves every backup, which takes up a great deal of disk space. It's a good idea to save at least three backups; it's a better idea to keep a week's worth of backups. If your company file becomes corrupt, you can go back several days to find a backup that isn't a backup of the corrupted file.

Backup Reminders

You can configure QuickBooks to remind you to back up and ask if you want to perform a backup every X times you close the software (where X is a number you select).

Verifying Files before Backup

Before performing a manual backup, you should verify the integrity of the file. QuickBooks checks the file to make sure its structure is valid. Data verification functions can detect corrupt files or corrupt portions of files. Your choices are

- Complete Verification (Recommended).This checks both the data in the database and the accuracy of your company file. This option is only available if the file is in single-user mode.

- Quicker Verification. Choose this option to check only the underlying database for corruption; your company file is not checked.

- No Verification. Only use this option if time is of the essence and you need a quick backup.

If the verification process results in a message that there are problems in the file, use File | Utilities | Rebuild Data to try to repair the damage. Verify the file again, and if problems persist, you'll have to contact QuickBooks support.

Scheduled Backups

You can schedule automatic backups of your company file, which is the preferred method for backing up—no excuses, no waiting around the office after hours, no possibility that somebody will forget to back up your data file.

The best time to schedule a backup is at night, when nobody is using the software. However, that plan doesn't work unless you remember the rules:

- Make sure your computer is running when you leave the office.

- If you're on a network, schedule the backup from the QuickBooks software installed on the computer that holds the company file. Make sure that computer is running when you leave the office.

- Before you leave, make sure you close QuickBooks (or close all company files if you leave the software running), because open files can't be backed up.

Use the following steps to configure this feature:

1. Choose File | Back Up Company | Create Local Backup.

2. In the Create Backup dialog, select Local Backup.

3. Click Next to open the backup type selection dialog. If you haven't set the default options for backups as described earlier in this section, QuickBooks opens the Options dialog. You must fill out the form before this dialog displays.

4. Choose Only Schedule Future Backups and click Next to open the Create Backup dialog seen in Figure 13-2.

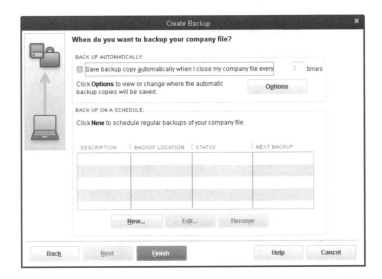

Figure 13-2: A scheduled backup is the best way to make sure your file is backed up regularly.

The top of the dialog has an option for configuring automatic backups when you close your company file. The word "close" is literal, so an automated backup takes place under either of the following conditions:

- While working in QuickBooks, you open a different company file or choose File | Close
- You exit QuickBooks

This can be a real drag, especially if you open and close your company file more than once a day. Unless you make a large number of entries during each QuickBooks session, it's also unnecessary, provided that you configure a scheduled backup every day.

To create a scheduled backup, click New to open the Schedule Backup dialog seen in Figure 13-3.

Figure 13-3: Schedule an automatic, unattended backup.

- Description is a name (a nickname) you give this backup configuration. For example, in Figure 13-3, the name of the target drive is the description.

- Location is the target drive or folder. This can be a removable drive, an external drive, a shared folder on another computer on your network, or a local folder (if you back up the local folder to another computer, removable media, or an online backup service every day). The location does not have to be the same location you configured in the Options dialog for manual backups.
- Number Of Backup Copies To Keep is your way of accumulating several backups in case your file becomes corrupted (and the last backup or two were, therefore, corrupt).
- Start Time is the time to perform the backup.

The bottom part of the dialog is where you create the schedule for this backup. The first scheduled backup should be at least five days a week (add Saturday and/or Sunday if users work on those days).

You can create additional schedules, such as a weekly backup that you save to a folder on your local computer and transfer to a CD.

Store password means that you enter a user name and password of a user who has permissions for the target folder or drive. The user name and password is a Windows user name and password, not a QuickBooks user name and password. The user may be you, or it may be a user on a remote computer who has full rights on the backup folder on that computer.

Offsite Storage of Backups

At least once a month (preferably once a week), you should make an additional backup and take the backup media offsite.

Offsite backups are your insurance against disasters beyond dead hard drives or computers. Fire, flood, or burglaries can rob you of your computer, your network, and your locally stored backup media.

If your organization has a web site with sufficient storage space, set aside a folder for holding backups. Use FTP software to upload the files.

(Your web-hosting company has instructions for completing this task on its support pages.)

ProAdvisor NOTE: *You can also subscribe (for a monthly fee) to the Intuit Data Protect service, which allows you to create online backups to the Intuit servers. Click the Try Now Or Learn More link in the Create Backup window for details.*

Restoring Backup Files

If you need to restore a company file, you must have your last backup at hand. If you're restoring your company file to a new computer or new hard drive, install QuickBooks and download the latest update.

If you backed up to removable media, put the disk that contains your last backup into its drive. If you backed up to a network share, be sure the remote computer is running. If you used an online backup service, be sure you're connected to the Internet.

When everything is ready, open QuickBooks and choose File | Open Or Restore Company. When the Open Or Restore Company dialog, seen in Figure 13-4, is displayed, use the following steps to restore your company file:

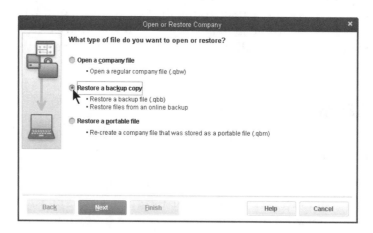

Figure 13-4: Use the Restore A Backup Copy feature for local or online backups.

1. Choose Restore A Backup Copy and click Next.

2. Choose Local Backup and click Next.

3. In the Open Backup Copy dialog, use the Look In drop-down list to navigate to the folder where you stored the backup. Select the file (it has the extension .QBB) and click Open.

4. In the next window, read the instructions and then click Next. The Save Company dialog should display the contents of the folder that holds your company file. If not, navigate to that folder.

5. Name the file and click Save, using the following guidelines:

   - Use the default name (the company name) to save the file, which overwrites the existing company file if one exists. Depending on the version of Windows you're using, you may see an error message telling you that the existing file is Read-Only and advising you to pick a different name. Instead of picking a different name, leave the Save File dialog open and navigate to the folder in Windows. Find the file (it has an extension .QBW). Right-click and choose Properties and deselect the Read-Only attribute. Then, return to the Save dialog and save the file with the original name (you have to confirm the overwrite).

   - If you are testing a backup to see if it restores properly or you have another reason not to overwrite the existing file, change the filename.

6. Click Save to have QuickBooks open the file.

ProAdvisor NOTE: *If this backup wasn't created yesterday (or after the last time you used your company file), you must re-create every transaction you made between the time of this backup and the last time you used QuickBooks.*

Cleaning Up Data File Corruption

QuickBooks offers a pair of utilities that help you keep your company file healthy. The first checks your data file for signs of corruption, while the second repairs many problems found.

This is one of those housekeeping tasks that many users fail to take seriously until problems arise. Since corrupted data files can result in erroneous report results, you run the risk of relying on faulty information if you fail to perform these tasks regularly.

Verify Data

The first utility is called Verify Data and should be run at least once a month; probably more often, depending on the number of users logging into QuickBooks. Ideally, it should be run weekly. It checks for damage to the list and transaction tables in the database, as well as to memorized reports. If you don't run the utility regularly, you should certainly run it when you see telltale signs of corruption:

- QuickBooks error messages
- QuickBooks crashes
- Report discrepancies
- List elements missing
- Missing transactions

You'll find the Verify Data utility on the File | Utilities submenu. Click the Verify Data command to run the utility. It starts immediately and informs you of the results—errors if it finds any, none if it hasn't found any. If you're running it as a regular housekeeping chore and it doesn't find any errors, you're good to continue working. However, if you have been encountering errors in QuickBooks and the utility doesn't find any errors, you may have to contact Intuit Support.

ProAdvisor TIP: *Before you run the Verify Data utility, close QuickBooks and reopen it. This will create a new Qbwin.log file, which keeps track of QuickBooks activity for the session (including the results of the Verify Data operation). The new file will be shorter, which will make it easier to locate errors in the event that the utility encounters any.*

Rebuild Data

If you run the Verify Data utility and it finds errors, it will advise you to run the Rebuild Data utility to correct the damage. However, before you run the utility, there are a few things you should do first:

- Make a backup of your company file. Not that you have a choice, since QuickBooks won't run the utility unless you first create a backup.

- Make sure that the company file is on a local computer with QuickBooks installed. In other words, don't run the utility over the network.

- Switch to single-user mode if you're in multi-user mode.

- Resort all your lists by opening each list, clicking the button at the bottom left corner of the list window, and selecting Re-Sort List. The button will be named for the list (Item, Account, etc.). The act of resorting can sometimes repair damage done to a list.

- Press F2 to open the Product Information window. From the File Information section, record the File Size, Total Transactions, Total Targets, Total Links, and DB File Fragments numbers. After the build, you can compare these numbers to assess the effects of the rebuild operation.

- Close all open QuickBooks windows.

> **ProAdvisor TIP**: *If, for some reason, you are unable to create a backup (one of the reasons being that you might be running the Rebuild Data utility), you can still run the utility by holding down the Ctrl key while selecting File | Utilities | Rebuild Data with your mouse. If you choose to use this method, be sure to make a copy of the folder containing the company file first.*

When you've completed the above-mentioned chores, you're ready to run the utility. Choose File | Utilities | Rebuild Data. QuickBooks insists that you make a backup copy. As soon as the backup is saved, QuickBooks runs the Rebuild Data utility. When the rebuild finishes, the Rebuild Has Completed message appears. Click OK to close it.

> **ProAdvisor TIP**: *If the rebuild crashes, open the Qbwin.log file and check the last line. Frequently, a corrupted transaction will cause the rebuild to crash. The last line of the Qbwin.log records the culprit. Open the transaction, save it as a memorized transaction, and delete it. Rerun the Rebuild Data utility to see if the problem is solved. If so, reenter the deleted transaction.*

To review the Qbwin.log file for errors, press F2 to display the Product Information window, and then press F3 to open the Tech Help window. Click the Open File tab, scroll down to the QBWIN.LOG file, and click the Open File button to the right. The file opens in NotePad.

> **ProAdvisor TIP**: *There's one more thing you can try if the Rebuild Data feature doesn't fix the problem. Create and restore a Portable Company File. The process re-indexes the company file, which frequently can resolve data issues. See Chapter 2 for more on Portable Company Files.*

Managing Users and Passwords

If more than one person is accessing the company file on the same computer, users and passwords should be set to protect sensitive financial data and to control who has access to that data. As a matter of fact, even if you're the only person accessing the company file (as the Admin), you should still create a password to prevent others from accessing the data while you're away from your computer.

Creating Users

Creating users is a multi-step process that can only be performed by the user named Admin. You have to complete the following tasks to create a user:

- Create a user name.
- Optionally assign a password to the user name.
- Set the permissions for the user.

Adding a User Name and Password

To add a user to your QuickBooks company file, choose Company | Set Up Users And Passwords | Set Up Users to open the User List dialog. All user names are displayed in the dialog and the notation (logged on) is next to the currently logged-on user (or users, if you're running a multi-user version of QuickBooks). If this is the first user you're creating, only the administrator appears in the list, as seen in Figure 13-5.

Figure 13-5: All user setup tasks start with the User List dialog.

To add a new user to the list, click Add User. A wizard appears to help you set up the new user. In the first wizard window, enter the user name, which is the name this user must type to log in to QuickBooks.

To establish a password for this user, enter and confirm the password. You can ask the user to give you a password or invent one yourself and pass it along to the user. (Users can change their own passwords at any time.)

> **ProAdvisor NOTE**: *If you don't create a password, QuickBooks issues a gentle warning, but you are free to omit the password (which is not a good idea).*

Setting User Permissions

When you click Next, the wizard asks whether you want to let this user have access to selected areas of QuickBooks or to all areas of QuickBooks. (Regardless of the choice you make, you can always return to this dialog and change the settings.)

If you choose the option All Areas Of QuickBooks, when you click Next, QuickBooks displays a message asking you to confirm that fact. Click Yes and then click Finish.

When you give blanket permissions to a new user, you're creating a virtual administrator. This person can do everything the administrator can do, except those tasks reserved specifically for the real administrator (create and modify users, change Company preferences, change company information, import and export data, and enable or disable credit card protection).

> **ProAdvisor NOTE**: *The third choice, External Accountant, provides the user with access to everything except customer credit card information and the ability to add, edit, or delete users. It also provides access to one additional feature that is unavailable to all other users (including the Admin)—the Client Data Review tool found in the Premier Accountant Edition. This utility enables you to review changes, reclassify transactions, and more.*

If you choose the option Selected Areas Of QuickBooks, clicking Next moves you through a series of wizard screens in which you specify the permissions for this user. Each of the ensuing wizard windows is dedicated to a specific QuickBooks component (see Figure 13-6). You can establish permissions for this user for each component.

Figure 13-6: Each component of QuickBooks has its own screen,
where you can set permissions for this user.

For each QuickBooks component, select one of the following permission options:

- No Access. The user is denied permission to open any windows in that component of QuickBooks.

- Full Access. The user can open all windows and perform all tasks in that component of QuickBooks except editing or deleting existing transactions (see the section "Changing or Deleting Transactions" later in this chapter).

- Selective Access. The user is permitted to view data and perform tasks as you specify.

If you choose Selective Access, you're asked to specify the rights this user should have. Those rights vary from component to component, but generally, you're asked to choose one of these permission levels:

- Create transactions
- Create and print transactions
- Create transactions and create reports

When you're configuring selective access, you can choose only one of the three levels. If you need to give the user rights to more than one of these choices, you can't custom-design a mix-and-match set of permissions. Instead, you must select Full Access for that component.

Notice that the list of permissions for selective access doesn't include any permissions for changing transactions or deleting transactions. The wizard handles those tasks separately. (See the section "Changing or Deleting Transactions" later in this chapter.)

As you move through the wizard windows, you can click Finish at any time. The components you skip are automatically set for No Access for this user. This means that when you're setting up a user who should only be able to access Purchases and Accounts Payable tasks, after you make your selections for that component, you can click Finish instead of moving through the remaining wizard windows.

Setting Permissions for Special Areas of QuickBooks

Two of the wizard windows display permissions settings that are not directly related to any specific component of the software: Sensitive Accounting Activities and Sensitive Accounting Reports.

Sensitive Accounting Activities Permissions

Sensitive accounting activities are those tasks that aren't directly related to specific QuickBooks components or transactions. They include tasks such as the following:

- Making changes to the Chart of Accounts
- Working in balance sheet account registers

- Using online banking
- Transferring funds between banks
- Reconciling bank accounts
- Creating journal entries
- Preparing an accountant's review
- Condensing data
- Working with budgets

The configuration window presents the same three permission levels as the windows for the other components. If you choose Selective Access as the permission level, the three access choices are the same as those for the other components.

Sensitive Accounting Reports Permissions

Sensitive financial reports are those reports that reveal important financial information about your company, such as:

- Profit & Loss reports
- Balance Sheet reports
- Budget reports
- Cash Flow reports
- Income Tax reports
- Trial Balance reports
- Audit Trail reports

The configuration window for Sensitive Accounting Reports presents the same three permission levels as the windows for the other components. If you choose Selective Access as the permission level, the following choices are offered:

- Create Sensitive Reports Only
- Create And Print Sensitive Reports

The difference between the permissions has to do with the user's ability to walk out of the office with sensitive reports.

Changing or Deleting Transactions Permissions

If a user has permissions for certain components, you can limit his or her ability to manipulate existing transactions within those areas. Figure 13-7 shows the wizard window that manages these permissions.

Figure 13-7: Set permissions for manipulating existing transactions.

If you choose Yes, the user can edit and delete transactions in any area where the user has been given access permissions.

If you choose No, the user can only edit and delete transactions that he or she created in the current QuickBooks session. Transactions created by other users and transactions created by this user in the past or in the future cannot be edited or deleted.

Closed Period Permissions

The Changing or Deleting Transactions window also covers transactions that are in a closed period (which means you've taken the steps described in Chapter 12 to enter a closing date and create a password for access to transactions dated on or before that closing date).

If you choose Yes, the user can edit and delete transactions entered on or before the closing date as long as the user knows the password needed to access those transactions.

If you choose No, the user cannot access transactions in the closed period, even if he or she knows the password.

Permissions Summary

When you have finished configuring user permissions for components and sensitive areas, the last wizard window displays a list of the permissions you've granted and refused. If everything is correct, click Finish. If there's something you want to change, use the Back button to back up to the appropriate window.

Changing User Settings

In addition to adding users, the administrator can remove users, change user passwords, and modify user permissions at any time. All user modifications are made in the User List dialog, which has the following functions available for the user name you select:

- Edit User. Opens the Change User Password And Access wizard, which is almost the same as the Add User wizard, so you can re-do the settings.

- Delete User. Removes the user from the User List.

- View User. Displays the summary page of the Set Up User Password And Access wizard, which shows all permissions set for this user.

ProAdvisor TIP: *If you're running a networked version of QuickBooks and want to see which users are logged on, simply open the User List and take a look. All logged on users have "(logged on)" next to their names.*

Updating QuickBooks

QuickBooks provides an automatic update service to make sure your QuickBooks software is up-to-date and trouble-free. This service provides you with any maintenance releases of QuickBooks that have been created since you purchased and installed your copy of the software.

An update (maintenance release) is distributed when a problem is discovered and fixed. This is sometimes necessary, because it's almost impossible to distribute a program that is totally bug-free (although our experience has been that QuickBooks generally releases without any major bugs, since Intuit does a thorough job of testing its software before it's released).

The Update QuickBooks service also provides enhancements to features along with notes from Intuit that help you keep up with new features and information about QuickBooks. Keep in mind, this service does *not* provide upgrades to a new version; it just provides updates to your current version.

The Update QuickBooks service is an online service, so you must have set up online access in QuickBooks. To check for updates and to configure update options, choose Help | Update QuickBooks to display the Update QuickBooks dialog (see Figure 13-8).

Configuring the Update Service

Click the Options tab to configure the Update feature. As you can see in Figure 13-8, you have several methods for updating your software components. You can change these options at any time.

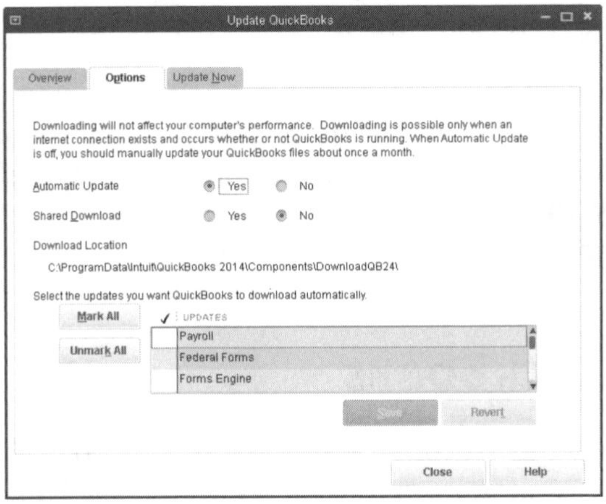

Figure 13-8: Configure the QuickBooks Update services.

Automatic Updates

Select Yes for Automatic Updates if you want to allow QuickBooks to check the QuickBooks update site on the Internet periodically (while you're connected). QuickBooks doesn't have to be open for this function to occur.

If new information is found, it's downloaded to your hard drive automatically, without any notification. If you happen to disconnect from the Internet while updates are being downloaded, the next time you connect to the Internet, QuickBooks will pick up where it left off.

If you don't like the idea of a software application downloading files without notifying you, select No to turn off the automatic option. However, you must periodically open the Update QuickBooks dialog and click Update Now to check for updates and install them.

ProAdvisor NOTE: *If you have any online services, such as Payroll or Online Banking, when you use those services, QuickBooks checks for updates. This occurs even if you've turned off automatic updates.*

Shared Downloads

If you're running QuickBooks on a network with multiple users, configure the Update QuickBooks service to share downloaded files with other users. The files are downloaded to the computer that holds the shared QuickBooks data files, and the location is noted on this dialog. Every user on the network must open his or her copy of QuickBooks and configure the Update options for Shared Download, pointing to the location on the computer that holds the shared data files.

Checking the Status of Updates

Click the Update Now tab to view information about the current status of the update service, including the last date that QuickBooks checked for updates and the names of any files that were downloaded.

Updating QuickBooks Manually

If you configured QuickBooks so that updates aren't automatically downloaded, click Get Updates on the Update Now tab to tell QuickBooks to check the Internet immediately and bring back any new files.

Most of the time, the files are automatically integrated into your system. However, sometimes an information message appears to tell you that the files will be installed the next time you start QuickBooks.

Importing and Exporting

There is often a need to exchange QuickBooks information with other users and other programs. When that need arises, you have several options.

Import Utilities

Bringing data into your company file is accomplished using one of the import utilities provided by QuickBooks and found on the File | Utilities | Import submenu:

- Excel Files. This feature opens the Add Your Excel Data To QuickBooks window, which enables you to import customer, vendor, and inventory data from Excel spreadsheets. You can either enter data into a spreadsheet created automatically for you, or you can import data from an existing spreadsheet.

- IIF Files. IIF (Intuit Interchange Format) files allow you to exchange data with other QuickBooks users and with some other software applications. You can export many of your lists, including the Chart of Accounts, item lists, customer lists, and more to IIF files. Other QuickBooks users can then import those files into their company files. It's also a great way to transfer lists between your own company files.

- Web Connect Files. If your bank does not offer the Direct Connect method for downloading transactions into QuickBooks, it probably does offer Web

Connect files. These are special files containing your transactions that can be downloaded and opened directly into QuickBooks. Check with your bank to see what they offer.

- Timer Activities. If you track time with the QuickBooks Timer, you'll need to import the data into your timesheets using the Timer Activities import feature.

- General Journal Entries. Journal entries are one of the QuickBooks activities that many users prefer to leave up to their accountants. To facilitate the process, accountants can create journal entries on their computers (using a copy of your company file) and send them to you via e-mail. Once you receive them, you can use this import utility to enter them into QuickBooks automatically.

ProAdvisor CAUTION: *Imports are great, but they have one drawback—they can't be reversed. Once you import data from an outside source, you're stuck with it, so be sure to review all data for errors and duplicate entries before importing.*

Export Utilities

In addition to providing import utilities, QuickBooks also offers a number of export features.

- Lists To IIF Files. If you want to save another user (or yourself when creating a new company file) a lot of time and aggravation, export some of your existing lists to IIF files. Choose File | Utilities | Export | Lists To IIF Files to display the Export dialog shown in Figure 13-9. You can choose one, more than one, or all of the lists by placing a check mark next to each list you want to export. When you click OK, they are all exported into a single IIF file that can be imported into other QuickBooks company files.

- Addresses To Text File. This is a handy little tool that will take names from your Customer, Vendor,

Employee, and Other Names lists and export them into a text file you can open in Word, NotePad, Excel, or another program to review and use.

- **Timer Lists.** If you're using the QuickBooks Timer to track time, you'll find this export tool indispensable. To utilize the QuickBooks Timer, you need to provide it with a list of all your customers, jobs, vendors, employees, other names, service items, and classes. This export feature creates an IIF file containing those items, which can be opened and used by the QuickBooks Timer.

- **Payroll To XML.** Select this option to generate an XML file containing payroll information (employees, payroll items, and payroll transactions) that you can exchange with other users or other applications.

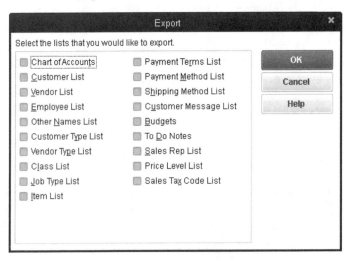

Figure 13-9: Exporting, then importing lists is a great time saver.

ProAdvisor NOTE: *Although QuickBooks timer lists are exported to IIF files, they are constructed differently from the IIF files that are exported by the Lists To IIF Files utility. In other words, don't think they are interchangeable. QuickBooks will balk if you try importing the wrong type.*

Third-Party Utilities

The import utilities included with QuickBooks are handy, but somewhat limited. If your import needs are more sophisticated, you might want to try one of the third-party utilities available for purchase. While there are several worthwhile programs on the market, we have found one to be particularly useful. It is called Transaction Pro Importer by Baystate Consulting (www.baystateconsulting.com).

It offers a wide range of import options, including the ability to import data from Excel files, Access database files, and a variety of text files (.csv, .tsv, .txt, and more). The type of data you can import is also impressive. In addition to list information, you can import transaction data, as well. As a matter of fact, you can import 12 different list types and 21 different transaction types, including invoices, bills, credits, item receipts, receive payments, and a lot more.

When you first open it, QuickBooks asks you to confirm that you want to allow the application to access the QuickBooks Company file. Provide the type of permission you want Transaction Pro Importer to have and click Continue to open the Transaction Pro Import Wizard (see Figure 13-10).

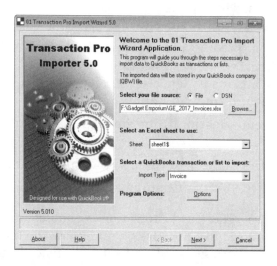

Figure 13-10: The wizard walks you through the steps to import your data.

The wizard offers a lot of import options that cover most concerns you might have when bringing new data into QuickBooks. For example, you can map incoming fields to match existing QuickBooks fields, you can tell the utility not to add new customers or vendors, etc. You can even enable custom fields created in QuickBooks.

Enabling Customer Credit Card Protection

These days, the only reason to retain credit card information from your customers is if they are repeat customers who continually use the same credit card to pay for purchases. In the event that you do retain credit card information, you must be sure that it is secure. As a matter of fact, failure to comply with the PCI Data Security Standard (PCI DSS) can result in penalties and the loss of ability to accept credit cards. Visit https://www.pcisecuritystandards.org/ for more information.

To ensure your retained credit card information is safe, you should enable the Customer Credit Card Protection feature in QuickBooks.

1. Select Company | Customer Credit Card Protection.
2. Click Enable Protection in the informational dialog that appears. This opens the Sensitive Data Protection Setup dialog seen in Figure 13-11.
3. Enter a "strong" password in the New Password and Confirm New Password fields. A "strong" password is one that contains at least seven characters in a combination of letters and numbers and upper and lower case.
4. Choose a question from the Challenge Question drop-down list.
5. Type the answer to the question in the Answer text box.
6. Click OK to turn Customer Credit Card Protection on.

Once Customer Credit Card Protection is enabled, anyone wishing to access the data must have permission and know the password. See the section entitled "Setting User Permissions" earlier in this chapter for more information.

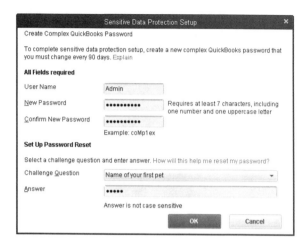

Figure 13-11: Use a complex password to secure credit card data.

CHAPTER 14:

Managing Equity

- Understanding Equity Accounts
- Proprietorships
- Partnerships
- LLCs and LLPs
- Multimember LLCs and LLPs
- Corporations
- C Corporations
- S Corporations

In this chapter, we'll explain how to post transactions related to the money you put into your business and the money you take out of the business. We'll discuss the following types of entities:

- Proprietorship. A business owned by a single individual.

- Partnership. A business owned by more than one individual.

- LLC (Limited Liability Company). A business that has one or more owners (called members instead of owners). Note that the "C" in LLC stands for company, not corporation. A single-member LLC is similar to a proprietorship, and a multimember LLC is similar to a partnership. An LLC provides more protection against personal liability than a proprietorship or a partnership. An LLC can request permission of the IRS to be treated as a corporation; if granted, the discussions in this chapter follow the rules of C Corporations.

- LLP (Limited Liability Partnership). Similar to a partnership, but providing more protection against personal liability. Each partner is called a member instead of partner.

- S Corporation. A hybrid organization with some characteristics of a proprietorship or partnership and some characteristics of a C Corporation.

- C Corporation. The entity type most controlled by rules, including the way the stockholder (owner) funds the corporation and withdraws funds.

For all of these entities, the discussions in this chapter involve the use of equity accounts in transactions that contribute money to and withdraw money from your business. Some of these transactions segregate information you use in preparing income tax returns. Income tax discussions, while mentioned in this chapter, are discussed in further detail in Chapter 12.

Understanding Equity Accounts

Equity is your business's capital, the difference between what it owns (assets) and what it owes (liabilities). Equity is increased by the money that owners put into the business (startup funds and additional funds for growth) and by the company's profit. Equity is decreased by business losses and by withdrawals (not including payroll) made by the business owners.

CPA NOTE: *For income tax purposes, owners are taxed on the profit and loss of the business, not the amount of funds they withdraw.*

The equity accounts are the best reminder of an important concept that some business owners don't understand: Not all of your bank deposits are income, and not all of your checks are expenses. Transactions that involve equity accounts are neither income nor expenses; these transactions don't affect the taxable profit/loss of the company.

The simplified definition of "equity" is, "What the owner's stake in the company is worth." The owner can be a proprietor, a partner, a member, or a stockholder. Equity transactions appear on the Balance Sheet report and not on the Profit & Loss report because the Profit & Loss report is only concerned with income and expenses. (Details about those reports and what they represent can be found in Chapter 11.)

There are a variety of equity accounts you use when you post equity-based transactions, and it's important to understand how and when to use each equity account. Equity accounts track the net effect of all of your company's past transactions and are the starting point in calculating the value of your business.

Using these accounts correctly also means that you won't have a hassle with the IRS because you incorrectly reported an equity transaction as an expense or because you failed to report the correct amount of personal income from the business on your personal tax return.

Proprietorships

A proprietorship (also called a sole proprietorship) has a single owner and doesn't file a business tax return. Instead, the profit for the business is reported on Schedule C of the owner's federal tax return (or Schedule E in the case of real estate rental activities) and is included on the owner's personal income tax return (Form 1040). There is no limit to the number of proprietorships that can be included on an individual tax return. Each proprietorship requires its own Schedule C (based on each individual company's Profit & Loss report), and the amount reported on Form 1040 is the sum of all the Schedule Cs included with the tax return.

It's best to run your proprietorship with a separate bank account dedicated to your business operations. Although this isn't strictly required, handling your business operations in this manner makes record keeping easier and provides a record that a third party (tax authority, a bank considering loaning your business money, etc.) could examine without confusing your personal finances with your business activities.

Funding Proprietorships

When you started your business, you probably funded it by transferring money from your personal bank account to the business account. Those startup funds are not income to the business and don't result in any taxable profit. You record this startup transaction using the Make Deposit window (see Figure 14-1).

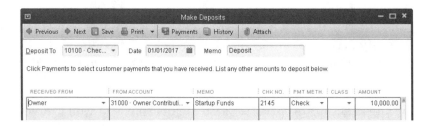

Figure 14-1: Deposit your startup funds using the correct equity account.

The postings for the deposit are shown in Table 14-1.

Account	Debit	Credit
10100—Bank Account	1000.00	
31000—Owner Contributions		1000.00

Table 14-1: The initial contribution of capital to a proprietorship is posted to an equity account—it isn't income.

Occasionally, you may find it necessary to add additional capital to the business in order to fund operations. The additional funding is recorded in exactly the same way.

Withdrawing Money from a Proprietorship

As your proprietorship makes money, you can withdraw funds. It's important to note that the proprietor cannot take payroll (although you can hire employees who are on the payroll).

When you withdraw money, you post the amount as a contra (negative) transaction to equity. It's best to create a separate equity account named Draw to track your withdrawals. That way, both your contributions and draws are easy to see. You record the transaction with a check written to the owner (added to the Other Names List), as seen in Figure 14-2.

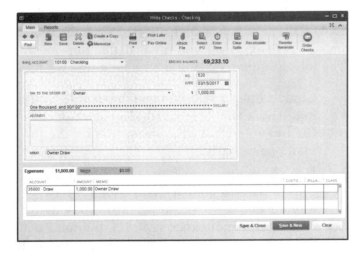

Figure 14-2: Add the owner to the Other Names List to record owner draws.

The postings for the check in Figure 14-2 are shown in Table 14-2.

Account	Debit	Credit
35000—Draw	100.00	
10100—Bank Account		100.00

Table 14-2: Record your withdrawal by posting the check to an equity account named Draw.

If you take money out of the cash register instead of writing a check to yourself, post the transaction to the account that tracks the register instead of the bank account.

ProAdvisor TIP: *To make tracking owner equity a little simpler, you can create a parent account called Owner Equity with three subaccounts—Beginning of Year Equity, Owner Contribution, and Owner Draw. This will enable you to see three key numbers and will also have the total appear on balance sheet reports in the parent account.*

Personal Expenses Paid by a Proprietorship

Many proprietors pay certain categories of expenses from the business bank account, even though those expenses are not deductible by the business. (Some of those expenses end up as deductions on your personal tax return.) The most common expenses managed this way are

- Charitable contributions. Charitable contributions made by a sole proprietorship are not deductible by the business, but are deductible by the proprietor as if made personally.

- Health insurance premiums. If your business contributes to health insurance premiums for you and for employees, the premium payment for your own health insurance is not a business deduction. Premium payments for employees are deductible.

- Retirement plan contributions. Payment of a proprietor's retirement plan contributions are not deductible by a business, although payments made for employees are a business deduction.

* Taxes. Many proprietors pay their income taxes from the business bank account, even though these payments are not a business expense.

You should set up a specific Draw account for each of these payment types instead of posting the payments to a single Draw account (reserving the account named Draw for general withdrawal of funds). This makes it easier to accumulate the totals for personal tax-deductible payments that are not deductible on the business's Schedule C when you're getting ready for tax time. When you use business funds to make these payments, the transaction journal should resemble Table 14-3.

Account	Debit	Credit
35500—Draw for Health Insurance	250.00	
35600—Draw for Taxes	800.00	
10100—Bank Account		1050.00

Table 14-3: Post payments for amounts that are transferred to the owner's personal tax return to specific Draw accounts.

In addition to these transactions, it's common for proprietorships to have payments made by the business that include some personal expenses in addition to business expenses (such as a credit card payment). It's efficient to pay the credit card bill from the business checking account instead of sending one business check and one personal check to the vendor. However, you must post the personal expenses to the owner's Draw account.

CPA NOTE: *It's best to use one credit card for business and another credit card for personal use. This makes your accounting tasks easier. However, many proprietors don't follow this advice, and these examples are presented as a way to deal with reality.*

For example, let's say you used your credit card for gasoline for company use ($75.00) and for gasoline for your personal use ($30.00). In addition, you purchased office supplies for your business ($100.00) and bought something personal ($20.00). The credit card bill comes in the amount of $225.00. The check in Figure 14-3 is used to pay the bill.

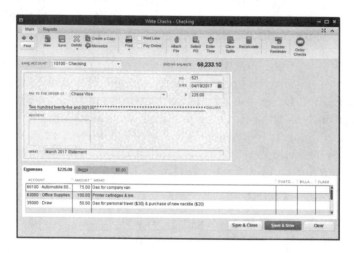

Figure 14-3: You must separate business and personal expenses.

The postings for the check are seen in Table 14-4.

Account	Debit	Credit
60100—Automobile Expense	75.00	
63000—Office Supplies	100.00	
35000—Draw	50.00	
10100—Bank Account		225.00

Table 14-4: This is the way to record the payment of a credit card bill that includes both business and personal expenses.

Partnerships

A partnership is an entity that operates like a proprietorship but has more than one owner. The funding and withdrawal methods used by a partnership are determined by the agreement of the partners. A partnership files its taxes using federal Form 1065 and provides each partner with a Schedule K-1, which the partner uses in preparing his/her personal tax return.

The recording of capital contributions, withdrawals, and payment of personal expenses is the same as explained for proprietorships in the preceding section. You need to create a separate equity account for each partner in your Chart of Accounts so that you can supply accurate financial information to each partner for that partner's personal tax return.

In some partnerships, the contributions, draws, and allocation of profits that are transferred to each partner's personal tax return are not the same for each partner. For example, your business may have three partners with different percentages of ownership:

- Partner A has a 50% interest.
- Partner B has a 30% interest.
- Partner C has a 20% interest.

CPA NOTE: *Usually, the capital contributions and draws match the percentage of ownership, but that's not a legal requirement. All partners might contribute the same amount of startup money, but their share of the company's profits (declared on their personal income tax returns) match the agreed upon percentages.*

Funding Partnerships

When you record the initial contribution of each partner, use the partners' individual equity accounts in the Make Deposits window (see Figure 14-4).

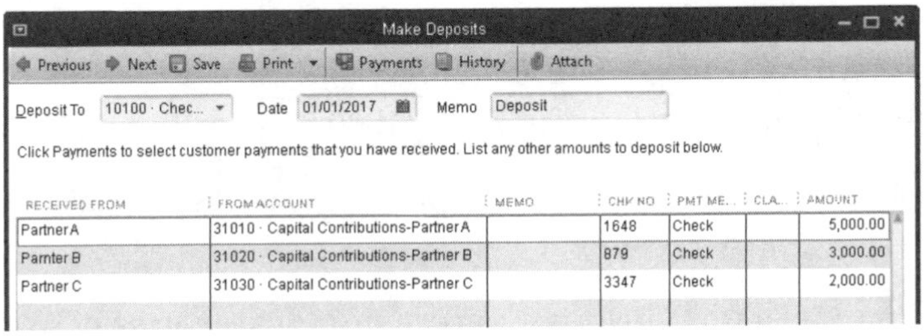

Figure 14-4: Partnership startup funds are assigned to the partner equity accounts.

You can see the postings for the deposit in Table 14-5.

Account	Debit	Credit
10100—Bank Account	10000.00	
31010—Capital Contributions, Partner A		5000.00
31020—Capital Contributions, Partner B		3000.00
31030—Capital Contributions, Partner C		2000.00

Table 14-5: Posting of capital contributions by partners.

As the partnership continues its operations, it may be necessary to add additional capital to the business to fund its continuing operations. The additional funding is recorded the same way.

ProAdvisor TIP: *Here, again, you might want to simplify the accounting by creating a parent account called Partnership Contributions with three subaccounts—one for each partner.*

Withdrawing Money from a Partnership

Withdrawals of cash by the partners may be spelled out in the partnership agreement, or the partners may instead periodically agree on the method of withdrawing money. As with a proprietorship, draw is not an expense; instead, it's an equity transaction. Draws are recorded as shown in Table 14-6.

Account	Debit	Credit
35010—Draw, Partner A	500.00	
35020—Draw, Partner B	300.00	
35030—Draw, Partner C	200.00	
10100—Bank Account		1000.00

Table 14-6: Distribution of cash to partners is tracked in individual Draw accounts.

Just like proprietorships, there are several categories of expenses that businesses commonly pay out of their operating accounts that are not deductible by the partnership. Table 14-7 illustrates the way health insurance premiums paid for partners are recorded. (Health insurance paid for non-owner employees is a deductible business expense.) The transactions are for the actual premiums paid for each partner and may not be in proportion to their ownership interest.

The same format applies to using the business checking account to remit retirement plan contributions and personal taxes (both federal and state) on behalf of each partner.

Account	Debit	Credit
35510—Draw Partner A, Health Insurance Premiums	500.00	
35520—Draw Partner B, Health Insurance Premiums	500.00	
35530—Draw Partner C, Health Insurance Premiums	250.00	
10100—Bank Account		1250.00

Table 14-7: Premium payments for partners' personal health insurance coverage are posted to each partner's equity account.

Paying Personal Expenses for Partners

As with a proprietorship, you may make payments of personal expenses on behalf of a partner to avoid sending multiple checks to the same vendor (such as a credit card payment that includes business and personal expenses). The personal expenses are posted to the appropriate partner's draw account, not to an expense account.

It's best to use one credit card for business and have each partner use a personal credit card for personal purchases. This makes your accounting tasks easier. However, many partnerships send business checks to vendors for amounts that include both business and personal expenses. Note that maintaining this paradigm can produce partnership balances that aren't in proportion to individual partner interests.

LLCs and LLPs

LLCs and LLPs provide more protection against personal liability than a proprietorship or a partnership. Owners are called members.

An LLC (Limited Liability Company) may be organized in either of the following ways:

- A single-member LLC, which is similar to a proprietorship
- A multi-member LLC, which is similar to a partnership

An LLP (Limited Liability Partnership) provides more protection against personal liability than a standard partnership. It is similar to a multi-member LLC and is frequently used by professional businesses (for example, accountants, attorneys, architects, engineers, etc.) due to state regulations that will not permit them to form the business as an LLC.

An LLC can provide continuity to a business that an LLP cannot if, over time, members are bought out. An LLC can have a single member, where an LLP cannot, and for that reason, an LLP that eventually has only one member would need to reorganize. Reorganization can require new federal, state, and local applications and obtaining new identification numbers (business taxes, sales taxes, payroll taxes, etc.). For that reason, many companies prefer to start as LLCs from their inception. This should be discussed with your attorney and accountant.

Single-Member LLC

A single-member LLC has only one owner, called a member. For federal income tax purposes, it is considered a disregarded entity (as if it does not exist) and is treated exactly the same as a proprietorship (discussed earlier in this chapter). The member files a Schedule C with his/her personal income tax return.

CPA NOTE: *While it is possible to request permission of the IRS to operate an LLC or an LLP as a corporation, it's unusual for a small business to do this.*

Funding a Single-Member LLC

Usually, a single-member LLC is funded by transferring money from your personal bank account to the business account. Your investment of these funds is not income to the business and does not result in any taxable profit. It is recorded by increasing your bank balance and the member contribution balance, as shown in Table 14-8.

Account	Debit	Credit
10100—Bank Account	1000.00	
31000—Member's Capital Contributions		1000.00

Table 14-8: Posting for the initial contribution of capital to a single-member LLC.

As the business continues its operations, you may find it necessary to add additional capital to the business to fund its continuing operations. The additional funding is recorded in exactly the same way as the initial capital contribution.

Withdrawing Funds from a Single-Member LLC

The net profit is available for withdrawal by the member. (As with a proprietorship, a single-member LLC owner cannot take payroll.) The withdrawals are recorded by increasing an account named Draw, which is a contra (negative) equity account and is recorded as seen in Table 14-9.

Account	Debit	Credit
35000—Member Draw	100.00	
10100—Bank Account		100.00

Table 14-9: Withdrawal of profits by the member.

If you take money out of the cash register instead of writing a check to yourself, post the transaction to the account that tracks the register instead of the bank account.

It's common for a single-member LLC to pay several categories of expenses from the business bank account that are not deductible by the business. Usually, these expenses are health insurance premiums, pension contributions, and payment of estimated income tax. As discussed earlier in this chapter about proprietorships, you should set up separate Draw accounts for each of these payments so that you can easily see the totals when you're preparing your personal tax return.

Multi-member LLCs and LLPs

The finances of multi-member LLCs and LLPs are managed the same as partnerships (which are discussed earlier in this chapter). The only difference is that the owners of an LLP or a multi-member LLC are called members instead of partners. Both of these entities file partnership tax returns (Form 1065) and provide each member with a Schedule K-1, which he or she uses in the preparation of personal income tax returns.

The funding and withdrawal methods used by an LLC are determined by the agreement of the members. The recording of capital contributions, withdrawals, and payment of business expenses not deductible specifically by the business and the payment of personal expenses is the same as explained previously with respect to partnerships, except that the word "member" would be used in place of the word "partner" in the Chart of Accounts.

Funding Multi-member LLCs and LLPs

The initial funding of an LLP or multi-member LLC is usually accomplished by having the members deposit money into the business bank account. (Assets other than cash could also be contributed, and their value needs to be acceptable to tax authorities and agreeable to the members.)

Initial contributions of cash or other assets are outlined in the organization agreement and need not be equal among the members. These funds are not income; instead, they are capital (equity). You post the transaction of startup capital as seen in Table 14-10.

Account	Debit	Credit
11000—Bank Account	10000.00	
31010—Member A, Contribution		5000.00
31020—Member B, Contribution		3000.00
31030—Member C, Contribution		2000.00

Table 14-10: Posting contributions of members of an LLP or multi-member LLC.

You use the same method to add additional capital to the business to fund its continuing operations.

Withdrawing Funds in Multi-member LLCs and LLPs

Withdrawals of profits by members should be spelled out in the organization agreement or by periodic agreement of the partners. These distributions are not an expense to the business; instead, they are withdrawals of equity. Table 14-11 displays the posting of withdrawal of equity funds by members.

Account	Debit	Credit
35010—Member A, Distribution	500.00	
35020—Member B, Distribution	300.00	
35030—Member C, Distribution	200.00	
10100—Bank Account		1000.00

Table 14-11: Distribution of funds to members of a LLP or multi-member LLC.

As with partnerships, several types of expenses (health insurance, retirement plan payments, and income taxes) paid for the members of multi-member LLCs and LLPs are not deductible by the business. Separate distribution accounts should be set up for each member so that the information can be easily tracked for reporting the amounts to each member on the Schedule K-1 he/she receives at the end of the year.

Guaranteed Payments for Multi-member LLCs and LLPs

Members of an LLC and LLP do not take salary. In some multi-member LLCs and LLPs, there are members who are active in the business and other members who are just passive investors. For the "working members," you can use a guaranteed payment to substitute for a salary. A guaranteed payment differs from payroll and draw (withdrawal of profits) in the following ways:

- Unlike payroll, no taxes are withheld from the payment. Instead, all applicable federal, state, and local taxes are paid by the individual members when they file their personal tax returns.

- Unlike a draw, a guaranteed payment is a tax-deductible expense to the company. You need to set up an expense account to post the guaranteed payment.

CPA TIP: *Tax reporting requires that each member's guaranteed payments be reported individually, so for each member, you should set up a separate guaranteed payment expense account in your Chart of Accounts.*

A guaranteed payment is recorded as shown in Table 14-12. Note that there is no guaranteed payment to Member B, who is a passive investor.

Account	Debit	Credit
65010—Guaranteed Payments, Member A	4000.00	
65020—Guaranteed Payments, Member C	2000.00	
10100—Bank Account		6000.00

Table 14-12: Posting of guaranteed payments paid to members actively working in the company.

Many multi-member LLCs and LLPs issue guaranteed payments to members when they issue payroll checks to employees. Since guaranteed payments are a substitute for payroll for working members, this makes sense.

If you do your payroll in-house, create the guaranteed payment checks the same day (but not through the payroll module, since these payments have no payroll taxes withheld and are not included on your payroll reporting forms to the various tax authorities).

If you outsource your payroll, you can ask the payroll service to issue the guaranteed payment checks. Make sure that the payroll service sets up the members as a separate unit/department so that reports from the payroll service clearly show the deductions for employees and the lack of deductions for the members.

Guaranteed payments are not the same as a distribution of profits to members. The company's profit is reduced by the amount of the guaranteed payments, because the guaranteed payments are considered direct expenses for the company.

The guaranteed payments are provided to each member on the Schedule K-1 he or she receives for income tax preparation at the end of the year. Members who receive guaranteed payments report both the guaranteed payments and their share of the profits on Schedule E of their personal tax returns (Form 1040).

Corporations

A corporation is the most formal form that an organization can choose. Part of the legal formation of a corporation is the issuance of stock (other parts include filing registrations in the business's home state and any other states in which the company does business). The number of authorized shares of stock is stated in the papers prepared by the corporation's attorney, as is the value of each share (called the par value).

Funding Corporations

To fund the corporation's startup, the corporation's founders purchase stock, usually purchasing only a portion of the authorized number of shares to reserve some shares for future issue. Usually, the corporation's founders provide startup funds in an amount larger than the par value of the stock they purchase. The amount contributed over the par value for their stock is called *paid in capital*.

Table 14-13 shows the way the startup funding is posted for a corporation that issued 1000 shares of stock to the founders with a par value of $1.00 per share. A total of $10,000.00 was provided for startup, so $9000.00 in paid in capital is received. Both the stock purchases and the additional paid in capital are posted to Equity accounts.

Account	Debit	Credit
10100—Bank Account	10000.00	
31000—Stock		1000.00
35000—Paid In Capital		9000.00

Table 14-13: Funding a corporation can be accomplished through stock purchases and additional capital contributed.

If the corporation requires additional funding to operate, additional stock can be issued, additional paid in capital can be received, or the corporation can borrow money.

Loans from Stockholders

It's common for stockholders to provide loans to the corporation. However, you must work closely with your attorney if a stockholder loans funds to the company. (There are strict rules about the way the loan must be documented and the amount of interest attached to the loan.)

Loans are liabilities (amounts owed by the corporation), and the loan amount is neither equity nor income. Table 14-14 displays the way a stockholder loan is posted.

Account	Debit	Credit
10100—Bank Account	25000.00	
25200—Loan Payable—Stockholder A		25000.00

Table 14-14: Create a liability account to track a loan from a stockholder.

C Corporations

C Corporations are the most formal types of corporations. Some of the rules concerning financial transactions that affect stockholders are different from the rules for S Corporations (covered in the next section), and we go over the important financial transactions for C Corporations in this section.

C Corporation Stockholder Compensation

An active stockholder in the business is considered an employee of the corporation, and his or her compensation (including both salary and benefits) is treated the same as for any other employee of the corporation. Salary for the stockholder/employee must be considered reasonable (neither too high, nor too low) as loosely defined by the federal tax regulations; no attempt at a discussion of reasonableness is made in this book. (Chapter 10 covers payroll.)

A corporation can also pay directors' fees to active owners serving on its Board of Directors in compensation for their oversight of the business. These payments are usually tied to attendance at Board meetings. They are paid as subcontractor fees and are recorded as a charge to an account named Director Fee Expense. The expense is tax deductible by the corporation. The payments are reported on Form 1099, which is sent to the recipient. (Chapter 10 covers 1099 expenses.) Directors' fees are recorded as shown in Table 14-15.

Account	Debit	Credit
72000—Directors' Fee Expense	1000.00	
10100—Bank Account		1000.00

Table 14-15: Payment of directors' fees for attendance at a Board of Directors meeting.

C Corporation Profit Distributions

Dividend payments to stockholders, while not used by many small corporations, are another way for the stockholders to take profit out of the business. The rules covering dividend payments are complicated, involving classes of stock, and you need to discuss this option and the way you post these transactions with your accountant.

Dividends are a reduction in equity and are a distribution of net income that was previously taxed to the C Corporation. Dividend payments are not expenses of the corporation, do not appear on the Profit & Loss report, and do not affect the net profit of the C Corporation.

C Corporation Taxation

A C Corporation is a taxable entity. It files and pays income taxes based on its Profit & Loss report using Form 1120.

S Corporations

An S Corporation can have either a single owner (stockholder) or multiple owners. An S Corporation must allocate all income and expense items in proportion to a stockholder's percentage ownership in the business's outstanding stock.

To take advantage of avoiding income taxes at the corporate level, consult with your attorney to be certain that forms have been filed with the appropriate tax authorities so that the business is considered an S Corporation by the tax authorities. These forms are normally prepared in conjunction with the other incorporation papers for the business.

S Corporation Stockholder Compensation

An active stockholder in an S corporation is considered an employee of the corporation, and his/her compensation (including salary and benefits) is treated the same as for any other employee of the corporation. All normal employee benefits are available to the owner/employee.

As with a C Corporation, the salary for the stockholder/employee must be considered reasonable (neither too high, nor too low) as loosely defined by the federal tax regulations. Again, discussion of "reasonableness" is beyond the scope of this book. You should talk to your accountant about this issue.

Health insurance paid for a stockholder who has more than 2% ownership is recorded as a health insurance expense in the business's books, as for any other employee, but there are complicated tax reporting issues for this benefit. Payroll tax consequences for this benefit should be discussed with your accountant and, if applicable, your outside payroll service.

Additionally, the corporation's tax return preparer needs to know the amounts of health insurance paid for each applicable stockholder so that the appropriate tax reporting can be transferred to Form 1120S and to each stockholder's Schedule K-1.

CPA CAUTION: *The IRS takes a dim view of active stockholder/employees taking no payroll while receiving other benefits from the business.*

An S Corporation can also pay directors' fees to owners actively serving on its Board of Directors in compensation for their oversight of the business. These payments are usually tied to attendance at Board meetings. They are paid like subcontractor fees (for which Form 1099 is issued) and are recorded as a charge to the Directors' Fee Expense account. This fee is tax deductible by the corporation. Directors' fees for an S Corporation are recorded the same as for a C Corporation, as discussed earlier in the section on C Corporations.

Draws from S Corporations

Distributions taken from the business by its stockholders are treated as draws (like partners in a partnership), using the postings shown in Table 14-16.

Account	Debit	Credit
35010—Draw, Stockholder A	500.00	
35020—Draw, Stockholder B	300.00	
35030—Draw, Stockholder C	200.00	
10100—Bank Account		1000.00

Table 14-16: Track stockholder draws in individual equity accounts for each stockholder.

The equity of an S Corporation is required to be allocated among its stockholders and needs to remain in proportion to the percentage of stock each stockholder owns. Annually, the operating income and expenses are allocated to the stockholders according to their percentage of stock ownership. This action increases and decreases their individual equity balances.

Equity is also reduced by each stockholder's distributions. Any items of draw that are not in proportion to stock ownership need to be corrected within the next fiscal year by issuing catch-up distributions to adjust the balances to their proper individual percentages according to stock ownership.

S Corporation Taxation

An S Corporation files its own corporate tax return (Form 1120S), which is similar to a partnership's tax return. The S Corporation provides each of its stockholders with a Schedule K-1 that includes each stockholder's share of net business income and several other classes of income, expenses, and credits that the stockholders report on their personal tax returns. When profit is taxed to the individual stockholder, but the total amount is not withdrawn, the undrawn amount is available for withdrawal at a later date with no income tax consequence.

Index

Numerics

940 Form, 350
941 Form, 350
1040, Form, 430, 431, 432, 470, 483
1065, Form, 431, 433, 474, 480
1096, Form, 428
1099 Form, 110, 353, 356, 373, 425–429, 434, 485
1099 QuickBooks feature, 426
1099 QuickBooks wizard, 427–428
1120 Forms, 434, 486, 488

A

Accountant's Copy
    and bank reconciliation, 61–62
    creating, 58–59
    delivering to accountant, 59
    dividing date, 58, 59
    and the Intuit server, 59
    and list elements, 60–61
    and passwords, 59
    restrictions on, 59–60
    and transactions, 60
    using, 416
accounting
    accrual basis method, 11–12, 156–157, 162, 395, 420
    cash basis method, 10–11, 156, 162, 395, 413, 419
    cash vs. accrual basis, 9–10
    categories, 4
    fiscal vs. calendar year, 13–14
    method selection, 12–13
accounts
    create new, 32
    creating, 78–80
    editing, 80
    naming, 74–75
    numbering scheme, 75–78
    registers, 18, 30
    Retained Earnings account, 244
    and subaccounts, 76
    tracking, 9
    transferring funds between, 247
accounts payable. See A/P (accounts payable)
accounts receivable. See A/R (accounts receivable)
Add/Edit Multiple List Entries
    about, 56–58
    Clear Column, 58
    Copy Down, 57
    Customize Columns, 57
    Duplicate Row, 57
    service items, 56–68
amortization, 5, 307, 332, 382, 413–415
A/P (accounts payable)
    account register, 18
    aging reports, 193
    Bill Pay window, 177
    as current liability, 6, 310
    header data, 165
    multiple currencies, 133
    posting bills, 167–168

reports, 390–391
vendor bills, 162–163, 167–168
A/R (accounts receivable)
account register, 18
aging reports, 159, 395
Allowance for Doubtful Accounts, 157
as current asset, 4
explanation of, 128–129
multiple currencies, 133
report, 388–391
tracking, 288
writing off, 155–156
assembled products
about, 221, 230–231
group items, 117, 221–223
WIP (Work In Progress), 230–231
assemblies, 115–116, 206, 235
asset accounts. See also A/R (accounts receivable); intangible assets; inventory
about, 4
cash, 4
fixed, 298–299, 300–301
inventory, 5, 218
loans (made to others), 5
long-term, 5
long term, 5
naming, 75
prepaid expenses, 5
subaccounts, 417
tracking, 77, 288
understanding, 3–5
audit trail, 229, 259, 262, 274, 325, 455

B

backorder tracking, 394
backup of files
configuring, 440
manual, 440
offsite storage, 445–446
restoring backup files, 446–447
scheduled, 443–445
utility for, 18
bad debt
about, 155–156
Allowance for Doubtful Accounts, 157
customer credit, 156
as expense category, 156–157
GAAP (Generally Accepted Accounting Principles), 157
journal entries, 157
and Profit & Loss, 156
writing off, 156
balance sheets
detail report, 378–379
liability accounts, 383–384
previous year comparison report, 380
standard report, 378
summary report, 379
balancing checkbook. See reconciling bank accounts
bank accounts. See also bounced checks; reconciling bank accounts
account register, 18
Bank Feed Setup wizard, 41, 276–277
chart of accounts, 242–243
configuring checking preferences, 244–246

Direct Connect, 279
Enter Opening Balance fields, 243
escrow, 322–325
online services, 41
opening account balances, 243–244
register, 253–254
security measures, 273–275
transferring funds between accounts, 247–250
virtual accounts, 305, 315–316
Web Connect, 279–280, 461

Bank Feeds Center
accessing, 41
and account registers, 42
display of, 42
setup wizard, 41

batch invoices
about, 58
Batch Invoice wizard, 132–133
creating, 132

bills
adjusting payment amounts, 180
applying credits toward payment, 180
duplicate bill numbers, 164
entering, 164–166, 209
inventory items, 209
memorized, 168–171
Pay Bills window, 210–212
paying, 175–176, 181, 210
payment method, 178–179
posting to A/P (accounts payable), 167–168
posting to expense accounts, 167
selecting for payment, 179–180
using Pay Bills window, 177–178, 210
using Write Checks window, 210
vendor, 12, 162–163, 167–168

bounced checks
adjusting account balances, 252–255
adjust using bank register, 253–254
adjust using journal entry, 254–255
bank charges for, 255
creating an item for re-invoicing, 256–257
creating an item for service charges, 257–258
creating new invoice, 258
General Journal Entries, 254
and journal entry, 254–255
Record Bounced Check feature, 251–252
re-invoicing customer, 256
required tasks, 250
subaccounts, 257
using Other Charge type item, 251, 256

business entities, types of
C corporations, 422, 434, 468, 484–486
LLCs, 6, 431, 433–434, 468, 477, 483
LLPs, 6, 422, 433, 468, 477–478, 480–483
partnerships, 6, 431–433, 468, 474–477
proprietorships, 6, 430–431, 468, 470–474
S corporations, 434, 468, 486–488

C

cash, definition of (in accounting), 288
Cash Payments Journal, 126
Cash Receipts Journal, 119, 390
cash sales
    cash register report, 120–122
    creating, 118–119
    over and short, 126–128
    recording sales in batches, 120
    sales receipts, 118
    tracking, 127
C corporations. See business entities, types of
CDR (Client Data Review), 452
Centers. See QuickBooks Centers
charitable contributions, 205, 230, 367, 472
chart of accounts
    about, 16, 73–74
    account numbering options, 75–76
    bank accounts, 242–243
    creating class divisions, 80–83
    creating new accounts, 78–80
    divisionalized with classes, 80
    editing existing accounts, 80
    explanation of, 73
    naming accounts, 74–75
    numbering scheme, 77–78
    numbering schemes, 75
    using account numbers, 75–76
classes
    about, 80
    assigning, 174
    creating list of classes, 81–82
    for divisionalized chart of accounts, 80
    enabling, 81
    and subclasses, 82
    tracking, 81, 131
Client Collaborator
    about, 28–29
    in Menu Bar, 28
closing the books, 435–437
COGS (Cost of Goods Sold)
    about, 8
    and inventory management, 203, 204, 213
    "purchase discount account," 176
    as variable expense, 387
Collections Center, 44
company setup
    about, 72
    about account numbers, 75
    advanced setup, 73
    chart of accounts, 73–74
    express start, 72
    naming accounts & conventions, 74–75
Cost of Sales. See COGS (Cost of Goods Sold)
credit cards. See also Customer Credit Card Protection
    account register, 42
    deposits, 126
    merchant fees for, 126
    retaining customer information, 103, 105, 464
    tracking transactions, 179
credits and debits, about, 74

credit side of ledger, 2–4
Customer Center
    about, 34
    Name List, 34–35
    Transactions list, 36
Customer Credit Card Protection
    about, 464
    enabling, 103, 464–465
    passwords, 464
Customer Relationship Management (CRM), 38
customers. See also Customer Credit Card Protection
    Add/Edit Multiple List Entries, 56–68
    create new, 32
    Credit Memos/Refunds form, 146–147
    Customer Job Type list, 89
    Customer Type list, 85–87
    discounts, 148–153
    Lead Center, 38
    naming, 102–103
    payments, 137–141
    records (creating), 102–106
    refunds, 127, 144–146
    register, 122
    retainers, 314–322
    returns, 7, 145, 227
    setting up in QuickBooks, 101–108
    statements, 153–154
    terms, types of, 85–86
    unpaid balances, 140–141
    upfront deposits, 292, 310–313
customizing QuickBooks. See QuickBooks Preferences

D

Daily Journal (from z-tapes), 120, 144
Daily Sales Summary, 122–124
database. See QuickBooks database
debit cards, 190–193
debit side of ledger, 2–4
deposits. See also upfront deposits
    adding missing deposits to register, 262–263
    cash and checks together, 125
    credit card, 126
    escrow account, 323
    Make Deposits window, 125–126, 262
    merchant card fees, 126
    returns of vendor deposit, 295
    sales tax items, 126
    subaccounts, 293
depreciation and amortization
    about, 413–414
    General Journal Entries, 415–416
    IRS Code Section 179, 302
    recording, 414
depreciation vs. expense, 301–302
Desktop View preferences. See also Left Icon Bar; Top Icon Bar
    about, 46
    administrator options, 49–50
    color scheme, 49

One Window vs. Multiple Window view, 47
Save options, 48, 49
Show Home Page option, 48
and windows settings, 49
Direct Connect, 279
direct deposit, 330, 360, 363, 365
direct disbursements, 181–184
Doc Center
about, 42–43
accessing, 42
adding documents and files, 43
attaching documents, 43
viewing documents, 43
double-entry bookkeeping, 2–4
draws (withdrawal of funds), 7

E

EasyStep Interview wizard, 73
Employee Center
about, 34
adding employees, 354–356
and Name List, 34–35
Payroll Center, 36
and Transactions list, 36
Enhanced Payroll subscription
additional fields, 355
and payroll liabilities, 371
as payroll service choice, 343
preferences in QuickBooks, 358–359

Workers' Comp, 356
equity
account registers, 18
accounts, 469–470
allocations, 421–422, 475
definition of, 469
explanation of, 6–7
escrow funds, 322–325
estimates, 24–26
Excel, Microsoft, 43, 219, 460, 461
exchanging information. See exporting company information; importing company information
expenses. See also bad debt; COGS (Cost of Goods Sold)
Cost of Goods Sold (COGS), 8
Cost of Sales, 8
discretionary, 387
explanation of, 7
fixed, 387
general and administrative, 8–9
loan payments, 332
overview of, 7–9
prepaid, 5
reimbursable, 374
reports, 193
tracking, 162–163
types of, 7–9
variable, 387
expense vs. depreciation, 301–302
exporting company information
from addresses to a text file, 461–462
from lists to IIF files, 461

payroll to XML file, 462
timer lists, 462
External Accountant, 452

F

FIFO (First In, First Out),
218–220
file backup. See backup of
files
file verification, 448–449
finance charges, 154
fixed assets
accounts, 298–299
definition of, 298
depreciation, 301–302
dispositions, 417
Fixed Asset Manager, 301, 414
item list, 300–301
opening balance for accounts,
298–299
overview of, 298
purchasing, 302–304
retirement of, 419
sale of, 417–419
subaccounts, 299, 417

G

GAAP (Generally Accepted
Accounting Principles), 157
garnishments, 368
General Journal Entries
for bank account opening balances, 243
depreciation/amortization,
415–416
for line of credit draw(s), 336
for organizational costs, 306

for receiving loan payments, 291
for returned (bounced) checks,
254
for virtual bank accounts, 316
General Ledger, 2–4, 73
General Preferences in
QuickBooks
audible confirmation of recording, 50
automatic decimal point, 50–51
automatic recall last transaction,
52
changing customer or vendor
information, 54
default dates, 52–53
keep QuickBooks running for
quick startups, 51–52
moving between fields, 50
one-time messages, 51
opening drop-down lists, 50
pop-up messages for products/
services, 51
pre-filling accounts, 52
retain or discard custom information, 53
saving transactions before printing, 54
time format, 53
ToolTips, 51
warn when deleting transactions,
51
warn when editing transactions,
51
year display, 53
Group Item, 117, 221–223
groups
about, 117
Billing, 133
creating group items, 221–222

Memorized Reports, 407–408
Memorized Transactions, 171–172
Sales Tax, 94, 99–101
Sales Tax Items, 118

H

Home Page
    about, 19
    icons, 20
    using, 20, 33

I

Icon Bar. See also Top Icon Bar
    adding commands, 22–23
    how to use, 30
    Left Bar versus Top Bar, 30
    placement of, 20
icons
    customizing, 20–21
    delete, 24
    Home Page, 20
    save, 24
    shortcuts, 19
IIF (Intuit Interchange Format) files, 460
importing company information
    journal entries, 461
    timer activities, 461
    using Excel files, 460
    using IIF files, 460
    using Web Connect files, 460–461
    warning about, 461
income
    and accounting method choice, 9–10
    explanation of, 7
    Income Tracker, 158–159
    interest income, 154
    overpayments, 155
    refunds and rebates received, 155
    reports, 159
    tracking, 157–159
independent contractor
    explanation of, 350–354
    W-9 form, 373
    working with, 373–374
information tables, 16
intangible assets
    about, 305
    amortization, 307
    goodwill, 307
    intellectual property, 305–306
    organizational costs, 306–307
    subaccounts, 305
intellectual property
    about, 305–306
    General Journal Entry, 306
interest income, 154
interest payments on loans (made to your company), 332
Intuit payroll service, 342–343
inventory. See also assembled products; inventory items; QOH (Quantity On Hand)
    accounting tasks, 203–212
    account register, 18
    acquiring inventory, 205
    adjusting for "freebies," 229–230
    adjustment account, 204–205

asset account, 203
as current asset, 5, 297
damaged, 227–229, 393
Damaged Inventory account, 229
Inventory Valuation Detail report, 392
Inventory Valuation Summary report, 392
pending builds, 235–236
physical inventory, 235, 412
receiving with bill, 208
receiving without bill, 207–208
reorder points, 236
reports, 235–236
tracking, 197
tracking inventory locations, 202
valuation problems report, 237–239

inventory items
    about, 196–197
    Add/Edit Multiple List Entries, 56–58
    adjusting, 223
    adjusting quantities, 226–227, 229
    asset account, 201
    average costing, 198, 214–218, 228
    COGS account, 200
    cost, 200, 212
    counting, 223–227
    count worksheet, 224–226
    creating, 198–199
    damaged, 227
    damaged inventory adjustments, 229
    description on purchase transactions, 200

description on sales transactions, 200
income account, 201
Inventory Stock Status by Item report, 236, 393
manufacturer's part number, 200
naming, 198
Physical Inventory worksheet, 235
preferred vendor, 201, 236
reorder point, 201, 236, 393
returned, 227
sales price, 201
selling, 213–214
subitems, 199
tax code, 201
tracking, 212
tracking for reordering, 236
value of, 212
WIP, 232

inventory reports
    customized for reorder points, 236
    pending builds, 235
    physical inventory, 224–225, 235
    running, 235–236
    valuation problems, 237–239

inventory valuation
    average cost, 215–216
    FIFO (First In, First Out), 218–220
    Inventory Valuation Summary report, 235
    LIFO (Last In, First Out), 220
    overview of, 214–215, 220–221
    QuickBooks Average costing, 216–218
    specific identification, 220–221

invoices

Add Available Time/Costs, 130
adding time and costs, 130
batch invoices, 132–133
bounced checks, 256
creating, 131–133
customizing, 24–25
explanation of, 129–130
posting, 134–136
sending/posting, 133–136
Send/Ship tab, 25–26
IRS (Internal Revenue Service)
    and accounting method choice, 12–13
    IRS Code, section 179, 302
Item List
    about, 16, 89
    active and inactive, 224
    adding items, 53
    adjusting quantities, 120
    creating items, 114–115
    custom fields, 89–90
    using Add/Edit Multiple List Entries feature, 115
Items
    Client Retainers, 315, 317
    Damaged Inventory, 228–229
    Discount, 117–118, 149
    Fixed Asset, 300
    Group, 117, 221–223
    inactive items, 224, 237, 238, 301
    Inventory, 116, 196–197, 198–199
    Non-Inventory Part, 116, 228–229
    Other Charge, 116–117, 127
    Over and Short, 127–128
    Payments, 118, 121–122

Physical Inventory, 220
Returned (bounced) check, 256–257
Sales Forms, 114–118
Sales Tax, 98–99, 118
Sales Tax Groups, 118
Service, 115
Service Charge, 257–258
Subtotal, 117
Taxable Sales, 120–121
tracking, 196
Untaxable Sales, 120–121
Upfront Deposit, 311, 312

J

jobs (definition for QuickBooks), 87–88
journal entries. See General Journal Entries

L

Layout Designer
    about, 67
    add data field, 68
    add image, 68
    add text box, 68
    arranging elements, 69
    margins and grids, 70
    modifying properties of elements, 69
    moving elements, 69
    resizing elements, 68–69
Lead Center, 38–39
ledger, 2–4
Left Icon Bar
    about, 19
    customizing icons, 20–21

My Shortcuts, 30
Open Windows, 30–31
Run Favorite Reports, 30
and shortcuts, 21
View Balances, 30
liabilities. See also A/P (accounts payable)
about, 5, 310
current vs. long term, 328
customer deposits, 310
explanation of, 5–6
line of credit, 335–339
overview of, 5–6
A/P (accounts payable), 310
payroll, 6, 366
sales tax, 6
liability accounts
Balance Sheet Loan, 384
credit card, 179
naming, 75
payroll, 368–369
LIFO (Last In, First Out), 220
line of credit, 335–339
lists
about, 16–17
adding custom fields, 89–90
Class List, 81–82
Customer & Jobs list, 106, 108
Customer & Vendor Profile List, 84–85
Customer List, 460
Customer Retainers List, 314
customers and jobs, 106–108
Customer Type List, 85–87
Job Type List, 87–89
Memorized Transactions List, 170–172
Other Names List, 289, 292

Payment Method List, 122, 318
QuickBooks Timer List, 462
Sales Tax Code List, 97–99
Terms List, 83
Timer List, 462
Transactions List, 281
Vendor Type List, 87
Lists menu, 17, 82, 170
list tables, 16
LLCs. See business entities, types of
LLCs and LLPs. See business entities, types of
Loan Manager, 332–335
loans (made to others)
account register, 18
as asset, 5
creating as Current Asset, 289–290
receiving payments, 291–292
sending payment invoices, 290–291
tracking, 289
using Other Charge type item for payments, 290
loans (made to your company)
account register, 18
entering in QuickBooks, 329
General Journal Entries, 291
as line of credit, 335
as long term liability, 6
making payments, 332
setting up lender as institution, 330–332
subaccounts, 289
tip for naming the loan account, 329
tracking, 328
tracking with Loan Manager,

332–335

M

maintenance of QuickBooks.
See QuickBooks maintenance
Make Deposits window,
125–126, 262, 295, 318, 320,
321, 324

Menu Bar
about, 19, 23
Alerts icon, 28
Client Collaborator icon,
28
Favorites menu, 28
how to use, 27–28
Reminders icon, 28

merging records, 111
multiple currencies, 133

N

Name List
Contacts tab, 35
To Do's tab, 35
drop-down lists, 35–36
Notes tab, 35
Sent Email tab, 35
Transactions tab, 35

non-inventory items
Add/Edit Multiple List Entries,
56–58, 115
and inventory valuation problems, 238–239
using non-inventory part type,
116, 121, 228
and Work In Process (WIP),
233

O

On Hand and Total Value,
201–202

online banking
about, 275–277
adding downloaded transactions, 284
adding transactions, 280–282
aliases for transactions, 283–
284
Bank Feeds Center, 41, 278–
285
Bank Feed Setup wizard, 276–
277
banking preferences, 284–285
Direct Connect, 275, 279
downloading transactions, 279
locating your bank, 276
QuickBooks preferences, 284–
285
transactions list, 280–281
using the Renaming Rules feature, 282–284
Web Connect, 275, 279–280
Web Connect vs. Direct connect,
275

opening balance
corrections, 410
and Fixed Asset accounts,
298–299
Opening Balance Equity account, 202, 410–411
and setting up QuickBooks, 105,
106–107

open item method, 137

Other Charge items
about, 116–117
Bad Debt, 157

Bounced Check, 251
Loan Payment, 290
Overage, 127
Shortage, 127
Overages and Shortages, 126–128

overhead expenses
    allocating to divisions, 421
    as expense category, 387
    tracking, 325

P

partnerships. See business entities, types of
passwords
    Accountant's Copy, 59, 416
    adding to users, 452
    changing settings for users, 457
    and creating users, 451–452
    Customer Credit Card Protection feature, 464
    electronic statements, 273
    online banking, 277
    and setting the closing date, 435–436
Payment Card Industry Data Security Standards (PCI DSS), 103, 464
payment item
    about, 121
    prepayment of invoice, 118
    setting up in QuickBooks, 122
    use with sales form, 118
Payment Method List, 122, 318
payments
    fee-based processing from Intuit, 26–27
    loans (made to others), 291–292
    methods of, 122, 147
    Receive Payments form, 26
    setting up, 122
    terms, 151, 154, 164
payroll
    about, 342–343
    adding employees, 354–358
    Add New Payroll Items wizard, 345, 349
    burden, 369
    charitable contributions, 367
    configuring manual payroll, 343–344
    configuring without wizard, 348–349
    Custom Setup method, 349–350
    employee benefits, 367
    Employee Center, 344
    employee setup, 345
    employee vs. independent contractor status, 350–354
    Enhanced payroll service, 343, 355, 359, 371
    expenses, 76, 368
    EZ Setup method, 346, 349
    garnishments, 368
    gross pay, 364–365
    independent contractor, 350–354, 373–374
    liabilities, 350, 366–373
    liabilities payments posting, 372–373
    liabilities posting, 369–370
    liability expenses, 76
    liability paying, 370–372
    net pay, 365
    preferences, 358–360

running payroll, 361–364
schedules for payroll, 360–361
setting up, 344–346
setup wizard, 346–348
subscribing to payroll service, 342–343
tax withholding, 366–367
Payroll Center
about, 36–37
accessing, 36
File Forms tab, 37
Pay Employees tab, 37
Pay Liabilities tab, 37
PDF (Portable Document Format) files, 134, 354, 373
permissions
changing or deleting specific, 456
closed period, 456–457
credit card, 103
External Accountant, 452
options, 453–454
Sensitive Accounting Activities, 276, 453–456
Sensitive Accounting Reports, 455
setting for users, 452–454
and Transaction Pro Importer, 463
virtual administrator, 452
petty cash
about, 184–185
debit card withdrawals, 192
putting money into, 185–186, 190
recording disbursements from, 186
tracking advances, 187–190
tracking disbursements, 186–

187
portable company file
about, 62
to rebuild corrupt company file, 450
posting
bill payments, 180–181
direct disbursements, 182, 184
explanation of, 73–74
invoices, 134–136
payroll liabilities, 369–370
preferences. See QuickBooks Preferences
prepaid expenses
as asset, 5
tracking, 293, 296
price levels
adding transactions, 106
custom pricing, 130
fixed percentage, 105
per item, 105
tracking, 102
printing
1099s, 428
checks in batches, 184
direct disbursement checks, 183
graphs, 395
invoices, 133
single checks, 183
proprietorships. See business entities, types of
ProSeries tax software, 430
prospective customers. See Lead Center
purchase orders
creating, 206
for inventory items, 205
preferences for, 197–198

using, 205–206
and WIP transactions, 234

Q

QOH (Quantity On Hand)
as inventory asset, 297
reorder point, 201, 393
warning options, 198
QuickBooks
about navigating, 27
basic structure of, 16–17
exchanging information. see
exporting company information;
importing company information
interface, 19–27
visual map of features, 33
QuickBooks Centers
about, 18, 33–34
Bank Feeds Center, 41–42
Collections Center, 44
Customer, Vendor and Employee Centers, 34
Customer Center, 18
Doc Center, 42–44
home page, 20
layout of features, 34
Lead Center, 38
Name List, 34–35
Payroll Center, 36
Report Center, 39–41
QuickBooks database
about, 16
corruption, 18, 62
tables, 16
QuickBooks Enterprise Edition
assembly items, 221
pending builds, 235

Per Item Price Levels, 105
QuickBooks maintenance
backing up, 440–445
cleaning up files, 448–450
customer credit card protection, 464–465
file verification, 448–449
importing/exporting company information, 460–464
managing users and passwords, 450–457
storing backup of files, 445–448
updating QuickBooks software, 457–460
QuickBooks Preferences. See also Desktop View preferences; General Preferences in QuickBooks
about, 44
accessing, 44–45
Company Preferences tab, 46
explanation of, 17–18
My Preferences tab, 45–46
Sales & Customers, 130
QuickBooks Premier Accountant Edition
CDR (Client Data Review) feature, 452
Fixed Asset Manager, 301, 414
QuickBooks Premier Edition
assembly items, 221
class tracking, 83
exporting customized reports, 408
Fixed Asset Manager, 301, 414
pending builds, 235
Per Item Price Levels, 105
QuickBooks Retail Edition,

122

R

rebates, 155
reconciling bank accounts
adding missing deposits to register, 262–263
adding missing disbursements to register, 261–262
adding transactions during, 266–267
adjusting entry, 270
bank statement, 260–261
Begin Reconciliation window, 263–264
clearing transactions, 265–266
deleting transactions during, 267
Discrepancy Report, 271–273
editing transactions during, 267–268
finishing up, 269
interest income, 264
manual search for discrepancy problem, 272–273
overview of, 259–260
pausing process, 270
preparing to reconcile, 261
resolving beginning balance difference, 271
resolving missing check numbers, 268
resolving problems, 269–270
service charges (bank charges), 264
switching between windows during, 267
using Eliminating Future Transactions for ease, 265

viewing Discrepancy report, 271–273
viewing transactions during, 266
voided checks, 272
refunds, receiving, 155, 173–175, 176, 263
Report Center
about, 39
Carousel view, 40–41
contributed customized reports, 40
favorite reports, 40
Grid view, 41
List view, 41
memorized reports, 40
pre-designed reports, 40
recent reports, 40
reports
about, 17
balance sheets, 378–380
bank account discrepancy, 271–273
creating filters for, 400–402
customizing, 396–407
Discrepancy, 271–273
favorites, 40
income tracking, 157
inventory, 235–236, 391–394
memorized, 40, 314, 407–408
Memorized Report Group, 407–408
payroll liability, 370–371
pre-designed, 40
Profit & Loss, 385–386
A/R (accounts receivable), 388
Report Center, 39–41
ribbon bar, 26
sales tax liability, 383
setting preferences for in Quick-

Books, 394–396
vendor, 193–194
Vendor Balance Summary, 413
Vendor Balance Summary report, 413
retained earnings
    definition of, 7
    and net income/loss, 386, 435
    Retained Earnings account, 224, 244
returned checks. See bounced checks
revenue. See income
Ribbon Bar
    about, 23–24
    Delete icon, 24
    Formatting tab, 24–25
    Main tab commands, 24
    Payments tab, 26
    Reports tab, 26
    Save icon, 24
    Send/Ship tab, 25–26

S

sales form
    discount items, 114
    group items, 117
    inventory part items, 116
    non-inventory part items, 116
    other charge items, 114, 116–117
    payment items, 118
    QuickBooks preferences, 130
    sales tax groups, 118
    sales tax items, 118
    service items, 115
    shipping, 130
    subtotal items, 117

taxable and untaxable sales, 120–121
Sales Journal, 131, 213
sales receipts
    customizing, 24–25
    Payments tab, 26
    Send/Ship tab, 25–26
sales tax
    account register, 18
    adjusting amounts due, 327–328
    codes, 97–98
    creating sales tax items, 91–93
    enabling use of, 91
    explanation of, 325
    laws, 11
    as liability, 6
    Manage Sales Tax feature, 326–327
    rates, 93–96
    remitting, 11, 326–327
    Sales Tax Code List, 97–98
    Sales Tax Groups, 94, 99–101, 118
    Sales Tax Items, 98–99, 118, 121
    Sales Tax Liability report, 383–384
    setting up, 90–99
    state, 11, 90–91
    statements, 95–96
    status, 96–97
    tracking, 11
Schedule C, 430, 431, 470, 478
S corporations. See business entities, types of
Send/Ship tab, 25–26
shipping, 102, 116, 130, 303,

387
shortages and overages in cash, 126, 127
shortcuts
  drop-down list transaction shortcut, 32
  icon bars, 21
  table of shortcut keys, 32
  using shortcut keys, 31–32
sole proprietorships. See proprietorships
stock
  as equity category, 6
  status by item report, 235
  status by vendor report, 235
subaccounts
  creating, 78–79
  for deposits, 293
  for fixed assets, 299, 417
  for intangible assets, 305
  making deposits into, 318
  for outstanding loans, 289
  for over and short accounts, 127–128
  for owner equity, 472
  for partnership contributions, 476
  and payroll liabilities, 350
  for prepayments, 293
  for returned (bounced) checks accounts, 257
  Show Lowest Subaccount Only option, 76
  for upfront deposits, 314
  using, 76
  and virtual bank account, 315–316
subcontractors
  1099 form, 13

Form 1099, 353–354
  and service items, 115
  tax settings, 110
subitems, 199
Summary Sales Transaction, 124–125

T

tax returns
  business, 429–430
  C Corp, 434–435
  LLC, 431
  LLP, 433–434
  partnership, 431–433
  proprietorship, 430–431
  S Corp, 434
templates. See also Layout Designer
  customizing, 25, 65–67
  Intuit Community Forms web page, 25
  memorized groups, 171–173
  memorized transactions, 55–56
  minor changes to, 64–65
  pre-designed, 65
  reports, 26
timer, 462
Top Icon Bar
  about, 19
  add separator, 22
  customizing, 21–22
  display options, 22
  search options, 22
transaction forms. See also templates
  about, 17, 18
  customizing, 64
  downloading, 279–280

memorized, 55–56, 270
ribbon bar, 19
ribbon bars, 24
summary sales, 124–125
Transaction Pro Importer, 463–464
transactions
about, 16
categories, 2–4, 36
Transactions List, 36
transaction tables, 16
Transfer Funds feature, 247
trust funds, 322–325
TurboTax software, 242, 430

U

Undeposited Funds account, 137, 252–254, 262, 312, 318
updating QuickBooks software
about, 457–458
checking status of, 459
manual, 460
shared downloads on a network, 459
Update QuickBooks service, 458–459
upfront deposits
accounts for, 310
customer, 305, 310–313
items for, 311
vendors, 292
users. See also passwords; permissions
about, 450–451
adding, 451–452
Admin, 451

changing, 457
changing user settings, 457
creating, 451
deleting, 457
External Accountant, 452
overview of, 450–457
utilities
about, 18
data file corruption, 448–450
Loan Manager, 333
Rebuild Data, 449–450
Transaction Pro Importer, 463
Verify Data, 448
verifying files for a manual backup, 442
web connection, 279–280

V

Vendor Center
about, 34
and Name List, 34–35
and Transactions list, 36
vendors
Add/Edit Multiple List Entries, 56–68
credits, 173–174
deposit return, 295–296
deposit return General Journal Entry, 296
deposits and prepaid expenses, 292–293
monthly services, 297
settings, 109
settings in QuickBooks, 109
terms, 83–84
Vendor Type list, 87
yearly payment allocation, 297
Verify Data utility, 448–449

virtual bank accounts, 305, 315–316
voided transactions, 272
voiding checks, 258–259

W

W-2 form, 423–425
W-9 form, 373, 426
Web Connect, 279–280, 461
What's New indicators, 19, 20
WIP (Work In Progress)
    about, 230–231
    redefined for small businesses, 231
    setting up in QuickBooks, 233–234
    tracking production costs, 231–232
    tracking transactions, 234–235
withdrawal of funds. See draws (withdrawal of funds)
writing off receivables, 155

X

XML files, 462

Y

year-end tasks
    adjustments, 412
    cash basis tax report adjustments, 419–421
    closing the books, 435–437
    Opening Balance Equity account, 410–411
    overhead expenses allocation, 421–422

reconcile accounts, 411
run reports, 412
tax forms and returns, 422–435

Z

Z-tape, 120, 144